209...

When should I travel to get the best airfare?
Where do I go for answers to my travel questions?
What's the best and easiest way to plan and book my trip?

www.frommers.travelocity.com

Frommer's, the travel guide leader, has teamed up with **Travelocity.com**, the leader in online travel, to bring you an in-depth, easy-to-use resource designed to help you plan and book your trip online.

At **www.frommers.travelocity.com**, you'll find free online updates about your destination from the experts at Frommer's plus the outstanding travel planning and purchasing features of Travelocity.com. Travelocity.com provides reservations capabilities for 95 percent of all airline seats sold, more than 47,⌐ ⌐⌐ 50 car rental companies. In addition, Travelocity.cor ⌐ ⌐ ⌐ ⌐ e packages. Tra ⌐ ⌐ vel planning with ⌐

Exper ⌐ rs
report ⌐

Best ⌐ to
travel ⌐

Fare ⌐
destin. ⌐

Dream Maps - a mapping feature that suggests travel opportunities based on your budget

Shop Safe Guarantee - 24 hours a day / 7 days a week live customer service, and more!

Whether traveling on a tight budget, looking for a quick weekend getaway, or planning the trip of a lifetime, Frommer's guides and Travelocity.com will make your travel dreams a reality. You've bought the book, now book the trip!

 Travelocity.com
A Sabre Company

 **Frommer's**

Other Great Guides for Your Trip:

Here's what the critics say about Frommer's:

"Amazingly easy to use. Very portable, very complete."
—Booklist

♦

"The only mainstream guide to list specific prices. The Walter Cronkite of guidebooks—with all that implies."
—Travel & Leisure

♦

"Complete, concise, and filled with useful information."
—New York Daily News

♦

"Hotel information is close to encyclopedic."
—Des Moines Sunday Register

♦

"Detailed, accurate and easy-to-read information for all price ranges."
—Glamour Magazine

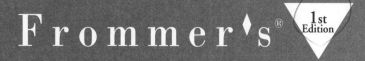

Frommer's® 1st Edition

Jamaica.

by Darwin Porter & Danforth Prince

IDG Books Worldwide, Inc.
An International Data Group Company
Foster City, CA • Chicago, IL • Indianapolis, IN • New York, NY

917.292
POR

IDG BOOKS WORLDWIDE, INC.

An International Data Group Company
919 E. Hillsdale Blvd.
Suite 400
Foster City, CA 94404

Find us online at **www.frommers.com**

ISBN 0-7645-6126-X
ISSN 1528-218X

Editors: Kate Welsh and Ron Boudreau
Production Editor: Tammy Ahrens
Photo Editor: Richard Fox
Design by Michele Laseau
Staff Cartographers: John Decamillis, Roberta Stockwell, and Elizabeth Puhl
Page Creation by IDG Books Indianapolis Production Department

SPECIAL SALES

For general information on IDG Books Worldwide's books in the U.S., please call our Consumer Customer Service department at 1-800-762-2974. For reseller information, including discounts, bulk sales, customized editions, and premium sales, please call our Reseller Customer Service department at 1-800-434-3422.

Manufactured in the United States of America

5   4   3   2   1

Ⅴ. JAMAICA -- DESCRIPTION + TRAVEL
Ⅰ. TITLE

Contents

v

List of Maps

ABOUT THE AUTHORS

A native of North Carolina, **Darwin Porter** was a bureau chief for the *Miami Herald* when he was 21 and later worked in television advertising. A veteran travel writer, he's the author of numerous best-selling Frommer's guides, notably to the Caribbean, England, Italy, and France. He's assisted by **Danforth Prince,** formerly of the Paris bureau of the *New York Times*. For years, they have been frequent travelers to Jamaica and have become intimately familiar with what's good there and what isn't. In this guide, they share their secrets and discoveries with you.

AN INVITATION TO THE READER

In researching this book, we discovered many wonderful places—hotels, restaurants, shops, and more. We're sure you'll find others. Please tell us about them, so we can share the information with your fellow travelers in upcoming editions. If you were disappointed with a recommendation, we'd love to know that, too. Please write to:

Frommer's Jamaica, 1st Edition
IDG Books Worldwide, Inc.
909 Third Avenue
New York, NY 10022

AN ADDITIONAL NOTE

Please be advised that travel information is subject to change at any time—and this is especially true of prices. We therefore suggest that you write or call ahead for confirmation when making your travel plans. The authors, editors, and publisher cannot be held responsible for the experiences of readers while traveling. Your safety is important to us, however, so we encourage you to stay alert and be aware of your surroundings. Keep a close eye on cameras, purses, and wallets, all favorite targets of thieves and pickpockets.

WHAT THE SYMBOLS MEAN

✪ Frommer's Favorites

Our favorite places and experiences—outstanding for quality, value, or both.

The following abbreviations are used for credit cards:

AE	American Express	ER	enRoute
CB	Carte Blanche	JCB	Japan Credit Bank
DC	Diners Club	MC	MasterCard
DISC	Discover	V	Visa

The following abbreviations are used in hotel listings:

AP (American Plan): Includes three meals a day (sometimes called *full board* or *full pension*).
CP (Continental Plan): A Continental breakfast (that is, bread, jam, and coffee) is included in the room rate.
EP (European Plan): This rate is always cheapest, as it offers only the room—no meals.
MAP (Modified American Plan): Sometimes called *half board* or *half pension*, this room rate includes breakfast and dinner (or lunch if you prefer).

FIND FROMMER'S ONLINE

www.frommers.com offers up-to-the-minute listings on almost 200 cities around the globe—including the latest bargains and candid, personal articles updated daily by Arthur Frommer himself. No other Web site offers such comprehensive and timely coverage of the world of travel.

The Best of Jamaica

You're flying off to Jamaica to relax and have a good time—not to waste precious vacation hours searching for the best deals and experiences. So take us along and we'll do the work for you.

We've tested the best beaches, reviewed countless restaurants, inspected the hotels, sampled the best scuba diving, and taken the best hikes. We've found the best buys, the hottest nightclubs, and even the best places to get away from it all when you want to escape the crowds. Here's our very opinionated selection, compiled after years of traveling through this island.

1 The Best Beaches

- **Doctor's Cave Beach** (Montego Bay): This 5-mile stretch of white sand made "Mo Bay" a tourist destination. Waters are placid and crystal clear, and there are changing rooms and a beach bar. This one is a family favorite. See chapter 3.
- **Cornwall Beach** (Montego Bay): Although it's often too crowded, this beach is covered with soft, white, sugary sand that's deep enough to really sink your toes into. The water is clean and warm, and it's a place to take your family. The admission charge entitles you not only to swim and sunbathe but also to use the changing room. The beach is near the main tourist strip and close to the popular and larger Doctor's Cave Beach (see above). The "higglers"—as local vendors are called—will seek you out and try to sell you everything from black-coral jewelry to drugs. See chapter 3.
- **Seven Mile Beach** (Negril): On the island's west coast, this beach stretches for 7 miles along the sea. It was once the haunt of the Caribbean's most notorious pirates. In the background are some of the most hedonistic resorts in the Caribbean, mixed in with a few family favorites. Many strips of these golden sands are fine for families, although there are several nudist patches where guests bare all. The nude-beach areas are sectioned off, even though some new oceanfront resorts have Peeping Tom views of these areas. See chapter 4.
- **Booby Cay** (Negril): Although it's X-rated, the aptly named Booby Cay is the haunt of snorkelers as well as nude sunbathers. Many folks come here from Hedonism II, Jamaica's answer to Club Med. Once they've landed by motor launch or even

by kayak, bathers in the buff—mainly male/female couples—disperse to seek out their own little white-sand patch of private heaven. See chapter 4.

- **Treasure Beach** (South Coast): Tired of fighting the crowds for your place in the sun? Head for Treasure Beach on Jamaica's dry, sunny, and isolated South Coast, a real hideaway that's a secret among young Jamaicans. There are drawbacks here: The undertow can be dangerous, so swimming is a bit tricky. These secluded sands are gray, and waves crash into the shore. It's one of the most dramatic beachscapes in Jamaica. See chapter 5.
- **Boston Beach** (Port Antonio): It's known not only for its white sands, but for its jerk pork stands. You can enjoy your unique beach barbecue while gazing out upon the incredibly clear waters of the bay. The beach has the biggest waves in Jamaica, and young men will rent you surfboards and even give you lessons. See chapter 7.

2 The Best Water-Sports Outfitters

- **Seaworld Resorts** (Montego Bay; ☎ 876/953-2180): Offering the best scuba diving in Montego Bay, the staff of qualified instructors here will take you to some intriguing dive sites where you can swim among some of the most spectacular offshore coral reefs in the Caribbean. See chapter 3.
- **Negril Scuba Centre** (Negril; ☎ 800/818-2963 in the U.S. or 876/957-9641): This is the best-equipped dive facility in this popular resort area. It has one of the most professional staffs on the island, all certified instructors. They'll take you for dives into a bay once frequented by some of the most notorious pirates (male and female) in the West Indies. See chapter 4.
- **Buccaneer Scuba Club** (Port Royal; ☎ 876/967-8061): Based at Morgan's Harbour Hotel and Beach Club, this operator is unique in the Caribbean. It offers the widest range of dive sites in Jamaica, including the *Texas* wreck, an American naval ship that sank in 1944. Other sites include South East Cays, a reef that runs alongside the south of Jamaica, and Sandra's Buoy, one of the largest reefs and filled with marine life, including coral growth. You can spot turtles, dolphins, and rays. See chapter 8.

3 The Best Golf Courses

- **Wyndham Rose Hall Golf & Beach Resort** (Montego Bay; ☎ 876/953-2650): Wyndham has been called one of the top-five courses in the world. That may be a bit of an exaggeration, but it is an unusual and challenging seaside and mountain course. The 10th fairway abuts the family burial grounds of the Barretts of Wimpole Street, and the 14th passes the vacation home of singer Johnny Cash. The 300-foot-high 13th tee offers a rare panoramic view of the sea and the roof of the hotel, and the 15th green is next to a 40-foot waterfall, once featured in a James Bond movie. See chapter 3.
- **Tryall Golf, Tennis & Beach Club** (Montego Bay; ☎ 876/956-5660): Jamaica's finest course, Tryall is the site of the annual Johnnie Walker World Championship. A par-71, 6,680-yard course, it crosses hills and dales on what was once sugarcane farmland. Some ruins, including an old waterwheel, remain. Wind direction can change suddenly, making the course more intriguing. One golfer whom we interviewed confessed he's played the course 50 times, and "each game was different." See chapter 3.

- **Half Moon Golf, Tennis & Beach Club** (Montego Bay; ☎ **800/626-0592** in the U.S. or 876/953-2211): This, the island's second championship course, was designed by Robert Trent Jones, Sr. in 1961. Played by the likes of former U.S. President George Bush, the course has manicured and diversely shaped greens, but it's not as challenging as the one at Tryall. See chapter 3.
- **Sandals Golf & Country Club** (Ocho Rios; ☎ **876/975-0119**): This 6,500-yard course is known for its panoramic vistas. Rolling terrain, lush vegetation, and flowers and fruit trees dominate the 120-acre course where Sandals guests play for free. Others are welcome for a fee. See chapter 6.

4 The Best Tennis Facilities

- **Half Moon Golf, Tennis & Beach Club** (Montego Bay; ☎ **800/626-0592** in the U.S. or 876/953-2211): Half Moon has Jamaica's best tennis—13 state-of-the-art courts, 7 of which are lit for night games. The head pro offers a clinic with a video playback. See chapter 3.
- **Wyndham Rose Hall Golf & Beach Resort** (Montego Bay; ☎ **876/953-2650**): Wyndham Rose Hall features six hard-surface courts, each lit for night games. Hotel guests play for free; others must pay a fee. There's also a resident pro on hand to offer lessons. See chapter 3.
- **Tryall Golf, Tennis & Beach Club** (Montego Bay; ☎ **876/956-5660**): Tryall is rivaled in Jamaica only by the Half Moon Club. It has nine hard-surface courts, three of which are lit for night games. Four pros on-site can help you improve your skills. See chapter 3.
- **Ciboney Ocho Rios** (Ocho Rios; ☎ **800/333-3333** in the U.S. or 876/974-1027): This Radisson franchise offers three clay courts and three hard-surface courts, all lit for nighttime play. There's a lot of emphasis here on tennis, including Pan-Caribbean competitions and even pan-parish tournaments. Twice-a-day clinics are sponsored, for both beginners and more-advanced players. See chapter 6.

5 The Best Natural Attractions

- **Martha Brae's Rafters Village** (Montego Bay; ☎ **876/952-0889**): Martha Brae's Rafters Village offers the best river-rafting experience in and around this popular resort. You sit on a raised dais on bamboo logs and watch the river scenery unfold before you. See chapter 3.
- **The Black River** (South Coast): You can explore what feels like real Tarzan country, with mangrove trees and crocodiles in the wild, on an outing with **South Coast Safaris** (☎ **876/965-2513**). At the mouths of the Broad and Black rivers, saltwater meets freshwater, and extensive red mangroves are formed with aerial roots of some 40 feet. Lots of wild things grow in these swamps. Birders: Look for ring-necked ducks, whistling ducks, herons, egrets, and even the blue-winged teal. See chapter 5.
- **Dunn's River Falls** (Ocho Rios): A favorite of cruise-ship passengers, these 600 feet of clear, cold mountain waters race over a series of stone steps. Visitors (and we mean *lots* of visitors) splash in the waters at the bottom of the falls or drop into the cool pools higher up between cascades of water. It's the best way to cool off on a hot day in Jamaica. Visitors hold hands climbing the falls and trust that the human chain won't have a weak link! See chapter 6.

- **Somerset Falls** (Port Antonio): This sun-dappled spot is not as touristy as Dunn's River. The waters from Daniels River race down a deep gorge split through a rain forest. Flowering vines, waterfalls, and foaming cascades form the lush backdrop. You can swim in the deep rock pools. See chapter 7.
- **Rafting on the Río Grande** (Port Antonio; ☎ 876/993-5778): Shades of Errol Flynn. This is the grandest rafting experience in Jamaica. Popularized by the late movie star, the rafts propelled by bamboo poles take you through Jungle Jim country on a soft adventure. See chapter 7.
- **Exploring the Blue Mountains** (outside Kingston; ☎ 876/920-8348): Sprawled across 192,000 acres, the Blue Mountain–John Crow Mountain National Park is one of the wildest and most lush in the Caribbean, ideal for exploring. You must hike 5 to 6 hours through thick vegetation and an amazing amount of bird life to reach the summit at about 3,000 feet above sea level. It's a heavy-duty trek, but well worth it if you have the stamina. See chapter 8.

6　The Best Honeymoon Resorts

- **Sandals** (Montego Bay, Negril, and Ocho Rios; ☎ 800/SANDALS in the U.S.): These resorts for male/female couples pride themselves on providing an all-inclusive environment where food and drink are spread out in abundance and you never have to carry cash or worry about tipping. Enthusiastic members of the staff bring heroic amounts of community spirit and enthusiasm to any weddings celebrated on-site. All of these resorts can provide a suitable setting, but the most favored ones are Sandals Royal Jamaican at Montego Bay and Sandals Dunn's River at Ocho Rios. See chapters 3, 4, and 6.
- **Half Moon Golf, Tennis & Beach Club** (Montego Bay; ☎ 800/626-0592 in the U.S. or 876/953-2211): This resort offers honeymooners deluxe ocean-view rooms fronting a near-perfect crescent-shaped beach. Newlyweds who didn't blow all their money on the wedding can opt for one of the large private "cottages," complete with their own swimming pool. Although there are plenty of nooks and crannies where you can retreat for romantic interludes, this is also the resort of choice for honeymooners who want lots of activities, such as aerobics, tennis, swimming, and, most definitely, golf. See chapter 3.
- **Jake's** (Treasure Beach; ☎ 800/OUTPOST): Funky and idiosyncratic, this is the offbeat choice of Jamaica for a honeymoon. No one will find you here, even the most intrepid of mothers-in-law. On the South Coast, and set adjacent to a rocky beach, this place is small scale and intensely personal, calling to mind something in the deserts of Morocco. See chapter 5.
- **Jamaica Inn** (Ocho Rios; ☎ 800/837-4608 in the U.S., or 876/974-2514): At one of the great hotels of the island, the "White Suite" is secluded on the brink of a promontory (Winston Churchill slept here), and it's quite a swanky place for a honeymoon if you can afford it. Otherwise, there are plenty of other spacious and classic rooms in which to begin your married life. The resort opens onto a private cove with powdery champagne-colored sand. The inn, with its colonial aura and a certain degree of formality, is a real contrast to the more free-for-all Sandals properties where anything (well, almost) goes. See chapter 6.
- **Ciboney Ocho Rios** (Ocho Rios; ☎ 800/333-3333 in the U.S., or 876/974-1027): The honeymoon villas at this stately, plantation-style spa and beach resort are set on lush hillside acreage and are perfect private retreats for newlyweds. Each has a private attendant and pool. Guests are pampered here

with complimentary massages, pedicures, and manicures. A private beach is reached by shuttle as the resort is not on the water. The resort is all-inclusive, and there's a range of sports facilities, such as tennis courts—but you'll be able to find some privacy to be with your new spouse. See chapter 6.

- **The Enchanted Garden** (Ocho Rios; ☎ **800/847-2535** in the U.S., or 876/974-1400): The island's most romantic retreat seems to have been designed just for honeymooners looking for their own Garden of Eden. Tropical plants and flowers are spread across some 20 acres of gardens, along with a series of waterfalls and streams. The rooms may be a bit small, but 30 come with their own private plunge pool. A shuttle will transport you to the nearest beach. Some of the resort's drinking and dining choices evoke *Arabian Nights,* which should put you in a romantic mood. See chapter 6.
- **Breezes Golf and Beach Resort** (Runaway Bay; ☎ **876/973-2436**): Lying 6 miles west of Ocho Rios, this all-inclusive hotel re-creates the South Seas but on Jamaican soil. It is stylish with luxurious accommodations and good food. One of the best gyms is found here, and activities even include reggae classes. See chapter 6.
- **Trident Villas & Hotel** (Port Antonio; ☎ **876/993-2602**): Here you can follow in the footsteps of that perpetual honeymooner, the late actor Errol Flynn. Poet Ella Wheeler Wilcox called Port Antonio "the most exquisite on earth," and if you're here there's no better hideaway than this posh hotel, enjoying a 14-acre setting on a rocky bluff at the edge of the Caribbean. White cottages and villas are staggered about the property to ensure maximum privacy. The main building has an English country-house tradition with formal service; the bedrooms feel very private and quiet, with only the sounds of the pounding surf, a large paddle fan, and pillow talk. See chapter 7.

7 The Best Family-Friendly Resorts

- **Coyaba** (Mahoe Bay, Little River, Montego Bay; ☎ **877/COYABA8** in the U.S. or 876/953-9150): With a graceful British colonial atmosphere, this small all-inclusive resort offers children 11 and under a 50% discount. This oceanfront retreat is intimate and inviting, and occupies a bucolic site that is a 15-minute drive east of the center of Montego Bay, opening onto a lovely strip of sandy beachfront. There's a nanny service to help you keep the little ones fed and entertained. See chapter 3.
- **Wyndham Rose Hall Golf & Beach Resort** (Montego Bay; ☎ **876/ 624-7326**): This is one of the island's most family-oriented resorts. It's set at the bottom of a rolling 30-acre site and opens directly onto a great white sandy beach. Its Kids Klub is one of the best on the island. See chapter 3.
- **Beaches Negril** (Negril; ☎ **800/BEACHES** in the U.S. or 876/957-9270): New in 1997, this is the family-oriented wing of the Sandals chain, whose resorts usually cater only to male/female couples. A roster of child and teen activities awaits youngsters on a highly desirable 20-acre lot studded with palms and sea grapes adjacent to a sandy beach. This resort's five separate restaurants include a grill for children only. See chapter 4.
- **Franklyn D. Resort** (Runaway Bay; ☎ **800/654-1FDR** in the U.S. or 876/ 973-4591): The FDR is the north-coast family favorite. All meals and activities are included in one net price, and families are housed in Mediterranean-style villas on the grounds 17 miles west of Ocho Rios. A personal attendant does all

the cooking, cleaning, and child care, and many programs are provided to keep your kids entertained. The Kiddies' Centre features everything from computers to arts and crafts. There are dinners for tots as well. See chapter 6.

- **Jamaica Grande Renaissance** (Ocho Rios; ☎ **800/330-8272**): In an area filled with couples-only places, this one is more democratic, catering to the family trade with a year-round children's program. It is also the largest hotel in Jamaica, with plenty of activities for the entire family. See chapter 6.

8 The Best Places to Get Away from It All

- **Lethe Estate** (Montego Bay; ☎ **876/956-4920**): Found 10 miles inland, away from the beach-loving hordes, this elite retreat occupies the grounds of a 150-acre banana plantation. Inspired by some of the great houses in the area, the structure was opened to the public in 1996. Bedrooms evoke Jamaica in the colonial age under British rule. See chapter 3.

- **Treasure Beach Hotel** (South Coast; ☎ **876/965-0110**): Lying on a lushly landscaped hillside above a sandy beach on Jamaica's unhurried South Coast, this is a place where no one will ever find you. It hardly competes with the grand megaresorts of Jamaica, but Treasure Beach offers tranquillity and a laid-back attitude. Bedrooms are in a series of outlying cottages, offering complete privacy. There's a freshwater pool, but most activities are those you organize yourself. It's cheap, too. See chapter 5.

- **Blue Harbour** (Port Maria; ☎ **876/994-0289**): The 1950s retreat of Sir Noël Coward, this is where the playwright and composer entertained the rich and famous of his day. Called "Coward's Folly," it is today rented in whole or part to paying guests who appreciate its funky type of nostalgia. See chapter 6.

- **Navy Island Marina Resort** (Port Antonio; ☎ **876/933-2667**): Once owned by the late actor Errol Flynn, this resort and marina is Jamaica's only private island getaway. Part of Flynn's hedonism still prevails, especially at the clothing-optional beach called Trembly Knee Cove. Accommodations are in studio cottages or villas, and ceiling fans and trade winds recapture the romantic aura of Jamaica's past. See chapter 7.

- **Strawberry Hill** (Blue Mountains; ☎ **876/944-8400**): This highland retreat has been called "a home-away-from-home for five-star Robinson Crusoes." Perched 3,100 feet above the sea, it's our favorite accommodation in all of eastern Jamaica. Set in a well-planted botanical garden, it is a cottage complex built on the site of a 17th-century great house. Multimillionaire Chris Blackwell is the owner, and he's created a memorable, lush retreat. See chapter 8.

9 The Best All-Inclusives

- **Sandals Montego Bay** (Montego Bay; ☎ **800/SANDALS** in the U.S. or 876/952-5510): This is a honeymoon haven in spite of the nearby airport and its zooming planes. This 19-acre all-inclusive resort (catering only to male/female couples) is one of the most popular in the Caribbean. Everything's included, even those notorious toga parties. It's mainly for couples wanting to have a good time. Guests tend to be extroverted and gregarious, and they usually eat and drink their money's worth. We think it's outclassed by some of the better resorts of Ocho Rios, but many vacationers prefer this Mo Bay location. See chapter 3.

- **Breezes Montego Bay** (Montego Bay; ☎ **876/940-1150**): This five-story SuperClub complex calls itself "a sandbox for your inner child" and is the only major hotel built on Doctor's Cave Beach, the beach that put Mo Bay on the tourist map. From intimate cabins to lavish suites, you can live it up in various styles and different price ranges. See chapter 3.

- **Grand Lido** (Negril; ☎ **800/859-7875** in the U.S. or 876/957-5010): This hedonistic resort is a class act. It's the grandest and most architecturally interesting along Negril's beach strip. Adjacent to the often raunchy Hedonism II, the Grand Lido is upscale and discreetly elegant. The smaller of its two beaches is reserved for nudists. Unlike many of Jamaica's resorts, it is not a male/female couples–only joint; it also welcomes singles and same-sex couples. It entertains and treats all guests in a grand style, which is far superior to the typical Club Med in the Caribbean. The dining options are the best in Negril. See chapter 4.
- **Ciboney Ocho Rios** (Ocho Rios; ☎ **800/333-3333** in the U.S. or 876/974-1027): This Radisson franchise is the leading all-inclusive resort in the Greater Ocho Rios area. Its accommodations consist of one-, two-, or three-bedroom villas, each with its own pool and fully equipped kitchen. The dining choices are the best of any of the competing resorts, including one restaurant with a menu of healthy haute cuisine. It's not directly on the beach, but there's a beauty spa and a health and fitness center. A nearby private beach club offers an array of water sports. See chapter 6.
- **Couples Ocho Rios** (Ocho Rios; ☎ **800/268-7537** in the U.S. or 876/975-4271): "Any man and woman in love" are pampered and coddled during their stay at Couples. The resort offers its own private island where couples can bask in the buff. Couples is more upscale and, we think, a little classier than either of the Sandals resorts in the Ocho Rios area. Accommodations are first-class, and the food is among the best in the area, with a choice of four restaurants featuring widely varied cuisine. See chapter 6.
- **Hedonism III** (Runaway Bay; ☎ **876/973-5029**): This is one of Jamaica's newest and best all-inclusives, charging moderate prices. It rents rooms to either singles or couples over 15 and is set on 15 acres of landscaped gardens. There are two good beaches: one where you can wear your suit, and another that is au naturel. See chapter 6.

10 The Best Restaurants

- **Sugar Mill Restaurant** (Montego Bay; ☎ **876/953-2314**): In the Half Moon Club, this is the premier restaurant at any of the megaresorts in the Mo Bay area. The chef creates unique taste sensations, for example, blending a classic Dijon mustard with the island's local pick-me-up, Pickapeppa. His smoked north-coast marlin is without equal, and he makes his own version of bouillabaisse á la Jamaican that is the island's finest. Guests dine by candlelight either indoors or on an open terrace with a view of the old waterwheel left from the days when there was a sugar plantation on-site. See chapter 3.
- **The Pork Pit** (Montego Bay; ☎ **876/952-1046**): It may look like a dump, but The Pork Pit is a classic, the best place on Jamaica's north coast for the famous jerk pork or jerk chicken. The highly spiced meat is barbecued slowly over wood fires until crisp and brown. Its taste is unique and will make you forget about any so-called barbecues you might have sampled elsewhere. Of course, only a Red Stripe beer would do to wash it all down. See chapter 3.
- **Belfield 1794** (Granville, outside Montego Bay; ☎ **876/952-2382**): Set in the hills above Montego Bay, this was once an 18th-century plantation before it was turned into an elegant restaurant featuring a savory international cuisine. Feast

on everything from filet of beef with a plantain and port wine sauce to filet of fish with three kinds of citrus butter. See chapter 3.

- **Rockhouse Restaurant** (Negril; ☎ 876/957-4373): Architecturally dramatic and perched high above the surging tides of a rocky inlet, this restaurant serves some of the best cuisine on the island. The food is international, and you get real flavor and taste here, ranging from smoked marlin to Jamaican peppered pork with yams and root vegetables. See chapter 4.

- **Bloomfield Great House** (Mandeville; ☎ 876/962-7130): Gourmets drive here from miles away to experience some of Jamaica's finest international cuisine. Set on 5 landscaped acres, in a 19th-century house that was once a part of a coffee plantation, the restaurant serves one of the island's best-orchestrated menus—everything from smoked marlin with black caviar to the finest pasta dishes in this part of Jamaica. See chapter 5.

- **Evita's Italian Restaurant** (Ocho Rios; ☎ 876/974-2333): Evita's reigns supreme in an area not noted for having top-notch restaurants outside of the hotels. Evita (actually Eva Myers) is a local culinary star, devoting at least half her menu to pastas. Her recipes are range from the north to the south of Italy. Try her snapper stuffed with crabmeat or the lobster and scampi in a buttery white-cream sauce—everything washed down with a good Italian vino. See chapter 6.

- **Mille Fleurs** (Port Antonio; ☎ 876/993-7267): In the Hotel Mocking Bird Hill, this restaurant is terraced, perched 600 feet above sea level with panoramic views. Even so, people come here for the delectable food, some of which has been praised by *Gourmet* magazine. Opt for the coconut and garlic soup and the fish with a spicy mango and shrimp sauce. See chapter 7.

- **Norma's on the Terrace** (Kingston; ☎ 876/968-5488): Kingston's best cuisine is served here under the supervision of Norma Shirley, the island's foremost female restaurateur. Ms. Shirley serves a nouvelle Jamaican cuisine that is without equal in the area. Try such delights as Jamaican chowder with crabmeat, shrimp, conch, and lobster, or else grilled smoked pork loin in a teriyaki and ginger sauce. See chapter 8.

- **Blue Mountain Inn** (near Kingston; ☎ 876/927-1700): The continental and Caribbean cuisine matches the elegant setting on the grounds of a coffee plantation from the 18th century, high on the slopes of Blue Mountain, which produces the world's best and most expensive coffee. Steaks and seafood dominate the repertoire, and the chef is never better than when preparing his lobster thermidor or tender chateaubriand with classic béarnaise sauce. See chapter 8.

- **Strawberry Hill** (Kingston; ☎ 876/944-8400): One of the best modern Jamaican restaurants on the island is found by taking a taxi ride into the Blue Mountains. Even if you don't stay at this elegant retreat, consider taking a meal here. You will experience a thrill in this remote setting as you partake of fresh grilled fish with jerk mango or grilled shrimp with fresh cilantro. See chapter 8.

11 The Best Shopping Buys

- **Art:** Its paintings may never rival those of the finest Haitian artists, but Jamaica is at least the second-best center for art in the Caribbean. Prices are still reasonable, too, even when the artist has a certain renown. Although paintings are sold all over the island, the finest art is found in Kingston at either the **Frame Centre Gallery** or the **Mutual Life Gallery,** the two leading display showcases for the best of the island's artistic talent. See chapter 8.

- **Handcrafts:** If you see something you like in Jamaica, you'd better purchase it on the spot, as it isn't likely to turn up again. Many Jamaicans produce unique creations, a one-time carving or a one-time straw basket, then vary their pattern if they make it again. Crafts come in many forms, ranging from alabaster and wood carvings to weavings. Some wood carvings show extreme style and others are so hideous you wonder why they were carved in the first place. Any outlet of **Things Jamaican,** including one in Montego Bay (see chapter 3), displays a good assortment of Jamaican crafts, as does **Harmony Hall** outside Ocho Rios on the north coast (see chapter 6).
- **Fashions:** Many artisans in Jamaica produce quality resort wear. (On many other islands, the clothing is inferior and often tacky.) Jamaican women are known as good seamstresses, and they often make quite passable copies based on the works of top designers and sell them at a fraction of the original's price. Some of the best resort wear—for both men and women—is found in Jamaica at **Caribatik Island Fabrics**, a famous outlet outside Falmouth (see chapter 3).
- **Jewelry and Watches:** Some watches at various outlets in Jamaica sell for 20% to 40% off stateside prices. Major international brands are sold, but you must buy from a reliable dealer—not from vendors hustling so-called gold Rolex watches. Jamaican gemstones include coral agate and black coral, and many fashionable pieces are made from these stones. Handmade necklaces are sold everywhere, even on the beach. Dozens of outlets in Jamaica, especially at shopping malls, sell a vast array of jewelry and watches, but you must shop carefully.

12 The Best After-Dark Fun

- **An Evening Cruise Aboard the *Calico*** (Montego Bay; ☎ 876/952-5860): This 55-foot wooden ketch sails from the Montego Bay waterfront. From Wednesday through Saturday, there is no better or more romantic way to spend an evening at Mo Bay than by taking this cruise. From 5 to 7pm, you sail into the sunset while enjoying drinks and the sound of reggae. See chapter 3.
- **Time 'n' Place** (Falmouth, east of Montego Bay; ☎ 876/954-4371): This is one of those places found only in Jamaica. A raffish beach bar, it is built of driftwood and looks as if it might blow away in the next hurricane. The setting is so authentic that many fashion magazines, including *Vogue,* have used it for background shots. The bartender makes the island's best daiquiris. See chapter 3.
- **Rick's Café** (Negril; ☎ 876/957-0380): At sundown in this popular South Coast resort, the gang meets at Rick's nightly to watch one of the most spectacular sunsets in the Caribbean. Still laid-back, the cafe is named for the old watering hole of Bogie's *Casablanca.* Ever had a papaya daiquiri? You can order that and dozens of other drinks in this bar that's been going strong since 1974. See chapter 4.
- **Jamaic'N Me Crazy** (Ocho Rios; ☎ 876/974-2201): The most popular club in this resort area, this hot spot has the best lighting and sound system not only in Ocho Rios, but perhaps on the island. Visiting yachties drop in for the fun, and at certain times of the year, especially in winter, the aura is virtually that of a New York club. Don't come here for an authentic Jamaican experience but for a good time instead. See chapter 6.
- **The Turntable Club** (Kingston; ☎ 876/924-0164): Since 1973, this battered, vintage nightclub has been going strong, maintaining its high energy level even to this day. The club evokes memories of Motown and the early years of reggae and still has great music. See chapter 8.

2

Planning a Trip to Jamaica

This chapter will give you all the nuts-and-bolts information about your trip to Jamaica—what you need to do before leaving home. We'll answer questions such as when to go, how to get the best airfare or package deal, what to take along, and what documents you'll need. In case you're not sure where in Jamaica you want to go, we begin with a rundown of the various major cities and areas.

1 Jamaica in Brief

MONTEGO BAY

The second-largest city in Jamaica, Montego Bay serves as the major tourist center and has a busy international airport. Here's where you'll find the greatest concentration of resorts and some of the island's finest beaches and golf courses. Tourists come to "Mo Bay" for its duty-free shopping, good restaurants, late-night discos, museums, historic buildings, and tours of nearby rum distilleries.

NEGRIL

Situated near Jamaica's relatively arid western tip, Negril enjoys a reputation as the nudist center of the West Indies, with a kind of gently provocative do-as-you-please attitude. Its **Seven Mile Beach** is one of the longest uninterrupted stretches of sand in the Caribbean. Because of a boom in hotel construction, the Negril region is no longer the hippie hideaway it was during the 1960s and early 1970s. The area has become big business and mainstream, competing aggressively for tourist dollars once headed almost exclusively to Montego Bay and Ocho Rios.

THE SOUTH COAST

The little-visited South Coast, lying east of Negril along the A2 (the road to Kingston), is undiscovered Jamaica—although it's becoming better known all the time. Contrary to the island's lush, tropical image, this area is dry and arid. Hotels are few and far between, and they are frequently of the mom-and-pop persuasion. The chief draw here is **Treasure Beach,** tucked away on the secluded coast. Savvy locals—many descended from Scottish seamen shipwrecked off the coast—consider their beachfront a secret on the verge of being discovered by the general public. Regrettably, undertow makes swimming a bit tricky, but the beach is secluded and tranquil, and dramatic waves crash into the gray sands.

MANDEVILLE

Located in south-central Jamaica, Mandeville is the country's highest-altitude town and is built in a style strongly influenced by the English. A gateway for tours of the Blue Mountains, Mandeville was the first community in Jamaica to receive tourists on a large scale (Victorian English visitors looking for a cool mountain retreat). It is now the center of the island's noted coffee cultivation. A sense of slow-paced colonial charm remains a trademark of the town.

THE NORTH COAST

The region's primary natural attractions include the steeply sloping terrain, which has challenged the architectural skill of Jamaica's most sophisticated hotel developers and provided the setting for panoramic public gardens and dramatic waterfalls.

Set on a deep-water harbor easily able to accommodate cruise ships, **Ocho Rios** boasts a dense concentration of resort hotels and other vacation spots. A relative new-comer to the tourist trade, the community lures visitors with its natural beauty and the aura of history left behind by Spanish colonists. Directly west of Ocho Rios is the satellite town of **Runaway Bay,** which boasts a handful of resorts opening onto some good beaches and has the distinct advantage of not being overrun, as many parts of Ocho Rios are.

The hub of verdant eastern Jamaica, **Port Antonio** has retained a sense of glamour ever since financier J. P. Morgan and actors Bette Davis, Ginger Rogers, and Errol Flynn took their vacations—and their paramours—here many years ago. Frequently photographed for its Victorian/Caribbean architecture (with slightly rotted gingerbread), the town is refreshing and not as touristy as Negril, Ocho Rios, and Montego Bay.

KINGSTON & SPANISH TOWN

Located on the southeast coast, Kingston is Jamaica's capital, largest city, and principal port. It's a cosmopolitan city with approximately 650,000 residents in its metropolitan area and serves as the country's main economic, cultural, and government center. Residents proudly say it is the world's reggae capital as well. The city's northern district, called New Kingston, includes most of the capital's high-rises, showcase modern buildings, chic hotels, and upscale private homes. There are, however, extensive poverty-stricken areas in Kingston, and it's not the safest place to be—it's not really a tourist destination.

Nearby are the remains of **Port Royal,** once an infamous lair of pirates and renegades, most of whom were unofficially pressed into service to the English Crown. Port Royal was superseded by Kingston after being destroyed by earthquakes in 1692 and again in 1907. Twenty minutes west of Kingston by car is **Spanish Town,** the country's capital from 1534 to 1872. It was the second town built by Spanish colonists in Jamaica after Nueva Sevilla (now abandoned). The slow-paced village today contains the Cathedral of St. James (early 16th century)—one of the oldest Spanish churches in the West Indies—and memorials to English colonization.

THE BLUE MOUNTAINS

A land of soaring peaks and deep valleys with luxuriant vegetation, the Blue Mountain range rises to the north of Kingston. Mountain roads wind and dip, and they are in bad repair, so don't try to visit on your own. Road signs do not exist in most places, and it's easy to get lost. However, travel agents in Kingston can hook you up with tours through this area, with its coffee plantations and rum factories. Maintained by the government, the prime part of the mountain range is the 192-acre Blue Mountain–John Crow Mountain National Park. The most popular climb begins at Whitfield Hall (see chapter 8), a high-altitude hostel and coffee estate 6 miles from the hamlet of Mavis Bank. The summit of Blue Mountain Peak towers 3,000 feet above sea level.

2 Visitor Information

TOURIST OFFICES

Before you go, you can get information from the **Jamaica Tourist Board** at the following U.S. addresses: 500 N. Michigan Ave., Suite 1030, **Chicago, IL** 60611 (☎ 312/527-1296); 1320 S. Dixie Hwy., Suite 1101, **Coral Gables, FL** 33146 (☎ 305/665-0557); 3440 Wilshire Blvd., Suite 805, **Los Angeles, CA** 90010 (☎ 213/384-1123); 801 Second Ave., **New York, NY** 10017 (☎ 212/856-9727). In **Atlanta,** information can be obtained only by phone at ☎ 770/452-7799.

In **Canada,** contact 1 Eglinton Ave. E., Suite 616, Toronto, ON M4P 3A1 (☎ 416/482-7850). Brits can contact the **London** office: 1–2 Prince Consort Rd., London SW7 2BZ (☎ 020/7224-0505).

Once on the island, you'll find tourist offices at 2 St. Lucia Ave., **Kingston** (☎ 876/929-9200); Cornwall Beach, St. James, **Montego Bay** (☎ 876/952-4425); Shop no. 29, Coral Seas Plaza, **Negril** (☎ 876/957-4243); in the Ocean Village Shopping Centre, **Ocho Rios** (☎ 876/974-2582); in City Centre Plaza, **Port Antonio** (☎ 876/993-3051); and in Hendriks Building, 2 High St., **Black River** (☎ 876/965-2074).

INFO ON THE WEB

The Internet is a great source of travel information. Jamaica is on the Internet at **www.jamaicatravel.com**. In addition, **Yahoo** (www.yahoo.com), **Excite** (www.excite.com), **Lycos** (www.lycos.com), **Infoseek** (www.infoseek.com), and the other major Internet indexing sites all have subcategories for travel, country/regional information, and culture—click on all three for links to travel-related Web sites.

Other good clearinghouse sites for information are **Microsoft's Expedia** (www.expedia.msn.com), **Travelocity** (www.travelocity.com), the **Internet Travel Network** (www.itn.com), and **TravelWeb** (www.travelweb.com). Another good site is **www.city.net/regions/caribbean**, which will point you toward a wealth of Caribbean travel information on the Web. Of the many, many online travel magazines, one of the best is **Arthur Frommer's Budget Travel Online** (www.frommers.com), written and updated by the guru of budget travel himself.

Web Sites for Divers

For useful information on scuba diving in the Caribbean, check out the Web site of the Professional Association of Diving Instructors (PADI) at **www.padi.com**. This site provides descriptions of dive destinations throughout the Caribbean and a directory of PADI-certified dive operators. *Rodale's Scuba Diving Magazine* also has a helpful Web site at **www. scubadiving.com**. Both sites list dive package specials and display gorgeous color photos of some of the most beautiful dive spots in the world.

That covers some of the top general Web sites. As often as possible throughout this chapter, we've included specific Web sites along with phone numbers and addresses. We've also given each resort's Web site if it has one, so you can see pictures of a property before you make your reservation.

You might also check out "The Unofficial Web Site on Jamaica" (**www.jamaicans. com**), the best all-around site, with some good pointers, cultural tidbits, a patois primer, and plenty of humor. This is one of the few Jamaica Web pages that isn't either a blatant ad, or just somebody's homepage with a few vacation pictures. City.Net (**www.city.net/countries/jamaica/**) also has pointers to several of the more official, and generally more staid, Jamaica sites on the Web. The Jamaica Tourist Board and the U.S. government weigh in here.

TRAVEL AGENTS

Travel agents can save you plenty of time and money by steering you toward the best package deals, hunting down the best airfare for your route, and arranging for cruise and rental cars. For the time being, most travel agents still charge nothing for their services—they're paid through commissions from the airlines and other agencies they book for you. Airlines, however, have begun to cut commissions, and increasingly agents are finding they have to charge a fee to hold the bottom line. In the worst instances, unscrupulous agents will offer you only travel options that bag them the juiciest commissions. Shop around and ask hard questions—use this book to become an informed consumer.

If you decide to use a travel agent, make sure the agent is a member of the **American Society of Travel Agents** (ASTA), 1101 King St., Alexandria, VA 22314 (☎ 703/739-8739; www.astanet.com). If you send a self-addressed stamped envelope, ASTA will mail you the free booklet *Avoiding Travel Problems.*

3 Entry Requirements & Customs

DOCUMENTS

U.S. and Canada residents do not need passports but must have proof of citizenship (or permanent residency) and a return or ongoing ticket. A passport is the best bet, but an original birth certificate (or a certified copy) plus photo ID will usually suffice. Do check on the latest entry requirements before you travel, as the rules can change. Our advice is to always bring a passport when you're going to another country.

Other visitors, including British citizens, need passports that are good for a maximum stay of 6 months.

Immigration cards are given to visitors at the airport arrivals desks. Hold onto it because you will need to surrender the document to Jamaican Customs when you leave the country.

Before leaving home, make two copies of your most valuable documents, including the identification pages of your passport, your driver's license, or any other identity document; your airline ticket; and hotel vouchers. If you're taking prescribed medication, make copies of the prescriptions.

PASSPORT INFORMATION

Safeguard your passport in an inconspicuous, inaccessible place like a money belt. If you lose it, visit the nearest consulate of your native country as soon as possible for a replacement. Passport applications are downloadable from the Internet sites listed below.

FOR RESIDENTS OF THE UNITED STATES   If you're applying for a first-time passport, you need to do it in person at one of 13 passport offices throughout the U.S.; a federal, state, or probate court; or a major post office (though not all post offices accept applications; call the number below to find the ones that do). You need to present a certified birth certificate as proof of citizenship, and it's wise to bring along your driver's license, state or military ID, and social security card as well. You also need two identical passport-sized photos (2 in. by 2 in.), taken at any corner photo shop (not one of the strip photos, however, from a photo-vending machine).

For people over 15, a passport is valid for 10 years and costs $60 ($45 plus a $15 handling fee); for those 15 and under, it's valid for 5 years and costs $40. If you're over 15 and have a valid passport that was issued within the past 12 years, you can renew it by mail and bypass the $15 handling fee. Allow plenty of time before your trip to apply; processing normally takes 3 weeks but can take longer during busy periods (especially spring). For general information, call the **National Passport Agency** (☎ 202/647-0518). To find your regional passport office, call the **National Passport Information Center** (☎ 900/225-5674, 35¢ per minute; http://travel.state. gov).

FOR RESIDENTS OF CANADA   You can pick up a passport application at one of 28 regional passport offices or most travel agencies. The passport is valid for 5 years and costs $60. Children under 16 may be included on a parent's passport but need their own to travel unaccompanied by the parent. Applications, which must be accompanied by two identical passport-sized photographs and proof of Canadian citizenship, are available at travel agencies throughout Canada or from the central **Passport Office,** Department of Foreign Affairs and International Trade, Ottawa, Ont. K1A 0G3 (☎ 800/567-6868; www.dfait-maeci.gc.ca/passport). Processing takes 5 to 10 days if you apply in person or about 3 weeks by mail.

FOR RESIDENTS OF THE UNITED KINGDOM   U.K. citizens need a passport to visit Jamaica. To pick up an application for a regular 10-year passport (the Visitor's Passport has been abolished), visit your nearest passport office, major post office, or travel agency. You can also contact the **London Passport Office** at ☎ 0990/210-410 or search its Web site at www.open.gov.uk/ukpass/ ukpass.htm. Passports are £21 for adults and £11 for children under 16.

FOR RESIDENTS OF IRELAND   You can apply for a 10-year passport, costing IR£45, at the **Passport Office, Setanta Centre,** Molesworth Street, Dublin 2 (☎ 01/ 671-1633; www.irlgov.ie/iveagh/foreignaffairs/services). Those under 18 and over 65 must apply for a IR£10 3-year passport. You can also apply at 1A South Mall, Cork (☎ 021/272-525) or over the counter at most main post offices.

FOR RESIDENTS OF AUSTRALIA   A passport is required to visit Jamaica. Apply at your local post office or passport office or search the government Web site at www.dfat.gov.au/passports/. Passports for adults are A$126 and for those under 18 A$63; they are valid for 10 years.

FOR RESIDENTS OF NEW ZEALAND   A passport is required to visit Jamaica. You can pick up a passport application at any travel agency or Link Centre. For more info, contact the **Passport Office,** P.O. Box 805, Wellington (☎ 0800/225-050). Passports for adults are NZ$80 and for those under 16 NZ$40; they are valid for 10 years.

CUSTOMS

WHAT YOU CAN BRING INTO JAMAICA   Most small island nations in the Caribbean let you go through Customs without a thorough check (but don't count on that!). Jamaica is an exception to the rule. The Jamaican government is concerned about drug-running and smuggling more than most other island nations. Therefore, your luggage might get a more thorough check in Jamaica than it would elsewhere.

If you're not carrying illegal substances or firearms, you'll generally pass the test; in general, you are allowed items intended for your personal use while on the island (but not for resale).

You can bring in 2 liters of alcohol, plus two cartons of cigarettes. You're allowed to bring in some duty-free goods, but there is confusion here. You're not supposed to bring in an "inordinate" amount of such goods. Your local Customs official has great leverage in interpreting what is meant by "inordinate." So, limit your import of duty-free goods to what you'll actually need to avoid paying a big import tax.

WHAT YOU CAN TAKE HOME   U.S. Customs   Returning U.S. citizens who have been away for 48 hours or more are allowed to bring back, once every 30 days, $600 worth of merchandise duty-free. You'll be charged a flat rate of 10% duty on the next $1,000 worth of purchases. Be sure to have your receipts handy. On gifts, the duty-free limit is $50. You cannot bring fresh foodstuffs into the United States; tinned foods, however, are allowed.

Joint Customs declarations are possible for members of a family traveling together.

Collect receipts for all purchases made abroad. You must also declare on your Customs form the nature and value of all gifts received during your stay abroad. It's prudent to carry proof that you purchased expensive cameras or jewelry on the U.S. mainland. If you purchased such an item during an earlier trip abroad, you should carry proof that you have previously paid Customs duty on the item.

Sometimes, merchants suggest a false receipt to undervalue your purchase. Be warned: You could be involved in a sting operation—the merchant might be an informer to U.S. Customs.

If you use any medication that contains controlled substances or requires injection, carry an original prescription or note from your doctor.

For more specifics, write to the **U.S. Customs Service,** 1301 Constitution Ave., P.O. Box 7407, Washington, DC 20044 (☎ **202/927-6724**), and request the free pamphlet *Know Before You Go.*

U.K. Customs   U.K. citizens returning from a non-EC country such as one of the Caribbean nations have a Customs allowance of 200 cigarettes; 50 cigars; 250 grams of smoking tobacco; 2 liters of still table wine; 1 liter of spirits or strong liqueurs (over 22% volume); 2 liters of fortified wine, sparkling wine, or other liqueurs; 60cc (ml) perfume; 250cc (ml) of toilet water; and £145 worth of all other goods, including gifts and souvenirs. People under 17 cannot have the tobacco or alcohol allowance. For more information, contact **HM Customs & Excise,** Passenger Enquiry Point, 2nd Floor Wayfarer House, Great South West Rd., Feltham, Middlesex, TW14 8NP (☎ **0181/910-3744,** or 44/181-910-3744 from outside the U.K.; www.hmce.gov.uk).

Canadian Customs   For a clear summary of Canadian rules, write for the booklet *I Declare,* issued by **Revenue Canada,** 2265 St. Laurent Blvd., Ottawa K1G 4KE (☎ **613/993-0534**). Canada allows its citizens a $750 exemption, and you're allowed to bring back duty-free 200 cigarettes, 2.2 pounds of tobacco, 40 imperial ounces of liquor, and 50 cigars. In addition, you're allowed to mail gifts to Canada from abroad at the rate of Can$60 a day, provided they're unsolicited and don't contain alcohol or tobacco (write on the package "Unsolicited gift, under $60 value"). All valuables should be declared on the Y-38 form before departure from Canada, including serial numbers of valuables you already own, such as expensive foreign cameras. *Note:* The $750 exemption can be used only once a year and only after an absence of 7 days.

Australian Customs   The duty-free allowance in Australia is A$400 or, for those under 18, A$200. Personal property mailed back from Jamaica should be marked "Australian goods returned" to avoid payment of duty. Upon returning to Australia, citizens can bring in 250 cigarettes or 250 grams of loose tobacco, and 1,125ml of alcohol. If you're returning with valuable goods you already own, such as foreign-made cameras, you should file form B263. A helpful brochure, available from Australian consulates or Customs offices, is *Know Before You Go*. For more information, contact Australian Customs Services, GPO Box 8, Sydney NSW 2001 (☎ **02/9213-2000**).

New Zealand Customs   The duty-free allowance for New Zealand is NZ$700. Citizens over 17 can bring in 200 cigarettes, or 50 cigars, or 250 grams of tobacco (or a mixture of all three if their combined weight does not exceed 250 grams); plus 4.5 liters of wine and beer, or 1.125 liters of liquor. New Zealand currency does not carry import or export restrictions. When you leave New Zealand, you should fill out a certificate of export, listing the valuables you are taking out of the country; that way, you can bring them back without paying duty. Most questions are answered in a free pamphlet available at New Zealand consulates and Customs offices: *New Zealand Customs Guide for Travellers, Notice no. 4*. For more information, contact New Zealand Customs, 50 Anzac Ave., P.O. Box 29, Auckland (☎ **09/359-6655**).

4 Money

CURRENCY

The unit of currency in Jamaica is the Jamaican dollar, with the same symbol as the U.S. dollar, "$." There is no fixed rate of exchange for the Jamaican dollar. It is traded publicly and is subject to market fluctuations.

Visitors to Jamaica can pay for any goods in U.S. dollars, *but be careful!* Unless clearly stated, always insist on knowing whether a price is quoted in Jamaican or U.S. dollars.

In this guide, we quote some prices in both Jamaican and U.S. dollars, though for the most part U.S. dollars are listed alone because the Jamaican dollar tends to fluctuate. U.S. dollar values give a better indication of costs. Prices given in Jamaican dollars are indicated by "J$"; all other prices are in U.S. dollars.

Many British travelers prefer to use U.S. dollars in Jamaica, especially if they also plan to visit Puerto Rico, the U.S. Virgin Islands, or the U.S. mainland.

There are Bank of Jamaica exchange bureaus at both international airports (Montego Bay and Kingston), at cruise-ship piers, and in most hotels.

There is no limit to the amount of foreign currency you can bring into or out of Jamaica.

Whenever you leave your hotel, take along some small bills and coins. They will come in handy, since tips are generally expected for any small service rendered.

ATMS

ATMs are linked to an international network that most likely includes your bank at home. **Cirrus** (☎ 800/424-7787; www.mastercard.com) and **Plus** (☎ 800/ 843-7587; www.visa.com/atms) are the two most popular networks; check the back

The Jamaican Dollar, the U.S. Dollar, the British Pound & the Canadian Dollar

The chart below gives rounded-off U.S. dollar, British pound, and Canadian dollar values for Jamaican prices. The chart's exchange rates of U.S.$1 = J$40.08, £1 = J$65.10, and CAN$1 = J$27.10 were in effect as this edition was printed but may be slightly different when you visit the island. Stated differently, J$1 equals about 2 U.S. cents, about 2 British pence, and about 4 Canadian cents.

Jamaican $	U.S. $	U.K. £	CAN $
5	0.12	0.08	0.18
10	0.25	0.15	0.36
25	0.62	0.38	0.92
50	1.24	0.76	1.84
75	1.87	1.15	2.76
100	2.49	1.53	3.68
200	4.98	3.06	7.36
300	7.47	4.59	11.04
400	9.96	6.12	14.72
500	12.45	7.65	18.40
750	18.67	11.47	27.60
1,000	24.90	15.30	36.80
5,000	124.50	76.50	184.00
10,000	285.00	153.00	368.00

of your ATM card to see which network your bank belongs to. Use the toll-free numbers to locate ATMs in your destination.

If you're traveling abroad, ask your bank for a list of overseas ATMs. Be sure to check the daily withdrawal limit before you depart, and ask whether you need a new personal ID number.

CREDIT CARDS

Credit cards are invaluable when traveling. They are a safe way to carry money, and they provide a convenient record of all your expenses. You can also withdraw cash advances from your credit cards at any bank (though you'll start paying hefty interest on the advance the moment you receive the cash, and you won't receive frequent-flyer miles on an airline credit card). At most banks, you don't even need to go to a teller; you can get a cash advance at the ATM if you know your PIN. (If you've forgotten your PIN or didn't even know you had one, call the phone number on the back of your credit card and ask the bank to send it to you. It usually takes 5 to 7 business days, though some banks will provide the number over the phone if you tell them your mother's maiden name or pass some other security clearance.)

TRAVELER'S CHECKS

Traveler's checks are something of an anachronism from the days before the ATM made cash accessible at any time. These days, traveler's checks seem less necessary, as most islands have 24-hour ATMs that allow you to withdraw small amounts of cash as needed. However, if you want to avoid ATM service charges, or if you just want the security of knowing you can get a refund in the event that your wallet is stolen, you may want to purchase traveler's checks, which you can do at almost any bank. American Express offers denominations of $10, $20, $50, $100, $500, and $1,000. You'll pay a service charge ranging from 1% to 4%. You can also get American Express traveler's checks over the phone by calling ☎ **800/221-7282;** by using this number, Amex gold and platinum cardholders are exempt from the 1% fee. AAA members can obtain checks without a fee at most AAA offices.

Visa offers traveler's checks at **Citibank** locations nationwide and several other participating banks. The service charge ranges from 1.5% to 2%; checks come in denominations of $20, $50, $100, $500, and $1,000. **MasterCard** also offers traveler's checks. Call ☎ **800/223-9920** for a location near you.

THEFT

Almost every credit-card company has an emergency toll-free number you can call if your wallet or purse is stolen. They may be able to wire you a cash advance off your credit card immediately, and in many places, they can deliver an emergency credit card in a day or two. The issuing bank's toll-free number is usually on the back of the credit card—though of course that doesn't help you much if the card was stolen. In that case, call the toll-free information directory at ☎ **800/555-1212. Citicorp Visa's** U.S. emergency number is ☎ **800/336-8472. American Express** cardholders and traveler's-check holders should call ☎ **800/221-7282** for all money emergencies. **MasterCard** holders should call ☎ **800/307-7309.**

Odds are that if your wallet is gone, the police won't be able to recover it for you. However, after you realize that it's gone and you cancel your credit cards, it is still worth informing them. Your credit-card company or insurer may require a police report number.

5 When to Go

HIGH SEASON VS. LOW SEASON: SOME PROS & CONS

With its fabled weather balmy all year, Jamaica is more and more a year-round destination. Nevertheless, it has a distinct **high season** running roughly from mid-December to mid-April. Hotels charge their highest prices during this peak winter period, when visitors fleeing from cold north winds crowd onto the island. (We've quoted each hotel's rack rates throughout this guide, but you don't have to pay that much, even in the high season, if you book a package instead of calling the hotel directly.) And let's face it: When it's snowy and 10° in Chicago, sometimes it's worth any price to save your sanity and go bask on a warm, sunny beach.

Reservations should be made 2 to 3 months in advance for trips during the winter. At certain hotels, it's almost impossible to book accommodations for the Christmas holidays or for the month of February.

The **off-season** in Jamaica (roughly from mid-April to mid-December, with variance from hotel to hotel) amounts to a summer sale. In most cases, hotel rates are slashed a startling 20% to 60%. Some package-tour charges are as much as 20% lower, and individual excursion airfares are reduced from 5% to 10%. In addition, airline seats and hotel rooms are much easier to come by. It's a bonanza for cost-conscious travelers, especially families who like to vacation together. In the chapters ahead, we'll spell out in dollars the specific amounts hotels charge during the off-season.

There are other advantages to off-season travel. Resort boutiques often feature summer sales, hoping to clear merchandise not sold in February to accommodate stock for the coming winter. After the winter hordes have left, a less-hurried way of life prevails on the island. You'll have a better chance to appreciate the food, culture, and local customs. Swimming pools and beaches are less crowded, sometimes not crowded at all. There's no waiting for a rental car (only to be told none are available), no long tee-up for golf, no queuing for tennis courts and water sports. You can often walk in unannounced and find a seat for dinner at a top restaurant that in winter would have required reservations far in advance. Also, when waiters are less hurried, they give better service.

The atmosphere is more cosmopolitan in the off-season than in the winter, mainly because of the influx of Europeans and Japanese. You'll no longer feel as if you're at a Canadian or American outpost. Also, the Jamaicans themselves travel in the off-season, and your holiday becomes more of a people-to-people experience.

Summer is also the time for family travel, not often possible during the winter season.

But let's not paint too rosy a picture: There are disadvantages of off-season travel to consider. Sometimes services are curtailed—restaurants might be closed because of lack of business. Entertainment, including bands and folkloric shows, will be greatly curtailed or may not exist at all until the winter season. Also, when business slows down in summer, many hotels use this time to renovate or even to launch new construction for the coming season. You're also taking a chance that the sun will be broiling—and the hurricane season in the Caribbean officially lasts from June 1 to November 30. Finally, a minus for singles, there are just fewer people, lowering your chances to meet Mr. or Ms. Right.

CLIMATE

Jamaica has one of the most varied climates of any Caribbean island. Along the seashore, where most visitors congregate, the island is air-conditioned by the northeast trade winds, and temperature variations are surprisingly slight. Coastal readings average between 71° and 88°F all year. The Jamaican winter is usually like May in the United States or northern Europe, however, and there can be really chilly times, especially in the early morning and at night. Winter is generally the driest season but can be wet in mountain areas; you can expect showers, especially in northeast Jamaica.

Inland, Jamaica's average temperatures decrease by approximately 1°F for every 300 feet increase in elevation. Temperatures atop the highest of the Blue Mountains might descend to a chilly 50°F, although most visitors find that a light jacket, sweater, or evening wrap is adequate for even the coldest weather on the island. In some cases, a wrap is a good idea even on the beach because of nighttime breezes or strong drafts from a dining room's air conditioner.

Average yearly precipitation in Jamaica is more than 80 inches. Rainfall is heaviest along the eastern edge of the island's north coast, with Port Antonio receiving some of the most intense downpours. The island has two rainy seasons, May and October to November, although with the recent trend toward global warming, there have been fewer strict seasonal variations.

THE HURRICANE SEASON   The curse of Jamaican weather, the hurricane season, officially lasts from June 1 to November 30—but there's no need for panic. Satellite weather forecasts generally give adequate warning so that precautions can be taken.

If you're heading for Jamaica during the hurricane season, you can call your nearest branch of the National Weather Service, listed in the phone directory under U.S. Department of Commerce, for a weather forecast.

Another easy way to receive the weather forecast in the city you plan to visit is by contacting the information service associated with The Weather Channel. It works like this: Dial ☎ **800/WEATHER** and listen to the recorded announcement. When you're prompted, enter the account number of a valid Visa or MasterCard. After the card is approved, at a rate of 95¢ per query, punch in the name of any of 1,000 cities worldwide whose weather is monitored by The Weather Channel. The report that's delivered might help you in deciding what to wear and how to pack.

HOLIDAYS

Jamaica observes the following public holidays: New Year's Day (January 1), Ash Wednesday, Good Friday, Easter Sunday and Monday, National Labor Day (late May), Independence Day (a Monday in early August), National Heroes Day (third Monday in October), Christmas Day (December 25), and Boxing Day (December 26).

Jamaica Calendar of Events

January

- **Accompong Maroon Festival,** St. Elizabeth. Annual celebration by the Maroons in Western Jamaica, with traditional singing and dancing. Maroon feasts and ceremonies, blowing of the abeng, and playing of Maroon drums. The festival dates back to the 19th century. Contact Kenneth Watson at ☎ **876/952-4546.** January 6.
- **Jamaica Sprint Triathlon,** Negril. Hundreds participate in a three-part competition joining swimming, cycling, and running in one sweat-inducing endurance test. Contact the Jamaica Tourist Board for details (see "Visitor Information," earlier in this chapter). January 23 to 25.

February

- **Tribute to Bob Marley—Symposium in Music,** Ocho Rios. Seminars for students of music as well as players of drums, guitar, and wind instruments. Contact the Jamaica Cultural Development Commission at ☎ **876/926-5726.** February 4 to 8.
- **Bob Marley Birthday Bash,** Montego Bay. Annual celebration of Bob Marley's birthday with a concert featuring popular reggae artists. Contact Marjorie Scott, at the Bob Marley Foundation, at ☎ **876/978-2991.** February 6.
- ✪ **Reggae Sunsplash,** Ocho Rios. Annual reggae festival featuring internationally acclaimed reggae musicians. Contact Rae Barrett, Reggae Sunsplash International, at ☎ **876/960-1904.** Call for dates.

March

- **Spring Break,** Negril, Montego Bay, and Ocho Rios. An annual program for students vacationing in Jamaica. Discounted rates at selected hotels, attractions, restaurants, and nightclubs. Featured are reggae concerts with live bands and beach-volleyball competitions; entry to concerts is free with valid student ID. Contact the Jamaica Tourist Board at ☎ **800/233-4582.**
- **Montego Bay Yacht Club's Easter Regatta.** An annual sailing event with several races staged along the north coast over a 4-day period at Easter time. Contact the Montego Bay Yacht Club (☎ **876/979-8038**).

April

- **Carnival in Jamaica,** Kingston, Ocho Rios, and Montego Bay. Weeklong series of fetes, concerts, and street parades, with flamboyantly costumed groups of all ages dancing through the streets of Ocho Rios, Kingston, and Montego Bay. Local tourist offices will provide more details. First week of April.

June

- **Ocho Rios Jazz Festival,** Ocho Rios and Montego Bay. International performers from Great Britain, Europe, Japan, the United States, and the Caribbean perform here along with Jamaican jazz artists. A series of jazz concerts is presented, along with jazz lunches, jazz teas, jazz feasts on the river, and even jazz barbecues. Contact the Jamaica Tourist Board at ☎ **800/233-4582** or 876/922-3544. June 13 to 20.

- **National Dance Theatre Company's Season of Dance,** Kingston. At the Little Theatre in Kingston, the island's internationally celebrated dance company presents this major cultural event. Creative dancers explore both traditional and modern choreography. The season also features notable singers. Call ☎ **876/926-6129** for information. June to August 31.

July

✪ **Reggae Sunsplash,** at Chukka Cove, St. Ann. An annual and internationally famous reggae festival featuring top local and international reggae performers. Call ☎ **876/929-9200** for dates.

August

- **Reggae Sunfest,** at Catherine Hall, Montego Bay. An annual 5-day music festival featuring international singers and top local talent. Call ☎ **876/940-5446** for more information. August 2 to 8.

September

- **Falmouth Blue Marlin Tournament,** Montego Bay. Although this fishing tournament outside Montego Bay attracts many world-class fishers, the big event remains in Port Antonio in October (see below). Nevertheless, in September, when there is little activity on the Jamaican calendar of events, it's somewhat of a big deal locally. For more information, contact ☎ **876/954-3338.** September 23 to 25.

October

✪ **Port Antonio International Fishing Tournament.** This tournament is one of the oldest and most prestigious sport-fishing events in the Caribbean, with participants from Europe and North America. Contact Sir Henry Morgan Angling Association at ☎ **876/923-8724.** October 11 to 15.

November

- **Air Jamaica Jazz & Blues Festival,** Montego Bay. Internationally acclaimed musicians and recording artists perform in a series of concerts at Rose Hall Great House over a long weekend. Call ☎ **876/929-4089** for more information. November 17 to 21.

December

- **Motor Sports Championship Series,** Dover Raceway, St. Ann. Prestigious championship event that features local, regional, and international motoring enthusiasts. Contact Motor Sports Ltd. at ☎ **876/960-9100** for information. December 5.

6 The Active Vacation Planner

If sports are important to you, you may want to learn more about the offerings of particular parts of Jamaica before deciding on a resort. Jamaica is so large that it isn't much fun to undertake a long day's excursion just to play golf, for example. The cost of most activities is generally the same throughout the island.

Your Choice of Resort

Most casual visitors to Jamaica pick a resort without paying undue attention to its location on the island. That is particularly true for guests who prefer to spend most of their time at an all-inclusive, venturing out occasionally for some handcrafts shopping or to see some of the local sights. Even so, knowing a bit about the different areas of Jamaica can help you find the perfect resort for you.

For example, it might be handy to know that most travelers who visit Kingston do so for business reasons, although for the true Jamaican culture buff it has the most museums, the best galleries, and some great historic sights. It also has more nightlife than most of the upscale resorts, ranging from jazz and reggae clubs to upscale supper clubs and English theater. But you hardly come here for beaches.

Port Antonio is for the elite traveler who wants to escape the mass package tours of Ocho Rios or even Montego Bay. Come here for some good beaches, plus great river rafting, scuba diving, and snorkeling.

To the west, Ocho Rios has some of the grandest and most traditional resorts in Jamaica as well as some of the leading Sandals properties. But it doesn't have the best beaches, shops, or scenic attractions. Nonetheless, if you're resort oriented, this might be your choice.

The grand dame of Jamaica is Montego Bay, which boasts three of the poshest resorts in the Caribbean: Half Moon, Round Hill, and Tryall. Aside from these deluxe resorts, Montego Bay—along with Negril—also features the largest number of acceptable resorts that are inexpensive or moderately priced. Although we prefer the beaches of Negril, those of Montego Bay are equally fine but overcrowded in winter. Shopping here is excellent for Jamaica, but the nightlife is surprisingly lackluster.

Negril, the final contender, is for the hedonist. It's a sleepy retreat of sybaritic singles and couples. If Montego Bay is a bit staid, Negril is young and hip. One visitor who flies in every year claims Negril is for "sand and sex," but not necessarily in that order. You don't have to be a refugee from the swinging 60s to enjoy Negril, however. Many of its resorts, such as Grand Lido Negril, have become subdued and quite respectable. Nonetheless, Negril is not for your aging maiden aunt. Take her to Montego Bay. But if you're with a spouse or partner who doesn't mind taking off his or her clothes, make it Negril.

Below is a summary to get you going and help you choose the destination that's right for you.

BEACHES

Many visitors want to do nothing more sporting than lie on the beach. For specific recommendations, refer to the regional chapters that follow, and to section 1 of chapter 1, "The Best Beaches." On the whole, the best beaches are as follows: the 7-mile stretch of sand at Negril, with many sections reserved for nudists (see chapter 4); Walter Fletcher Beach at Montego Bay, with especially tranquil waters (see chapter 3); the unfortunately crowded Doctor's Cave Beach, also at Montego Bay, with water sports and changing rooms (see chapter 3); and San San Beach, at Port Antonio on the north coast, with clean white sand, plenty of water sports, and a favorite picnic area (see chapter 7).

BIRDING

Victor Emanuel Nature Tours (☎ 800/328-8368) offers weeklong birding trips to Jamaica, costing from U.S.$1,995 per person. Jamaica is home to some 30 species of birds found nowhere else in the world. Trips are conducted by a Jamaican ornithologist. Visits are to the Blue Mountains (north of Kingston, the capital) and to the ponds and lagoons of Mandeville in the southwest.

DEEP-SEA FISHING

The waters off north Jamaica are world-renowned for game fish, including dolphinfish, kingfish, wahoo, blue and white marlin, sailfish, tarpon, Allison tuna, barracuda, and bonito. The **Port Antonio International Fishing Tournament** lures fishers from around the world every October. Most major hotels from Port Antonio to Montego Bay offer deep-sea fishing, and there are many charter boats. See chapters 3 and 7.

GOLF

Jamaica has the best golf courses in the West Indies, with Montego Bay alone sporting four championship links. Those at **Wyndham Rose Hall Golf & Beach Resort** (☎ 876/953-2650) are ranked as among the top five golf courses in the world, according to an expert assessment. It is an unusual and challenging seaside and mountain course, built on the shores of the Caribbean.

The excellent course at **Tryall Golf, Tennis & Beach Club** (☎ 876/956-5660) is the site of the Jamaica Classic Annual.

The **Half Moon** (☎ 876/953-2560) at Rose Hall features a championship course designed by Robert Trent Jones. **Ironshore Golf & Country Club** (☎ 876/953-3681) is another well-known 18-hole golf course with a 72 par. See chapter 3 for details about these Montego Bay courses.

On the north shore, there's **SuperClub's Runaway Golf Club** (☎ 876/973-4820) at Runaway Bay and **Sandals Golf & Country Club** (☎ 876/975-0119) at Ocho Rios. See chapter 6.

In Mandeville, **Manchester Country Club,** Brumalia Road (☎ 876/962-2403), is Jamaica's oldest golf course but with only nine greens. Beautiful vistas unfold from 2,201 feet above sea level. See chapter 5.

HIKING

Unlike many of its neighboring islands, Jamaica offers mountain peaks of up to 7,400 feet. The flora, fauna, waterfalls, and panoramas of those peaks have attracted increasing numbers of hikers, each determined to experience the natural beauty of the island firsthand. Because of possible dangers involved, it's often best to go on an organized tour, the best of which are offered by **Sunventure Tours,** 30 Balmoral Ave., Kingston 10, Jamaica W.I. (☎ 876/920-8348). For more information, refer to chapter 8.

HORSEBACK RIDING

The best riding is on the north shore. Jamaica's most complete equestrian center is **Chukka Cove Polo Club** (☎ 876/972-2771), at Richmond Llandovery, less than 4 miles east of Runaway Bay (see chapter 6). The best ride here is a 3-hour jaunt to the sea, where you can unpack your horse and swim in the surf.

Another good program is offered at the **Rocky Point Riding Stables** (☎ 876/953-2286), Half Moon Club, Rose Hall, Montego Bay, which is housed in the most beautiful barn and stables in Jamaica (see chapter 3).

SCUBA DIVING

Diving is sometimes offered as part of all-inclusive packages by the island's major hotels. There are also well-maintained facilities independent of the hotels.

Jamaica boasts some of the finest waters for diving in the world, with depths averaging 35 to 95 feet. Visibility is usually 60 to 120 feet. Most diving is on coral reefs, which are protected as underwater parks. Fish, shells, coral, and sponges are plentiful on them. Experienced divers can also see wrecks, hedges, caves, drop-offs, and tunnels.

Near Montego Bay, **Seaworld Resorts** (☎ 876/953-2180), at the Cariblue Hotel, Rose Hall Main Road, offers scuba-diving excursions to offshore coral reefs that are among the most spectacular in the Caribbean. There are also PAIC-certified dive guides, one dive boat, and all necessary equipment for either inexperienced or certified divers. See chapter 3.

Outside Kingston, the **Buccaneer Scuba Club,** Morgan's Harbour, Port Royal (☎ 876/967-8061), is one of Jamaica's leading dive and water-sports operators. It offers a wide range of dive sites to accommodate various divers' tastes—from the incredible *Texas* shipwreck to the unspoiled beauty of the Turtle Reef. See chapter 8.

Negril is a hotbed of diving. **Negril Scuba Centre** (☎ 800/818-2963 or 876/957-9641), in the Negril Beach Club Hotel, Norman Manley Boulevard, is the area's most modern, best-equipped scuba facility. Equally as good is **Marine Life Divers,** a PADI-approved five-star dive shop located at the Drumville Cove Hotel (☎ 876/957-6290). See chapter 4.

TENNIS

All-Jamaica Hardcourt Championships are played in August at the **Manchester Country Club,** Brumalia Road, P.O. Box 17, Mandeville (☎ 876/962-2403). The courts are open for general play during the rest of the year. See chapter 5.

Ciboney Ocho Rios, Main Street, Ocho Rios (☎ 876/974-1027), focuses more on tennis than does any other resort in the area. It offers three clay-surface and three hard-surface courts, all lit for nighttime play. Residents play free either day or night, but nonresidents must call and make arrangements with the manager. See chapter 6.

In Montego Bay, you'll find excellent tennis facilities at **Wyndham Rose Hall Golf & Beach Resort,** at Rose Hall (☎ 876/953-2650); **Half Moon Golf, Tennis & Beach Club** (☎ 876/953-2211); and **Tryall Golf, Tennis & Beach Club,** St. James (☎ 876/956-5660). See chapter 3.

7 Health & Insurance

Traveling to Jamaica should not adversely affect your health. Finding a good doctor in Jamaica is no real problem, and all of them speak English, of course.

STAYING HEALTHY

Keep the following suggestions in mind:

- It's best to drink bottled water during your trip.
- If you experience diarrhea, moderate your eating habits and drink only bottled water until you recover. If symptoms persist, consult a doctor.
- The Jamaican sun can be brutal. Wear sunglasses and a hat and use sunscreen liberally. Limit your time on the beach the first day. If you do overexpose yourself, stay out of the sun until you recover. If your exposure is followed by fever or chills, a headache, or a feeling of nausea or dizziness, see a doctor.

- Some of the biggest health menaces are the "no-see-ums," which appear mainly in the early evening. You can't see these gnats, but you sure can "feel-um." Screens can't keep these critters out, so carry your favorite bug repellent.

WHAT TO DO IF YOU GET SICK AWAY FROM HOME

Finding a good doctor in Jamaica is not a problem, and they speak English. See the "Fast Facts" section in each chapter for specific names and addresses on each individual area.

If you worry about getting sick away from home, you may want to consider medical travel insurance (see the section on travel insurance later in this chapter). In most cases, however, your existing health plan will provide all the coverage you need. Be sure to carry your identification card in your wallet.

If you suffer from a chronic illness, consult your doctor before your departure. For conditions like epilepsy, diabetes, or heart problems, wear a **Medic Alert Identification Tag** (☎ 800/825-3785; www.medicalert.org), which will immediately alert doctors to your condition and give them access to your records through Medic Alert's 24-hour hot line. Membership is $35, plus a $15 annual fee.

Pack prescription medications in your carry-on luggage. Bring written prescriptions in generic, not brand-name, form. Also bring along copies of your prescriptions in case you lose your pills or run out.

If you wear contact lenses, pack an extra pair in case you lose or tear one.

Contact the **International Association for Medical Assistance to Travelers** (IAMAT) (☎ 716/754-4883 or 416/652-0137; www.sentex.net/~iamat) for tips on travel and health concerns in the countries you'll be visiting. The **United States Centers for Disease Control and Prevention** (☎ 404/332-4559; www.cdc.gov) provides up-to-date information on necessary vaccines and health hazards by region or country (by mail, their booklet is $20; on the Internet, it's free).

Once you're abroad, if you do get sick, you may want to ask the concierge at your hotel to recommend a local doctor—even his or her own. This will probably yield a better recommendation than any toll-free number would. If you can't find a doctor who can help you right away, try the emergency room at the local hospital. Many emergency rooms have walk-in clinics for emergency cases that are not life-threatening.

INSURANCE

There are three kinds of travel insurance: trip-cancellation, medical, and lost-luggage coverage.

Trip-cancellation insurance is a good idea if you have paid a large portion of your vacation expenses up front, say, by purchasing a package or a cruise. Trip-cancellation insurance should cost approximately 6% to 8% of the total value of your vacation. (Don't buy it from the same company from which you've purchased your vacation—talk about putting all your eggs in one basket!) Trip-cancellation insurance can fall into two categories: one if the trip gets cancelled—say, because not enough people sign up. The other, which we recommend, is in case you need to cancel your trip because of sickness or death. Say you've signed up for a $3,000 cruise. If you can't go because a relative has died, you may be out every cent.

Lost luggage and your health may be covered by existing policies. Rule number one: Check your existing policies before you buy any additional coverage. Note, however, that in many cases, existing health coverage does not include emergency evacuation, and Medicare often doesn't cover all medical expenses overseas. For example, if you need to be flown off a cruise ship, you could lose a fortune.

Your existing health insurance should cover you if you get sick on vacation (though if you belong to ahealth maintenance organization [HMO], you should check to see whether you are fully covered while you're away from home). If you need hospital treatment, most health insurance plans and HMOs will cover out-of-country hospital visits and procedures, at least to some extent. Most make you pay the bills up front at the time of care, however, and you'll get a refund only after you've returned and filed all the paperwork. Members of **Blue Cross/Blue Shield,** however, can now use their cards at select hospitals in most major cities worldwide (☎ **800/810-BLUE** or www.bluecares.com for a list of hospitals). Note that **Medicare** covers U.S. citizens traveling only in Mexico and Canada.

Your homeowner's insurance should cover stolen luggage. The airlines are responsible for $1,250 if they lose your luggage on domestic flights; if you plan to carry anything more valuable than that, keep it in your carry-on bag.

If you do require additional insurance, try one of the following companies: **Access America,** 6600 W. Broad St., Richmond, VA 23230 (☎ **800/284-8300**); **Travel Guard International,** 1145 Clark St., Stevens Point, WI 54481 (☎ **800/284-1300**); **Travel Guard International, Inc.,** P.O. Box 280568, East Hartford, CT 06128 (☎ **800/243-3174**); **Columbus Travel Insurance,** 279 High St., Croydon CR01QH (☎ **020/7375-0011** in London; www.columbusdirect.co.uk). For medical coverage, try **MEDEX International,** P.O. Box 5375, Timonium, MD 21094-5375 (☎ **888/MEDEX-00** or 410/453-6300; fax 410/453-6301; www.medexassist.com); or **Travel Assistance International** (Worldwide Assistance Services, Inc.), 1133 15th St. NW, Suite 400, Washington, DC 20005 (☎ **800/821-2828** or 202/828-5894; fax 202/828-5896). The **Divers Alert Network** (DAN) (☎ **800/446-2671** or 919/684-2948) insures scuba divers.

CAR RENTER'S INSURANCE   For information on car renter's insurance, see "Getting Around," later in this chapter.

8 Tips for Travelers with Special Needs

FOR TRAVELERS WITH DISABILITIES

Hotels rarely give much publicity to the facilities, if any, they offer persons with disabilities, so it's always wise to contact the hotel directly, in advance. Tourist offices probably won't be able to help you with such questions.

A disability shouldn't stop anyone from traveling. There are more resources out there than ever before. *A World of Options,* a 658-page book of resources for travelers with disabilities, covers everything from biking trips to scuba outfitters. It costs $35 ($30 for members) and is available from **Mobility International USA,** P.O. Box 10767, Eugene, OR 97440 (☎ **541/343-1284** voice and TDD; www.miusa.org). Annual membership for Mobility International is $35, which includes their quarterly newsletter, *Over the Rainbow.*

The **Moss Rehab Hospital** (☎ **215/456-9600**) has been providing friendly and helpful phone advice and referrals to travelers with disabilities for years through its **Travel Information Service** (☎ **215/456-9603;** www.mossresourcenet.org).

You can join the **Society for the Advancement of Travel for the Handicapped** (SATH), 347 Fifth Ave. Suite 610, New York, NY 10016 (☎ **212/447-7284;** fax 212/725-8253; www.sath.org), for $45 annually, $30 for seniors and students, to gain access to a vast network of connections in the travel industry. SATH provides information sheets on travel destinations and referrals to tour operators that specialize in traveling with disabilities; its quarterly magazine, *Open World for Disability and*

Mature Travel, is full of good information and resources. A year's subscription is $13 ($21 outside the U.S.).

Travelers with disabilities may also want to consider joining a tour that caters specifically to them. One of the best operators is **Flying Wheels Travel,** 143 West Bridge (P.O. Box 382), Owatonna, MN 55060 (☎ **800/535-6790**). It offers various escorted tours and cruises, with an emphasis on sports, as well as private tours in minivans with lifts. Other reputable specialized tour operators include **Access Adventures** (☎ 716/889-9096), which offers sports-related vacations; **Accessible Journeys** (☎ 800/TINGLES or 610/521-0339), for slow walkers and wheelchair travelers; **The Guided Tour, Inc.** (☎ 215/782-1370); **Wilderness Inquiry** (☎ 800/728-0719 or 612/379-3858); and **Directions Unlimited** (☎ 800/533-5343).

Travelers with vision impairments should contact the **American Foundation for the Blind,** 11 Penn Plaza, Suite 300, New York, NY 10001 (☎ **800/232-5463**), for information on traveling with Seeing Eye dogs.

FOR BRITISH TRAVELERS   The **Royal Association for Disability and Rehabilitation** (RADAR), Unit 12, City Forum, 250 City Rd., London, EC1V 8AF (☎ **0171/250-3222;** fax 0171/250-0212), publishes holiday "Fact Packs," three in all, which sell for £2 each or all three for £5. The first one provides general information, including planning and booking a holiday, insurance, finances, and useful organization and holiday providers. The second outlines transportation available when going abroad and equipment for rent. The third deals with specialized accommodations.

FOR GAYS & LESBIANS

Jamaica is the most homophobic island in the Caribbean, with harsh anti-gay laws, even though there's a large local gay population.

Many all-inclusive resorts, notably the famous Sandals of Jamaica, have discriminatory policies. Although Sandals started off welcoming "any two people in love," they quickly switched to allowing only male/female couples. Gays are definitely excluded from their love nests. However, not all all-inclusives practice such blatant discrimination. Hedonism II, a rival of Sandals in Negril, is a couples-only resort, but any combination will do. The Grand Hotel Lido, a more upscale all-inclusive in Negril, will welcome whatever combination shows up (even singles, for that matter).

The **International Gay & Lesbian Travel Association** (IGLTA) (☎ **800/ 448-8550** or 954/776-2626; fax 954/776-3303; www.iglta.org) links travelers with the appropriate gay-friendly service organization or tour specialist. With around 1,200 members, it offers quarterly newsletters, marketing mailings, and a membership directory that's updated quarterly. Membership often includes gay or lesbian businesses but is open to individuals for $150 per year, plus a $100 administration fee for new members. Members are kept informed of gay-friendly hoteliers, tour operators, and airline and cruise-line representatives. Contact the IGLTA for a list of its member agencies, who will be tied into IGLTA's information resources.

General gay and lesbian travel agencies include **Family Abroad** (☎ **800/999-5500** or 212/459-1800, gay and lesbian); and **Above and Beyond Tours** (☎ **800/ 397-2681,** mainly gay men).

There are also two good biannual English-language gay guidebooks; both focus on gay men but include information for lesbians as well. You can get the *Spartacus International Gay Guide* or *Odysseus* from most gay and lesbian bookstores, or order them from **Giovanni's Room** (☎ **215/923-2960;** e-mail giophilp@netaxs.com) or **A Different Light Bookstore** (☎ **800/343-4002** or 212/989-4850; www.adlbooks. com). Both lesbians and gays might want to pick up a copy of *Gay Travel A to Z* ($16).

The Ferrari Guides (www.q-net.com) is yet another very good series of gay and lesbian guidebooks.

Out and About, 8 W. 19th St. #401, New York, NY 10011 (☎ **800/929-2268** or 212/645-6922), offers guidebooks and a monthly newsletter packed with good information on the global gay and lesbian scene. A year's subscription to the newsletter costs $49. *Our World,* 1104 North Nova Rd., Suite 251, Daytona Beach, FL 32117 (☎ **904/441-5367**), is a slicker monthly magazine that promotes and highlights travel bargains and opportunities. Annual subscription rates are $35 ($45 outside the U.S.).

Several companies now assemble gay travel packages. **RSVP Vacations** (☎ **800/ 328-RSVP** or 612/379-4697; www.rsvp.net), based in Minneapolis, offers gay cruises on ships both large and small in the Caribbean. **Atlantis Events** (☎ **800/628-5268** or 310/281-5450); www.atlantisevents.com), based in West Hollywood, books Club Med resorts for all-gay, all-inclusive vacations; they also do all-gay cruises, often in the Caribbean.

Many travel agencies are affiliated with the **International Gay Travel Association,** based in Key West. Any of these agencies can work with you to choose gay-friendly destinations and accommodations. (You'll find a list of gay-friendly travel agencies across the U.S. on the RSVP Vacations and Out and About Web sites mentioned above.) One gay-friendly agency is **Islanders' Kennedy Travel** (☎ **800/988-1181** or 516/352-4888). There are many others, all over the United States.

FOR SENIORS

Don't be shy about asking for discounts, but always carry some kind of identification, such as a driver's license, that shows your date of birth. Also, mention the fact that you're a senior citizen when you first make your travel reservations; many hotels offer senior discounts.

Members of the **American Association of Retired Persons** (AARP), 601 E St. NW, Washington, DC 20049 (☎ **800/424-3410** or 202/434-2277), get discounts not only on hotels but also on airfares and car rentals. AARP offers members a wide range of special benefits, including *Modern Maturity* magazine and a monthly newsletter.

The **National Council of Senior Citizens,** 8403 Colesville Rd., Suite 1200, Silver Spring, MD 20910 (☎ **301/578-8800**), a nonprofit organization, offers a newsletter six times a year (partly devoted to travel tips) and discounts on hotels and car rentals. Annual dues are $13 per person or couple.

Mature Outlook, P.O. Box 9390, Des Moines, IA 50306 (☎ **800/336-6330**), began as a travel organization for people over 50, though it now caters to people of all ages. Members receive a bimonthly magazine and discounts on hotels. Annual membership is $19.95, which entitles members to discounts and, often, free coupons for discounted merchandise from Sears.

The Mature Traveler, a monthly 12-page newsletter on senior travel, is a valuable resource. It's available by subscription ($30 a year) from GEM Publishing Group, Box 50400, Reno, NV 89513-0400 (☎ **800/460-6676**). Another helpful publication is *101 Tips for the Mature Traveler,* available from Grand Circle Travel, 347 Congress St., Suite 3A, Boston, MA 02210 (☎ **800/221-2610** or 617/350-7500; fax 617/346-6700).

Grand Circle Travel is also one of the hundreds of travel agencies that specialize in vacations for seniors. Many of these packages, however, are of the tour-bus variety, with free trips thrown in for those who organize groups of 10 or more. Seniors seeking more independent travel should probably consult a regular travel agent. **SAGA International Holidays,** 222 Berkeley St., Boston, MA 02116 (☎ **800/343-0273**), offers inclusive tours and cruises for those 50 and older. SAGA also sponsors the more

---

Tying the Knot in Jamaica

In high season, some Jamaican resorts witness several weddings a day. Many of the larger resorts can arrange for an officiant, a photographer, and even the wedding cake and champagne. Some resorts will even throw in your wedding with the cost of your honeymoon at the hotel. Both the Jamaican Tourist Board and your hotel will assist you with the paperwork. Participants must reside on Jamaica for 24 hours before the ceremony. Bring birth certificates and affidavits saying you've never been married before. If you've been divorced or widowed, bring copies of your divorce papers or a copy of the deceased spouse's death certificate. The license and stamp duty costs $200. The cost of the ceremony can range from $50 to $200, depending on how much legwork you want to do yourself. You may apply in person at the **Ministry of National Security and Justice,** 12 Ocean Blvd., Kingston, Jamaica (☎ **876/906-4909**).

---

substantial **Road Scholar Tours** (☎ **800/621-2151**), which are fun loving but with an educational bent.

FOR FAMILIES

Several books on the market offer tips to help you travel with kids. Most concentrate on the U.S., but two, *Family Travel* (Lanier Publishing International) and *How to Take Great Trips with Your Kids* (The Harvard Common Press), are full of good general advice that can apply to travel anywhere. Another reliable tome, with a worldwide focus, is *Adventuring with Children* (Foghorn Press).

Family Travel Times is published 6 times a year by TWYCH (Travel with Your Children; ☎ **888/822-4388** or 212/477-5524) and includes a weekly call-in service for subscribers. Subscriptions are $40 a year. A free publication list and a sample issue are available by calling or sending a request to the above address.

Jamaica is one of the top family-vacation destinations in the Caribbean. The smallest toddlers can spend blissful hours on sandy beaches and in the shallow seawater or in swimming pools constructed with toddlers in mind. There's no end to the fascinating pursuits offered for older children, ranging from boat rides to shell collecting to horseback riding, hiking, and dancing. Some children are old enough to learn to snorkel and to explore an underwater wonderland. Skills such as swimming and windsurfing are taught, and a variety of activities are unique to the island.

Many of the island's resorts realize that Mom and Dad's idea of fun may not be quite what the kids had in mind. So, they offer perks like daily supervised children's activities, baby-sitters, family discounts, and kid's meals, helping kids have a great vacation while parents gain some freedom to relax, too.

Boscobel Beach Resort in Ocho Rios, not too far from Jamaica's famous landmark, Dunn's River Falls, was the island's first all-inclusive hotel designed specifically for the family. This resort offers parents the atmosphere of a country club, and children aged 14 and under always stay free.

Regrettably, we think the hotel hasn't been well maintained lately, and many readers have complained—justifiably—about the state of their rooms. So, in spite of the wide publicity this resort gets, we don't feel we can recommend it in this edition. However, there are many other family-oriented places in better shape.

Just a half hour to the west of Ocho Rios is Runaway Bay (see p. 11), home of the **Franklyn D. Resort,** Jamaica's all-suite, all-inclusive family resort. FDR offers families an incredible service—a nanny is assigned to each one-, two-, and three-bedroom suite. This warm, friendly Jamaican woman will look after both parents and children while they're at FDR. She will cook, clean, and act as companion to the children day or night. And, if the kids want to mingle with other youngsters, they may do so at the resort's fully supervised Mini Club, complete with satellite television, Nintendo, and other diversions. And best of all, children under 16 sharing their parents' room stay, eat, and play completely free.

Montego Bay, on the northwest coast, is the resort capital of Jamaica, so it's no surprise to find here three special resorts that welcome families on vacation.

A member of the Elegant Resorts group, the **Half Moon Golf, Tennis & Beach Club** (see p. 59) welcomes children to its Children's Activity Centre. The center features an array of indoor/outdoor recreational and educational games and activities including a kiddies' swimming pool, duck pond, thatched play houses, a horseshoe court, and tennis courts. Trained professionals guide children in arts and crafts, nature walks, tennis and golf lessons, treasure hunts, and culinary lessons, among other activities. The center caters to children ages 3 to 14 and is open from 8am to noon and from 2 to 6pm. Daytime and evening nanny service is also available for an additional cost.

Handsomely situated on an old sugar plantation, the **Wyndham Rose Hall Golf & Beach Resort** (see p. 63) keeps children entertained in their Kids Klub, while parents enjoy their four restaurants, three cocktail bars, and complete athletic facility. The Kids Klub at Wyndham operates Monday through Saturday from 10am until 4pm and offers separate activities for children according to age group—5 to 8 years or 9 to 12 years. The facility runs activities such as building sand castles, a mini-Olympics, movies, volleyball, and swim races. The resort also features an expanded kid's menu and gives families discounts of up to 50% if you book your kids an adjoining or separate room.

Holiday Inn SunSpree (see p. 68) is located just 10 minutes from Montego Bay's airport, and after a massive renovation program, now has an emphasis on families with children. The resort's innovative Kids Spree Vacation Club welcomes youngsters from 6 months to 12 years absolutely free. Granny's Nursery (for those up to 2 years old) features trained Jamaican nannies—noted for having a way with children—who will rock a restless little guest to a local lullaby. From there on up, different activities are planned for children in different age groups, including nature walks, story times, reggae dance lessons, and pizza parties.

Within a 20-minute drive of all the attractions and activities of Montego Bay is **Sea Castles Resort** (see p. 64), a luxury all-suite resort set on 14 acres overlooking the Caribbean. This resort offers one-, two-, and three-bedroom units, and as part of the Kiddies Club, fully trained nannies are on hand to keep children busy. Families can take advantage of the kitchen or kitchenette in each unit as a way of cutting down on expenses. On-site is a freshwater pool, and families will also find laundry facilities. The staff can arrange baby-sitting.

Nestled among the private coves of Negril's Bloody Bay, the 256-unit **Point Village Resort** (see p. 100) is an all-inclusive family resort. Coupled with the casual, laid-back flavor of Negril, Point Village pays special attention to the needs of its littlest guests. Point Village boasts the Kiddie's Club, with fully trained nannies on hand to keep children busy. Amenities for children include a kiddie restaurant, an arts-and-crafts pavilion, and a video room. Teens find advanced video games, a music video room with snacks, and more.

Jamaica's newest family resort, **Beaches Negril** (see p. 98), opened in February 1997. Located on 20 acres of lush landscape, with more than 1,400 feet of white-sand beach, Beaches Negril has a total of 225 rooms including beachfront suites. There are five restaurants including the Beach Grill, which features live entertainment and caters only to children from 5 to 9pm; parents may be included at the child's special invitation. The resort offers an endless variety of land and water sports and child-oriented activities for kids as well as facilities catering specifically to teens. There are two freshwater pools—one of which has a swim-up soda fountain and a toddler's paddling pool.

FOR WOMEN

Several Web sites offer women advice on how to travel safely and happily. The **Executive Woman's Travel Network** (www.delta-air.com/womenexecs/) is the official women's travel site of Delta airlines and offers women tips on staying fit while traveling, eating well, finding special airfares, and dealing with many other feminine travel issues. **WomanTraveler** (www.womantraveler.com) is an excellent guide that suggests places where women can stay and eat in various destinations. The site is authored by women and includes listings of women-owned businesses such as hotels and hostels.

Several books on the market cater to the concerns of the female traveler. *Safety and Security for Women Who Travel*, by Sheila Swan Laufer and Peter Laufer, is well worth $12.95, and *Adventures in Good Company: The Complete Guide to Women's Tours and Outdoor Trips*, is a very good resource at $16.95.

FOR SINGLES

Many people prefer traveling alone save for the relatively steep cost of booking a single room, which usually costs well over half the price of a double. **Travel Companion** (☎ 516/454-0880) is one of the nation's oldest roommate finders for single travelers. Register with them and find a trustworthy travel mate who will split the cost of the room with you and be around as little, or as often, as you like during the day.

Several tour organizers cater to solo travelers as well. **Experience Plus** (☎ 800/685-4565; fax 907/484-8489) offers an interesting selection of single-only trips. **Travel Buddies** (☎ 800/998-9099) runs single-friendly tours with no singles supplement. **The Single Gourmet Club** (133 E. 58th St., New York, NY 10022; ☎ 212/980-8788; fax 212/980-3138) is an international social, dining, and travel club for singles, with offices in 21 cities in the U.S. and Canada, and one in London.

You may also want to research the **Outdoor Singles Network** (P.O. Box 781, Haines, AK 99827). An established quarterly newsletter (since 1989) for outdoor-loving singles ages 19 to 90, the network will help you find a travel companion, pen pal, or soul mate within its pages. A one-year subscription costs $45, and your own personal ad is printed free in the next issue. Current issues are $15. Write for free information or check out the group's Web site at www.kcd.com/bearstar/osn.html.

9 Flying to Jamaica

THE MAJOR AIRLINES

There are two **international airports** on Jamaica: Donald Sangster in Montego Bay (☎ 876/952-3124) and Norman Manley in Kingston (☎ 876/924-8452). The most popular flights to Jamaica are from New York and Miami. Remember to reconfirm all flights, coming and going, no later than 72 hours before departure. Flying time from Miami is 1¼ hours; from Los Angeles, 5½ hours; from Atlanta, 2½ hours; from Dallas, 3 hours; from Chicago and New York, 3½ hours; and from Toronto, 4 hours.

Some of the most convenient service to Jamaica is provided by **American Airlines** (☎ 800/433-7300 in the U.S.; www.aa.com) through its hubs in New York and Miami. Throughout the year, one daily nonstop flight departs from New York's

Kennedy Airport for Montego Bay. From Miami, at least two daily flights depart for Kingston and two daily flights for Montego Bay.

US Airways (☎ 800/428-4322; www.usairways.com) has one daily flight. **Northwest Airlines** (☎ 800/225-2525; www.nwa.com) flies directly to Montego Bay daily from Minneapolis and Tampa.

Air Jamaica (☎ 800/523-5585 in the U.S.; www.airjamaica.com) operates about 14 flights a week from New York, most of which stop at both Montego Bay and Kingston, and even more frequent flights from Miami. The airline has connecting service within Jamaica through its reservations network to **Air Jamaica Express,** whose planes usually hold between 10 and 17 passengers. Air Jamaica Express flies from the island's international airports at Montego Bay and Kingston to small airports around the island, including Port Antonio, Boscobel (near Ocho Rios), Negril, and Tinson Pen (a tiny airport near Kingston).

Air Canada (☎ 888/247-2262 in Canada, or 800/776-3000 in the U.S.; www.aircanada.ca) flies from Toronto to Jamaica daily. **British Airways** (☎ 0345/222-111 in England; www.british-airways.com) has four nonstop flights weekly to Montego Bay and Kingston from London's Gatwick Airport.

TIPS FOR FLYING IN COMFORT

- You'll find the most legroom in a bulkhead seat, in the front row of each airplane cabin. Consider, however, that you will have to store your luggage in the overhead bin, and you won't have the best seat in the house for the in-flight movie.
- When you check in, ask for one of the emergency-exit-row seats, which also have extra legroom. They are assigned at the airport, usually on a first-come, first-served basis. In the unlikely event of an emergency, however, you'll be expected to open the emergency-exit door and help direct traffic.
- Ask for a seat toward the front of the plane. That way, you'll be one of the first to disembark after the gangway is in place.
- When you make your reservation, order a special meal if you have dietary restrictions. Most airlines offer a variety of special meals: vegetarian, macrobiotic, kosher, and meals for the lactose-intolerant among them.
- Wear comfortable clothes and dress in layers. The climate in airplane cabins is unpredictable. You'll be glad to have a sweater or jacket to put on or take off as the temperature on board dictates.
- Pack some toiletries for long flights. Airplane cabins are notoriously dry places. Take a travel-size bottle of moisturizer or lotion to refresh your face and hands at the end of the flight. If you're taking an overnight flight (a.k.a. the red eye), don't forget to pack a toothbrush. If you wear contact lenses, take them out before you get on board and wear glasses instead—or at least bring eye drops.
- If you're flying with a cold or chronic sinus problems, use a decongestant ten minutes before ascent and descent to minimize pressure buildup in the inner ear.
- Try to acclimate yourself to the local time as quickly as possible. Stay up as long as you can the first day, then try to wake up at a normal hour the next morning.
- Drink plenty of water before your departure and during your flight to avoid dehydration.
- If you're flying with kids, don't forget a deck of cards, toys, extra bottles, pacifiers, diapers, and chewing gum (to help them relieve inner-ear pressure buildup during ascent and descent).

FINDING THE BEST AIRFARE

If you're willing to visit in the off-season, you shouldn't have to pay full fare. That's especially true if you're willing to plan on the spur of the moment. If a flight is not fully booked, an airline will discount tickets to try to fill it up.

Before you do anything else, read the section below on "Package Tours." But if you decide a package isn't for you, and you need to book your airfare on your own, read on, and we'll give you lots of money-saving tips.

If you fly in summer, spring, and fall, you're guaranteed substantial reductions on airfares to Jamaica. You can also ask if it's cheaper to fly Monday through Thursday. And don't forget to consider air-and-land packages, which offer considerably reduced rates.

Most airlines charge different fares according to the season. Peak season, which is winter in Jamaica, is most expensive; basic season, in the summer, offers the lowest fares. *Shoulder season* refers to the spring and fall months in between.

- **Keep an eye out for sales.** Check your newspaper for advertised discounts or call the airlines directly and ask if any promotional rates or special fares are available. You'll rarely see a sale during the peak winter vacation months of February and March or during the Thanksgiving or Christmas seasons; but in periods of low-volume travel, you should be able to find a discounted fare. If your schedule is flexible, ask if you can get a cheaper fare by staying an extra day or by flying mid-week. (Many airlines won't volunteer this information.) If you already hold a ticket when a sale breaks, it may even pay to exchange your ticket, which usually incurs a $50 to $75 charge. Note, however, that the lowest-priced fares are often nonrefundable, require advance purchase of 1 to 3 weeks and a certain length of stay, and carry penalties for changing dates of travel.
- **Consolidators (a.k.a. bucket shops) are sometimes a good place to find low fares.** Consolidators buy seats in bulk from the airlines and then sell them back to the public at prices below even the airlines' discounted rates. But tread carefully here. In some cases, consolidator tickets cost more than tickets from the airlines, particularly when there's a special sale going on. Make sure that the consolidator fares offered are lower than the airline's published rates before going the bucket-shop route. Their small, boxed ads usually run in the Sunday travel section at the bottom of the page. Before you pay a consolidator, however, ask for a record locator number and confirm your seat with the airline itself. Be prepared to book your ticket with a different consolidator—there are many to choose from—if the airline can't confirm your reservation. Also be aware that bucket-shop tickets are usually nonrefundable or rigged with stiff cancellation penalties, often as high as 50% to 75% of the ticket price.
- **Council Travel** (☎ 800/226-8624; www.counciltravel.com) and **STA Travel** (☎ 800/781-4040; www.sta.travel.com) cater especially to young travelers, but their bargain-basement prices are available to people of all ages. **Travel Bargains** (☎ 800/AIR-FARE; www.1800airfare.com) was formerly owned by TWA but now offers the deepest discounts on many other airlines, with a 4-day advance purchase. Other reliable consolidators include **1-800-FLY-CHEAP** (www.1800flycheap.com); **TFI Tours International** (☎ 800/745-8000 or 212/736-1140), which serves as a clearinghouse for unused seats; or "rebaters" such as **Travel Avenue** (☎ 800/333-3335 or 312/876-1116) and the **Smart Traveller** (☎ 800/448-3338 in the U.S., or 305/448-3338; www.smarttraveller@juno.com), which rebate part of their commissions to you.
- **Consider a charter flight.** Discounted fares have pared the number of charter flights available, but they can still be found. Most charter operators advertise and

sell their seats through travel agents, thus making these local professionals your best source of information for available flights. Before deciding to take a charter flight, however, check the restrictions on the ticket. You may be asked to purchase a tour package, to pay in advance, to be flexible if the day of departure is changed, to pay a service charge, to fly on an airline with which you're unfamiliar (this usually is not the case), or to pay harsh penalties if you cancel—but be understanding if the charter doesn't fill up and is canceled 10 days before departure. Summer charters fill up more quickly than others and are almost sure to fly, but if you decide on a charter flight, seriously consider cancellation and baggage insurance.

- **Join a travel club,** such as **Moment's Notice** (☎ 718/234-6295) or **Sears Discount Travel Club** (☎ 800/433-9383, or 800/255-1487 to join), which supplies unsold tickets at discounted prices. You pay an annual membership fee to get the club's hot-line number. Of course, you're limited to what's available, so you have to be flexible.

- **Search for the best deal on the Web.** The Web sites highlighted below are worth checking out, especially since all services are free. Always check the lowest published fare, however, before you shop for flights online.

   Arthur Frommer's Budget Travel (www.frommers.com) offers detailed information on destinations around the world and up-to-the-minute ways to save dramatically on flights, hotels, car rentals, and cruises. Book an entire vacation online and research your destination before you leave. Consult the message board to set up "hospitality exchanges" in other countries, to talk with other travelers who have visited a hotel you're considering, or to direct travel questions to Arthur Frommer himself. The newsletter is updated daily to keep you abreast of the latest-breaking ways to save, to publicize new hot spots and best buys, and to present veteran readers with fresh, ever-changing approaches to travel.

   Microsoft Expedia (www.expedia.com) offers a Fare Tracker that e-mails you weekly with the best airfare deals from your hometown on up to three destinations. The site's Travel Agent will steer you to bargains on hotels and car rentals, and with the help of hotel and airline-seat pinpointers, you can book everything right online. Before you depart, log on for maps and up-to-date travel information, including weather reports and foreign travel exchange rates.

   The Trip (www.thetrip.com) is really geared toward the business traveler, but vacationers-to-be can also use its exceptionally powerful fare-finding engine, which will e-mail you weekly with the best city-to-city airfare deals for as many as 10 routes. The Trip uses the Internet Travel Network, another reputable travel-agent database, to book hotels and restaurants.

   Travelocity (www.travelocity.com) is one of the best travel sites out there, especially for finding cheap airfares. In addition to its Personal Fare Watcher, which notifies you via e-mail of the lowest airfares for up to five different destinations, Travelocity will track the three lowest fares for any routes on any dates in minutes. You can book a flight, then find the best hotel or car-rental deals via the SABRE computer reservations systems. Click on "Last Minute Deals" for the latest travel bargains.

   Here's a partial list of airlines and their Web sites, where you can not only get on the e-mailing lists, but also book flights directly: **Air Jamaica** (www.airjamaica.com); **American Airlines** (www.aa.com); **British Airways** (www.british-airways.com); **BWIA** (www.bwee.com); **Canadian Airlines**

International (www.cdnair.ca); **Continental Airlines** (www.flycontinental.com); **Delta** (www.delta-air.com); and **US Airways** (www.usairways.com).

10 Escorted & Package Tours

You may want to consider booking your flight as part of a travel package such as an escorted tour or a package tour. What you lose in adventure, you'll gain in time and money saved when you book accommodations, and maybe even food and entertainment, along with your flight.

ESCORTED TOURS

Packaged travel may not be the option for you if you like to explore strange places at whim. If you like to plan your coordinates in advance, however, many package options will enable you to do just that—and save you money in the process.

Some people love escorted tours. They let you relax and take in the sights while a bus driver fights traffic for you; they spell out your costs up front; and they take you to the maximum number of sights in the minimum amount of time with the least amount of hassle. If you do choose an escorted tour, you should ask a few simple questions before you buy:

- What is the **cancellation policy**? Is a deposit required? Can they cancel the trip if they don't get enough people? Do you get a refund if *they* cancel? Do you get a refund if *you* cancel? How late can you cancel if you are unable to go? When do you pay in full?
- How busy is the **schedule**? How much sightseeing do they plan each day? Do they allow ample time for relaxing by the pool, shopping, or wandering?
- What is the **size** of the group? The smaller the group, the more flexible the itinerary, and the less time you'll spend waiting for people to get on and off the bus. Tour operators may be evasive about this because they may not know the exact size of the group until everybody has made their reservations; but they should be able to give you a rough estimate. Some tours have a minimum group size and may cancel the tour if they don't book enough people.
- What is included in the **price**? Don't assume anything. You may have to pay for transportation to and from the airport. A box lunch may be included in an excursion, but drinks might cost extra. Beer might be included, but wine might not. Can you opt out of certain activities, or does the bus leave once a day, with no exceptions? Are all your meals planned in advance? Can you choose your entree at dinner, or does everybody get the same chicken cutlet?

Note: If you choose an escorted tour, think strongly about purchasing travel insurance from an independent agency, especially if the tour operator asks you to pay up front. See the section on travel insurance above. One final caveat: Because escorted tour prices are based on double occupancy, the single traveler is usually penalized.

PACKAGE TOURS

Package tours are not the same thing as escorted tours. They are simply a way to buy airfare and accommodations at the same time. For popular destinations such as Jamaica, they are a smart way to go because they save you a lot of money. In many cases, a package that includes airfare, hotel, and transportation to and from the airport will cost you less than just the hotel alone would have, had you booked it yourself. That's because packages are sold in bulk to tour operators, who resell them to the public at a cost that drastically undercuts standard rates.

Packages, however, vary widely. Some offer a better class of hotels than others. Some offer the same hotels for lower prices. Some offer flights on scheduled airlines, while others book charters. In some packages, your choice of accommodations and travel days may be limited. Some packages let you choose between escorted vacations and independent vacations; others allow you to add on just a few excursions or escorted day trips (also at lower prices than you could locate on your own) without booking an entirely escorted tour. Each destination usually has one or two packagers that offer lower prices than the rest because they buy in even greater bulk. If you spend the time to shop around, you will save in the long run.

Visitors flock to the Caribbean not just to visit the beaches but also to dine in various restaurants. Many land-and-sea packages include meals, so you might find yourself locked into your hotel dining room every night where your meals are prepaid. If you're seeking a more varied dining experience, avoid **AP (American Plan),** which means full board, and opt for **MAP (Modified American Plan),** meaning breakfast and either lunch or dinner. That way, you'll at least be free for one main meal of the day and can sample a variety of an island's regional fare. Another way you can avoid being hotel-bound for meals is to book an apartment or condo. Then you can either cook in if there's a kitchenette, or take all your meals outside.

The best place to start your search is the travel section of your local Sunday newspaper. Also check the ads in the back of national travel magazines like *Arthur Frommer's Budget Travel, Travel & Leisure, National Geographic Traveler,* and *Condé Nast Traveler.* **Liberty Travel** (☎ **888/271-1584** to be connected with the agent closest to you; www.libertytravel.com) is one of the biggest packagers in the Northeast and usually boasts a full-page ad in Sunday papers. You won't get much in the way of service, but you will get a good deal. **American Express Vacations** (☎ **800/241-1700;** www.americanexpress.com) is another option. Check out its **Last Minute Travel Bargains** site, offered in conjunction with Continental Airlines (www.americanexpress.com), with deeply discounted vacation packages and reduced airline fares that differ from the E-savers bargains that Continental e-mails weekly to subscribers. **Northwest Airlines** offers a similar service. Posted on Northwest's Web site every Wednesday, its **Cyber Saver Bargain Alerts** offer special hotel rates, package deals, and discounted airline fares.

Another good resource is the airlines themselves, which often package their flights with accommodations. Fly-by-night packagers are uncommon, but they do exist; when you buy your package through an airline, however, you can be pretty sure that the company will still be in business when your departure date arrives. Among the airline packagers, your options include **American Airlines FlyAway Vacations** (☎ **800/ 321-2121), Delta Dream Vacations** (☎ **800/872-7786),** and **US Airways Vacations** (☎ **800/455-0123).** Pick the airline that services your hometown most frequently.

The biggest hotel chains and resorts also offer package deals. If you already know where you want to stay, call the resort itself and ask if it offers air-and-land packages.

To save time comparing the prices and values of all the package tours out there, consider calling **TourScan, Inc.,** P.O. Box 2367, Darien, CT 06820 (☎ **800/962-2080** or 203/655-8091). Every season, the company computerizes the contents of travel brochures that contain about 10,000 different vacations at 1,600 hotels in the Caribbean, the Bahamas, and Bermuda. TourScan selects the best-valued vacation at each hotel and condo. Two catalogs are printed each year, which list a choice of hotels in all price ranges on most of the Caribbean islands. Write to TourScan for their catalogs, the price of which ($4) is credited to any TourScan vacation.

Other tour operators include **Caribbean Concepts Corp.,** 99 Jericho Turnpike, Jericho, NY 11793 (☎ **800/423-4433** or 516/867-0700), which offers low-cost air-and-land packages to the islands, including apartments, hotels, villas, and condo

What the Meal Plans Mean

AP (American Plan): This plan includes three meals a day (sometimes called *full board* or *full pension*).

CP (Continental Plan): A continental breakfast (that is, bread, jam, and coffee) is included in the room rate.

EP (European Plan): This rate is always cheapest, as it offers only the room— no meals.

MAP (Modified American Plan): Sometimes called *half board* or *half pension*, this room rate includes breakfast and dinner (or lunch if you prefer).

rentals, plus local sightseeing (which can be arranged separately). **Horizon Tours,** 1010 Vermont Ave. NW, Suite 202, Washington, DC 20005 (☎ **888/SUN-N-SAND** or 202/393-8390), specializes in good deals for all-inclusive resorts in The Bahamas, Jamaica, Aruba, Puerto Rico, Antigua, and St. Lucia. **Globus,** 5301 S. Federal Circle, Littleton, CO 80123 (☎ **800/851-0728,** ext. 7518), gives escorted island-hopping expeditions to three or four islands, focusing on the history and culture of the West Indies.

FOR BRITISH TRAVELERS

Caribbean Connection, Concorde House, Forest St., Chester CH1 1QR (☎ **01244/355-300**), offers all-inclusive packages (airfare and hotel) to the Caribbean and customizes tours for independent travel. It publishes two catalogs of Caribbean offerings, one featuring more than 160 properties on all the major islands, and a 50-page catalog of luxury all-inclusive properties.

Other Caribbean specialists operating out of England include **Kuoni Travel,** Kuoni House, Dorking, Surrey RH5 4AZ (☎ **01306/742-222**). **Caribtours,** 161 Fulham Rd., London SW3 6SN (☎ **020/758-3517**), is a small, very knowledgeable specialist, tailoring itineraries to meet your demanding travel requirements.

11 Cruises

Here's a brief rundown of some of the major cruise lines that serve the Caribbean. For more detailed information, pick up a copy of *Frommer's Caribbean Cruises & Ports of Call.*

CRUISE LINES

- **Carnival Cruise Lines** (☎ 800/327-9501): Offering affordable vacations on some of the biggest and most brightly decorated ships afloat, Carnival is the boldest, brashest, and most successful mass-market cruise line in the world. More than twelve of its vessels depart for the Caribbean from Miami, Tampa, New Orleans, Port Canaveral, and San Juan. Eight of them specialize in 7-day-or-longer tours that feature stopovers at selected ports throughout the eastern, western, and southern Caribbean (ports include St. Lucia, San Juan, Guadeloupe, Grenada, Grand Cayman, and Jamaica). Four others offer 3- to 5-day itineraries visiting such ports as Nassau, Key West, Grand Cayman, and Playa del Carmen/Cozumel. Its fleet has many ships, including eight 2,000-passenger *Fantasy* class ships, such as the smoke-free *Paradise*. Most of the company's Caribbean cruises offer good value and feature nonstop activities. Food and party-colored drinks are plentiful, and the overall atmosphere is comparable to a floating theme park. Lots of single passengers opt for this line, as do families attracted by the lines well-run children's program. The average onboard age is a relatively youthful 42, although ages range from 3 to 95.

- **Celebrity Cruises** (☎ 800/327-6700): Celebrity maintains five newly built, stylish, medium-to-large ships with cruises that last between 7 and 14 nights to ports such as Key West, San Juan, Grand Cayman, St. Thomas, Ocho Rios, Antigua, and Cozumel, to name a few. It's classy but not stuffy, several notches above mass-market, and provides an experience that's both elegant and fun—and all for a competitive price. Accommodations are roomy and well equipped, cuisine is more refined than that offered by any of its competitors, and its service is impeccable.

- **Commodore Cruise Line** (☎ 800/237-5361): Commodore's two ships are both small, solid, not particularly glamorous, but highly seaworthy vessels and are based year-round in New Orleans. The *Enchanted Isle* sails through the western Caribbean and usually spends 3 full days of its 7 cruise days at sea, occupying the remaining 4 days at ports in Montego Bay, Jamaica; the Cayman Islands; and either Mexico or Honduras. The *Enchanted Capri* sails 2- and 5-night cruises: The former sails the Gulf of Mexico, visiting no ports, while the latter visits Progreso (a beach resort on the tip of Mexico's Yucatán peninsula) and Cozumel, where passengers can opt for a day excursion to Cancún. Both ships lack state-of-the-art facilities, but their low rates make a Caribbean cruise a reality for many first-time cruisers without a lot of cash. Theme cruises are especially popular aboard the *Enchanted Isle,* while the *Enchanted Capri* is very gambling oriented, particularly on its 2-night sails. Both ships attract goodly numbers of unattached singles.

- **Costa Cruise Lines** (☎ 800/462-6782): Costa, the U.S.-based branch of a cruise line that has thrived in Italy for about a century, maintains hefty to megasize vessels. Two of Costa's vessels offer virtually identical jaunts through the western and eastern Caribbean on alternate weeks, each of them departing from Fort Lauderdale. Ports of call during the eastern Caribbean itineraries of both vessels include stopovers in San Juan, St. Thomas, Serena Cay (a private island off the coast of the Dominican Republic known for its beaches), and Nassau. Itineraries through the western Caribbean include stopovers at Grand Cayman; either Ocho Rios or Montego Bay, Jamaica; Key West; and Cozumel. There's an Italian flavor and lots of Italian design on board here, and an atmosphere of relaxed indulgence.

- **Holland America Line-Westours** (☎ 800/426-0327): Holland America is the most high-toned of the mass-market cruise lines, with eight respectably hefty and good-looking ships. They offer solid value, with very few jolts or surprises, and attract a solid, well-grounded clientele of primarily older travelers (late-night revelers and serious partyers might want to book cruises on other lines, such as Carnival). Cruises stop at deep-water mainstream ports such as Ocho Rios and last an average of 7 days, but in some cases 10 days, visiting such ports as Key West, Grand Cayman, St. Maarten, St. Lucia, Curaçao, Barbados, and St. Thomas.

- **Princess Cruises** (☎ 800/421-0522): Currently operating 7 megavessels, six of which cruise through Caribbean and Bahamian waters, Princess offers a cruise experience that's one part Carnival- or Royal Caribbean–style party-time fun and one part Celebrity-style classy enjoyment. The *Ocean Princess, Dawn Princess,* and *Sea Princess,* almost identical vessels all built in the late nineties, offer the bulk of Princess's Caribbean itineraries, with the *Dawn* and *Ocean* running two alternating 7-night southern Caribbean itineraries round-trip from San Juan, while the *Sea* sails 7-night western Caribbean runs round-trip from Fort Lauderdale. Depending on the exact itinerary, ports on the southern Caribbean runs include Curaçao, Isla Magarita (Venezuela), La Guaira/Caracas (Venezuela), Grenada, Dominica, St. Vincent, St. Kitts, St. Thomas, Trinidad, Barbados, Antigua, Martinique, St. Lucia, and St. Maarten. Western Caribbean itineraries visit Ocho Rios (Jamaica), Grand Cayman, Cozumel, and Princess Cays, the line's private island. The *Grand Princess,* a megaship at 109,000 tons, sails 7-night eastern Caribbean itineraries round-trip from Fort Lauderdale, visiting St. Thomas, St. Maarten, and Princess Cays. All of the line's ships are stylish and comfortable, though the *Grand* ups it a notch in the style department, offering amazing open deck areas and some really beautiful indoor public areas.

- **Royal Caribbean International (RCI)** (☎ **800/327-6700** or 305/539-6000): RCI leads the industry in the development of megaships. Most of this company's dozen or so vessels weigh in at around 73,000 tons. Its unbelievably enormous *Voyager of the Seas* weighs in at 142,000 tons, carrying 3,114 passengers, and offering such cruise- ship firsts as an ice-skating rink and a rock-climbing wall. A mass-market company that has everything down to a science, RCI encourages a house-party theme that's just a little less frenetic than the mood aboard Carnival. There are enough onboard activities to suit virtually any taste and age level. Though accommodations are more than adequate, they are not upscale and tend to be a bit more cramped than the industry norm. Using either Miami, Fort Lauderdale, or San Juan as their home port, Royal Caribbean ships call regularly at St. Thomas, San Juan, Ocho Rios, St. Maarten, Grand Cayman, St. Croix, Curaçao, and one or the other of the line's private beaches—one in The Bahamas, the other along an isolated peninsula in northern Haiti. Most of the company's cruises last 7 days, although some weekend jaunts from San Juan to St. Thomas are available for 3 nights, and some Panama Canal crossings last for 11 and 12 nights.

- **Seabourn Cruise Line** (☎ **800/929-9595**): Seabourn is deservedly legendary for the unabashed luxury aboard its elegant, small-scale ships. The *Seabourn Pride* conducts 7- to 10-day cruises, offered in winter from November to March, in the Caribbean as part of a year-long itinerary devoted mostly to Europe and Asia. Its identical twin, the *Seabourn Legend,* spends the entire winter from home ports of San Juan and Fort Lauderdale. Ports of call for both ships include Jamaica, St. Barts, St. Martin, St. Lucia, Bequia, Tobago, Barbados, St. Croix, and Virgin Gorda, some of which are visited before or after transits of the Panama Canal. There are more activities than you'd expect aboard such a relatively small ship (10,000 tons), and an absolutely amazing amount of onboard space per passenger. The cuisine is superb, served in a dining room that's unapologetically formal. Other small ships in the fleet include the 4,250-ton *Seabourn Goddess I* & *II,* usually sailing between St. Thomas and Barbados on 7-night jaunts from November to April. Throughout every venue, the emphasis is on top-notch service, luxury, discretion, and impeccably good taste. All in all, you get what you pay for—and you pay *a lot.*

BOOKING YOUR CRUISE

How should you book your cruise and get to the port of embarkation before the good times roll? If you've developed a relationship over the years with a favorite travel agency, then by all means, leave the details to the tried-and-true specialists. Many agents will propose a package deal from the principal airport closest to your residence to the airport nearest to the cruise-departure point. It's possible to purchase your air ticket on your own and book your cruise ticket separately, but in most cases, you'll save big bucks by combining the fares into a package deal.

You're also likely to save money—sometimes *lots* of money—by contacting a specialist who focuses on cruise bookings. He or she will be likely to match you with a cruise line whose style suits you and can also steer you toward any of the special promotions that come and go as frequently as Caribbean rainstorms.

Here are some travel agencies to consider: **Cruises, Inc.,** 5000 Campuswood Dr. E., Syracuse, NY 13057 (☎ 800/854-0500 or 314/463-9695); **Cruise Fairs of America,** Century Plaza Towers, 2029 Century Park E., Suite 950, Los Angeles, CA 90067 (☎ 800/456-4FUN or 310/556-2925); **The Cruise Company,** 10760 Q St., Omaha, NE 68127 (☎ 800/289-5505 or 402/339-6800); **Kelly Cruises,** 1315 W. 22nd St., Suite 105, Oak Brook, IL 60523 (☎ 800/837-7447 or 630/990-1111); **Hartford Holidays Travel,** 129 Hillside Ave., Williston Park, NY 11596 (☎ 800/828-4813 or 516/746-6670); and **Mann Travel** and **Cruises American Express,** 6010 Fairview Rd., Suite 104, Charlotte, NC 28210 (☎ 800/849-2301 or 704/556-8311). These companies stay tuned to last-minute price wars; cruise lines don't profit if these megaships don't fill up near peak capacity, so sales pop up all the time.

You'll likely sail from Miami, which has become the cruise capital of the world. Other departure ports include San Juan, Port Everglades, New Orleans, Tampa, and (via the Panama Canal) Los Angeles.

12 Getting Around

BY RENTAL CAR

Jamaica is big enough—and public transportation is unreliable enough—that a car is a necessity if you plan to do much independent sightseeing. Unfortunately, prices of car rentals in Jamaica have skyrocketed; it's now one of the most expensive rental scenes in the Caribbean. In all likelihood, you can book a rental car as part of a package tour, but if you're reserving one on your own, here are some tips.

SAVING MONEY ON A RENTAL   Car-rental rates vary even more than airline fares. The price you pay will depend on the size of the car, where and when you pick it up and drop it off, the length of the rental period, where and how far you drive the car, whether you purchase insurance, and a host of other factors. Asking a few key questions could save you hundreds of dollars:

- Are weekend rates lower than weekday rates? Ask if the rate is the same for pickup Friday morning, for instance, as it is for Thursday night.
- Is a weekly rate cheaper than the daily rate? If you need to keep the car for four days, it may be cheaper to keep it for five, even if you don't need it that long.
- Does the agency assess a drop-off charge if you do not return the car to the same location where you picked it up? Is it cheaper to pick up the car at the airport compared to a downtown location?
- Are special promotional rates available? If you see an advertised price in your local newspaper, be sure to ask for that specific rate; otherwise, you may be charged the standard cost. The terms change constantly.
- Are discounts available for members of AARP, AAA, frequent-flyer programs, or trade unions? If you belong to any of these organizations, you are probably entitled to discounts of up to 30%.
- How much tax will be added to the rental bill? Local tax? State use tax?
- What is the cost of adding an additional driver's name to the contract?

- How many free miles are included in the price? Free mileage is often negotiable, depending on the length of your rental.
- How much does the rental company charge to refill your gas tank if you return with the tank less than full? Though most rental companies claim these prices are "competitive," fuel is almost always cheaper in town. Try to allow enough time to refuel the car yourself before returning it.

Some companies offer "refueling packages," in which you pay for an entire tank of gas up front. The price is usually fairly competitive with local gas prices, but you don't get credit for any gas remaining in the tank. If a stop at a gas station on the way to the airport will make you miss your plane, then by all means take advantage of the fuel purchase option. Otherwise, skip it.

DEMYSTIFYING RENTER'S INSURANCE   Before you drive off in a rental car, be sure you're insured. Hasty assumptions about your personal auto insurance or a rental agency's additional coverage could end up costing you tens of thousands of dollars—even if you're involved in an accident that is clearly the fault of another driver.

If you already hold a **private auto insurance** policy, you are most likely covered in the United States for loss of or damage to a rental car and liability in case of injury to any other party involved in an accident. Coverage probably doesn't extend outside the U.S., however. Be sure to find out whether you are covered in the area you are visiting, whether your policy extends to all persons who will be driving the rental car, how much liability is covered in case an outside party is injured in an accident, and whether the type of vehicle you are renting is included under your contract. (Rental trucks, sport utility vehicles, and luxury vehicles such as Jaguars may not be covered.)

Most **major credit cards** provide some degree of coverage as well—provided they were used to pay for the rental. Terms vary widely, however, so be sure to call your credit-card company directly before you rent.

If you are **uninsured or driving abroad,** your credit card provides primary coverage as long as you decline the rental agency's insurance. This means that the credit card will cover damage or theft of a rental car for the full cost of the vehicle. (In a few states, however, theft is not covered; ask specifically about state law where you will be renting and driving.) If you already have insurance, your credit card will provide secondary coverage—which basically covers your deductible.

Credit cards **will not cover liability** or the cost of injury to an outside party and/or damage to an outside party's vehicle. If you do not hold an insurance policy, you may seriously want to consider purchasing additional liability insurance from your rental company. Be sure to check the terms, however; some rental agencies cover liability only if the renter is not at fault. Even then, the rental company's obligation varies from state to state.

Bear in mind that every credit-card company has its own peculiarities. Most American Express Optima cards, for instance, provide no insurance. American Express does not cover vehicles valued at over $50,000 when they are new, luxury vehicles such as Porsche, or vehicles built on a truck chassis. MasterCard does not provide coverage for loss, theft, or fire damage, and covers collision only if the rental period does not exceed 15 days. Call your own credit-card company for details.

The basic insurance coverage offered by most car-rental companies, known as the **Loss/Damage Waiver (LDW)** or **Collision Damage Waiver (CDW)**, can cost as much as $20 per day. It usually covers the full value of the vehicle with no deductible if an outside party causes an accident or other damage to the rental car. In all states but California, you will probably be covered in case of theft as well. Liability coverage varies according to the company policy and state law, but the minimum is usually at least $15,000. If you are at fault in an accident, however, you will be covered for the full replacement value of the car but not for liability. Some states allow you to buy additional liability coverage for such cases. Most rental companies require a police report in order to process any claims you file, but your private insurer will not be notified of the accident.

PACKAGE DEALS   Many packages are available that include airfare, accommodations, and a rental car with unlimited mileage. Compare these prices with the cost of booking airline tickets and renting a car separately to see if these offers are good deals.

ARRANGING CAR RENTALS ON THE WEB   Internet resources can make comparison shopping easier. **Microsoft Expedia** (www.expedia.com) and **Travelocity** (www.travelocity.com) help you compare prices and locate car-rental bargains from various companies nationwide. They'll even make your reservation for you once you've found the best deal.

WHERE TO RENT   Try **Budget Rent-a-Car** (☎ **800/527-0700** in the U.S., 876/952-3838 at the Montego Bay Airport, or 876/924-8762 in Kingston); with Budget, a daily collision-damage waiver is mandatory and costs another $15. **Hertz** (☎ **800/654-3001** in the U.S.) operates branches at the airports at both Montego Bay (☎ **876/979-0438**) and Kingston (☎ **876/924-8028**).

If you'd like to shop for a better deal with one of the local companies in Montego Bay, try **Jamaica Car Rental,** 23 Gloucester Ave. (☎ **876/952-5586**), with a branch at the Sangster International Airport at Montego Bay (☎ **876/952-9496**). Daily rates begin at $55. You can also try **United Car Rentals,** 49 Gloucester Ave. (☎ **876/952-3077**), which rents Mazdas, Toyotas, Hondas, and Suzuki jeeps, costing from $48 per day for a two-door car without air-conditioning.

In Kingston, try **Island Car Rentals,** 17 Antigua Ave. (☎ **876/926-5991**), with a branch at Montego Bay's Sangster International Airport (☎ **876/952-5771**). It rents Hondas and Samurais with rates beginning at $88 daily in winter and $66 in the off-season.

DRIVING IN JAMAICA   *Driving is on the left side of the road,* not on the right side as in the United States, Canada, and most of Europe. You should exercise more than usual caution because of the unfamiliar terrain, and be especially cautious at night. Speed limits in towns are 30 m.p.h., and 50 m.p.h. outside towns. Gas is measured by the imperial gallon (a British unit of measurement that is 25% more than a U.S. gallon); most stations don't accept credit cards. Your valid driver's license from home is acceptable for short-term visits to Jamaica.

ROAD MAPS   The major highways of Jamaica tend to be well marked and easily discernible because of their end destination, which is often adequately signposted. More complicated are secondary roads, urban streets, and feeder roads, whose markings sometimes are infuriatingly unclear. Recognizing this problem, the Jamaica Tourist Board has issued one of the best maps of the island available anywhere, the "Discover Jamaica" road map. Conforming to international cartographic standards, it contains a detailed overview of the entire island, as well as blowups of the Kingston, Montego Bay, Negril, Mandeville, Spanish Town, Port Antonio, and Ocho Rios areas. The map includes a very useful street index to Kingston. A copy of the map is usually available from any branch of the Jamaica Tourist Board or from car-rental agencies. It's best to obtain one before your visit (see "Visitor Information," above), as local branches might be out of stock.

MILEAGE INFORMATION   Subject to many variations depending on road conditions, driving time from Montego Bay to Negril (about 52 miles) is 1 1/2 hours; from

Montego Bay to Ocho Rios (67 miles), 1¹/₂ hours; from Ocho Rios to Port Antonio (66 miles), 2¹/₂ hours; from Ocho Rios to Kingston (54 miles), 2 hours; from Kingston to Mandeville (61 miles), 1¹/₂ hours; and from Kingston to Port Antonio (61 miles), 2 hours. Following is a more-detailed mileage chart.

	Black River	Falmouth	Kingston	Mandeville	Montego Bay	Negril	Ocho Rios	Port Antonio	St. Ann's Bay
Black River	0	62	107	43	46	49	94	156	87
Falmouth	62	0	91	53	23	75	44	110	37
Kingston	107	91	0	61	119	153	54	61	59
Mandeville	43	53	61	0	70	92	72	117	62
Montego Bay	46	23	119	70	0	52	67	133	60
Negril	49	75	153	92	52	0	117	181	110
Ocho Rios	94	44	54	72	67	117	0	66	7
Port Antonio	156	110	61	117	133	181	66	0	73
St. Ann's Bay	87	37	59	62	60	110	7	73	0

AUTO BREAKDOWNS   In case of a breakdown, telephone your car-rental agency for assistance. The staff will contact the nearest garage with which it has an affiliation, and a tow truck or mechanic will be dispatched to help you.

BY TAXI & BUS

Most cabs in Jamaica are old vehicles that were made in the United States. Taxis in Kingston don't have meters, so agree on a price before you get in the car. In Kingston and the rest of the island, special taxis and buses for visitors are operated by JUTA (Jamaica Union of Travellers Association) and have the union's emblem on the side of the vehicle. All prices are controlled, and any local JUTA office will supply a list of rates. JUTA drivers do nearly all the ground transfers, and some offer sightseeing tours. We've found them to be pleasant, knowledgeable, and good drivers.

BY BIKE & SCOOTER

These can be rented in Montego Bay; you'll need a valid driver's license. **Montego Honda/Bike Rentals,** 21 Gloucester Ave. (☎ **876/952-4984**), rents Honda scooters for $30 to $35 a day (24 hours), plus a $300 deposit. Bikes cost $10 a day, plus a $150 deposit. Deposits are refundable if the vehicles are returned in good shape. Hours are daily from 7:30am to 5pm.

BY PLANE

Most travelers enter the country via Montego Bay (although American Airlines also flies to Kingston). If you want to fly elsewhere on the island, you'll need to use the island's domestic air service, which is provided by Air Jamaica Express. Reservations are handled by **Air Jamaica** (☎ **800/523-5585** in the U.S., or 876/923-8680), which has consolidated its reservation system. You can also reserve before you leave home through a travel agent or through Air Jamaica.

Air Jamaica Express offers 30 scheduled flights daily, covering all the major resort areas. For example, there are 11 flights a day between Kingston and Montego Bay and three flights a day between Negril and Port Antonio. (Incidentally, Tinson Pen Airport in the heart of downtown Kingston is for domestic flights only.) Car-rental facilities are available only at the international airports at Kingston and Montego Bay.

Air SuperClub (☎ 876/940-7746) also provides shuttle service between Montego Bay and Ocho Rios, and between Montego Bay and Negril.

13 Tips on Accommodations

Because of the island's size and diversity, Jamaica offers the widest array of accommodations in the Caribbean.

Accommodations can range from intimate inns, with no more than six or seven rooms (and the very visible on-site presence of the owner/manager), to giant megahotels with an enviable array of services and such facilities as tennis compounds, therapeutic spas, and golf courses.

One increasingly popular option is the **all-inclusive resort.** Well-publicized, solidly financed, and boasting a wealth of facilities, these tend to be large resorts where all your drinking, dining, and sporting diversions are offered within the hotel compound as part of one all-inclusive price. Although they tend to limit your exposure to local life, they are undeniably convenient; they usually operate as self-sufficient planets with few incentives to travel beyond the fences that surround them. For carefree vacations, however, they're hard to beat, especially since your total cost will be made explicitly clear before you ever leave home.

An equally attractive option might be a **European-style hotel.** Jamaica offers many of these, a few of which are the finest in the Caribbean. There, on any given day, you'll be given an option of dining either within the hotel or at any of the small and charming restaurants that flourish nearby. Although you'll have to arrange evening transportation between your hotel and these independent restaurants, a battalion of taxis is almost always available throughout the evening to carry you there and back.

Other options include renting a **self-catering villa or apartment,** where you can save money by making your own meals in your own kitchen. Also noteworthy are Jamaica's simple but decent **guest houses,** where low costs combine with maximum exposure to local life. Unfortunately, these sometimes lie far from beaches and offer almost none of the diversions and activities that vacationers seem to crave and will probably not appeal to clients who insist on problem-free luxury.

Regardless of what you select, be assured that every choice has its own style, flavor, and methods of operating. Any will contribute richly to your understanding of the kaleidoscopic tapestry that is Jamaica.

HOTELS & RESORTS

There's no rigid classification of Jamaican hotels. The word *deluxe* is often used—or misused—when *first class* might be a more appropriate term. First class itself often isn't apt. We've presented fairly detailed descriptions of the properties mentioned in this book, so you'll get an idea of what to expect once you're there. Even in deluxe and first-class properties, however, don't expect top-rate service and efficiency. "Things," as they're called in Jamaica, don't seem to work as well in the tropics as they do in certain fancy California or European resorts. When you go to turn on the shower, sometimes you get water and sometimes you don't. You may even experience island power failures.

Facilities often determine the choice of a hotel. For example, if golf is your passion, you may want to book into a hotel resort such as Tryall outside Montego Bay. If scuba diving is your goal, then head, say, for Negril. Regardless of your particular interest, there is a hotel catering to you.

TIPS FOR SAVING ON YOUR ROOM   The *rack rate* is the maximum rate that a hotel charges for a room. It's the rate you'd get if you walked in off the street and asked for a room for the night. Hardly anybody pays these prices, however, and there are many ways around them.

- **Don't be afraid to bargain.** Get in the habit of asking for a lower price than the first one quoted. Most rack rates include commissions of 10% to 25% or more for travel agents, which many hotels will cut if you make your own reservations and haggle a bit. Always ask politely whether a less-expensive room is available than the first one mentioned or whether any special rates apply to you. You may qualify for corporate, student, military, senior citizen, or other discounts. Be sure to mention membership in AAA, AARP, frequent-flyer programs, or trade unions, which may entitle you to special deals as well.

- **Rely on a qualified professional.** Certain hotels give travel agents discounts in exchange for steering business their way, so if you're shy about bargaining, an agent may be better equipped to negotiate discounts for you.

- **Dial direct.** When booking a room in a chain hotel, call the hotel's local line, as well as the toll-free number, and see where you get the best deal. A hotel makes nothing on a room that stays empty. The clerk who runs the place is more likely to know about vacancies and will often grant deep discounts in order to fill up.

- **Remember the law of supply and demand.** Resort hotels are most crowded and therefore most expensive on weekends, so discounts are usually available for mid-week stays. To the contrary, business hotels in downtown locations are busiest during the week; expect discounts over the weekend. Avoid high-season stays whenever you can; planning your vacation just a week before or after official peak season can mean big savings.

- **Look into group or long-stay discounts.** If you come as part of a large group, you should be able to negotiate a bargain, since the hotel can then guarantee occupancy in a number of rooms. Likewise, when you're planning a long stay in town (usually from five days to a week) you'll qualify for a discount. As a general rule, you will receive one night free after a seven-night stay.

- **Avoid excess charges.** When you book a room, ask whether the hotel charges for parking. Most hotels have free, available space, but many urban or beachfront hotels don't. Also, find out before you dial whether your hotel imposes a surcharge on local or long-distance calls. A pay phone, however inconvenient, may save you money.

- **Watch for coupons and advertised discounts.** Scan ads in your local Sunday travel section, an excellent source for up-to-the-minute hotel deals. Also research the local *Entertainments* directory books sold by school groups and some local bookstores.

- **Consider a suite.** If you are traveling with your family or another couple, you can pack more people into a suite (which usually comes with a sofa bed), and thereby reduce your per-person rate. Remember that some places charge for extra guests, though some do not.

- **Book an efficiency.** A room with a kitchenette enables you to grocery shop and eat some meals in. Especially during long stays with families, you're bound to save money on food this way.

- **Investigate reservation services.** These outfits usually work as consolidators, buying up or reserving rooms in bulk, and then dealing them out to customers at a profit. They do garner special deals that range from 10% to 50% off; but remember, these discounts apply to rack rates, inflated prices that people rarely

Jamaica Accommodations

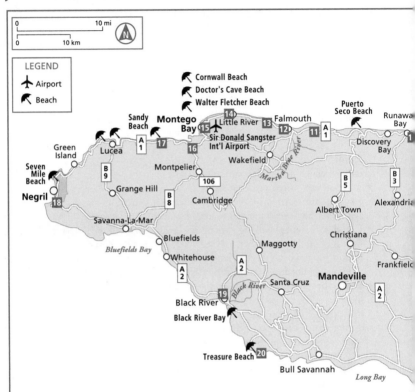

LEGEND
✈ Airport
🏖 Beach

0 — 10 mi
0 — 10 km

N

Cornwall Beach
Doctor's Cave Beach
Walter Fletcher Beach

Puerto Seco Beach

Sandy Beach
Montego Bay
Little River
Falmouth
Runawa Bay

Green Island
Lucea
Sir Donald Sangster Int'l Airport
Discovery Bay

Seven Mile Beach
Montpelier
Wakefield

Negril
Grange Hill
Cambridge
Albert Town
Alexandria

Savanna-La-Mar
Christiana

Bluefields
Maggotty
Frankfiel

Bluefields Bay
Whitehouse
Mandeville

Santa Cruz
Black River

Black River
Bull Savannah
Long Bay

Black River Bay

Treasure Beach

C a r i b b e a n   S e a

Altamont Court Hotel **2**
Banana Shout **18**
Beaches Negril **18**
Blue Caves Castle **18**
Blue Harbour **5**
Blue Harbour Hotel **15**
Bonnie Vue Plantation Hotel **4**
Breezes Golf and Beach Resort **10**
Breezes Montego Bay **15**
Caribbean Isle Hotel **10**
The Caves **18**
Charela Inn **18**
Chukka Cove Farm & Resort **10**
Ciboney Ocho Rios **8**
Club Ambiance Jamaica **10**
Club Jamaica Beach Resort **7**
Coco La Palm Resort **18**
Coconuts **18**
Coral Cliff Hotel **15**
Country, Country **18**
Couples Negril **18**

Couples Ocho Rios **7**
Courtleigh Hotel **2**
Coyaba **19**
Crowne Plaza Kingston **2**
Crystal Waters **18**
De Montevin Lodge Hotel **4**
Devine Destiny **18**
Doctor's Cave Beach Hotel **15**
Dragon Bay **4**
Drumville Cove Resort **18**
Eaton Hall Beach Hotel **10**
El Greco Resort **15**
The Enchanted Garden **8**
F.D.R. Franklyn D. Resort **10**
Fern Hill Club **4**
Firefly Beach Cottages **18**
Fisherman's Inn
  (Rose's by the Sea) **20**
Foote Prints **18**
Goblin Hill Villas at San San **4**
Goldeneye **4**

Golf View Hotel **21**
Good Hope **12**
Grand Lido **18**
Grand Lido Braco **11**
Grand Lido San Souci **6**
Half Moon Golf, Tennis &
  Beach Club **13**
Hedonism II **18**
Hedonism III **10**
Hibiscus Lodge Hotel **8**
High Hope Estate **9**
Holiday Inn Sun Spree **13**
Home Sweet Home **18**
Hotel Four Seasons **2**
Hotel Mocking Bird Hill **4**
Indies Hotel **1**
Invercauld Great House
  & Hotel **19**
Irie Sandz Hotel **19**
Jack Tar Village Montego Bay **15**
Jackie's on the Reef **18**

end up paying. You're probably better off dealing directly with a hotel, but if you don't like bargaining, this is certainly a viable option. Most of them offer online reservation services as well. Here are a few of the more reputable providers: **Accommodations Express** (☎ **800/950-4685;** www.accommodationsexpress.com); **Hotel Reservations Network** (☎ **800/96HOTEL;** www.180096HOTEL.com); **Quikbook** (☎ **800/789-9887,** includes fax on demand service; www.quikbook.com); and **Room Exchange** (☎ **800/846-7000** in the U.S., 800/486-7000 in Canada).

Online, try booking your hotel through **Arthur Frommer's Budget Travel** (www.frommers.com) and save up to 50%. **Microsoft Expedia** (www.expedia.com) features a "Travel Agent" that will also direct you to affordable lodgings.

LANDING THE BEST ROOM   Somebody has to get the best room in the house. It might as well be you. Always ask for a corner room. They're usually larger, quieter, and closer to the elevator. They often have more windows and light than standard rooms, and they don't always cost more.

When you make your reservation, ask if the hotel is renovating; if it is, request a room away from the renovation work. Many hotels now offer nonsmoking rooms; if smoke bothers you, by all means ask for a nonsmoking room. Inquire, too, about the location of the restaurants, bars, and discos in the hotel—these could all be a source of irritating noise. If you aren't happy with your room when you arrive, talk to the front desk. If they have another room, they should be happy to accommodate you, within reason.

GUEST HOUSES

An entirely different type of accommodation is the guest house, where most of the Jamaicans themselves stay when they travel. In Jamaica, the term "guest house" can mean anything. Sometimes so-called guest houses resemble simple motels built around swimming pools. Others are made up of small individual cottages with kitchenettes, constructed around a main building often containing a bar and a restaurant serving local food. Some are surprisingly comfortable, often with private baths and a swimming pool. You may or may not have air-conditioning. The rooms are sometimes cooled by ceiling fans, or by breezes entering through open windows at night.

Guest houses can't be topped for value. You can usually go to a big beach resort to enjoy its seaside facilities for only a small charge. Although bereft of frills, the guest houses we've recommended are clean and safe for families or single women. On the other hand, the least expensive are not places where you'd want to spend much time because of their simple furnishings, diversions, and amenities.

CONDOS, COTTAGES & VILLAS

If you're going as a family or group of friends, a housekeeping holiday can be one of the least-expensive ways to vacation in Jamaica. Self-catering accommodations are now available at many locations.

The more upscale villas have a staff, or at least a maid who comes in a few days a week, and they also provide the essentials for home life, including bed linens and cooking paraphernalia. Condos usually come with a reception desk and are often comparable to life in a suite in a big resort hotel. Nearly all condo complexes provide swimming pools (some have more than one pool).

Some private apartments in Jamaica are rented, either with or without maid service. This is more of a no-frills option than are the villas and condos. The apartments may not be in buildings with swimming pools, and they may not maintain a front desk to help you.

Cottages are the most freewheeling way to live in the four major categories of vacation homes. Most are fairly simple, many ideally opening onto a beach, although others may be clustered around a communal swimming pool. Many contain no more than a simple bedroom with a small kitchen and bath. In the peak winter season, reservations should be made at least 5 or 6 months in advance.

The savings, especially for a family of three to six people, or two or three couples, can range from 50% to 60% of what a hotel would cost. If there are only two in your party, these savings don't apply.

The savings will be on the rent, not on the groceries, which are sometimes 35% to 60% more costly than on the U.S. mainland. Grocery tabs reflect the fact that many food items must be imported. Even so, preparing your own food will be a lot cheaper than dining around, as most restaurants, even the so-called inexpensive places, are likely to be more expensive than what is considered cheap in your hometown.

Villas of Distinction, P.O. Box 55, Armonk, NY 10504 (☎ **800/289-0900** in the U.S., or 914/273-3331; fax 914/273-3387; www.villasofdistinction.com), offers private villas with one to six bedrooms and a pool. Domestic help is often included. They have offerings on St. Martin, Anguilla, Mustique, Barbados, the U.S. and British Virgin Islands, the Cayman Islands, St. Lucia, St. Barts, and Jamaica. Descriptions, rates, and photos are available online.

At Home Abroad, 405 E. 56th St., Suite 6-H, New York, NY 10022-2466 (☎ **212/421-9165;** fax 212/752-1591), has a roster of private upscale homes for rent on Barbados, Jamaica, Mustique, St. John, St. Lucia, St. Martin, St. Thomas, Tortola, and Virgin Gorda, most with maid service included.

VHR, Worldwide, 235 Kensington Ave., Norwood, NJ 07648 (☎ **800/633-3284** in the U.S. and Canada, or 201/767-9393; fax 201/767-5510), offers the most comprehensive portfolio of luxury villas, condominiums, resort suites, and apartments for rent in not only the Caribbean, but the Bahamas, Mexico, and the United States as well. The company can also arrange for airfare and car rental. Its more than 4,000 homes and suite resorts are handpicked by the staff, and these accommodations are generally less expensive than comparable hotel rooms.

Hideaways International, 767 Islington St., Portsmouth, NH 03801 (☎ **800/ 843-4433** in the U.S., or 603/430-4433; fax 603/430-4444; www.hideaways.com), publishes *Hideaways Guide,* a pictorial directory of home rentals throughout the world. Locations include the Caribbean, especially the British Virgin Islands, the Cayman Islands, Jamaica, and St. Lucia; the directory includes full descriptions so you know what you're renting. Rentals range from cottages to staffed villas to whole islands! On most rentals, you deal directly with owners. For condos and small resorts, Hideaways offers member discounts. Other services include yacht charters, cruises, airline ticketing, car rentals, and hotel reservations. Annual membership is $99; a 4-month trial membership is $39. Membership information, listings, and photos are available online.

Heart of the Caribbean Ltd., 17485 Penbrook Dr., Brookfield, WI 53045 (☎ **800/231-5303** or 414/783-5303; fax 414/781-4026; www.hotcarib.com), is a villa wholesale company offering travelers a wide range of private villas and condos on several islands, including St. Maarten/St. Martin, Barbados, and St. Lucia. Accommodations range from one to six bedrooms and from modest villas and condos to palatial estates. Homes have complete kitchens and maid service. Catering and car rentals can also be provided. Rates, listings, and photos are available online.

Villa Net, 7200 34th Ave. NW, Seattle, WA 98117 (☎ **800/488-RENT** or 206/789-9377; fax 206/789-9379; www.rentavilla.com), maintains an inventory of several thousand properties, specializing in condos and villas with weekly rates ranging from $700 to $25,000. It arranges bookings for weeklong or longer stays. For a color catalog including prices, descriptions, and pictures, send $15, which will be applied to your next rental. Prices, descriptions, and pictures are also available online.

Sometimes, local tourist offices will also advise you on vacation-home rentals if you write or call them directly.

14 Tips on Dining Out

The bad news is that dining in Jamaica is generally more expensive than in either the United States or Canada. Restaurant prices are in tune with Europe rather than North America. Virtually everything must be imported, except the fish or Caribbean lobster that is caught locally and some fruits and vegetables. Service is automatically added to most restaurant tabs, usually 10% to 15%. Even so, if service has been good, it's customary to tip extra.

To save money, many visitors prefer the Modified American Plan (MAP), which includes room, breakfast, and one main meal per day, almost always dinner. You can then have lunch somewhere else, or if your hotel has a beach, order a light à la carte lunch at the hotel, the cost of which is added to your bill. The American Plan (AP), on the other hand, includes all three meals each day. Drinks, including wine, are usually extra.

If you want to eat your main meals outside the hotel, book a Continental Plan (CP), which includes only breakfast. To go one step further, choose the European Plan (EP), which includes no meals.

Before booking a hotel, it's wise to have a clear understanding of what is included in the various meal plans offered.

If you're planning on eating out, here are some tips you may find useful:

- In summer, only the most sophisticated and posh establishments require men to wear jackets.
- Check to see if reservations are required. In the winter, you may find all the tables gone at some of the more famous places. At all places, wear a cover-up if you're lunching; don't enter a restaurant attired in a bikini.
- To save money, stick to regional food whenever possible. For a main dish, that usually means Caribbean lobster or fish (see "A Taste of Jamaica," in the appendix).
- You may want to avoid too much red meat; it's probably flown in and may have been waiting on the island long before you arrived on the beach.
- If you go out for dinner, consider taking a taxi. All taxi drivers know the badly marked roads well, so finding that special, off-the-beaten-track restaurant won't be as difficult as it would be if you drove your rental car. (Roads are narrow and poorly lit; complicating matters for Americans, Canadians, and Europeans, Jamaicans drive on the left side of the road, as in Great Britain.) Once at the restaurant, you can arrange for the taxi to pick you up at an agreed-upon time or else have the restaurant call the taxi when you are ready to leave. Some upscale restaurants will arrange to have a minivan pick you up and return you to your hotel if you call in advance.

15 Tips on Shopping

If your shopping tastes run toward the electronic, you might discover an occasional bargain in audio equipment in the marketplaces of Jamaica, as well as a scattering of

Digging into Jerk Pork

Wherever you go in Jamaica, you'll encounter ramshackle stands selling jerk pork. There is no more authentic local experience than stopping at one of these stands and ordering a lunch of jerk pork, preferably washed down with a Red Stripe beer. Jerk is a special way of barbecuing highly spicy meats on slats of pimento wood over a wood fire set in the ground. One is never sure what goes into the seasoning, but the taste is definitely of peppers, pimento, and ginger. You can also order jerk chicken, sausage, fish, and even lobster. The cook will haul out a machete and chop the meat into bite-size pieces for you, then throw them into a paper bag.

wristwatches, discounted gold chains, and a small appliance or two. Much more appealing, however, are the thousands of handcrafted items whose inspiration seems to spring from the creative depths of the Jamaican soul.

The arts are not a new tradition in Jamaica. During the 1700s, Jamaican wig holders, combs, boxes, and art objects were considered charming decorative objects as far away as London. Today, the tradition of arts and handcrafts continues to flourish, with a far greater array of purchasable possibilities.

In Jamaica, as everywhere else, the distinction between what is art and what is merely a craft is often a matter of personal preference. However varied your artistic background and tastes may be, an estimated 50,000 artisans labor long and hard to produce thousands of paintings, wood carvings, textiles, and whatnots, any of which might serve as an evocative reminder of your Jamaican holiday. It is estimated that there are at least 500 wood-carving stands set beside the road between Montego Bay and Ocho Rios, and many dozens of others scattered throughout the rest of Jamaica as well.

Usually chiseled from mahogany or a very hard tropical wood known as lignum vitae, **wood carvings** run the gamut from the execrably horrible to the delicately delightful, with many works of power and vision in between. Frequently, pieces have been carved with such crude tools as antique iron chisels and (sometimes) nothing more than a graduated set of pocketknives and nails. Also available are all sizes of **baskets** woven from palm fronds or the straw of an island plant known as the *jipijapa,* calabash (gourds) etched with illustrations of hummingbirds and vines, and hammocks woven into designs handed down from the time of the Arawak Indians.

Although many of Jamaica's crafts are distributed by entrepreneurial middlepeople, it always (at least for us) gives an item an especially subjective memory when the purchase is made directly from the hands that crafted it.

The island's inventory of wood carvings and weavings is supplemented by establishments selling **leather goods** (sandals and shoes are often a good buy); locally made jewelry fashioned from gold, silver, onyx, and bone; and garments (especially casual wear and sportswear) whose light textures nicely complement the heat of the tropics. Also noteworthy are the many handbags woven from straw or palm fronds, which are sometimes rendered more ornate through colorful embroidery applied by any of the island's "straw ladies."

Many people head home with several bottles of the heady **spices** whose seasonings flavor the best of Jamaica's dishes. Vacuum-sealed plastic containers filled with **Blue Mountain coffee** are enviable gifts for loved ones back home, as well as any of the bottles of specialty rums whose flavors (orange, coconut, and coffee, among others) can evoke the heat of Jamaica even during a snow-blanketed northern winter.

Jamaica Dining

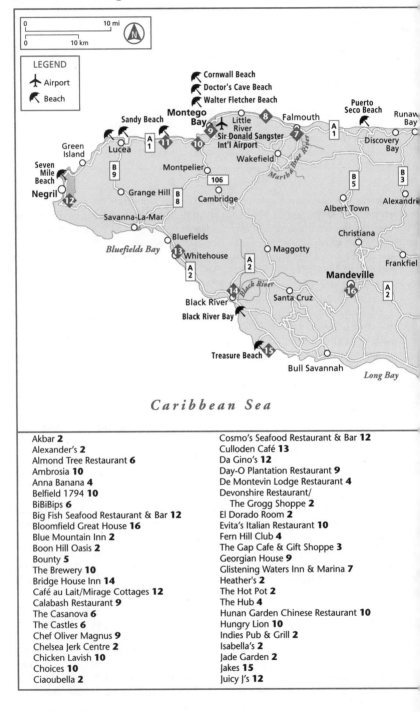

LEGEND

✈ Airport
🏄 Beach

Cornwall Beach
Doctor's Cave Beach
Walter Fletcher Beach
Montego Bay
Sandy Beach
Little River
Falmouth
Puerto Seco Beach
Runaway Bay
Sir Donald Sangster Int'l Airport
Discovery Bay
Green Island
Lucea
Wakefield
Seven Mile Beach
Montpelier
Negril
Grange Hill
Cambridge
Albert Town
Alexandria
Savanna-La-Mar
Christiana
Bluefields
Frankfield
Bluefields Bay
Whitehouse
Maggotty
Mandeville
Black River
Santa Cruz
Black River Bay
Treasure Beach
Bull Savannah
Long Bay
Martha Brae River
Black River

Caribbean Sea

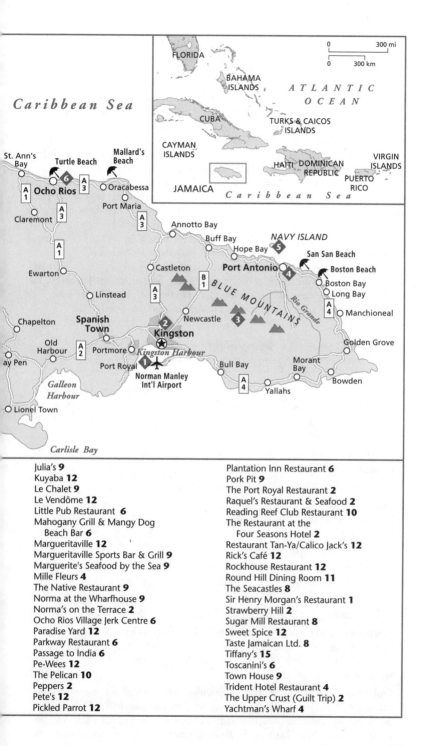

Especially noteworthy is the handful of **art galleries** that stock the paintings of local artists. Jamaica's impressive inventory of painters has been well documented in art galleries throughout Europe and North America. You'll probably find dozens of paintings for sale. Some critics say the island's most valuable export, after aluminum, is its art. These paintings range from the banal and uninspired to richly evocative portrayals of universal themes. If the painting speaks to you, consider buying it. Before investing in a major purchase, however, we suggest you consult with an expert at one of the island's better-known galleries, where paintings can easily cost several thousand dollars. Lesser works, or works by as-yet-unknown artists, are sometimes available for as little as U.S.$20 each on sidewalks throughout the country.

Polite and good-natured **bargaining** is usually expected, especially in the informal markets. In fact, if you bargain with goodwill and humor, you might get some pleasant insights into the interpersonal dynamics that are part of the island's daily life. And you should get a discount of around 15% to 20%. In more formal environments, bargaining often will simply not work. The aura projected by the owner or salesperson will quickly communicate the degree to which bargaining is welcomed.

Although shopping possibilities abound in virtually every tourist resort, every serious shopper should visit an outlet of the government-funded **Things Jamaican.** The quality of inventory varies widely from outlet to outlet, but they all offer a sampling of some of the best products of the island under one roof. See chapter 3.

Fast Facts: Jamaica

Airports   See "Flying to Jamaica" and "Getting Around" in this chapter.

Business Hours   Banks are open Monday through Friday from 9am to 5pm. Store hours vary widely, but as a general rule most business establishments open at 8:30am and close at 4:30 or 5pm Monday through Friday. Some shops are open on Saturday until noon.

Car Rentals   See "Getting Around," earlier in this chapter.

Climate   See "When to Go," earlier in this chapter.

Currency   See "Money," earlier in this chapter.

Currency Exchange   There are Bank of Jamaica exchange bureaus at both international airports (near Montego Bay and Kingston), at cruise-ship piers, and in most hotels.

Doctors   Many major resorts have doctors on call. If you need any particular medicine or treatment, bring evidence, such as a letter from your own doctor.

Documents Required   See "Entry Requirements & Customs," earlier in this chapter.

Driving Rules   See "Getting Around," earlier in this chapter.

Electricity   Most places have the standard electrical voltage of 110, as in the U.S. However, some establishments operate on 220 volts, 50 cycles. If your hotel is on a different current than your U.S.-made appliance, ask for a transformer and adapter.

Embassies, Consulates & High Commissions   Calling embassies or consulates in Jamaica is a challenge. Phones will ring and ring before being picked up, if they are answered at all. Extreme patience is needed to reach a live voice on the other end. The embassy of the **United States** is at the Jamaica Mutual Life

Meeting the Jamaicans

The Jamaica Tourist Board operates a **Meet-the-People program** in Kingston and the island's five major resort cities and towns. Through the program, visitors can meet Jamaican families who volunteer to host them free for a few hours or even a whole day.

More than 650 families are registered in the project with the tourist board, which keeps a list of their interests and hobbies. All you need do is give the board a rough idea of your interests, and they will arrange for you to spend the day with a similar family. You go along with whatever the family does, sharing their life, eating at their table, accompanying them to a dinner party. You may end up at a beach barbecue, afternoon tea with neighbors, or just sitting and expounding theories, arguing, and talking far into the night. The program does not include overnight accommodation.

If you have a particular interest—birds, butterflies, music, ham radio, stamp collecting, or spelunking in Jamaica's many caves—the tourist board will find you a fellow enthusiast. Lasting friendships have developed because of this unique opportunity to meet people.

Although the service is entirely free, your hostess will certainly enjoy receiving flowers or a similar token of appreciation after your visit.

In Jamaica, apply at any of the local tourist board offices (see "Visitor Information," earlier in this chapter).

Another program is offered by **World Learning,** founded in 1932 as The U.S. Experiment in International Living, Kipling Rd., P.O. Box 676, Brattleboro, VT 05302-0676 (☎ **800/336-1616** or 802/ 257-7751). Their College Semester Abroad program in Jamaica focuses on women and development and life and culture in Jamaica. Participants become one of the family, taking part in its daily activities, while studying in the region. The program includes fieldwork and an independent study project.

Centre, 2 Oxford Rd., Kingston 5 (☎ **876/929-4850**). The High Commission of **Canada** is in the Mutual Security Bank Building, 30–36 Knutsford Blvd., Kingston 5 (☎ **876/926-1500**), and there's a consulate at 29 Gloucester Ave., Montego Bay (☎ **876/952-6198**). The High Commission of the **United Kingdom** is at 28 Trafalgar Rd., Kingston 10 (☎ **876/926-9050**).

Emergencies   For police and air rescue, dial ☎ **119;** to report a fire or call an ambulance, dial ☎ **110.**

Holidays   See "When to Go," earlier in this chapter.

Hospitals   In Kingston, the **University Hospital** is at Mona (☎ **876/ 927-1620**); in Montego Bay, the **Cornwall Regional Hospital** is at Mount Salem (☎ **876/952-5100**); and in Port Antonio, the **Port Antonio General Hospital** is at Naylor's Hill (☎ **876/993-2646**).

Mail   Instead of going to a post office, you can, in most cases, give mail to your hotel's reception desk. Most hotels sell postage stamps. A hotel worker will give your mail to a mail carrier at the time of mail delivery or include it in the hotel mail when a staff member goes to the post office. Parcels can often be mailed by a hotel worker. Allow about 1 week for an airmail postcard or letter to reach the

---

A Word on Marijuana

You'll almost certainly be approached by someone selling ganja (marijuana), and, to be frank, that's why many travelers come here. However, we should warn you that drugs (including marijuana) are illegal, and imprisonment is the penalty for possession. Don't smoke pot openly in public. Of course, hundreds of visitors do and get away with it, but you may be the one who gets caught—the person selling to you might even be a police informant. Above all, don't consider for a second bringing marijuana back into the United States. There are drug-sniffing dogs stationed at the Jamaican airports, and they will check your luggage. U.S. Customs agents, well aware of the drug situation on Jamaica, have also easily caught and arrested many who have tried to take a chance on bringing some home.

North American mainland. Increases in postal charges can be implemented at any time, so find out the current rate before depositing mail. Call ☎ **876/ 922-9430** in Kingston for any problems or questions about mail in Jamaica. If you want to be sure of delivery, consider using a courier service like DHL or Federal Express.

Maps   See "Getting Around," earlier in this chapter.

Newspapers & Magazines   Jamaica supports three daily newspapers (*Daily Gleaner*, *The Jamaica Record*, and the *Daily Star*), several weekly periodicals, and a handful of other publications. U.S. newsmagazines, such as *Time* and *Newsweek*, as well as occasional copies of *The Miami Herald*, are available at most newsstands.

Nudity   Nude sunbathing and swimming are allowed at a number of hotels, clubs, and beaches (especially in Negril), but only where signs state that swimsuits are optional. Elsewhere, law enforcers will not even allow topless sunbathing.

Pharmacies   In Montego Bay, try **Overton Pharmacy,** 49 Union St., Overton Plaza (☎ **876/952-2699**); in Ocho Rios, **Great House Pharmacy,** Brown's Plaza (☎ **876/974-2352**); and in Kingston, **Moodie's Pharmacy,** in the New Kingston Shopping Centre (☎ **876/926-4174**). Prescriptions are accepted by local pharmacies only if issued by a Jamaican doctor. Hotels have doctors on call. If you need any particular medicine or treatment, bring evidence, such as a letter from your own physician.

Police   Dial ☎ **119.**

Radio & TV   Jamaica is served by two major radio broadcasters, both of which are instantly recognizable to thousands of island residents. Radio Jamaica (RJR) is the more popular of the two, partly because of its musical mix of reggae, rock and roll, and talk show material of everyday interest to Jamaicans. The broadcaster is owned by the Jamaican government, its employees, and members of the Jamaican community. RJR's two islandwide services are known as Supreme Sound and FAME FM. The second broadcaster is Jamaica Broadcasting Corporation (JBC), run by a board appointed by the government. JBC also operates the island's only television station (JBC-TV, established in 1963), which transmits from at least two different points on the island.

The availability of Jamaican radio and TV stations does not prevent many island residents from tuning in TV and radio programming from the U.S. mainland, South America, and other Caribbean islands. Many of Jamaica's better hotels offer Cable News Network (CNN) and other satellite broadcasts. Hotels also offer in-house video movies transmitted from a central point in the establishment.

Safety   You can get into a lot of trouble in Jamaica or you can have a carefree vacation—much depends on what you do and where you go. Major hotels have security guards to protect the grounds. Under no circumstances should you accept an invitation to see "the real Jamaica" from some stranger you meet on the beach. Exercise caution when traveling around the country. Safeguard your valuables and never leave them unattended on a beach. Likewise, never leave luggage or other valuables in a car's passenger compartment or trunk. Many private residences on the island have protected their windows with iron grills, and guard dogs are commonplace—even some beaches have guards hired by the resorts to protect their clients from muggers. For the latest advisories, call the **U.S. State Department** (☎ 202/647-5225).

Taxes   The government imposes a 12% room tax. You'll be charged a J$750 ($21.40) departure tax at the airport, payable in either Jamaican or U.S. dollars. There's also a 15% government tax on rental cars and a 15% tax on all overseas phone calls.

Taxis   See "Getting Around," earlier in this chapter.

Telephone, Telex, & Fax   All overseas telephone calls are subject to a government tax of 15%. Most calls can be made from the privacy of your hotel room or, in some budget or moderate hotels, from the lobby. Even the island's smallest hotels maintain their own fax machines. For telexes, and in case your hotel isn't equipped with suitable phone or fax equipment, contact the local branch of **Telecommunications of Jamaica,** the country's telecommunications operators. In Kingston, its address is 47 Halfway Tree Rd. (☎ 876/926-9700).

Time   In the winter, Jamaica is on eastern standard time. When the United States is on daylight savings time, however, it's 6am in Miami and 5am in Kingston because Jamaica does not switch to DST.

Tipping   Tipping is customary in Jamaica. Typically, 10% or 15% is expected in hotels and restaurants on occasions when you would normally tip. Most places add a service charge to the bill. Tipping is not allowed in the all-inclusive hotels.

Useful Telephone Numbers   Ambulance, 110; fire, 110; police, 119; time, 117; toll operator and telephone assistance on local and intra-island calls, 112; overseas calls operator, 113; and **Post and Telegraph Department,** ☎ 876/922-9430.

Water   It's usually safe to drink tap water islandwide, as it is filtered and chlorinated; however, it's prudent to drink bottled water, if available.

Weather   See "When to Go," earlier in this chapter.

3

Montego Bay

Montego Bay made its first appearance on the world's tourism stage in the 1940s when wealthy travelers discovered the warm, spring-fed waters of Doctor's Cave Beach. Now Jamaica's second-largest community, the town of Mo Bay—as the locals call it—lies on the northwest coast of the island. In spite of its large influx of visitors, Montego Bay retains its own identity. A thriving business and commercial center, it functions as the main market town for most of western Jamaica. It supports cruise-ship piers and a growing industrial center at the free port.

Montego Bay is served by its own airport, **Donald Sangster International,** so vacationers coming to Jamaica have little need to visit Kingston, the island's capital, unless they want to see its cultural and historic attractions. Otherwise, you'll find everything in Mo Bay, the most cosmopolitan of Jamaica's resort areas.

Some 23 miles east of Montego Bay, the small 18th-century port town of **Falmouth** is one of the most interesting morning or afternoon excursions from Mo Bay. (Ocho Rios and Runaway Bay are other good choices; they're covered in chapter 6.) Falmouth is not really a tourist town. The community revolves around farming and fishing; more than any resort town, it is the "real" Jamaica. We'll take you there at the end of this chapter.

1 Where to Stay

The Montego Bay region boasts a superb selection of hotels, ranging from very expensive world-class inns to notable bargains. There's also an amazing selection of all-inclusive resorts, which are all reviewed together for easy comparison at the very end of this section. Most of the big full-service resorts are frequently included in package tours. Booking a package will make the rates much more reasonable. See "Escorted & Package Tours" and "Tips on Accommodations" in chapter 2.

The big hotel news in Montego Bay for 2001 will be the opening of **The Ritz Carlton** at Rose Hall. It'll offer the ambience of a traditional Jamaican great house in tropical gardens with an 18-hole golf course designed by Robert von Hagge. If plans go according to schedule, it will become one of the great resort hotels of the Caribbean. To check its status at the time of your visit, consult a travel agent, call ☎ **800/ 241-3333,** or log on to **www.ritzcarlton.com**.

VERY EXPENSIVE

✪ Half Moon Golf, Tennis, & Beach Club. Rose Hall (P.O. Box 80), Montego Bay, Jamaica, W.I. ☎ **800/626-0592** in the U.S., or 876/953-2211. Fax 876/953-2731. www. halfmoon.com.jm. E-mail: reservation@halfmoonclub.com. 418 units. A/C TV TEL. Winter $390–$480 double; from $590 suite; from $1,650 villa. Off-season $220–$280 double; from $320 suite; from $1,320 villa. MAP (breakfast and dinner) $65 per person extra. AE, MC, V.

About 8 miles east of Montego Bay's city center and 6 miles from the international airport, the Half Moon Golf, Tennis & Beach Club is a classic, and one of the 300 best hotels in the world, according to *Condé Nast Traveler*. It was established as a private club in 1954 by a group of well-heeled U.S.-based investors, but took its present form only after the ascension of the present manager and part owner, Austrian-born Hans Simonitsch, who has imbued the place with an aesthetic that reflects the best days of the Hapsburgs. Even the public areas at this hotel are the best furnished, most tasteful, and most grand of any hotel in Jamaica. It has far more activities, excitement, amenities, restaurants, and a better beach than either Round Hill or Tryall. One of the largest resorts in the Caribbean, it's scattered over 400 acres of sea-fronting property that has won virtually every award for eco-sensitivity, with a varied collection of lodgings including conventional hotel rooms, suites, and a relatively new collection of villas. Most of these have private pools and a full-time staff. Each unit is comfortably furnished with an English colonial/Caribbean motif. Queen Anne–inspired furniture is set off by bright Jamaican paintings, and many units have mahogany four-poster beds.

Dining/Diversions: The Sugar Mill restaurant, our favorite restaurant in Montego Bay, is set beside a working waterwheel from a bygone sugar estate on the property (see "Where to Dine," below). The Seagrape Terrace (named after the 80-year-old sea grapes on the property) offers delightful meals alfresco. Il Giardino, set within a convincing replica of a Renaissance palazzo, serves savory Italian cuisine. Also on the premises are an Asian (Japanese and Chinese) restaurant, a steak house, and an English pub. Evening entertainment includes music from a resident band and nightly folklore and musical shows.

Amenities: This is the best-accessorized hotel in Jamaica. The most recently built of the 52 pools is an Olympic-size lap pool that local professional athletes pronounce the finest in Jamaica. There's a state-of-the-art health club where yoga and aerobics are offered nearly every day, as well as 13 tennis courts (7 floodlit at night), and 4 lit squash courts. There are facilities for sailing, windsurfing, snorkeling, scuba diving, and deep-sea fishing. There's also an outstanding 18-hole golf course designed by Robert Trent Jones, Sr., and a riding stable that's one of the best equipped and well recommended in Jamaica. Also on the premises are two separate shopping villages (with a pharmacy; dozens of unusual, high-profile shops; and a beauty salon). Room service is available from 7am to midnight, as well as laundry, baby-sitting, massage, and instruction in various water sports.

✪ Round Hill Hotel and Villas. Rte. A1 (P.O. Box 64), Montego Bay, Jamaica, W.I. ☎ **800/ 972-2159** in the U.S., or 876/956-7050. Fax 876/956-7505. www.roundhilljamaica.com. E-mail: roundhill@cwjamaica.com. 74 units. A/C TEL. Winter $390–$470 double; $570–$780 villa. Off-season $240–$290 double; $340–$510 villa. Extra person $65. MAP (breakfast and dinner) $70 per person extra. AE, DC, MC, V.

Opened in 1953 and now a Caribbean legend, this is one of the most distinguished hotels in the West Indies. It stands on a lushly landscaped 98-acre peninsula that slopes gracefully down to a sheltered cove, where the elegant reception area and social

Montego Bay

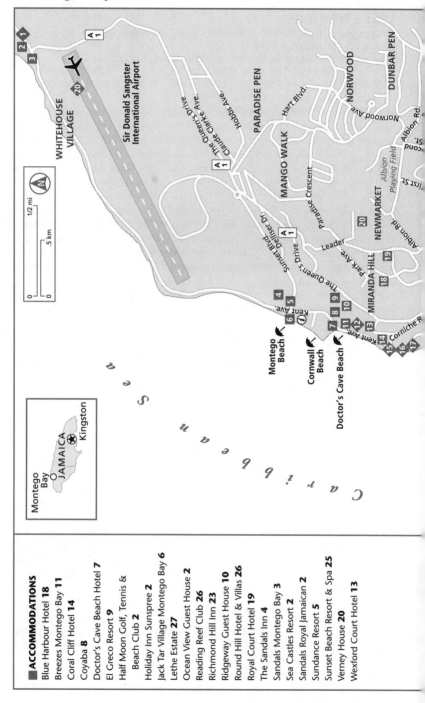

ACCOMMODATIONS

Blue Harbour Hotel **18**
Breezes Montego Bay **11**
Coral Cliff Hotel **14**
Coyaba **8**
Doctor's Cave Beach Hotel **7**
El Greco Resort **9**
Half Moon Golf, Tennis & Beach Club **2**
Holiday Inn Sunspree **2**
Jack Tar Village Montego Bay **6**
Lethe Estate **27**
Ocean View Guest House **2**
Reading Reef Club **26**
Richmond Hill Inn **23**
Ridgeway Guest House **10**
Round Hill Hotel & Villas **26**
Royal Court Hotel **19**
The Sandals Inn **4**
Sandals Montego Bay **3**
Sea Castles Resort **2**
Sandals Royal Jamaican **2**
Sundance Resort **5**
Sunset Beach Resort & Spa **25**
Verney House **20**
Wexford Court Hotel **13**

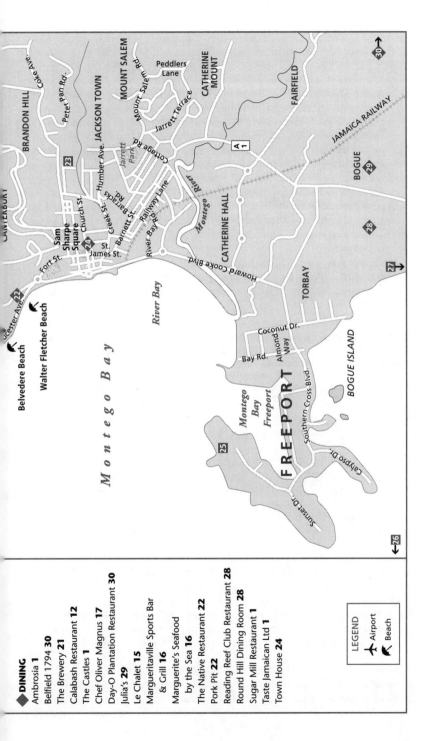

◆ DINING

Ambrosia **1**
Belfield 1794 **30**
The Brewery **21**
Calabash Restaurant **12**
The Castles **1**
Chef Oliver Magnus **17**
Day-O Plantation Restaurant **30**
Julia's **29**
Le Chalet **15**
Marguueritaville Sports Bar & Grill **16**
Marguerite's Seafood by the Sea **16**
The Native Restaurant **22**
Pork Pit **22**
Reading Reef Club Restaurant **28**
Round Hill Dining Room **28**
Sugar Mill Restaurant **1**
Taste Jamaican Ltd **1**
Town House **24**

LEGEND
✈ Airport
⚲ Beach

center stand. If you're Harrison Ford or Steven Spielberg, you check in here, wanting an elitist retreat far removed from the madding crowd. Surrounded by landscaped tropical gardens, Round Hill accommodates some 200 guests, who enjoy its private beach, the views of Jamaica's north shore and the mountains, and the colonial elegance of the resort. There are full spa services, lots of water sports, and fine tennis facilities. The guest rooms are in a richly appointed seaside building known as the Pineapple House, and each opens onto views of the water and beach. Each unit has a plantation-style decor with refinished antique furniture and twin beds with luxury mattresses, plus spacious bathrooms. The most deluxe rooms are upstairs. There are also privately owned villas dotting the hillside, most available for rental when the owners are not in residence. Each is individually decorated, sometimes lavishly, and rates include the services of a uniformed maid, a cook, and a gardener.

Dining/Diversions: Informal luncheons are held in an intimate straw hut with an open terrace in a little sandy bay. Standard Jamaican and continental dishes are served on a candlelit terrace or in the Georgian colonial room overlooking the sea. The entertainment is varied.

Amenities: Pool, fitness center (with aerobics classes), top-quality tennis courts (lit at night), safety-deposit boxes, windsurfing, glass-bottom-boat rides, scuba diving, horseback riding, sailing, paddleboats, rubber-sided inflatable boats, water-skiing. Room service (from 7:30am to 9:30pm), concierge, laundry, baby-sitting, valet service.

✪ **The Tryall Club.** St. James (P.O. Box 1206), Montego Bay, Jamaica, W.I. ☎ **800/ 238-5290** in the U.S., or 876/956-5660. Fax 876/956-5673. www.tryallclub.com. E-mail: tryallclub@cwjamaica.com. 68 units. A/C TEL. Winter $500 double; from $1,080 villa. Off-season $350 double; from $429 villa. Extra person $70 in winter, $55 in off-season. MAP (breakfast and dinner) $66 per person extra. AE, MC, V.

With more spacious grounds than almost any other hotel on Jamaica, this stylish and upscale resort sits 12 miles west of town on the site of a 2,200-acre former sugar plantation. It doesn't have the fine beach that Half Moon does, nor the house-party atmosphere of Round Hill, but it's noteworthy nevertheless. Known as one of the grandest resorts of Jamaica, the property lies along a 1.5-mile seafront and is presided over by a 165-year-old Georgian-style great house. It's a top choice for vacationers who are serious about their golf game. The accommodations, in either modern wings or luxurious villas, are decorated in cool pastels with English colonial touches. All contain ceiling fans and air-conditioning, along with picture windows framing sea and mountain views. Guest rooms are exceedingly spacious with luxurious beds, safes, coffeemakers, private patios or terraces, and tile floors. Bathrooms are roomy, with plenty of counter space. The resort's famous villas are set amid lush foliage and designed for privacy. Each villa comes with a full-time staff, including a cook, maid, laundress, and gardener. All have private pools.

Dining/Diversions: The most formal of the resort's dining areas is in the great house, where an elegant, delicious, and refined cuisine is presented nightly, featuring the finest ingredients, both domestic and imported. More-casual meals are served in a beachside cafe. A resident band plays everything from reggae to slow-dance music every night during dinner. Afternoon tea is served in the great house.

Amenities: Championship 18-hole par-71 golf course (site of many world-class golf competitions and the pride of this elegant property), nine Laykold tennis courts, 2-mile jogging trail, pool with a swim-up bar, windsurfing, snorkeling, deep-sea fishing, paddleboats, glass-bottom boats. Room service, baby-sitting, laundry, massage; lessons given in golf, tennis, and water sports.

EXPENSIVE

✪ **Coyaba.** Mahoe Bay, Little River, Montego Bay, Jamaica, W.I. ☎ **877/COYABA8** or 876/953-9150. Fax 876/953-2244. www.coyabajamaica.com. E-mail: coyaba@n5.com.jm. 50 units. A/C TV TEL. Winter $260–$360 double. Off-season $180–$240 double. All meals $70 per person extra. Children 11 and under get a 50% discount. AE, MC, V.

With only 50 rooms and a graceful British colonial atmosphere, this is one of the smaller and more elegant all-inclusive resorts. It was established in 1994 by American/Jamaican-Chinese entrepreneurs, the Robertson family, and built from scratch at a cost of $4 million. Set on a lovely strip of beachfront, a 15-minute drive east of the center of Montego Bay, it's centered around an adaptation of a 19th-century great house. Accommodations in the main building overlook the garden; those in the pair of three-story outbuildings lie closer to the beach and are somewhat more expensive. The decor is British colonial, with traditional prints, expensive chintz fabrics, French doors leading onto private patios or verandas, carved mahogany furniture, and other reminders of the plantation age. Hand-carved bedsteads, often four-posters, are fitted with luxury mattresses. The roomy bathrooms have combination shower/tubs.

Dining/Diversions: The hotel's main and most formal restaurant, the Vineyard, serves first-rate Jamaican and continental dinners. Less upscale is Docks Caribbean Bar & Grill, where there's a daily salad bar. Three bars are scattered about the grounds.

Amenities: Tennis court lit at night, rectangular pool, exercise room, outdoor hot tub, water-sports center, gift shop. Afternoon teas, room service, massage, laundry, and nanny service for care and feeding of children.

✪ **Lethe Estate.** Lethe (P.O. Box 32), Montego Bay, Jamaica, W.I. ☎ **876/956-4920.** Fax 876/956-4927. 13 units. A/C TEL. Winter $140 double; off-season $125 double. Rates include continental breakfast. AE, DC, MC, V.

In 1996, the Tulloch family, owners of a 150-acre banana plantation, decided to diversify their holdings by building this riverfront hotel, which lies 10 miles inland. Fronted by a veranda and set beneath a green roof that blends into the surrounding forest, the structure was inspired by the region's many antique plantation houses and allows guests close exposure to the Great River's bird and animal life. It's definitely not a beach resort; all activities revolve around the river, such as rafting expeditions that carry participants from points 2 miles upriver back down to a point near the hotel. Bedrooms are airy, open to breezes, and equipped with comfortably formal furnishings that evoke Jamaica's English colonial age.

Dining: The restaurant facilities of the estate are open only to guests of the hotel. A respectable Jamaican and continental cuisine is served, a rather standard fare of chicken, fish, steaks, and pasta, with a frequently changing menu.

Amenities: The resort contains a swimming pool set into a verdant lawn, a restaurant, and easy access to the river and several hiking trails radiating out into the surrounding forest.

Wyndham Rose Hall Golf & Beach Resort. Rose Hall (P.O. Box 999), Montego Bay, Jamaica, W.I. ☎ **800/624-7326** in the U.S., or 876/953-2650. Fax 876/953-2617. www.wyndham.com. 708 units. A/C TV TEL. Winter $215–$260 double; from $460 suite. Off-season $160–$200 double; from $355 suite. MAP (breakfast and dinner) $65 per person extra. AE, DC, MC, V.

Wyndham Rose Hall sits at the bottom of a rolling 30-acre site along the north-coast highway, 9 miles east of the airport. On a former sugar plantation that once covered 7,000 acres, the hotel abuts the 200-year-old home of the legendary "White Witch of Rose Hall," now a historic site, and has a thin strip of sandy beach. If you have to be directly on a great beach, this place isn't for you. But if you want to escape the more impersonal and chain-operated all-inclusives, and want a more authentic Jamaican experience, then check in. The seven-story H-shaped structure features a large and attractive lobby on the ground floor; upstairs, guest rooms all have sea views and rather unremarkable furnishings. Most units have two queen beds, and each accommodation has a small private balcony. The tiled bathrooms are well maintained.

Dining/Diversions: There are five restaurants, each serving excellent food, and it's never more than a short walk to one of the many bars scattered around the property. Wednesday nights in winter feature a poolside buffet and a Caribbean variety show with dancers, fire-eaters, and calypso and reggae performances.

Amenities: Three pools, complimentary sailboats, top-rated golf course meandering over part of the grounds, tennis complex (with six lit all-weather Laykold courts) headed by pros who offer a complete tennis program, air-conditioned fitness center. Room service (from 7am to 11pm), baby-sitting, laundry, massage, Kids Klub.

MODERATE

○ Doctor's Cave Beach Hotel. Gloucester Ave. (P.O. Box 94), Montego Bay, Jamaica, W.I. **☎ 800/44-UTELL** in the U.S., or 876/952-4355. Fax 876/952-5204. www.doctorscave. com. E-mail: info@doctorscave.com. 90 units. A/C TEL. Winter $145–$155 double; $170 suite for 2. Off-season $120–$130 double; $150 suite for 2. Extra person $30. MAP (breakfast and dinner) $29 per person extra. AE, DISC, MC, V.

Across the street from the well-known Doctor's Cave Beach in the bustle of the town's commercial zone, this three-story property offers great value. It has its own gardens, a pool, a Jacuzzi, and a small gymnasium, all set on 4 acres of tropical gardens. The rooms are simply but comfortably furnished, and suites have kitchenettes. Rooms are rented standard or superior, the latter more spacious with balconies opening onto a view. All units have tile floors; floral spreads on queen or twin beds, each fitted with a good mattress; and small but efficiently organized tiled bathrooms with combination tub/showers. Hair dryers are available upon request from the front desk. The two restaurants are the Coconut Grove, whose outdoor terrace is floodlit at night, and the less formal Greenhouse. The good cuisine is more authentically Jamaican here than at the other deluxe resorts previously recommended. In the Cascade Bar, where a waterfall tumbles down a stone wall, you can listen to a piano duo during cocktail hours.

Sea Castles Resort Rte. A1, Rose Hall (P.O. Box 55), Montego Bay, St. James, Jamaica, W.I. **☎ 876/953-3250.** Fax 876/953-3062. 198 units. A/C MINIBAR TV TEL. Winter $330 suite. Off-season $280 suite. Rates are all inclusive. AE, MC, V.

This, one of the most architecturally dramatic hotels in the region, was built in 1991 along an isolated seafront 11 miles east of Montego Bay. Its development included at least a 50% participation by the Jamaican government, which helped to market many of the units as privately owned condominiums. The result is an airy, widely separated compound of postmodern buildings vaguely influenced by English colonial models. The resort contains only suites, each with kitchen or kitchenette, all scattered among a half dozen outbuildings ringed with greenery and capped with cedar-shingled roofs. Lawns slope down to the beach, past arbors, gazebos, bars, and water-sports kiosks. The staff organizes activities like beer-drinking contests, volleyball on the beach, shows with staff and guests, bingo, and diving contests. The Castles restaurant (see "Where to Dine," below) overlooks the graceful freshwater swimming pool; less formal meals and drinks are offered in the Clifftop Bar. Other amenities include laundry, baby-sitting, water-sports facilities, and a tour desk for island tours.

Reading Reef Club. Rte. A1, on Bogue Lagoon, at the bottom of Long Hill Rd. (P.O. Box 225), Reading, Montego Bay, Jamaica, W.I. ☎ **800/315-0379** in the U.S., or 876/952-5909. Fax 876/952-7217. www.montego-bay-jamaica.com/jhta/reefclub. E-mail: rrc@n5.com.jm. 34 units. A/C TEL. Winter $115–$135 double; $265 2-bedroom suite; $325 3-bedroom suite. Off-season $85–$125 double; $220 2-bedroom suite; $270 3-bedroom suite. AE, MC, V.

This small, informal inn reflects a sense of style and flair. Located on 2.5 acres, the hotel is a 15-minute drive west of Montego Bay, on a 350-foot sandy beach where people relax in comfort, undisturbed by beach vendors. The complex of four buildings overlooks beautiful reefs once praised by Jacques Cousteau for their aquatic life. The accommodations, which include two- and three-bedroom suites, open onto a sea view. All have air-conditioning and ceiling fans and a light Caribbean motif. The luxury rooms contain minibars, and the two- and three-bedroom suites offer kitchenettes. Quality mattresses and fine linens are found on the most comfortable beds, and the medium-size bathrooms contain adequate shelf space. An excellent restaurant is located on-site. There's also a bar/lounge and a beachside luncheon barbecue specializing in Jamaican (jerk) sausages, English sausages, and Tex-Mex food. Services include laundry, valet, and drivers for island tours. Guests also enjoy the freshwater pool and free water sports, including snorkeling, windsurfing, and sailing in a 12-foot sailboat; scuba diving costs extra.

Wexford Court Hotel. 39 Gloucester Ave. (P.O. Box 108), Montego Bay, Jamaica, W.I. ☎ **876/952-2854.** Fax 876/952-3637. www.montego-bay-jamaica.com/wexford. E-mail: wexford@cwjamaica.com. 61 units. A/C TV TEL. Winter $115.50–$132 double; $150 apt. Off-season $104.50–$121 double; $115.50 apt. MAP (breakfast and dinner) $33 per person extra. AE, MC, V.

Stay here for economy, not style. About 10 minutes from downtown Mo Bay, near Doctor's Cave Beach, this hotel has a small pool and a patio (where calypso is enjoyed in season). The apartments have living/dining areas and kitchenettes, so you can cook for yourself. All the back-to-basics rooms contain patios shaded by gables and Swiss chalet–style roofs. The Wexford Grill includes a good selection of Jamaican dishes, such as chicken deep-fried with honey. Guests can enjoy drinks in a bar nearby.

Winged Victory Hotel. 5 Queens Dr., Montego Bay, Jamaica, W.I. ☎ **800/74-CHARMS** in the U.S., or 876/952-3892. Fax 876/952-5986. www.hotelbook.com 30 units. A/C. Winter $120–$150 double; $175–$225 suite. Off-season $80–$100 double; $110–$150 suite. MAP (breakfast and dinner) $30 per person extra. AE, MC, V.

On a hillside road in Montego Bay, in the Miranda Hill District, this tall and modern hotel delays revealing its true beauty until you pass through its comfortable public rooms into a Mediterranean-style courtyard in back. Here, urn-shaped balustrades enclose a terraced garden, a pool, and a veranda looking over the faraway crescent of Montego Bay. The veranda's best feature is the Calabash Restaurant. The owner, Roma Chin Sue, added hotel rooms to her already well-known restaurant in 1985. All but five have a private balcony or veranda, along with an eclectic decor that's part Chinese, part colonial, and part Iberian. The bedrooms are of generous size and are well maintained with firm mattresses renewed as frequently as needed, along with average-size bathrooms.

INEXPENSIVE

✪ **Blue Harbour Hotel**. 6 Sewell Ave. (P.O. Box 212), Montego Bay, Jamaica, W.I. ☎ **876/952-5445.** Fax 876/952-8930. http://fly.to/jamaica. E-mail: robbyg@cwjamaica.com. 23 units. A/C TV. Winter $70–$112 double. Off-season $56–$95 double. Children 11 and under stay free in parents' room. AE, MC, V.

On a hillside overlooking the harbor, midway between the airport and town off Route A1, this small hotel offers basic service in a friendly atmosphere. The beach is a 5-minute walk from the hotel, which provides free transportation to and from the shore. The rooms are simple, while the suites offer kitchenettes to help you save even more money. For dinner, the hotel offers the option of a dine-around plan that includes 10 of Montego Bay's restaurants. (Transportation to and from the restaurants is provided.) The facilities include a swimming pool, an air-conditioned lounge, and a coffee shop serving breakfast and a light lunch. Tennis is nearby and arrangements can be made for golf, deep-sea fishing, scuba diving, and island tours.

✪ **Coral Cliff Hotel.** 165 Gloucester Ave. (P.O. Box 253), Montego Bay, Jamaica, W.I. ☎ 876/952-4130. Fax 876/952-6532. www.montego-bay-jamaica.com/coralcliff. E-mail: coralclif@usa.net. 30 units. A/C TEL. Winter $85–$95 double; $97–$115 triple; from $160 suite. Off-season $80–$90 double; $92–$105 triple; from $140 suite. MC, V.

For a good value, the Coral Cliff may be your best bet in Montego Bay. The hotel grew from a colonial-style building that was once the private home of Harry M. Doubleday (of the famous publishing family). It's located about a mile west of the center of town but only 2 minutes from Doctor's Cave Beach. The Coral Cliff also offers its own luxurious pool. Many of the light, airy, and spacious bedrooms open onto a balcony with a view of the sea. The rooms, as befits a former private house, come in a wide variety of shapes and sizes, most of them containing old colonial furniture, wicker, and rattan. Most units also have twin beds with firm mattresses. The bathrooms are small in the older bedrooms, but more spacious in the newer wing out back. Each is tidily maintained and has a combination tub/shower. The hotel's breeze-swept restaurant overlooking the bay is appropriately called the Verandah Terrace, specializing in Jamaican and international dishes, with succulent tropical fruit. The food features local produce and fresh seafood whenever available.

El Greco Resort. 11 Queens Dr. (P.O. Box 1624), Montego Bay, Jamaica, W.I. ☎ 876/940-6116. Fax 876/940-6115. www.montego-bay-jamaica.com/jhta/elgreco/index.html. E-mail: elgreco@n5.com.jm. 96 apts. TV TEL. $139 1-bedroom apt for 2; $169 2-bedroom apt for 4. AE, MC, V.

This three-story, cream-colored hotel sits at the top of a rocky bluff, high above the surf, sand, and well-oiled bodies of Doctor's Cave Beach. A private elevator links the hotel's cliff-top site to a point near the beachfront. Surrounded by a landscaped garden into which is nestled both a swimming pool and a pair of tennis courts that are lit for night play, the resort is well maintained and well priced. It's smack in the middle of Montego Bay's densest concentration of honky-tonk commercialism. But the location allows guests to rise above the congestion a bit; the hotel catches the trade winds, and most (but not all) of the rooms offer a sweeping view over the sea. Apartments contain full kitchenettes and have pure white ceramic floor tiles. The bedrooms are air-conditioned, but not the living rooms, which have ceiling fans instead. All of the two-bedroom units (32 in all) occupy the building's uppermost floor. There's both a bar and a restaurant on the premises, although many of the guests opt to cook at least some of their meals in-house.

Ocean View Guest House. 26 Sunset Blvd. (0.5 mile west of Sangster airport; P.O. Box 210), Montego Bay, Jamaica, W.I. ☎ 876/952-2662. 12 units. A/C. Winter $38 double; $43–$55 triple. Off-season $31.50 double; $45 triple. No credit cards.

Stay here for a great deal; you won't get state-of-the-art maintenance or service, but the price is adjusted accordingly. Originally established in the 1960s, when the grandparents of the present owners began to rent extra rooms in their private home, this super bargain lies a half mile from the airport and the same distance from a public beach. The simple and uncomplicated bedrooms are supplemented with a small library and TV room (satellite reception is available). Most open onto a veranda or the spacious front porch. It's quietest at the back. Dinner is offered for guests only; reservations must be made by 2pm. The large and extremely reasonable menu features such fare as T-bone steak, pork chops, roast chicken, and fresh fish.

Richmond Hill Inn. Union St. (P.O. Box 362), Montego Bay, Jamaica, W.I. ☎ **876/952-3859.** Fax 876/952-6106. 20 units. A/C TV TEL. Winter $115 double; $160 1-bedroom suite; $300 3-bedroom suite. Off-season $90 double; $135 1-bedroom suite; $250 3-bedroom suite. AE, MC, V.

If you're an avid beach lover, you should know in advance that the nearest beach (Doctor's Cave Beach) is a 15-minute drive away from this hotel. Set high on a forested slope, 500 feet above sea level and the commercial center of Montego Bay, this place was originally built as the homestead of the Dewar family (the scions of scotch). Very little of the original villa remains, but what you'll find is a hilltop aerie ringed with urn-shaped concrete balustrades, a pool terrace suitable for sundowner cocktails, and comfortable, slightly fussy bedrooms with lace-trimmed curtains, homey bric-a-brac, and pastel colors. Maid service is included in the rates, and there's both a bar and a restaurant (featuring vistas over the blinking lights of Montego Bay).

Ridgeway Guest House. 34 Queens Dr., Montego Bay, Jamaica, W.I. ☎ **876/952-2709.** 8 units. Winter $65 double. Off-season $35–$55 double. Children 11 and under stay free in parents' room. DC, DISC, MC, V.

This warm B&B, far removed from the impersonal megaresorts (and their megaprices), is a great find. The helpful owners offer free pickup from the airport and transport to Doctor's Cave Beach, a 15-minute walk or 5 minutes by car. They are constantly improving their property, a two-story white-painted building set among flowers and fruit trees from which guests may help themselves, perhaps having an orange and grapefruit salad. Guests may partake of before-dinner drinks in the roof garden, enjoying a view of the airport and ocean. The large rooms are decorated in a tropical motif with two or three queen-size beds. The marble baths have modern fixtures, and TV is available in a public area. The more expensive rooms (see above) contain air-conditioning, TV, and phone; the less expensive units are equipped with ceiling fans without TV and phone. Next door is the Chatwick Garden Hotel, with a restaurant open to Ridgeway guests.

Royal Court Hotel. Sewell Ave. (P.O. Box 195), Montego Bay, Jamaica, W.I. ☎ **876/952-4531.** Fax 876/952-4532. www.drvendrxes.com. 20 units. A/C TEL. Winter $80–$90 double; $150 suite. Off-season $70 double; $100 suite. AE, MC, V.

This reasonable choice is located on the hillside overlooking Montego Bay, above Gloucester Avenue and off Park Avenue. The small rooms are outfitted in bright, tasteful colors, and all have patios and decent beds; the larger ones have fully equipped kitchenettes. This hotel is clean and attractive, has a charming atmosphere, and is a good value. Meals are served in the Pool Bar and Eatery. Its restaurant, Leaf of Life, specializes in vegetarian food, among other selections. Free transportation is provided to the town, the beach (a 10-minute ride away), and the tennis club. Amenities and facilities include massage, gym, steam room, Jacuzzi, TV room, conference room, and a doctor on the premises. There's also a wellness center, offering holistic health consultations, hypnotherapy sessions, and other personalized programs.

Sundance Resort. 1 Kent Ave. (P.O. Box 467), Montego Bay, Jamaica, W.I. ☎ **876/952-4370.** Fax 876/952-6591. www.best-caribbean.com/sundance/info.html. E-mail: sundance@cwjamaica.com. 72 units. A/C. Winter $80 double. Off-season $70 double. AE, DISC, MC, V.

The Sundance Resort is a 5-minute walk from Doctor's Cave Beach. Its location beside the busy main thoroughfare of downtown Montego Bay is either an advantage or a disadvantage, depending on how much you value easy access to the resort's inexpensive bars and restaurants. Despite the traffic and crowds around it, the almond, mango, and grapefruit trees that surround the two-story main building, a series of individual cottages, and two swimming pools create a sense of rural isolation. You'll also find a restaurant serving Jamaican cuisine, a flower shop, a mini-gym, a bandstand for the rare concerts presented here, and a bar where a TV set provides at least some of the entertainment. The bedrooms have either a terrace or a balcony. The hotel is also a showcase for Jamaican and foreign art.

Verney House Resort. 3 Leader Ave. (P.O. Box 18), Montego Bay, Jamaica, W.I. ☎ **876/952-2875.** Fax 876/979-2944. 25 units. A/C TV TEL. Winter $50 double; $65 triple; $75 quad. Off-season $45 double; $55 triple; $65 quad. AE, MC, V.

In a verdant setting just far enough away from the urban congestion of Montego Bay, this hotel offers a feeling of remote calm. You can still get to where the action is by taking a short trek downhill, or head to one of several beaches, such as Cornwall Beach, that are only 5 minutes away on foot. The inn also provides transportation to and from the beach. The two-story structure was originally built on steeply sloping land in 1945. In 1995, the pastel-colored bedrooms were freshened up. Each accommodation has white walls and simple furnishings and creates the sense that you're in a private home. The restaurant (the Kit-Kat) and bar overlook the swimming pool. The staff is usually gracious.

ALL-INCLUSIVE RESORTS

Breezes Montego Bay. Gloucester Ave., Montego Bay, Jamaica, W.I. ☎ **800/859-SUPER** or 876/940-1150. Fax 876/940-1160. www.superclubs.com/resorts/Breezes/MontegoBay/index.html. E-mail: info@superclubs.com. 124 units. A/C TV TEL. All-inclusive rates for 3 nights: Winter $1,330–$1,922 double. Off-season $1,062–$1,754 double. AE, MC, V. No children under 16 accepted.

Built in 1995 in a boomerang-shaped five-story complex, this SuperClub is defined as "a sandbox for your inner child." It's the only major hotel perched directly on the sands of Montego Bay's most popular public beach, Doctor's Cave. The venue is adult and indulgent, but without the emphasis on raucous partying that's the norm at Hedonism II (a member of the same chain). Bedrooms are simply furnished and breezy, overlooking either the beach or the garden that separates the hotel from the traffic of Montego Bay's main commercial boulevard, Gloucester Avenue. Rooms range from intimate cabins to lavish suites. The cabin rooms, 31 in all, are similar to a ship's cabin, very intimate with a queen bed. Slightly larger are the deluxe rooms, with twins or a king bed. The best are the deluxe oceanfront rooms, with king beds, and the oceanfront suites.

Dining/Diversions: Informal but good meals are served at Jimmy's Buffet, a terrace overlooking the pool and the beach. The more formal, with a more refined cuisine, is served at the candlelit Martino's, an Italian rooftop restaurant.

Amenities: Freshwater pool; rooftop Jacuzzi; full range of water sports; tennis courts (lit at night); fitness center with Nautilus equipment and aerobics and water-aerobics classes.

Holiday Inn SunSpree. 5 miles east of Montego Bay International Airport (P.O. Box 480), Rose Hall, Jamaica, W.I. ☎ **800/HOLIDAY** or 876/953-2485. Fax 876/953-2840. www.where2stay.com/islands/resorts/425.html. 523 units. A/C TV TEL. Winter $450–$500 double; from $500 suite for 2. Off-season $250–$310 double; from $350 suite. Rates are all inclusive. AE, MC, V.

This is the only Holiday Inn resort in the world that can be booked on all-inclusive terms. It opened in 1995 following a $13 million renovation. It continues a tradition of catering to singles, couples, and honeymooners, but the resort has a new emphasis on programs for families with children. The 12-acre property fronts nearly half a mile of white-sand beach on Jamaica's north shore. The well-furnished, modern rooms and suites are for the most part spacious and are housed in eight free-standing buildings; all have such amenities as hair dryers and a private balcony or patio. Of these, 76 are oceanfront, and 23 suites come complete with indoor Jacuzzi.

Dining/Diversions: A wide range of dining options is available even though the resort is all inclusive. In the main building, the Mo Bay Festival offers views of the Caribbean and other specialties along with international menus, whereas Vista's, also with an ocean view, features a more formal setting and a continental cuisine. The Barefoot Bar & Grill at poolside is for heavy snacking, and the Beach Hut Bar is known for its Jamaican delicacies. Two nights each week are devoted to buffet theme nights, when guests dine on the beach and listen to live Jamaican music and dance. The Sports Bar with a large TV is a macho hangout, while the Witches Disco attracts a younger crowd.

Amenities: Spacious interlocking tropical-style freshwater swimming pools of varying depths, four night-lit tennis courts, water-sports center, basketball court, volleyball court, fitness center with Nautilus equipment, Kids Spree Vacation Club staffed by trained counselors, baby-sitting, and shopping and sightseeing excursions.

Jack Tar Village Montego Bay. 2 Gloucester Ave. (P.O. Box 144), Montego Bay, Jamaica, W.I. ☎ **800/858-2258** or 876/952-4340. Fax 876/952-6633. www.allegroresorts.com. E-mail: info@jtmgobay.allegroresorts.com. 131 units. A/C TV TEL. Winter $185 per person double occupancy. Off-season $145–$150 per person double occupancy. AE, MC, V. No children accepted.

Adults-only Jack Tar isn't as upscale as many of the other all-inclusives on Jamaica, but it does offer an affordable, worry-free beach vacation for couples on a budget. (The Sandals Inn next door is far superior, even though it's Sandals' budget property.) This 3.25-acre beachfront resort encompasses a pair of buildings 2 miles north of the commercial core of Montego Bay. This is one of the smaller members of a chain known for generous (if not blue-chip) food and drink policies. In 1996 the resort underwent a $4-million renovation, in which each of the bedrooms was upgraded. The guest units are modern but bland, and they sit a few steps from the beach, with a view of the water. Private balconies open directly onto Montego Bay, and guests practically live in their bathing suits.

Dining/Diversions: Lunch is served beachside or in the main dining room, and there is nightly entertainment. The international food isn't wildly creative or refined, but it's plentiful.

Amenities: Freshwater pool, tennis clinic and tennis courts (for daytime), sauna, windsurfing, water-skiing, snorkeling, sailing, reggae dance lessons, massage.

The Sandals Inn. Kent Ave. (P.O. Box 412), Montego Bay, Jamaica, W.I. ☎ **800/SANDALS** in the U.S. and Canada, or 876/952-4140. Fax 876/952-6913. www.sandals.com. 52 units. A/C TV TEL. All-inclusive rates for 4 days/3 nights: Winter $1,380–$1,560 double. Off-season $1,310–$1,620 double. AE, MC, V. No children accepted.

The Sandals Inn is a couples-only (male-female) hotel built around a large pool and patio, with a beach a short walk across a busy highway. This is the least expensive, least glamorous, least spacious, and least attractive of the Sandals all-inclusive resorts scattered across Jamaica. But it's a trade-off: You don't get luxury, but you do get proximity to downtown Montego Bay, reasonable rates, and free day passes (including free transportation) to both of the Sandals resorts of Montego Bay. Thirty-eight rooms open onto the pool; all units contain king beds with good mattresses. There is now so-called environmentally friendly linen service, so that sheets and towels are not changed unless you request it. Bathrooms are small but equipped with hair dryers.

Dining/Diversions: Food is served in bountiful portions in the resort's only dining room, and there's nightly entertainment. A specialty restaurant, Caryle, specializing in flambé dishes, breaks the routine of the main dining room.

Amenities: Recreational and sports program, exercise room, saunas, Jacuzzi, tennis courts, pool, room safes. Room service (from 9am to 10pm), free round-trip airport transfers.

Sandals Montego Bay. Kent Ave. (P.O. Box 100), Montego Bay, Jamaica, W.I. ☎ **800/ SANDALS** in the U.S. and Canada, or 876/952-5510. Fax 876/952-0816. www.sandals.com. 244 units. A/C TV TEL. All-inclusive rates for 4 days/3 nights: Winter $1,690–$2,100 double; from $2,380 suite for 2. Off-season $1,620–$2,040 double; from $2,350 suite for 2. AE, MC, V. No children accepted.

Located 5 minutes northeast of the airport, this honeymoon haven next to Whitehouse Village lies on a 19-acre site. It is a couples-only (male-female), all-inclusive resort, opening onto the largest private beach in Montego Bay, far greater sands than the challenging Sandals Royal Jamaican property (see below). The place has a great big party atmosphere in contrast to the more refined Sandals below. Everything is covered in the price—meals, snacks, nightly entertainment (including those notorious toga parties), unlimited drinks night or day at one of four bars, tips, and round-trip airport transfers and baggage handling from the Montego Bay airport. Lots of entertainment and sports facilities are available on the property, so many guests never leave. In con-trast to its somewhat more laid-back nearby counterpart (the Sandals Royal Jamaican), this resort offers many different activities for a clientele and staff who tend to be extro-verted and gregarious. The accommodations are either in villas spread along 1,700 feet of white-sand beach or in the main house, where all bedrooms face the sea and con-tain private balconies. Try to avoid booking into a room over the dining room; these don't have balconies and may be noisy. The best units are the grande luxe ocean or beachfront units, with private balconies or patios.

Dining/Diversions: The food is in the typical Sandals chain style—plenty of it but nothing too imaginative. Options include the main dining room; Tokyo Joe's, serving six-course Asian meals; the Beach Grill; and the Oleander Deck, with "white-glove ser-vice," featuring Jamaican and Caribbean cuisine. The Oleander offers the finest din-ing in the Sandals chain. The late-night disco often has rum and reggae nights.

Amenities: Water-skiing, snorkeling, sailing, scuba diving daily with a certification program (PADI or NAUI), windsurfing, paddleboats and a glass-bottom boat, two freshwater pools, three Jacuzzis, tennis courts (lit at night), fully equipped fitness cen-ter. Free shuttle bus to the resort's twin, the Sandals Royal Jamaican, whose facilities are open without charge to residents here.

✪ **Sandals Royal Jamaican.** Mahoe Bay (P.O. Box 167), Montego Bay, Jamaica, W.I. ☎ **800/SANDALS** in the U.S. and Canada, or 876/953-2231. Fax 876/953-2788. www.san-dals.com. 190 units. A/C TV TEL. All-inclusive rates for 4 days/3 nights: Winter $1,790–$2,480 double; from $2,930 suite for 2. Off-season $1,730–$2,410 double; from $2,860 suite for 2. AE, MC, V. No children accepted.

This all-inclusive, couples-only (male-female) resort has a more tranquil and genteel atmosphere than Sandals Montego Bay. The building lies on its own private beach (which, frankly, isn't as good as the one at the Sandals Montego Bay). Some of the British colonial atmosphere remains (the formal tea in the afternoon), but there are

---

Catch a Fire: Jamaica's Reggae Festivals

Every August, Jamaica comes alive with the pulsating sounds of **Reggae Sunsplash,** the world's largest annual reggae festival. This weeklong music extravaganza has featured some of the most prominent reggae groups and artists, including Ziggy Marley, Cocoa Tea, and the Melody Makers. Sunsplash takes place at different venues; check with Jamaican tourist boards for the latest details.

Sometime during the second week of August, **Reggae Sunfest** takes place in Montego Bay. Usually this is a 4-day musical event. Some of the biggest names in reggae, both from Jamaica and worldwide, perform. Many local hotels are fully booked for the festival, so advance reservations are necessary.

The Jamaican Tourist Board's U.S. and Canadian offices can give you information about packages and group rates for the festivals and fill you in on other reggae concerts and events held throughout the year on Jamaica.

---

modern touches as well, including a private, clothing-optional island reached by boat. The spacious rooms come in a wide range of categories, from standard to superior to deluxe, but each has a king bed with a luxury mattress and a private safe. Most desirable are the grand luxe beachfront rooms with private patios or balconies. Each unit has a small but well-equipped private bathroom.

Dining/Diversions: The cuisine seems more varied here than at the other Sandals. The Regency Suite and Deck is the Jamaican-inspired main dining room. Bali Hai is an Indonesian restaurant on the previously mentioned offshore island. The Courtyard Grill serves such items as grilled sirloin, grilled snapper, and smoked marlin. There are four bars, food and drink available throughout the day, and live music by a local reggae band.

Amenities: Scuba diving, windsurfing, sailing, three tennis courts, pool. Laundry, massage, free shuttle bus to the resort's twin Sandals (whose facilities are available without charge to any resident).

Sunset Beach Resort & Spa. Montego Freeport Peninsula, P.O. Box 1168, Montego Bay, Jamaica. W.I. ☎ **876/979-8800.** Fax 876/953-6744. www.sunsetbeachresorts.spa.com. E-mail: sunsethbeach@cwjamaica.com. 420 units. A/C TV TEL. Winter $240–$300 double; $480 suite for 2. Off-season $220–$280 double; $400 suite for 2. Rates include accommodations, all meals, drinks, entertainment, and most land and water sports. AE, MC, V.

This all-inclusive hotel opened in 1998 and aims for a marketing niche less glamorous (and less expensive) than that occupied by the Beaches and Sandals groups. The complex consists of three separate beaches; two pale-pink, 11-story towers containing a total of 300 units; and a 120-room annex, the Beach Inn, whose low-rise design allows guests closer and more immediate access to the sands. Accommodations are outfitted in a subdued motif that includes vague references to tropical design, but that tends to be more soothing, even blander, than the decor of many of its competitors. Rooms are fairly spacious with excellent mattresses on comfortable beds, plus medium-size bathrooms.

Dining/Diversions: Meals, featuring a varied cuisine, are served at each of the property's four restaurants and are included in the all-inclusive rates. The Silk Road offers Pacific Rim cuisine, Botticelli serves Italian cuisine, and the Sunset Grill is an indoor/outdoor pool and beach restaurant. The Banana Walk is the resort's all-purpose dining room, with an ongoing roster of buffets, served in a style that might remind you of Club Med. There's nightly entertainment.

Amenities: Three pools, four tennis courts, a frilly gazebo that's sometimes used as a site for weddings, shuffleboard courts, jogging trails, giant chess and checker boards, beachfront volleyball, fitness center, supervised children's program.

2 Where to Dine

The Montego Bay area offers some of the finest—and most expensive—dining on Jamaica. But if you're watching your wallet and don't have a delicate stomach, some intriguing food is sold right on the street. For example, on Kent Avenue, you might try jerk pork. Seasoned spareribs are also grilled over charcoal fires and sold with extra-hot sauce. Naturally, it goes down better with a Red Stripe beer. Cooked shrimp are also sold on the streets of Mo Bay; they don't look it, but they're very hotly spiced, so be warned. If you're cooking your own meals, you might also want to buy fresh lobster or the catch of the day from Mo Bay fishers.

EXPENSIVE

Julia's. Julia's Estate, Bogue Hill. ☎ **876/952-1772**. Reservations required. Fixed-price dinner $35–$45. AE, MC, V. Daily 5:30–10:30pm. Private van transportation provided; ask when you reserve. ITALIAN.

The winding jungle road you take to reach this place is part of the before-dinner entertainment. After a jolting ride to a setting high above the city and its bay, you pass through a walled-in park that long ago was the site of a private home built in 1840 for the Duke of Sutherland. Today, the focal point is a long, low-slung modern house with sweeping, open-sided views over the rolling hills and faraway coastline. Neville and Gisela Roe, the Jamaican-German couple running the place, draw on the cuisine of both the Caribbean and central Europe in the preparation of filet of fresh fish with lime juice and butter, lobster, shrimp, and about 10 different kinds of pasta. Also look for such German dishes as schnitzels of chicken or pork; goulash with noodles or dumplings; cheesecake of the day; and Schwarzwald torte (Black Forest cake). The food, although competently prepared with fresh ingredients whenever possible, can hardly compete with the view.

Norma at the Wharfhouse. Reading Rd. ☎ **876/979-2745**. Reservations required. Main courses $29–$35. MC, V. Tues–Sun 6:30–10pm. Closed May–Nov. Drive 15 minutes west of the town center along Rte. A1. NOUVELLE JAMAICAN.

Set within a coral-stone warehouse whose two-foot-thick walls are bound together with molasses and lime, this is one of the most unusual and noteworthy restaurants in Montego Bay, thanks to its long-time association with restaurant diva and international entrepreneur Norma Shirley. Originally built in 1780, this Montego Bay monument was restored during the 1950s by Millicent Rogers, heiress of the Standard Oil fortune, before its present role as a restaurant. Between December and April, you can dine either on a large pier built on stilts over the coral reef (where a view of Montego Bay glitters in the distance), or within an elegant and very formal 19th-century dining room illuminated only with hurricane lamps and flickering candles. The restaurant's service is impeccable, and the food is reliable. Menu specialties include grilled deviled crab backs, smoked marlin with papaya sauce, chicken breast with callaloo, nuggets of lobster in a mild curry sauce, and chateaubriand larded with pâté in a peppercorn sauce. Dessert might be a rum-and-raisin cheesecake or a piña-colada mousse. Look also for the daily specials.

✪ **Sugar Mill Restaurant.** At the Half Moon Club, Half Moon Golf Course, Rose Hall, along Rte. A1. ☎ **876/953-2314**. Reservations required. Main courses $18.50–$39.50. AE, MC, V.

Daily noon–3pm and 7–10pm. A minivan can be sent to most hotels to pick you up. INTERNATIONAL/CARIBBEAN.

This restaurant, near a stone ruin of what used to be a water-wheel for a sugar plantation, is reached after a drive through rolling landscape. Despite newer, trendier restaurants in town, including the Italian restaurant on the grounds of Half Moon, this remains the perpetual favorite of everyone at Half Moon, by far the most appealing and the most endearing. Guests dine by candlelight either indoors or on an open terrace with a view of a pond, the waterwheel, and plenty of greenery. Lunch can be a relatively simple affair, perhaps an akee burger with bacon, preceded by Mama's pumpkin soup and followed with homemade rum-and-raisin ice cream. For dinner, try one of the chef's zesty jerk versions of pork, fish, or chicken. He also prepares the day's catch with considerable flair. Smoked north-coast marlin is a specialty. On any given day, you can ask the waiter what's cooking in the curry pot. Chances are it will be a Jamaican specialty such as goat, full of flavor and served with island chutney. Top your meal with a cup of unbeatable Blue Mountain coffee.

MODERATE

Ambrosia. Across from the Wyndham Rose Hall Resort, Rose Hall. ☎ **876/953-2650.** Reservations recommended. Main courses $20–$27. AE, MC, V. Thurs–Tues 6:30–10pm. MEDITERRANEAN.

Ambrosia sits across from one of the largest hotels in Montego Bay. With its cedar-shingled design and trio of steeply pointed roofs, it has the air of a country club. Once you enter the courtyard, complete with a set of cannons, you find yourself in one of the loveliest restaurants in the area. You'll enjoy a sweeping view over the rolling lawns leading past the hotel and down to the sea, interrupted only by Doric columns. Not everything is ambrosia on the menu, but the cooks turn out a predictable array of good pasta and seafood dishes. Many of the flavors are Mediterranean, especially the lobster tails and other seafood dishes. The chefs handle the Long Island duckling expertly, although it arrives frozen on the island.

✪ **Belfield 1794.** Barnett Estate, Granville. ☎ **876/952-2382.** Reservations recommended. Main courses $15.75–$19.75. AE, DISC, MC, V. Daily noon–10pm. INTERNATIONAL.

You can expect more than just a well-prepared meal if you opt to visit this unusual blend of fine dining and Jamaican colonial history. Although this restaurant is owned and operated by the prestigious Half Moon Resort, it is set in the hills above Montego Bay, several miles from the hotel. The dining experience typically begins with a get-acquainted drink at a bar that's set on what used to be the threshing floor of an antique sugarcane mill. After that, you order the components of your meal and are then ushered through a 15-minute tour of the nearby great house, a late 18th-century plantation home. A guide will point out its construction of coral stone and mahogany and some of the mahogany furniture that was made on the premises by slaves working in the British style. After the tour, you return to a different area of the sugarcane mill and enjoy dishes that are usually served either within a "Dutchie" (a shallow cast-iron pot with a tightly fitting cover) or on a carved wooden platter covered with a breadfruit leaf. Menu items include filet of beef with a plantain/port wine sauce and sweet-potato pudding, filet of fish with three kinds of citrus butter (grapefruit, orange, and lime), a jerk combination platter, and curried goat. Shuttle bus service to the restaurant is offered at regular intervals from both the Half Moon and Round Hill resorts. Austrian-born Roland Heitzeneder is your host, working hard to configure an appealing blend of good food and antique charm.

The Castles. In the Sea Castles Resort, Rose Hall (along A1 east of Montego Bay, toward Falmouth). ☎ **876/953-3250.** Reservations required. Main courses $18–$25. AE, DC, MC, V. Tues–Wed and Sun 6:30–10pm. INTERNATIONAL.

One of the most elegant restaurants between Montego Bay and Falmouth is The Castles in the Sea Castles Resort (see "Where to Stay," earlier in this chapter). Its chefs scour the globe in their search for dishes such as gazpacho from Spain and spicy spaghetti in meat sauce from Italy as an appetizer; beef consommé julienne is the chef's specialty appetizer. In a formal setting, open to the breezes, guests peruse a menu that is usually divided among seafood selections, such as a delicious lobster thermidor, or main dishes and roasts, perhaps tenderloin of pork with honey and thyme, or a savory roast prime rib of beef. Every night, there is a selection of Italian dishes, ranging from veal parmigiano to chicken with peppers, although these tend to vary in quality. Carrot cake is the pastry chef's prized dessert. Although the restaurant serves its regular guests nightly, it is open to the general public only on Tuesday, Wednesday, and Sunday.

Chef Oliver Magnus. Corniche Rd. ☎ **876/952-2988.** Main courses J$545–J$785 ($15.55–$22.35). DC, MC, V. Daily 6:30–10:30pm. INTERNATIONAL.

Set on a hill overlooking faraway cruise ships, this restaurant is housed in a villa with a tile roof. Oliver Magnus is the chef in this former private home dating from the 1930s. Service is on a bilevel terrace, and patrons include a wide assortment of business people, expats, and many visitors. The cookery is good and reflects the chef's long experience. He'll dazzle you with an array of appetizers ranging from gazpacho to smoked marlin. His salads are always interesting, especially the marinated papaya with the tangy balsamic green-onion vinaigrette. The choice of excellently prepared main dishes features snapper Camembert with a ranch sauce topped with cheese and toasted almonds. We're also fond of the *misto dimare,* a medley of shrimp, crab, and other fish stewed in a tomato pesto ragout. The grilled lamb from New Zealand is given added Jamaican flair with the use of a mild jerk spice.

Day-O Plantation Restaurant. Barnett Estate Plantation, Lot 1, Fairfield, P.O. Box 6, Granville P.O., Montego Bay. ☎ **876/952-1825.** Reservations required. Main courses $13–$30. AE, DC, DISC, MC, V. Tues–Sun 7–11pm. It's an 8-minute drive west of town off Rte. A1 leading toward Negril; minivan service will pick up diners at any of the Montego Bay hotels and return them after their meal. INTERNATIONAL/JAMAICAN.

This place was originally built in the 1920s as the home of the overseer of one of the region's largest sugar producers, the Barnett Plantation. Established as a restaurant in 1994, it occupies a long, indoor-outdoor dining room that's divided in half by a dance floor and a small stage. Here, owner Paul Hurlock performs as a one-man band, singing and entertaining the crowd while his wife, Jennifer, and their three children manage the dining room and kitchen.

Every dish is permeated with Jamaican spices and a sense of tradition. Try the chicken made plantation style, with red-wine sauce and herbs; filet of red snapper in Day-O style, with olives, white wine, tomatoes, and peppers; or, even better, one of the best versions of jerked snapper in Jamaica. We also like the grilled rock lobster with garlic butter sauce.

The establishment's unusual name derives from a long-ago Harry Belafonte song about life aboard a banana boat. Near the restaurant's entrance, don't overlook the curious-looking custom-made electric-driven car designed and built over many years of labor by the restaurant's owner, Paul Hurloch. Shaped in a futuristic one-of-a-kind design that might remind you of the wing of a seagull, it's the owner's pride and (not particularly cost-effective) joy, and the subject of many articles in the local press.

Marguerite's Seafood by the Sea and Margueritaville Sports Bar & Grill. Gloucester Ave. ☎ **876/952-4777.** Reservations recommended for Marguerite's Seafood by the Sea. Main courses (in restaurant) $19–$38; platters, sandwiches, and snacks (in sports bar) $5–$21. AE, DC, MC, V. Restaurant daily 6–10:30pm; sports bar daily 10am–3am. INTERNATIONAL/ SEAFOOD.

This two-in-one restaurant across from the Coral Cliff Hotel specializes in seafood served on a breeze-swept terrace overlooking the sea. There's also an air-conditioned lounge with an adjoining "Secret Garden." The chef specializes in exhibition cookery at a flambé grill. The menu is mainly devoted to seafood, including fresh fish, but there are also numerous innovative pastas and rather standard meat dishes. The changing dessert options are homemade, and a reasonable selection of wines is served. The sports bar and grill features a 110-foot hydroslide, live music, satellite TV, water sports, a sundeck, a CD jukebox, and a straightforward menu of seafood, sandwiches, pasta, pizza, salads, and snacks—nothing fussy. Naturally, the bartenders specialize in margaritas.

Richmond Hill Inn. 45 Union St. ☎ **876/952-3859.** Reservations recommended. Main courses $16.50–$28.50. AE, MC, V. Daily 7:30am–9:30pm. Take a taxi (a 4-minute ride uphill, east of the town's main square) or ask the restaurant to have you picked up at your hotel. INTERNATIONAL/CONTINENTAL.

This plantation-style house was originally built in 1806 by owners of the Dewar's whiskey distillery, who happened to be distantly related to Annie Palmer, the "White Witch of Rose Hall." Today, it's run by an Austrian family that prepares well-flavored food for an appreciative clientele. Dinners include a shrimp-and-lobster cocktail, an excellent house salad, different preparations of dolphin (mahimahi), breaded breast of chicken, surf-and-turf, Wiener schnitzel, filet mignon, and a choice of dessert cakes. Many of the dishes are of a relatively standard international style, but others, especially the lobster, are worth the trek up the hill.

Town House. 16 Church St. ☎ 876/952-2660. Reservations recommended. Main courses $15–$30. AE, DC, MC, V. Mon–Sat 11:30am–3:30pm; daily 6–10:30pm. Free limousine service to and from many area hotels. JAMAICAN/INTERNATIONAL.

Housed in a red-brick building dating from 1765, the Town House is a tranquil luncheon choice. It offers sandwiches and salads or more elaborate fare if your appetite demands it. At night, it's floodlit, with outdoor dining on a veranda overlooking an 18th-century parish church. You can also dine in what used to be the cellars, where old ship lanterns provide a warm atmosphere. Soups, which are increasingly ignored in many restaurants, are a specialty here. The pepper pot or pumpkin soup is a delectable start to a meal. The chef offers a wide selection of main courses, including the local favorite, red snapper en papillote (wrapped in parchment paper). We're fond of the chef's large rack of barbecued spareribs, with the owners' special Tennessee sauce. The pasta and steak dishes are also good, especially the homemade fettuccine with whole shrimp and the perfectly aged New York strip steak. The restaurant often attracts the rich and famous.

Round Hill Dining Room. In the Round Hill Hotel and Villas, along Rte. A1, 8 miles west of the center of Montego Bay. ☎ **876/956-7050.** Reservations required for 10 or more. Main courses $24–$48. AE, DC, MC, V. Daily 12:30–2:30pm and 7:30–9:30pm. INTERNATIONAL.

One of the top dining rooms in Montego Bay, this place has attracted a smattering of celebrities with its sophisticated surroundings. To reach the dining room, you'll have to pass through the resort's open-air reception area and proceed through a garden. Many visitors opt for a drink in the large and high-ceilinged bar area, designed by Ralph Lauren, before moving on to their dinner, which is served either on a terrace perched above the surf or (during inclement weather) under an open-sided breezeway. Although many dishes are classic, the same recipes fed to Noël Coward or Cole Porter, other more innovative dishes reflect a taste of Jamaica. The menu changes nightly, offering an array of well-prepared dishes, from Mediterranean to Jamaican, from American to Italian pastas. For example, shrimp and pasta Caribe is sautéed with chopped herbs, cream, and wine; and Rasta pasta is tossed with vegetables and basil. Caribbean veal is stuffed with spicy crabmeat and seared, and the catch of the day is served jerked, broiled, or steamed with butter, herbs, and ginger. Of course, you can also order more classic dishes, including rack of lamb or a medallion of lobster sautéed with cream and served over fettuccine. Afternoon tea and sandwiches are served daily at 4pm in the English style.

INEXPENSIVE

The Brewery. In Miranda Ridge Plaza, Gloucester Ave. ☎ **876/940-2433.** Main courses J$220–J$750 ($6.25–$21.40). AE, MC, V. Daily 11am–2am. AMERICAN/JAMAICAN.

This is more a bar than a full-scale restaurant, but lunch and dinner are served. Basic hamburgers, salads, and sandwiches are available, and there's also a nightly Jamaican dinner special, a bargain at about J$200 ($5.70). You can enjoy drinks and your meal on the outside patio overlooking the ocean. The best time to come for drinks is during happy hour, from 4 to 6pm daily. Drinks made with local liquor are all half price. If you're really daring, you might want to try the bartender's specialty "fire water"; he won't disclose the ingredients but promises that it lives up to its name. On Wednesday, Saturday, and Sunday nights, live entertainment is offered, and the bar has karaoke on Tuesday and Friday.

Calabash Restaurant. In the Winged Victory Hotel, 5 Queens Dr. ☎ **876/952-3892.** Reservations recommended. Main courses $6–$25. AE, MC, V. Daily 7:30am–10pm. INTERNATIONAL/JAMAICAN.

Perched on the hillside road in Montego Bay 500 feet above the distant sea, this well-established restaurant has amused and entertained Peter O'Toole, Robert McNamara, Leonard Bernstein, Francis Ford Coppola, and Roger Moore. The restaurant was opened more than 25 years ago in this Mediterranean-style courtyard and elegantly simple eagle's-nest patio. The menu of seafood, international favorites, and Jamaican classics includes curried goat, lobster dishes, and the house specialty—baked stuffed Jamaican she-crab, plus a year-round version of a Jamaican Christmas cake.

Le Chalet. 32 Gloucester Ave. ☎ **876/952-5240.** Main courses $3–$16 lunch, $6–$20 dinner. AE, MC, V. Mon–Sat 11am–10:30pm, Sun 4–10:30pm. INTERNATIONAL/JAMAICAN.

Set in the densest concentration of stores and souvenir shops of Montego Bay's "tourist strip," this high-ceilinged restaurant lies across Gloucester Avenue from the sea and looks somewhat like a Howard Johnson's. Food is served in copious portions and includes a lunchtime menu of burgers, sandwiches, barbecued ribs, and salads, and a more substantial selection of evening platters. These might include chicken, steak, fresh fish, and lobster, which seems to taste best here if prepared with Jamaican curry. The staff is articulate and helpful and proud of their straightforward and surprisingly well-prepared cuisine.

The Native Restaurant. 29 Gloucester Ave. ☎ **876/979-2769.** Reservations recommended. Main courses $7.70–$32. AE, MC, V. Daily 7:30am–10pm. JAMAICAN/ INTERNATIONAL.

Open to the breezes, this casual restaurant with panoramic views serves some of the finest Jamaican dishes in the area. Appetizers include jerk reggae chicken and akee and salt fish, or smoked marlin. This can be followed by such old favorites as steamed fish or fried or jerk chicken. The most tropical offering is "goat in a boat" (that is, a pineapple shell). A more recent specialty is Boonoonoonoos; billed as "A Taste of Jamaica," it's a big platter with a little bit of everything—meats and several kinds of fish and vegetables. Although fresh desserts are prepared daily, you may prefer to finish with a Jamaican Blue Mountain coffee.

The Pelican. At the Pelican, Gloucester Ave. ☎ **876/952-3171.** Reservations recommended. Main courses $5–$25. AE, DC, MC, V. Daily 7am–11pm. JAMAICAN.

A Montego Bay landmark, the Pelican has been serving good food at reasonable prices for more than a quarter of a century. Most of the dishes are at the lower end of the price scale, unless you order shellfish. It's ideal for families, as it keeps long hours. Many diners come here at lunch for one of the well-stuffed sandwiches, juicy burgers, or barbecued chicken. You can also choose from a wide array of Jamaican dishes, including stewed peas and rice, curried goat, Caribbean fish, fried chicken, and curried lobster. A "meatless menu" is also featured, and includes such dishes as a vegetable plate or vegetable chili. Sirloin and seafood are available as well, and the soda fountain serves old-fashioned sundaes with real whipped cream, making it one of the best choices for kids in the area.

✪ **Pork Pit.** 27 Gloucester Ave. ☎ **876/952-1046.** 1 pound of jerk pork $11. No credit cards. Daily 11am–11:30pm. JAMAICAN.

The Pork Pit is the best place to go for the famous Jamaican jerk pork and jerk chicken, and the location is right in the heart of Montego Bay, near Walter Fletcher Beach. In fact, many beach buffs head over here for a big, reasonably priced lunch. Picnic tables encircle the building, and everything is open-air and informal. A half-pound of jerk meat, served with a baked yam or baked potato and a bottle of Red Stripe, is usually sufficient for a meal. The menu also includes steamed roast fish.

Reading Reef Club Restaurant. On Bogue Lagoon, on Rte. A1 at the bottom of Long Hill Rd. (4 miles west of the town center). ☎ **876/952-5909.** Reservations recommended. Main courses $8–$14 at lunch, $10–$22 at dinner. AE, MC, V. Daily 6:30am–10pm. ITALIAN/CONTINENTAL/CARIBBEAN.

This restaurant no longer has the glamour it did in the 1990s when you might have seen Lady Sarah Churchill and others dining here, but it is still quite good and most reasonable in price. On a second-floor terrace overlooking Bogue Lagoon, the Reading Reef serves exceptional cuisine based on quality ingredients. The chef is known for his soups—too often neglected in many kitchens nearby. Here, you are likely to be given a selection that includes pumpkin (a Jamaican favorite), pepper pot, conch, and red pea. Pastas are regularly featured, including the now-classic Rasta pasta with fresh vegetables and cream sauce. The jerk chicken here is zesty and spicy, or else you can order it curried, along with curried shrimp and lobster dishes, even a New York strip steak, if you're not feeling too experimental. Desserts always feature a homemade pie of the day.

3 Hitting the Beach, Hitting the Links & Other Outdoor Pursuits

BEACHES

Cornwall Beach (☎ 876/952-3463) is a long stretch of white sand with dressing rooms, a bar, and a cafeteria. The grainy sand has made Cornwall a longtime favorite. Unlike some of Jamaica's remote, hard-to-get-to beaches, this one is near all the major hotels, especially the moderately priced ones. Regrettably, especially in winter, there isn't a lot of room for seclusion. Swimming is excellent all year, although we've noticed that the waters are coolest in January and February. As swimming is safe, the beach is often a playground for children—but parents should watch that their children don't venture out too far. The ocean bottom is shallow, gently sloping down to deeper waters. The beach is almost always occupied by tourists; it doesn't seem to be popular with the Jamaicans themselves. It's open daily from 9am to 5pm. Admission is J$60 ($1.70) for adults, J$30 (85¢) for children.

Across from the Doctor's Cave Beach Hotel is **Doctor's Cave Beach,** on Gloucester Avenue (☎ 876/952-2566). This beach, arguably the loveliest stretch of sand bordering Montego Bay, helped launch the resort area in the 1940s. Its gentle surf, golden sands, and fresh turquoise water make it one of the most inviting places to swim. Popular with families (the placid waters rarely become turbulent unless a storm is brewing), it's the best all-around beach in Montego Bay, although some prefer Cornwall or Walter Fletcher. Sometimes, schools of tropical fish weave in and out of the waters, but usually the crowds of frolicking people scare them away. Since it's almost always packed, especially in winter, you must go early to stake out a beach-blanket-sized spot. Admission is $2.75 for adults, $1.40 for children 12 and under. Dressing rooms, chairs, umbrellas, and rafts are available from 8:30am to 5pm daily.

One of the premier beaches of Jamaica, **Walter Fletcher Beach** (☎ 876/979-9447), in the heart of Mo Bay, is noted for its tranquil waters, which makes it a particular favorite for families with children. This is one of the most beautiful beaches along the southern coast of Jamaica. Easy to reach, it's generally crowded in winter and enjoyed by visitors and locals alike. Some people bring a picnic, but you must be careful not to litter, or else face a fine. From December to March, there seems to be a long-running beach party here. Somehow, regardless of how many people show up, there always seems to be a place in the sun for them. Visitors show up in almost anything (or lack thereof), although actual nudity is prohibited. There are changing rooms, a restaurant, and lifeguards. Hours are daily from 9am to 5pm. Admission is $3 for adults, $1.50 for children.

Frankly, you may want to skip all these public beaches entirely and head instead for the **Rose Hall Beach Club** (☎ 876/953-2323), on the main road 11 miles east of Montego Bay. The club offers a half mile of secluded white-sand beach with crystal-clear water, plus a restaurant, two bars, a covered pavilion, an open-air dance area, showers, rest rooms, changing rooms, beach-volleyball courts, beach games, a full water-sports program, and live entertainment. Admission is $8 for adults, $5 for children. Hours are daily from 10am to 6pm. This beach club is far better equipped than any of the beaches previously recommended.

SPORTS & OUTDOOR PURSUITS

DEEP-SEA FISHING   **Seaworld Resorts,** whose main office is at the Cariblue Hotel, Rose Hall Main Road (☎ 876/953-2180), operates flying-bridge cruisers, with deck lines and outriggers, for fishing expeditions. A half-day fishing trip costs $350 for up to six participants.

DIVING, SNORKELING & OTHER WATER SPORTS   **Seaworld Resorts** (see above) also operates scuba-diving excursions, plus sailing, windsurfing, and more. Its dives plunge to offshore coral reefs, among the most spectacular in the Caribbean. There are three certified dive guides, one dive boat, and all the necessary equipment for both inexperienced and already-certified divers. One-tank dives cost $35; night dives are $60.

In Montego Bay, the waters right on the beach are fine for snorkeling. However, it's more rewarding to go across the channel to Cayaba Reef, Seaworld Reef, and Royal Reef, which are full of barjacks, blue and brown chromis, yellow-headed wrasses, and spotlight parrot fish. You must have a guide here, as the currents are strong and the wind picks up in the afternoon. If you're not staying at a resort offering snorkeling expeditions, then Seaworld is your best bet. For a cost of usually $25 per hour, the guide swims along with you and points out the various tropical fish.

GOLF ○ **Wyndham Rose Hall Golf & Beach Resort,** Rose Hall (☎ 876/953-2650), has a noted course with an unusual and challenging seaside and mountain layout, built on the shores of the Caribbean. Its eighth hole skirts the water, then doglegs onto a promontory and a green thrusting 200 yards into the sea. The back nine are the most scenic and interesting, rising up steep slopes and falling into deep ravines on Mount Zion. The 10th fairway abuts the family burial grounds of the Barretts of Wimpole Street, and the 14th passes the vacation home of singer Johnny Cash. The 300-foot-high 13th tee offers a rare panoramic view of the sea and the roof of the hotel, and the 15th green is next to a 40-foot waterfall once featured in a James Bond movie. Amenities include a fully stocked pro shop, a clubhouse, and a professional staff. Guests at the Wyndham pay $70 for 18 holes, $40 for 9 holes. Nonguests pay $80 for 18 holes, $60 for 9 holes. Mandatory cart rental is $40 for 18 holes, and the use of a caddy (also mandatory) is another $14 for 18 holes.

The excellent course at the ○ **Tryall** (☎ 876/956-5660), 12 miles from Montego Bay, is so regal, it's often been the site of major golf tournaments, including the Jamaica Classic Annual and the Johnnie Walker Tournament. For 18 holes, guests of Tryall are charged $80 in winter, $40 the rest of the year. In winter, the course is usually closed to nonguests; the rest of the year, they pay a steep $150.

Half Moon, at Rose Hall (☎ 876/953-2560), features a championship course designed by Robert Trent Jones, Sr., with manicured and diversely shaped greens. Half Moon hotel guests pay $100 for 18 holes; nonguests pay $130. Carts cost $35 for 18 holes, and caddies (which are mandatory) are hired for $15.

The ○ **Ironshore Golf & Country Club,** Ironshore, St. James, Montego Bay (☎ 876/953-3681), is another well-known 18-hole, 72-par course. Privately owned, it's open to all golfers who show up. Greens fees for 18 holes are $57.50.

HORSEBACK RIDING A good program for equestrians is offered at the **Rocky Point Riding Stables,** at the Half Moon Club, Rose Hall, Montego Bay (☎ 876/953-2286). Housed in the most beautiful barn and stables in Jamaica, built in the colonial Caribbean style in 1992, it offers around 30 horses and a helpful staff. A 90-minute beach or mountain ride costs $50.

RAFTING **Mountain Valley Rafting,** 31 Gloucester Ave. (☎ 876/956-4920), offers excursions on the Great River, which depart from the Lethe Plantation, about 10 miles south of Montego Bay. This is hardly the most exciting rafting trip in Jamaica and is in fact a bit bland but fun for some. The best rafting is on the Río Grande at Port Antonio, but since so few visitors make it to Port Antonio, this may have to do. Rafts are available for $36 for up to two people. Trips last 45 minutes and operate daily from 8am to 5pm. The rafts are composed of bamboo trunks with a raised dais to sit on. In some cases, a small child can accompany two adults on the same raft, although due caution should be exercised if you choose to do this. Ask about pickup by taxi at the end of the rafting run to return you to your rented car. For $45 per person, a half-day experience will include transportation to and from your hotel, an hour's rafting, lunch, a garden tour of the Lethe property, and a taste of Jamaican liqueur.

TENNIS   Wyndham Rose Hall Golf & Beach Resort, Rose Hall (☎ 876/
953-2650), outside Montego Bay, is an outstanding tennis resort, though it's not the
equal of Half Moon or Tryall (see below). Wyndham offers six hard-surface courts,
each lit for night play. As a courtesy, nonguests are sometimes invited to play for free,
but permission has to be obtained from the manager. You cannot play unless you're
invited. The resident pro charges $30 per hour or $20 for 30 minutes for lessons.

Half Moon Golf, Tennis, and Beach Club, outside Montego Bay (☎ 876/
953-2211), has the finest courts in the area, even outclassing Tryall. Its 13 state-of-
the-art courts, 7 of which are lit for night games, attract tennis players from around
the world. Lessons cost $20 to $30 per half hour, $35 to $55 per hour. Residents play
free, day or night. The pro shop, which accepts reservations for court times, is open
daily from 7am to 9pm. If you want to play after those hours, you switch on the lights
yourself. If you're not a hotel guest, you must purchase a day pass ($50 per person) at
the front desk; it allows access to the resort's courts, gym, sauna, Jacuzzi, pools, and
beach facilities.

Tryall Golf, Tennis, and Beach Club, St. James (☎ 876/956-5660), offers nine
hard-surface courts, three lit for night play, near its great house. Day games are free for
guests; nonguests pay $30 per hour. All players are assessed $10 per hour for nighttime illumination. Four on-site pros provide lessons for $15 to $30 per half hour, or
$20 to $50 per hour.

4 Seeing the Sights

If you ever feel like deserting Montego Bay's sandy beaches, there are several notable
sights and activities in the area.

TOURS & CRUISES

The **Croydon Plantation,** P.O. Box 1348, Catadupa, St. James (☎ 876/979-8267),
is a 25-mile ride from Montego Bay. It can be visited on a half-day tour from Montego
Bay (or Negril) on Wednesday and Friday. Included in the $50 price are round-trip
transportation from your hotel, a tour of the plantation, a taste of tropical fruits in season, and a barbecued-chicken lunch. Most hotel desks can arrange this tour, which is
rather touristy and not worth a half day for most visitors, who'd rather spend more
time on the beach instead. But if you have a serious interest in seeing what plantation
life was like back in the old days, this at least will give you a decent preview.

To see plantations, go on a **Hilton High Day Tour,** through Beach View Plaza
(☎ 876/952-3343). The tour includes round-trip transportation on a scenic drive
through historic plantation areas, but not Croydon. Your day starts with continental
breakfast at an old plantation house. You can roam the 100 acres of the plantation and
visit the German village of Seaford Town or St. Leonards village nearby. Calypso music
is played throughout the day, and a Jamaican lunch is served at 1pm. The cost is $55
per person for the plantation tour, breakfast, lunch, and transportation. Tour days are
Tuesday, Wednesday, Friday, and Sunday.

Day and evening cruises are offered aboard the *Calico,* a 55-foot gaff-rigged wooden
ketch that sails from Margaritaville on the Montego Bay waterfront. An additional vessel, *Calico B,* also carries another 40 passengers. You can be transported to and from
your hotel for either cruise. The day voyage, which departs at 10am and returns at 1pm,
offers sailing, sunning, and snorkeling (with equipment supplied). The cruise costs $35
and is offered daily. On the *Calico's* evening voyage, which goes for $25 and is offered
Wednesday to Saturday from 5 to 7pm, cocktails and wine are served as you sail

The White Witch of Rose Hall

Annie Mary Paterson, a beautiful bride of only 17, arrived at the Rose Hall Great House near Montego Bay on March 28, 1820, to take up residence with her new husband, John Palmer. The house was said to have affected her badly from the moment she entered it.

When John Palmer found out she was having an affair with a young slave, he is said to have beaten her with a riding whip. John Palmer died that night, and before long, rumors were swirling that his young wife had poisoned his wine.

With her husband buried, Annie Palmer began a reign of terror at Rose Hall. Fearing her slave lover might blackmail her, she watched from the back of a black horse while he was securely tied, gagged, and flogged to death. Legend says that she then began to drift into liaison after liaison with one slave after another. But she was fickle; when her lovers bored her, she had them killed.

Her servants called her the "Obeah (voodoo) woman," the daughter of the devil, and "the White Witch of Rose Hall."

Although some scholars claim that they can produce no evidence of this legendary figure's cruelty or even of her debauchery, her story has been the subject of countless paperback Gothic novels.

When Ms. Palmer was found strangled in her bed in 1833, few speculated who her murderer might have been. Her household servants just wanted her buried as soon as possible in the deepest hole they could dig.

through the sunset. For information and reservations, call Capt. Bryan Langford, **North Coast Cruises** (☎ 876/952-5860). A 3-day notice is recommended.

MEETING SOME FEATHERED FRIENDS

Rocklands Wildlife Station. Anchovy, St. James. ☎ **876/952-2009.** Admission J$300 ($8.55). Daily 2:30–5pm.

It's a unique experience to have a Jamaican doctor bird perch on your finger to drink syrup, to feed small doves and finches millet from your hand, and to watch dozens of other birds flying in for their evening meal. Don't take children 5 and under to this sanctuary, as they tend to bother the birds. Rocklands is about a mile outside Anchovy on the road from Montego Bay.

THE GREAT HOUSES

Occupied by plantation owners, each great house of Jamaica was built on high ground so that it overlooked the plantation itself and was in sight of the next house in the distance. It was the custom for the owners to offer hospitality to travelers crossing the island by road; travelers were spotted by the lookout, and bed and food were given freely. All the great houses below can be toured in 1 day.

Barnett Estates and Belfield Great House. Barnett Estates. ☎ **876/952-2382.** Admission $10. Daily 9:30am–5pm.

Once a totally private estate sprawled across 50,000 acres, a 15-minute drive west of Montego Bay, this great house has hosted everybody from John F. Kennedy to Winston Churchill and even Queen Elizabeth II over the years. Now anybody who pays the entrance fee can come in and take a look. The domain of the Kerr-Jarret family during 300 years of high society, this was once the seat of a massive sugar plantation. At its center is the 18th-century Belfield Great House. Restored in 1994, it is a grand example of Georgian architecture, though not as ornate as Rose Hall (see below). Guides in costumes offer narrated tours of the property. After the tour, drop in at the old Sugar Mill Bar for a tall rum punch.

Greenwood Great House. On Rte. A1, 14 miles east of Montego Bay. ☎ **876/953-1077.** Admission $12 adults, $6 children under 12. Daily 9am–6pm.

Some people find the 15-room Greenwood even more interesting than Rose Hall (see below) because it's less restored and has more literary associations. Erected on its hillside perch between 1780 and 1800, the Georgian-style building was the residence of Richard Barrett, cousin of poet Elizabeth Barrett Browning. Elizabeth Barrett Browning herself never visited Jamaica, but her family used to be one of the largest landholders here. An absentee planter who lived in England, her father once owned 84,000 acres and some 3,000 slaves. On display is the original library of the Barrett family, with rare books dating from 1697 (including the H. G. deLisser book *White Witch of Rose Hall*) along with oil paintings of the family, Wedgwood china, rare musical instruments, and a fine collection of antique furniture. The house was built by John Palmer, a wealthy British planter, during the years 1778 to 1790. At its peak, this was a 6,600-acre plantation, with more than 2,000 slaves. However, it was Annie Palmer, wife of the builder's grandnephew, who became the focal point of fiction and fact. Called "Infamous Annie," she was said to have dabbled in witchcraft. She took slaves as lovers and then killed them off when they bored her. Servants called her "the Obeah woman" (*Obeah* is Jamaican for voodoo). Annie was said to have murdered several of her husbands while they slept and eventually suffered the same fate herself. Long in ruins, the house has now been restored and can be visited by the public. Annie's Pub is on the ground floor.

5 Shopping

Be prepared to be pursued persistently by aggressive vendors. Since selling a craft item may mean the difference between having a meal or going hungry, there's often a feverish attempt to peddle goods to potential customers, all of whom are viewed as rich.

The main shopping areas are at **Montego Freeport,** within easy walking distance of the pier; **City Centre,** where most of the duty-free shops are, aside from those at the large hotels; and **Holiday Village Shopping Centre.**

The **Old Fort Craft Park,** a shopping complex with 180 vendors (all licensed by the Jamaica Tourist Board), fronts Howard Cooke Boulevard (up from Gloucester Avenue in the heart of Montego Bay, on the site of Fort Montego). A market with a varied assortment of handcrafts, it's grazing country for both souvenirs and more serious purchases. If you have time for only one shopping complex, make it this one, as its crafts are more varied. You'll see wall hangings, handwoven straw items, and wood

Warning

Some so-called "duty-free" prices are actually lower than stateside prices, but then the government hits you with a 10% "general consumption tax" on all items purchased. Even so, you can still find good duty-free items here, including Swiss watches, Irish crystal, Italian handbags, Indian silks, and liquors and liqueurs. Appleton's rums are an excellent value. Tía Maria (coffee-flavored) and Rumona (rum-flavored) are the best liqueurs. Khus Khus is the local perfume. Jamaican arts and crafts are available throughout the resorts and at the Crafts Market (see below).

sculpture. You can even get your hair braided. Vendors can be very aggressive, so be prepared for major hassles. If you want something, also be prepared for some serious negotiation, as persistent bargaining on your part will lead to substantial discounts.

At the **Crafts Market,** near Harbour Street in downtown Montego Bay, you can find a good selection of handmade souvenirs of Jamaica, including straw hats and bags, wooden platters, straw baskets, musical instruments, beads, carved objects, and toys. That *jijipapa* hat is important if you're going to be out in the island sun.

One of the newest and most intriguing places for shopping is an upscale mini-mall, **Half Moon Plaza,** on the coastal road about 8 miles east of the commercial center of Montego Bay. It caters to the shopping and gastronomic needs of guests of one of the region's most elegant hotels, the Half Moon Club. Merchandise here is far more elegant, refined, and expensive than that found in the native craft markets recommended above. On the premises are a bank and about 25 shops, each arranged around a central courtyard and selling a wide choice of carefully selected merchandise.

The **Ambiente Art Gallery,** 9 Fort St. (☎ 876/952-7919), is housed in a 100-year-old clapboard cottage set close to the road. The Austrian-born owner, Maria Hitchins, is one of the doyennes of the Montego Bay art scene. She has personally encouraged and developed scores of fine artworks and prints by local artists. **Neville Budhai Paintings,** Budhai's Art Gallery, Reading Main Road, Reading, 5 miles east of town on the way to Negril (☎ 876/979-2568), is the art center of a distinguished artist, Neville Budhai, the president and co-founder of the Western Jamaica Society of Fine Arts. He has a distinct style, and his work captures the special flavor of the island and its people. **Sun Art,** Half Moon Shopping Village, Half Moon Plaza (☎ 876/853-8455), is one of the major galleries of Jamaica, with an array of the country's finest artists along with a well-chosen selection of Haitian and other Caribbean art. If you're seeking Jamaican art, there is nothing finer—an exciting selection of paintings, sculpture, ceramics, and prints.

Klass Kraft Leather Sandals, 44 Fort St. (☎ 876/952-5782), next door to Things Jamaican, offers sandals and leather accessories made on location by a team of Jamaican craftspeople. At **Blue Mountain Gems Workshop,** at the Holiday Village Shopping Centre (☎ 876/953-2338), you can take a tour to see the raw stone turned into finished pieces. Wooden jewelry, local carvings, and one-of-a-kind ceramic figurines are also sold. **Golden Nugget,** 8 St. James Shopping Centre, Gloucester Ave. (☎ 876/952-7707), is a duty-free shop with an impressive collection of watches for both women and men and a fine assortment of jewelry, especially gold chains. The shop also carries leading brand-name cameras and a wide assortment of French perfumes.

Copasetic, Half Moon Shopping Village (☎ 876/953-3838), is a good outlet for Jamaican crafts, including pottery and jewelry. There are also good buys here in straw products. For the antique collector, the best offerings are at **The Antique Collection,** Blue Diamond Shopping Centre (☎ 876/953-2982), where any purchase can be shipped. **Bob Marley Experience,** Half Moon Shopping Village, Half Moon Plaza (☎ 876/953-3449), has the largest collection of Marley recordings in Montego Bay, on CD or tape. There is also an interesting collection of reggae T-shirts and posters. There's also a small theater seating 69 showing a 15-minute documentary on Marley's life and music.

Mezzaluna, Half Moon Shopping Village, Half Moon Plaza (☎ 876/953-9683), is an upscale women's boutique, selling lingerie, perfumes, and various garments along with chic accessories such as belts. **Isaacs for Men,** Half Moon Shopping Village, Half Moon Plaza (☎ 876/953-9318), is one of the best outlets for men's wear both formal and semiformal. Men will delight in the selection of casual sportswear as well, ideal for the Jamaican climate if you didn't bring the right stuff.

Things Jamaican Ltd., 44 Fort St. (☎ 876/952-5605), is affiliated with the government and set up to encourage the development of Jamaican arts and crafts. The store is a showcase for the talents of the artisans of this island nation. There's a wealth of Jamaican products on display, even food and drink, including rums and liqueurs, along with jerk seasoning and such jellies as orange pepper. Look for Busha Browne's fine Jamaican sauces, especially their spicy chutneys such as banana, their spicy piquant sauce, and their spicy tomato (called love apple) sauce, which is not to be confused with catsup. These recipes are prepared and bottled by the Busha Browne Company in Jamaica just as they were 100 years ago. Many items for sale are carved from wood, including not only sculptures, but salad bowls and trays as well. You'll also find large handwoven Jamaican baskets and women's handbags made of bark (in Jamaica, these are known unflatteringly as "old-lady bags").

Look also for reproductions of the Port Royal collection, named for the wicked city buried by an earthquake and tidal wave in 1692 (see chapter 8). After resting in a sleepy underwater grave for 275 years, beautiful pewter items were recovered and are living again in reproductions (except the new items are lead-free). Impressions were made, and molds were created to reproduce them. They include rat-tail spoons, a spoon with the heads of the monarchs William and Mary, splay-footed Lion Rampant spoons, and spoons with Pied-de-Biche handles. Many items were reproduced faithfully, right down to the pit marks and scratches. To complement this pewter assortment, Things Jamaican created the Port Royal Bristol-Delft Ceramic Collection, based on original pieces of ceramics found in the underwater digs.

6 Montego Bay After Dark

There's a lot more to do here at night than go to the dance clubs, but the area certainly has those, too. Much of the entertainment is offered at the various hotels.

The **Cricket Club,** at Wyndham Rose Hall (☎ 876/953-2650), is more than just a sports bar; it's where people go to meet and mingle with an international crowd. Televised sports, karaoke sing-alongs, tournament darts, and backgammon are all part of the fun. It's open daily from 7pm to 1am; there's no cover. We've enjoyed the atmosphere at **Walter's,** 39 Gloucester Ave. (☎ 876/952-9391), which has an authentic Jamaican laid-back feel—complete with a constant flow of calypso and reggae music from as early as 10am daily (for the diehards) until 2am. There's never a cover, and they have live bands on the weekends.

If you want to stick to the more familiar, try **Witches Nightclub,** Holiday Inn Sunspree Resort (☎ 876/953-2485). Nonguests of the hotel can pick up a pass at the front desk for $50, which allows them all-inclusive privileges at the nightclub. The pass includes a buffet and all the drinks and dancing you can handle. The house/disco/jazz music is as imaginative as what you'll find at a club in the United States. It's open daily from 6pm to 2am.

Margueritaville, Gloucester Avenue (☎ 876/952-4777), is the Montego Bay branch of an establishment that's bigger and brighter in Negril. It sits on a narrow strip of land between Gloucester Road and the sea. Into its three-story premises, its developers crammed a restaurant and bar, a disco, and an array of fun-in-the-sun diversions that include a giant water slide. The result combines an "Animal House goes tropical" motif with reggae, bright colors, a floating trampoline, and a laissez-faire design that can be either impossibly juvenile or a lot of distracting fun. Burgers and sandwiches are served throughout the day, along with party-colored drinks, but the place is at its most appealing after 10:30pm. Then, there's a cover charge of J$100 ($2.85) per person for a beat that goes on and on and on. **The Brewery,** Gloucester Avenue (☎ **876/940-2433**), is one of the city's most popular nightlife hangouts, evoking a mixture of an English pub and an all-Jamaican jerk pork pit. There's a woodsy-looking bar where everyone is into Red Stripe and reggae, lots of neo-medieval memorabilia à la Olde England, and a covered veranda in back where clients overlook the traffic on busy Gloucester Avenue.

When you tire of your fellow visitors and want to escape to a place where time has stood still—the way Jamaica used to be—head for the appropriately named ✪ **Time 'n' Place,** just east of Falmouth (☎ **876/954-4371**). From Montego Bay, you'll spot the sign by the side of the road before you reach Falmouth, reading, "If you got the time, then we got the place." On an almost deserted 2-mile beach sits this raffish beach bar, built of driftwood and looking like it's just waiting for the next hurricane to blow it away. Sit back in this relaxed, friendly place and listen to the reggae from the local stations. You can order the island's best daiquiris, made from fresh local fruit, or stick around for peppery jerk chicken or lobster. Of course, Time 'n' Place isn't as completely undiscovered as we've made it out to be; the fashion editors of *Vogue* have swooped down on the place, using it as a backdrop for beach-fashion shots.

7 A Side Trip to Falmouth

This port town lies on the north coast of Jamaica, about 23 miles east of Montego Bay. The **Trelawny Beach Hotel** originally put it on the tourist map (though we no longer recommend staying there, as it's a bit worn down). The town itself is interesting but ramshackle. There's talk about fixing it up for visitors, but no one has done anything yet. If you'd like to see what a Jamaican town looked like in the early 50s, before all the megaresorts took over, give this place a short visit.

Leave your car at Water Square; you can explore the town on foot in about an hour. The present courthouse was reconstructed from the early 19th-century building, and fisherfolk still congregate on Seaboard Street. You'll pass the Customs office and a parish church dating from the late 18th century. Later, you can go on a shopping expedition outside town to Caribatik.

RIVER RAFTING NEAR FALMOUTH

Rafting on the **Martha Brae** is an adventure. To reach the starting point from Falmouth, drive approximately 3 miles inland to **Martha Brae's Rafters Village** (☎ **876/952-0889**). The rafts are similar to those on the Río Grande, near Port Antonio; you sit on a raised dais on bamboo logs. The cost is $40, with two riders allowed on a raft, plus a small child if accompanied by an adult (but use caution). The trips last 1 hour and 15 minutes and operate daily from 9am to 4pm. If you have time for only one river-rafting experience in the Mo Bay area, make it this one instead of the better publicized Mountain Valley Rafting reviewed earlier. Along the way, you can stop and order cool drinks or beer along the banks of the river. There's a bar, a restaurant, and two souvenir shops in the village.

Market Day

On Wednesday morning, Falmouth hosts the biggest flea market in the country, with hundreds of booths linking the marketplace and overflowing into the streets. Buyers from all over the island flock here to pick up bargains (later sold at inflated prices). Take time out to buy a loaf of *bammy* (cassava bread) and pick up the makings of a picnic.

A SHOPPING EXPEDITION FOR BATIKS

Two miles east of Falmouth on the north-coast road is **Caribatik Island Fabrics,** at Rock Wharf on the Luminous Lagoon (☎ **876/954-3314**), which is open Tuesdays through Saturdays from 9am to 4pm (closed in September and on national holidays). You'll recognize the place easily, as it has a huge sign painted across the building's side. This is the private domain of Keith Chandler, who established the place with his late wife, Muriel, in 1970. Today, the batiks Muriel Chandler created before her death in 1990 are viewed as stylish and sensual garments by the chic boutiques in the States.

The shop has a full range of fabrics, scarves, garments, and wall hangings, some patterned after such themes as Jamaica's doctor bird and various endangered animal species of the world. The gallery continues to sell a selection of Muriel's original batik paintings. Either Keith or a member of the staff will be glad to describe the intricate process of batiking.

WHERE TO STAY

Fisherman's Inn (Rose's by the Sea). Rock Falmouth, Jamaica, W.I. ☎ **876/954-4078.** For reservations, contact 534 West Manchester Rd., Inglewood, CA 90301 ☎ 310/671-9649. Fax 310/671-4343. 12 units. A/C TV TEL. $111–$122 double. Rates include continental breakfast. AE, MC, V.

Set on the coastal road just outside the commercial center of Falmouth, immediately adjacent to the also-recommended Glistening Waters, this is a well-designed roadside inn that might remind you of a pub-hotel in Britain. Much attention is devoted to the woodsylooking restaurant, where main courses at lunch cost from $4.50 to $12, and where main courses at dinner range from $13 to $30. Menu items include filet mignon, stir-fried beef with soy and oriental herbs, and chicken breast stuffed with cheese and chopped callaloo. Despite its appeal as a restaurant, there's an interesting hotel configuration here as well: It includes a swimming pool set in a concrete wharf jutting into the waters of the phosphorescent bay, a gazebo-style pool bar, and a walkway/wooden pier accessing the establishment's dozen bedrooms—built on pilings above the sea. Each of these has a private veranda or patio, white tile floors, white-painted furniture, and a sense of low-key coziness that only a small, intimately organized hotel can convey.

WHERE TO DINE

Glistening Waters Inn and Marina. Rock Falmouth (between Falmouth and the Trelawny Beach Hotel). ☎ **876/954-3229.** Main courses $8–$23. AE, MC, V. Daily 9:30am–10pm. SEAFOOD.

Residents of Montego Bay often make the 28-mile drive out here, along Route A1, just to sample the ambience of Old Jamaica. This well-recommended restaurant, with a veranda overlooking the lagoon, is housed in what was originally a private clubhouse for the aristocrats of nearby Trelawny. The furniture here may remind you of a stage set for *Night of the Iguana*. Menu items usually include local fish dishes, such as snapper or kingfish, served with *bammy* (a form of cassava bread). Other specialties are three different lobster dishes, three different preparations of shrimp, three different conch viands, fried rice, and pork chops. The food is just what your mama would make (if she came from Jamaica). The waters of the lagoon contain a rare form of phosphorescent microbe, which, when the waters are agitated, glows in the dark. Ask about evening booze cruises, which cost $10 per person, including one drink. Departures are nightly at about 7:15pm.

Negril   4

On the arid western tip of Jamaica, **Negril** has had a reputation for bacchanalia, hedonism, marijuana smoking, and nude bathing since hippies discovered its sunny shores during the late 1960s (long before they helped establish Negril's reputation for debauchery, it was noted for the buccaneer Calico Jack, famous for carousing with the infamous women pirates Ann Bonney and Mary Read—see the box "Ann Bonney & Her Dirty Dog," later in this section). The resort became more mainstream in the early 1990s as the big-money capitalists of Kingston and North America built several new megaresorts, most of them managed by Jamaica's SuperClubs. Not all of the old reputation has disappeared, however, for some resorts here reserve stretches of their beach for nude bathers, and illegal ganja is peddled openly.

Whether clothed or unclothed, visitors are drawn to Negril's Seven Mile Beach of white sand and some of the best snorkeling and scuba diving in Jamaica. Opening onto a tranquil lagoon protected from the Caribbean by a coral reef, this great beach is set against a backdrop of sea grapes and coconut palms. Local authorities mandate that no building can be taller than the highest palm tree, resulting in an ecologically conscious setting, with the resorts blending gracefully into the flat and sandy landscape.

There are really two Negrils. The West End is the site of many little authentic restaurants with names like Chicken Lavish, and of modest cottages that still take in paying guests. The other Negril is on the east end, along the road from Montego Bay. The best hotels, such as Negril Gardens, line the panoramic beachfront. The actual town itself may have power and phones these days, but it has little of interest to travelers. The only building of any historic note in the area is Negril Lighthouse, at the westerly tip of Jamaica. Built in 1894, it offers a chance to climb some 100 steps for a view of Negril Point, the bay, and the sea inlet. An automatic light flashes every 2 seconds throughout the night. You can still see the old kerosene lamps that were used until the 1940s, when they were replaced by gas lamps.

Chances are, however, your main concern will be staking out your own favorite spot along Negril's Seven Mile Beach. You don't need to get up for anything; somebody will be along to serve you. Perhaps it'll be the banana lady, with a basket of fruit perched on her head. Maybe the ice-cream man will set up a stand right under a coconut palm. Surely, the beer lady will find you as she strolls along the beach, a carton of Red Stripe on her head and a bucket of ice in her hand. And just like in the old days, hordes of young men peddling illegal ganja will seek you out. At some point, you'll want to leave the beach long enough to explore Booby Key (or Cay), a tiny islet off the Negril coast. It was featured in the Walt Disney film *20,000 Leagues Under the Sea*.

Negril is 50 miles (about a 2-hour drive) southwest of the Montego Bay international airport, along a winding road, past ruins of sugar estates and great houses. It's 150 miles (about a 4-hour drive) west of Kingston. If you're going to Negril, you'll fly into **Donald Sangster Airport** in Montego Bay. Most hotels, particularly the all-inclusive resorts, will pick you up and drive you directly to your hotel. Be sure to ask when you book.

If your hotel doesn't provide transfers, you have a few options. You can fly on from Montego Bay to Negril's small airport aboard the independent carrier, **Air Jamaica Express,** booking your connection through the Air Jamaica reservations network (☎ **800/523-5585** in the U.S.). The airfare is $55 one way. If you don't want to deal with another flight, public and private bus companies have desks in the Montego Bay airport, all offering a U.S.$20 one-way fare to get you to Negril. The public bus is not a comfortable way to go for the 2-hour trip. Two private companies making the run are **Tour Wise** (☎ **876/979-1027** in Montego Bay, or 876/957-2223 in Negril) and **Caribic Vacations** (☎ **876/953-9874** in Montego Bay, or 876/974-9106 in Ocho Rios). All buses make one refreshment stop at a halfway point during the trip. Buses depart as flights arrive and will drop you off at your hotel once you reach Negril.

Yet another option is renting a car. Information on car rentals is given in chapter 2. From Montego Bay, drive 52 miles west along Route A1. Because of conditions, plan for a 90-minute drive. A final option is to take a taxi; dozens are available at the airport. A typical one-way fare from Montego Bay to Negril is from $50 to $60. Always negotiate and agree upon the fare before getting into the taxi.

1 Where to Stay

Refer to the end of this section for a complete rundown on all-inclusive resorts.

VERY EXPENSIVE

The Caves. P.O. Box 15, Lighthouse Station, Negril, Jamaica, W.I. ☎ **800/OUT-POST** in the U.S., or 876/957-0270. Fax 876/957-4930. www.islandoutpost.com. E-mail: thecaves@ islandoutpost.com. 6 cottages. Winter $450–$950 double. Off-season $325–$625 double. Rates include all meals and self-service bar. AE, MC, V. Closed Sept 8–Oct 8.

Although not on the beach, this inn still has its discerning devotees who seek out the most atmospheric and elegant small inn in Negril. A short ride into Negril will deposit you on a good beach. This place might be well suited for groups of friends traveling together or for a family reunion. This small-scale hotel was established in 1990 on 2 acres of land that's perched above a honeycombed network of cliffs, 32 feet above the surf on a point near Negril's lighthouse, close to Jamaica's westernmost tip. Accommodations are in breezy units within five cement and wood-sided cottages, each with a thatched roof and sturdy furniture. Matisse could have designed them. None has air-conditioning, and the windows are without screens. A TV and VCR can be brought in if you request them.

In spite of its fame, there are drawbacks here. Of all the members of Chris Blackwell's Outpost hotels, generally the finest in the Caribbean, there's a sense of snobbishness, and the prices are very high when stacked up against the competition. The hotel's physical setting, though lavishly publicized, is difficult to negotiate with its stairwells and catwalks.

Negril

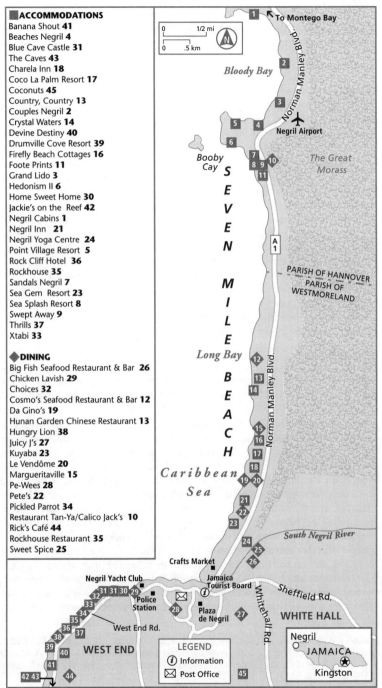

ACCOMMODATIONS
Banana Shout **41**
Beaches Negril **4**
Blue Cave Castle **31**
The Caves **43**
Charela Inn **18**
Coco La Palm Resort **17**
Coconuts **45**
Country, Country **13**
Couples Negril **2**
Crystal Waters **14**
Devine Destiny **40**
Drumville Cove Resort **39**
Firefly Beach Cottages **16**
Foote Prints **11**
Grand Lido **3**
Hedonism II **6**
Home Sweet Home **30**
Jackie's on the Reef **42**
Negril Cabins **1**
Negril Inn **21**
Negril Yoga Centre **24**
Point Village Resort **5**
Rock Cliff Hotel **36**
Rockhouse **35**
Sandals Negril **7**
Sea Gem Resort **23**
Sea Splash Resort **8**
Swept Away **9**
Thrills **37**
Xtabi **33**

DINING
Big Fish Seafood Restaurant & Bar **26**
Chicken Lavish **29**
Choices **32**
Cosmo's Seafood Restaurant & Bar **12**
Da Gino's **19**
Hunan Garden Chinese Restaurant **13**
Hungry Lion **38**
Juicy J's **27**
Kuyaba **23**
Le Vendôme **20**
Margueritaville **15**
Pe-Wees **28**
Pete's **22**
Pickled Parrot **34**
Restaurant Tan-Ya/Calico Jack's **10**
Rick's Café **44**
Rockhouse Restaurant **35**
Sweet Spice **25**

To Montego Bay

Bloody Bay

Negril Airport

Booby Cay

The Great Morass

SEVEN MILE BEACH

Long Bay

PARISH OF HANNOVER
PARISH OF WESTMORELAND

Caribbean Sea

South Negril River

Crafts Market

Negril Yacht Club

Jamaica Tourist Board

Sheffield Rd.

Police Station

Plaza de Negril

WHITE HALL

West End Rd.

Whitehall Rd.

WEST END

LEGEND
(i) Information
⊠ Post Office

Negril
JAMAICA
Kingston

Dining: Sumptuous meals are prepared only for guests and are included, along with domestic Jamaican drinks from the bar, as part of the all-inclusive price.

Amenities: Spa treatments, sauna, bikes, airport transfers, snorkeling equipment. Many sports, such as horseback riding, kayaking, scuba diving, and golf, can be arranged, as can yoga instruction. There's a saltwater pool and Jacuzzi on-site.

EXPENSIVE

Sea Splash Resort. Norman Manley Blvd. (P.O. Box 123), Negril, Jamaica, W.I. ☎ **800/ 254-2786** in the U.S., or 876/957-4041. Fax 876/957-4049. E-mail: seasplash@mail. cwjamaica.com. 15 units. A/C TV TEL. Winter $199 suite for 2. Off-season $135 suite for 2. Extra person $20. Full board $33 per person extra. AE, CB, DC, MC, V.

Partly because of its small size, this beachfront resort often has a friendly, personable feeling. In deliberate contrast to the megaresorts nearby, it lies on a small but carefully landscaped sliver of beachfront land planted with tropical vegetation. The suites are spacious and stylishly decorated with wicker furniture and fresh pastel colors. All are the same size and contain the same amenities—a kitchenette, a balcony or patio, large closets, and either a king-size bed or twin beds—although those on the upper floor have higher ceilings and feel more spacious. Living areas contain sofa beds, ideal for small families. The small bathrooms come with hair dryers.

Dining: The resort contains two different restaurants, Calico Jack's (a simple lunchtime *bohio*) and the more elaborate Tan-Ya's (see "Where to Dine," below). There's also a poolside bar.

Amenities: Guests have use of a small gym, a Jacuzzi, and a pool. Baby-sitting, laundry, and room service are also offered.

MODERATE

✪ Charela Inn. Norman Manley Blvd. (P.O. Box 33), Negril, Jamaica, W.I. ☎ **800/ 423-4095** in the U.S., or 876/957-4648. Fax 876/957-4414. www.charela.com. 49 units. A/C TEL. Winter $158–$210 double. Off-season $108–$148 double. MAP (breakfast and dinner) $38 per person extra. 3-night minimum stay. AE, MC, V.

A seafront inn reminiscent of a Spanish hacienda, this place sits on the main beach strip on 3 acres of landscaped grounds. The building's inner courtyard, with a tropical garden and a round, freshwater pool, opens onto one of the widest (250 feet) sandy beaches in Negril. The inn attracts a loyal following of visitors seeking a home away from home. Try for one of the 20 or so rooms with a view of the sea, as these are the most desirable. Accommodations are generally spacious, often with a bit of Jamaican character with their wicker furnishings and ceiling fans. All the rooms have either private patios or balconies. Most of the good-size bathrooms have combination tub/showers, though some have shower stalls only. Le Vendôme, facing the sea and the garden, offers both an á la carte menu and a five-course fixed-price meal that changes daily (see "Where to Dine," below). Sunsets are toasted on open terraces facing the sea. Sunset cruises, lasting 3¹/₂ hours, are offered, along with Sunfish sailing, windsurfing, and kayaking. Thursday and Saturday nights, there's live entertainment. Simplicity, a quiet elegance, and excellent value for the money are the hallmarks of the inn.

Coco La Palm Resort. Norman Manley Blvd., Negril, Jamaica, W.I. ☎ **800/320-8821** or 876/957-4227. Fax 876/957-3460. www.cocolapalm.com/rates.html. 41 units. A/C MINIBAR TV TEL. Winter $155–$175 double; $185–$195 suite. Off-season $125–$145 double; $150–$160 suite. MC, V.

This is a well-conceived hotel with very little plastic or glitter and lots of opportunity for relaxation and rest. Wedged directly at the edge of Negril's long and sandy beach between another hotel and a vacant lot, behind a screen of sea grapes, this is one of Negril's newest resorts, the brainchild of a Minnesota-based real-estate developer who fell in love with Jamaica during his many vacations here. It consists of a pair of long and narrow two-story buildings whose slender ends face the beach, and whose long sides form the edges of a carefully landscaped garden containing a Jacuzzi and a kidney-shaped swimming pool. Rooms are shaped like an octagon, and each has its own patio or balcony, a safety-deposit box, white-painted furniture, and a coffeemaker. On the premises are a bar and a restaurant (The Seaside).

Coconuts. Little Bay, Negril, Jamaica, W.I. ☎ **800/962-5548** in the U.S., or 876/997-5013. Fax 715/686-7143. 10 cottages. Winter $695 per person per week, cottage for 2. Off-season $645 per person per week, cottage for 2. Children 14–17 $395 extra; ages 6–13 $295 extra; ages 5 and under $195 extra. Rates include all meals. MC, V.

In a fishing village on a quiet country road on the South Coast, 8 miles east of Negril on the way to Savanna-la-Mar, this getaway offers a respite from the hustle and bustle of life. Guests stay in cedar-and-stone cottages that have their own private garden patios surrounded by flowers. Only two units have full baths; the rest contain half baths. The philosophy here is, in a climate as beautiful as Jamaica's, why lather up in an indoor cubicle when you can enjoy the garden and ocean views offered by the four totally private coral-stone showers located in the terraced gardens? Your stay includes the use of the saltwater pool and sporting equipment, including snorkeling and fishing gear. Island tours and excursions into Negril or Savanna-la-Mar can be arranged. Your meals consist of freshly caught fish and lobster, chicken, fresh local vegetables, and local fruits and juices that you can enjoy at the seaside restaurant or on your private patio served by the staff.

Crystal Waters. Norman Manley Blvd. (P.O. Box 3018), Negril Beach, Negril, Jamaica, W.I. ☎ **876/957-4284.** Fax 876/957-4889. www.crystalwaters.net. E-mail: crystalwaters@cwjamaica.com. 10 villas. A/C TV. Winter $135–$150 1-bedroom villa; $235–$275 2-bedroom villa; $385 3-bedroom villa. Off-season $100–$110 1-bedroom villa; $160–$200 2-bedroom villa; $270 3-bedroom villa. Maximum of 2 people per room. AE, MC, V.

This is an excellent choice for families with children. The housekeeper assigned to your unit takes over all the cooking and baby-sitting duties, much to the relief of visiting parents. The place is a long-established old-timer and much respected locally, a solidly reliable choice. Located on Negril Beach, a 1½-hour drive from the international airport in Montego Bay, this hotel offers simple accommodations at reasonable prices. Nehru Caolsingh owns and operates these villas, which were opened in the mid-1960s. The accommodations are tropically decorated, furnished with a mixture of hardwoods and wicker. The villas include ceiling fans (plus air-conditioning) and full kitchens, and each is staffed with a housekeeper who will cook breakfast, lunch, and dinner for you. There's also a freshwater pool.

Jackie's on the Reef. West End Rd., Negril, Jamaica, W.I. ☎ **876/957-4997** or 718/469-2785 in New York state. 3 units, 1 cottage. Winter $150 per person. Off-season $125 per person. Rates include breakfast, dinner, and yoga class. No credit cards. Drive 2.5 miles past the oldest lighthouse in Negril; just keep heading out the West End until you come to the sign. No children permitted.

The setting is a soaring concrete building that leaves the impression that it was never completed; whether this is due to a lack of funds or because of the artfully angular postindustrial look the setting provides, only Jackie Lewis, the ultra New York–raised owner, will ever really know. The result evokes a postmodern cathedral, thanks to long corridors that spill into sunlit communal areas. In Jackie Lewis's own irreverent words, "This is a healing joint," welcoming a revolving series of practitioners imported for temporary sojourns from Manhattan's SoHo or East Village. Treatments are likely to include facials, body massages, reflexology, and more. Treatments are individually priced at between $47 and $95 each. Don't expect culinary or hotel-related grandeur. Meals are served in communal settings, and relatively early (dinner is at 6pm). Two of the rooms have openings between the top of their walls and the ceiling, allowing conversations, or whatever, to be overheard by anyone in the communal area. And attentive service rituals are simply not part of the scene here, as it's viewed more as a holistic commune than a "snap-your-fingers-and-get-what-you-thought-you-wanted" resort hotel. But if you're looking for a holistic escape from the ordinary, it might be perfect for you. Among the New-Age crowd in Negril, it's rather famous, and who knows what might arise from a renewed contact with your inner child? The bedrooms are generous in size with mosquito netting draped over the beds in the old plantation style. However, there are no TVs, phones, air-conditioning, or even fans. Furnishings are simple, usually twin beds and small tables in the rooms. The hotel lies 7 miles from the nearest beach but there's a small seawater pool and a ladder down to the reef for swimming.

✪ **Negril Cabins.** Ruthland Point, Negril, Jamaica, W.I. ☎ **800/330-8272** in the U.S., or 876/957-5350. Fax 876/957-5381. www.negrilcabins.com. E-mail: negrilcabins@cwjamaica.com. 86 units. Winter $195–$225 cabin for 2; $230–$255 cabin for 3. Off-season $150–$180 cabin for 2; $185–$210 cabin for 3. Children under 12 stay free in parents' room. AE, MC, V.

Except for the palm trees and the sandy beach, you might imagine yourself at a log-cabin complex in the Maine woods. In many ways, this is the best bargain in Negril, suitable for the budget-conscious traveler eager to get away from it all. The cabins are in a forest, across the road from a beach called Bloody Bay (where the infamous 18th-century pirate, Calico Jack, was captured by the British). The 9 acres of gardens are planted with royal palms, bull thatch, and a rare variety of mango tree. The unadorned cabins are really small timber cottages, none more than two stories high, rising on stilts. Each accommodation offers two spacious and comfortable bedrooms, plus a balcony. Many units have been recently upgraded and improved. The best are rented as "executive suites," with a sunken living and dining area, plus a pull-out queen-size sofa bed for small families. All have private safes; the executive suites also come with air-conditioning and an iron and ironing board. Bathrooms are small but well maintained. The bar and restaurant serve tropical punch, a medley of fresh Jamaican fruits, and flavorful but unpretentious Jamaican meals. A children's program is also available, and live entertainment is offered on some nights.

INEXPENSIVE

Banana Shout. 4 West End Rd. (P.O. Box 4), Negril, Jamaica, W.I. ☎ and fax **876/957-0384.** 7 cottages. Winter $50–$100 cottage for 1 or 2; $85–$120 cottage for 4; $200 cottage for 8. Off-season $35–$60 cottage for 1 or 2; $60–$70 cottage for 4; $160 cottage for 8. MC, V.

Set on 2.5 acres of landscaped grounds with waterfalls, lily ponds, tropical flowers, and fruit trees, this property comprises seven cottages with three units poised on a cliff overlooking the sea. A series of tiered decks with concrete steps leads down the rocks to water. The garden cottages are located across the road with private access to the beach. Each of the secluded units contains a kitchenette and ceiling fan. The rooms are furnished with locally crafted pieces and artwork from Indonesia and Bali. The best deal at this hideaway is the cottage with the patio barbecue. For a group of eight, each person would spend only U.S.$20 to U.S.$25, depending on the time of year for your visit. Rick's Café is across the street.

✪ **Blue Cave Castle.** Lighthouse Rd., Negril, Jamaica, W.I. ☎ and fax **876/957-4845.** 10 units. Winter $75 double. Off-season $50 double. Extra person U.S.$10. No credit cards.

Filled with a sense of whimsy and fun, this little mock castle is a terrific deal. It's been featured by the Jamaica Tourist Board in its TV ads, and the Dallas Cowboy cheerleaders calendar for 1997 was shot here. Battlements and turrets re-create medieval days, and the resort, covering an acre, is built over a cave. It was built in the 1980s by a Czech expatriate who escaped from Czechoslovakia's communist regime in 1968; his creation beside the sea in Negril duplicates one of the 2,500 castles of Czechoslovakia. As such, it is a deliberate departure from the hippie/Rastafarian architecture that dominates many neighboring resorts. There are steps down to the cave from the garden, where local wedding receptions are held regularly. The guest rooms are decorated with handmade mahogany furniture and antique Turkish carpets covering the walls. Many of the objects decorating the castle were collected by the owner, Susan Evanko, during her globetrotting days. Three rooms are air-conditioned, although there are no room phones or TVs. There's no pool either, although you can swim off the cliffs in lieu of a beach. All rooms have sea views, refrigerators, ceiling fans, and balconies. A good restaurant in front is open to the public, but the oceanside dining area is reserved for guests only. You can take breakfast and lunch by the sea and enjoy a daily sunset barbecue.

✪ **Country, Country.** Norman Manley Blvd., Negril, Jamaica, W.I. ☎ **876/957-4273.** Fax 876/957-4342. www.countrynegril.com. E-mail: countrynegril@cwjamaica.com. 14 units. A/C. Dec 15–April 14 $110–$125 double. Off-season $80–$95 double. AE, MC, V.

The owners of one of Negril's newest and smallest hotels were determined to outclass their older competitors when it came to the construction of their property. Consequently, they labored to develop an all-new concept, turning to celebrity decorator Ann Hodges (the creative force behind the decor within many of the much more expensive Island Outpost properties) to define its aesthetics. The result is much talked about in hotel circles in Western Jamaica. Lining either side of a narrow meandering path stretching from the coastal boulevard to the beach are a collection of neo-Creole, clapboard-sided buildings that drip with elaborate gingerbread and cove moldings, each inspired by an idealized vision of vernacular Jamaican colonial architecture. More intriguing are the colors of the buildings: A rainbow of peacock hues highlights the separate architectural features of each building. There's nothing else like it in Negril, and if you stay here, you might never interpret house paint in quite the same way. Inside, concrete floors keep the spacious interiors cool. Each has a vaguely Victorian feel, comfortable furnishings, and a refrigerator. On the premises, adjacent to the beach, is a semicircular bar and grill, Arnella's by the Sea. Near the hotel's entrance, adjacent to the boulevard, is the only Chinese restaurant in Negril, the Hunan Garden. Set within a scarlet-lacquered pavilion, whose wicker furniture evokes Shanghai during the British colonial era, it's open daily from noon to 10pm. Main courses cost $8 to $20.

Devine Destiny. Summerset Rd., West End (P.O. Box 117), Negril, Jamaica, W.I. ☎ **876/957-9184.** Fax 876/957-3846. 44 units. Winter $59–79 double; $145 suite. Off-season $49–$69 double; $95 suite. Children 11 and under stay free in parents' room. AE, MC, V.

This is one of the best and best-designed resorts on Negril's West End, one that's utterly devoid of the funky-hippie motif that permeates most of its competitors. Set in an isolated neighborhood 400 yards from the rocky cliffs of the West End's seafront, it's a full-fledged, relatively large resort plunked in the middle of what's always been viewed as a counterculture neighborhood that until recently shunned conventional resorts.

Ann Bonney & Her Dirty Dog

It was at Bloody Bay, off the coast of Negril, that one of the most notorious pirates of all time, Calico Jack Rackham, was finally captured in 1720. His is a name that will live in infamy, along with Blackbeard's. He was captured with his lover Ann (also Anne) Bonney, the most notorious female pirate of all time. (The bay isn't called "bloody," however, because of these pirates. Whalers used to disembowel their catch here, turning the waters red with blood.)

After tracking her husband, a penniless ne'er-do-well sailor named James Bonney, to a brothel in the Virgin Islands, Ann slit his throat. However, she soon fell for Captain Jack Rackham, who was known as "Calico Jack." Some say he came by his nickname because of the colorful shirts he wore; others claim it was because of his undershorts.

Until he met this lady pirate, Calico Jack hadn't done so well as a pirate, but she inspired him to greatness. In a short time, they became the scourge of the West Indies. No vessel sailing the Caribbean Sea was too large or too small for them to attack and rob. Ann is said to have fought alongside the men, and, according to reports, was a much tougher customer than Calico Jack himself. With her cutlass and marlinespike, she was usually the first to board a captured vessel.

It was late in October, off the Negril coast, when Calico Jack and all the pirates were getting drunk on rum, that a British Navy sloop attacked. Calico Jack ran and hid, but Ann fought bravely, according to reports. She flailed away with a battle-ax and cutlass.

Calico Jack and the other captured pirates were sentenced to be hanged. Ann, however, pleaded with "milord" that she was pregnant. Since British law did not allow the killing of unborn children, she got off though her comrades were sentenced to death. Her final advice to Calico Jack: "If you'd fought like a man, you wouldn't be hanged like the dirty dog you are." So much for a lover's parting words. Ann's father in Ireland purchased her release and she opened a gaming house in St. Thomas where she prospered until the end.

The architecture might remind you of an upscale hacienda in Argentina, with sprawling wings, terra-cotta, tile work, mahogany furniture, and such additional decorative touches as a stone column in the lobby where water drip-drip-drips from a fountain. More than any of the nearby competitors, this place gives the feeling of a coherently planned "important" resort. There's a shuttle bus carrying clients to Negril's Seven Mile Beach, which you'll certainly want to take as a means of avoiding a 2-hour walk. One on-site restaurant serves simple fare three times a day, although after a few days, many guests opt to dine out in any of several restaurants on the West End. There's a pool on the premises, two bars, a TV room, sundeck, game room, and tour desk. Many of the clients are part of European-derived tour groups.

Drumville Cove Resort. West End Rd. (P.O. Box 72), Negril, Jamaica, W.I. ☎ **876/ 957-4369.** Fax 876/957-0198. 30 units. Winter $70 double; $90 for cabana up to 4. Off-season $60 double; $70 for cabana up to 4. AE, MC, V.

It's set on a rocky, irregular terrain of dusty, battered footpaths that meander—sometimes precariously—among arid, thirsty vegetation. The resort is named after a small but treacherous-looking rocky inlet (Drumville Cove) into whose surging waves descends a ladder for cool, saltwater dips. In other words, don't expect a conventional sandy beach. The rooms here are housed in cream-colored structures trimmed in brown, overlooking the sea near the lighthouse, whereas the cottages are scattered throughout the property. All the rooms and cottages have ceiling fans, but only seven of the rooms and none of the cottages are air-conditioned; five rooms offer TVs. Included on the property is a restaurant serving Jamaican specialties with a few American dishes. The nearest good beach is a 5-minute drive away (the hotel provides transportation), and there's a freshwater swimming pool for guest use.

Firefly Beach Cottages. Norman Manley Blvd. (P.O. Box 54), Negril, Jamaica, W.I. ☎ **876/957-4358.** Fax 876/957-3447. E-mail: firefly@jamaicalink.com. 19 units. Winter $105–$180 double. Off-season $75–$136 double. AE, MC, V.

With a lot of Jamaican flair, this laid-back hodgepodge of several white concrete and wooden buildings opens directly onto the beach. There's even a so-called penthouse in the garden with sleeping lofts. In addition to these, there are various studios and cottages, including one large two-bedroom unit that can sleep up to eight in cramped conditions. Most of the units are cooled by air-conditioning and ceiling fans, and many beds are canopied. When they rent "rooms with a view" here, they mean it; the hotel opens onto a stretch of clothing-optional beach. All rooms have verandas and kitchens as well, but there's no restaurant, although many little local spots are within walking distance. There's no pool, but the beach is close at hand (and you don't even have to put on your bathing suit to enjoy it).

Foote Prints. Norman Manley Blvd. (P.O. Box 100), Negril, Jamaica, W.I. ☎ **876/957-4300.** Fax 876/957-4301. www.negril.com. E-mail: footeprints@cwjamaica.com. 31 units. A/C TV TEL. Winter $232 double; $250 double with kitchenette. Off-season $85 double; $115 double with kitchenette. Extra person $30 in winter, $20 in off-season. AE, MC, V.

Dane and Audrey Foote started this enterprise with one building in the mid-1980s; it has since expanded to three. Located on Seven Mile Beach next door to the Swept Away resort, this place offers its best deals during the off-season (mid-April to mid-December). The rooms, four of which contain kitchenettes, are tropically decorated with hardwood furnishings, air-conditioning, and private baths. The hotel's restaurant, Robinson Crusoe's, serves breakfast, lunch, and dinner, specializing in a mix of Jamaican and American dishes. On Friday nights, a barbecue with local bands livens up the place.

Home Sweet Home. West End Rd., Negril, Jamaica, W.I. ☎ and fax **800/925-7418** in the U.S., or 876/957-4478. E-mail: negril_resort@simplycom.net. 16 units. Winter $110–$210 double; $180 penthouse. Off-season $74–$160 double; $140 penthouse. Extra person $15. Children 11 and under stay free in parents' room. AE, DC, MC, V.

On the cliff side, this is a cozy, down-home place. At times, it seems to re-create Negril's hippie heyday of the swinging 60s. You may find your groove here, as the writer Terry McMillan did when she visited many little inns while doing research for her hot seller, *How Stella Got Her Groove Back.* "Home" is a concrete building with a garden with lots of greenery and flowering plants. There's also a pool and a Jacuzzi. When you see the bedrooms, you'll know that many visitors have slept here before you. All accommodations have ceiling fans, a radio and cassette player, and a balcony or veranda, but no TV or phone. There's a sundeck on the cliffs, and you can swim, dive, or snorkel. A simple restaurant serves three inexpensive Jamaican-style meals a day.

Negril Yoga Centre. Norman Manley Blvd. (P.O. Box 48), Negril, Jamaica, W.I. ☎ and fax **876/957-4397.** www.negrilyoga.com. E-mail: negrilyoga@cwjamaica.com. 12 units. Winter $33–$66 double. Off-season $27.50–$55 double. V.

The success of this resort can be judged by the dozens of clients who opt to return year after year to its unpretentious and relatively underfurnished premises. Its owner and founder is Raquel Austin, a wise and well-intentioned matriarch who seems moderately embarrassed by the adulation of her pupils, many of whom wouldn't dream of missing one of her five-times-a-week yoga classes. Set into 3^1/$_2$ flat and verdant acres of thriving botany, across the boulevard from the beach, it offers a collection of artfully mismatched accommodations that evolved over time as the need for more rooms arose. This place has survived longer than most of the other hotels in Negril, basking in its role as the first-established yoga school in a resort that today follows the ritual more aggressively than any other in Jamaica. Three of the units lie within La Casa Blanca, a cement-sided building from the 1980s whose angularity evokes a work by Le Corbusier. The remaining units all lie within funky-looking wood-and-concrete cottages, each with a ceiling fan but no air-conditioning. Overall, the aura is artfully Spartan and carefully synchronized with nature, permeated with a Zen-like calm. The social center is an open-aired pavilion where Ms. Austin teaches hatha yoga. Classes are conducted every Monday through Friday from 9:30 to 10:30, at a price of $8 each. Massage is available at the rate of $45 per hour. If you phone in advance, and if there's a table not occupied by a resident guest, you might want to attend a meal here as a kind of dining oddity. Dress as you would to meet the Dalai Lama, and expect to be surrounded by a hardcore group of urban escapists and yoga aficionados. Meals cost from $6 to $15 and are served at 6pm and 7pm, depending on which seating is available.

Rock Cliff Hotel. West End Rd. (P.O. Box 3067), Negril, Jamaica, W.I. ☎ **876/957-4331.** Fax 876/957-4108. 33 units. A/C. Winter $143.75 double; $333 suite for 2. Off-season $80–$115 double; $240 suite for 2. AE, MC, V.

This hotel is one of the better of the dozens of raffish guest houses that lie among the palms and sea grapes west of Negril's center. Set atop a low cliff overlooking the sea, and popular with divers, it features a restaurant, two bars, and a Sunday-night all-you-can-eat lobster buffet. There's a pool on the premises, and you can inch your way down the cliff for sea dips offshore from the rocks, though most people trek 2 miles to the nearest beach. The suites (but not the conventional bedrooms) contain kitchenettes. The bedrooms have mahogany furniture, pastel-colored draperies, and off-white walls. Maid service is included, and baby-sitting and laundry can be arranged. There's a Jacuzzi, volleyball and basketball courts, a kiosk for sundries and souvenirs, and a well-recommended PADI-affiliated dive shop.

✪ **Rockhouse.** West End Rd. (P.O. Box 24), Negril, Jamaica, W.I. ☎ and fax **876/957-4373.** 28 units. MINIBAR. Winter $100 studio; $185 villa. Off-season $85 studio; $120 villa. Extra person $25. Children 11 and under stay free in parents' unit. AE, MC, V.

This boutique inn stands in stark contrast to the hedonistic all-inclusive resorts, evoking both a South Seas island retreat and an African village, with thatched roofs capping stone-and-pine huts. A team of enterprising young Aussies recently restored and expanded this place, which was one of Negril's first hotels (the Stones hung out here in the 1970s). The rooms have ceiling fans and fridges. You'll really feel you're in Jamaica when you go to bed in a mosquito-draped four-poster or take a shower in the open air (mercifully, the toilet facilities are inside). One cottage is divided into two studios; other units contain queen-size beds; and four cottages have sleeping lofts with extra-queen-size beds. A quarter mile from the beach, Rockhouse has a ladder down to a cove where you can swim and snorkel; equipment is available for rent. After a refreshing dip in the cliff-side pool, you can dine in the open-sided restaurant pavilion serving spicy local fare three times a day.

Sea Gem Resort. Norman Manley Blvd., Negril, Jamaica, W.I. ☎ **876/957-4318.** Fax 876/957-9765. 22 units. A/C. Winter $62–$97 double; $106 suite. Off-season $48–$77 double; $88 suite. Extra person $12 per night. Rates include continental breakfast. AE, MC, V.

This is one of the newer and more appealing hotels along Negril Beach, with an artfully designed collection of bedrooms and a clientele that has included the ambassadors from both Mexico and Chile. It occupies a long and narrow strip of sandy soil stretched between the coastal road and the beach. Accommodations are within buff-colored, Iberian-inspired, two-story buildings that contain terra-cotta floors, mahogany four-poster beds; lots of mahogany louvers and trim, and rates that—considering the quality of the rooms—are a relative bargain. The suites are especially good value. Part of the appeal of this place derives from the in-house, beachfront restaurant, the Kuyaba. Permeated with the kind of Polynesian whimsy you might have expected in Hawaii, it has the most elaborately engineered setting of any restaurant along Negril's beachfront (see separate recommendation in "Where to Dine").

Thrills. West End (P.O. Box 99, Negril Post Office), Westmoreland, Jamaica, W.I. ☎ **876/957-4390.** Fax 876/957-4153. 25 units. Winter $65 double; $75 triple. Off-season $50 double; $65 triple. MC, V.

Southwest of the center of Negril, on sloping, palm-dotted land that descends toward a rocky beach, this is a simple but well-managed resort. It's set about a half-mile inland from the far-western end of West End Road, inconveniently uphill, way up in "the gush" from the West End's rocky coastline and dining and drinking facilities. It's small and receives lots of England-derived package tours. Its centerpiece is a hexagonal tower set adjacent to a low-slung motel-like complex containing the bedrooms. Each room is simply decorated with white walls, island-made mahogany furniture and louvered doors, and tiled floors. A few contain air-conditioning and TV. An in-house restaurant serves international cuisine.

Beach lovers negotiate a 10-minute drive (or a 20-minute walk) eastward to the famous sands of Negril's legendary beach, and Thrills also provides shuttle service. Snorkelers, however, find ample opportunities for pursuing their favorite sport off the low cliffs and caves along the coast. The resort has its own tennis courts and swimming pool, and a wide choice of dive shops and water-sports facilities is nearby.

Xtabi. West End Rd., Negril, Jamaica, W.I. ☎ **876/957-4336.** Fax 876/957-0827. www.xtabi-negril.com. E-mail: xtabiresort@cwjamaica.com. 24 units. Winter $55–$65 double; $160 seafront cottage for 2. Off-season $45–$55 double; $110 seafront cottage for 2. Extra person $8–$12 each. MC, V.

The land that's owned by this resort is bisected by West End Road in a way that places the simpler, less-expensive units on the landward side, and the larger, more-glamorous units (in this case, cottages) near the establishment's bar and restaurant, on a cliff above the sea. Units on the landward side have air-conditioning and efficient, unpretentious layouts and furnishings. Those near the sea don't have air-conditioning but are larger and benefit from more-direct access to ocean breezes. If you stay here, don't expect direct access to a sandy beach. Ladders head, somewhat precariously, down to a set of rock-sided inlets where the surf roils around during heavy seas. Safer and easier is a dip in the hotel's pool. Management cites a quintet of caves scattered throughout the property as an additional incentive for staying here. The resort's social center is an octagonal bar area, with a large ocean-fronting patio. Drinks are an ongoing venue at virtually any hour of the day or evening; lunches are simple affairs featuring conch burgers and salads; dinners are more elaborate, with grilled pork chops and filet mignon, lobster thermidor, and conch steaks.

ALL-INCLUSIVE RESORTS

Beaches Negril. Norman Manley Blvd., Negril, Jamaica, W.I. ☎ **800/BEACHES** or 876/957-9270. Fax 876/957-9269. 215 units. A/C TV TEL. All-inclusive rates for 3 nights: Winter $1,070–$1,240 per person double; $1,310–$1,605 per person in a suite. Off-season $1,035–$1,205 per person double; $1,275–$1,555 per person in a suite. AE, MC, V.

One of the newest resorts in Negril was established in 1997 as the family-oriented wing of the Sandals chain, an all-inclusive outfit that remains stoically opposed to allowing children in its other resorts. The resort occupies a highly desirable 20-acre lot studded with palms and sea grapes adjacent to a sandy beach. At Beaches Negril, you can either spend time with your kids or relax on the beach in the knowledge that they're entertained and supervised elsewhere, thanks to a roster of child and teen activities in segregated areas (where adults enter only at their children's specific invitation!). Accommodations are clustered into three individual villages (Savannah, Montpellier, and Santa Cruz), each of which is subdivided into a cluster of cement and wood buildings accented with cedar shingles.

Dining/Diversions: The resort's five separate restaurants include a completely unpretentious Beach Grill, which is reserved for children only, between 5 and 9pm every night, and the most formal of the five, the Seville Room, where the international cuisine and the decor evoke Andalusia. There's live entertainment nightly (usually music from a local reggae band).

Amenities: Services include concierge laundry, a tour desk that will arrange visits to other parts of the island, as well as lessons in tennis, sailing, and scuba diving. Facilities include two tennis courts, two freshwater swimming pools with swim-up bars, three Jacuzzis, a gym/sauna/steam room/health club, and a fine beach. Most water sports (including scuba and sailing) are included in the resort's all-inclusive price.

Couples Negril. Bloody Bay, Negril, Jamaica, W.I. ☎ **800/268-7537** or 876/957-5960. Fax 876/957-5858. www.changes.com/couples/negril/rates.html. E-mail: info@couples.com. 234 units. A/C TV TEL. All-inclusive rates for 3 nights: Winter $1,670–$2,110 double; from $2,510 suite for 2. Off-season $1,620–$1,850 double; from $2,180 suite for 2. AE, DC, MC, V.

If you're *a man and a woman* in love (others, stay away!), you're welcomed at this romantic resort. The formula worked in Ocho Rios (see below), so it was repeated here. A rival of Sandals properties, this love-nest site is the scene of many a wedding or at least a honeymoon. On 18 acres facing crescent-shaped Bloody Bay, it opens onto 1,000 feet of white sandy beach, 5 miles from Negril. This resort caters to those who want back-to-back scheduled activities, ranging from tennis tournaments to fashion shows. Each good-size unit has a view of the bay or of the lush gardens. Furnishings, though standardized, are comfortable, and everything is new. The best doubles are the deluxe beachfront units. All units have balconies or patios, along with king-size beds. No building in the complex is higher than the tallest coconut tree. On the east side of the property, *au naturel* sunbathing is permitted.

Dining/Diversions: The food is good, and you have a choice of three restaurants, including Otaheite, serving a Caribbean fusion cuisine. Mediterranean and continental menus are also served. The breakfast buffet is among the most generous in Negril. There's a resident band nightly and special entertainment planned throughout the week, including Caribbean dinner buffets with music.

Amenities: Glass-bottom-boat trips, gigantic swimming pool with adjacent Jacuzzis, tennis courts, game room, fitness room, basketball court, currency exchange, tour desk, water-sports shop.

✪ **Grand Lido.** Bloody Bay (P.O. Box 88), Negril, Jamaica, W.I. ☎ **800/859-7873** in the U.S., 800/553-4320 in Canada, or 876/957-5010. Fax 876/957-5517. www.superclubs.com. 210 units. A/C MINIBAR TV TEL. All-inclusive rates for 4 days/3 nights: Winter $2,310–$3,126 suite for 2. Off-season $1,860–$2,700 suite for 2. Minimum stay of 4 days/3 nights. AE, MC, V. Children not allowed.

The grandest and most architecturally stylish hotel of its chain, the Grand Lido sits on a flat and lushly landscaped stretch of beachfront adjacent to Hedonism II. It's much more subdued than its neighbor. This is the most upscale and deliciously luxurious of the string of resorts known as Jamaica's SuperClubs. Each spacious suite contains either a patio or a balcony that (except for a few) overlooks the beach. Most units are bilevel, with stereos, king or twin beds (each with a quality mattress and fine linen), and large bathrooms with tub/showers. The elegant hardwood furniture in the rooms was handmade in Jamaica. The smaller of the resort's two beaches is reserved for nudists. If you don't like looking at nude bathers outside your window, ask for a "swimwear-side" unit.

Dining/Diversions: In addition to the cavernous and airy main dining room, a trio of restaurants serves excellent nouvelle, continental, and Italian cuisine. Guests also enjoy an all-night disco, a piano bar, pool tables, and nine bars. Even after the four restaurants close, there are three different dining enclaves that remain open throughout the night.

Amenities: Four tennis courts, two pools, four Jacuzzis, gym/sauna/health club, spa facility, and one of the most glamorous yachts in the West Indies, the *M-Y Zein*, given by Aristotle Onassis to Prince Rainier and Princess Grace of Monaco as a wedding present. Twenty-four-hour room service, concierge, laundry, free airport transfers.

Hedonism II. Negril Beach Rd. (P.O. Box 25), Negril, Jamaica, W.I. ☎ **800/859-7873** in the U.S. or 876/957-5200. Fax 876/957-4289. E-mail: info@superclubs.com. 280 units. A/C. All-inclusive rates for 4 days/3 nights: Winter $1,450–$1,620 double. Off-season $1,164–$1,512 double. AE, MC, V. Children not accepted.

Devoted to the pursuit of pleasure, Hedonism II packs the works into a one-package deal, including all the drinks and partying anyone could want. There's no tender of any sort, and tipping is not permitted. Of all the members of the SuperClubs chain, this is the most raucous. It's a meat market, deliberately inviting its mainly single guests to go wild for a week. To provide a sense of the ambience, we'll tell you that one manager boasted that the resort holds the record for the most people in a Jacuzzi at once. The rooms are stacked in two-story clusters dotted around a sloping 22-acre site about 2 miles east of the town center. Most of the guests, who must be at least 18 years of age, are Americans. Closed to the general public, this is not a couples-only resort; singles are both accepted and encouraged. The hotel will find you a roommate if you'd like to book on the double-occupancy rate. Accommodations don't have balconies but are very spacious. Each has a king or twin beds, fitted with firm mattresses and fine linen, with mirrors hanging over the beds. Bathrooms have combination tub/showers. On one section of this resort's beach, clothing is optional. It's called the "Nude" section; the other is known as "the Prude." The resort also has a secluded beach on nearby Booby Cay, where guests are taken twice a week for picnics.

A Note on Nudity

Nude bathing is allowed at a number of hotels, clubs, and beaches (especially in Negril), but only where there are signs stating "swimsuits optional." Elsewhere, the law will not even allow topless sunbathing.

Dining/Diversions: There's nightly entertainment, along with a live band, a high-energy disco, and a piano bar. International cuisine, a bit bland, is served in daily buffets. There's also a clothing-optional bar, a prude bar, and a grill.

Amenities: Sailing, snorkeling, water-skiing, scuba diving, windsurfing, glass-bottom boat, clothing-optional Jacuzzi, pool, six tournament-class tennis courts (lit at night), two badminton courts, basketball court, two indoor squash courts, volleyball court, table tennis, Nautilus and free-weight gyms, aerobics, indoor games room, massage, free airport transfers.

Negril Inn. Norman Manley Blvd. (P.O. Box 59), Negril, Jamaica, W.I. ☎ **876/957-4209.** Fax 876/957-4365. 46 units. A/C. Winter $200 double; $180 triple. Off-season $110 double; $90 triple. Rates are per person and all inclusive, including airport transfers. AE, MC, V. Children not accepted in winter.

Located about 3 miles east of the town center in the heart of the Seven Mile Beach stretch, this is one of the smallest all-inclusive resorts in Negril. Because of its size, the atmosphere is much more low-key than what you'll find at its larger competitors, such as Hedonism II. The resort, not confined to couples only, offers very simple but comfortably furnished guest rooms with private balconies, in a series of two-story structures in a garden setting. The helpful staff offers a host of activities, day and night. Included in the package are all meals, all alcoholic drinks (except champagne), and nightly entertainment (including a disco). Meals are consumed in the resort's only restaurant, which serves pretty good food; there are also bars in the disco and beside the pool. Amenities include a range of water sports (windsurfing, water-skiing, scuba diving, snorkeling, hydrosliding, and aqua bikes), two floodlit tennis courts, a Jacuzzi, a piano room, a Universal weight room, and a freshwater pool. Room service (for breakfast only), laundry, round-trip transfers to and from the airport at Montego Bay, and filtered water are also available.

Point Village Resort. Rutland Point (P.O. Box 105), Negril, Jamaica, W.I. ☎ **800/752-6824** or 876/957-5170. Fax 876/752-6824. www.pointvillage.com. E-mail: pt-village@cwjamaica.com. 256 units, 177 of which are available for rentals. A/C TV TEL. Winter $288–$360 double; $356–$430 suite for 2. Off-season $248–$280 double; $278–$310 suite for 2. Rates are all inclusive. AE, MC, V.

This condo complex is especially family-friendly, so couples with children make up a large part of the clientele. It's a cluster of three-story, tile-roofed buildings nestled within the edges of a 14-acre sandy peninsula dotted with sea grapes and salt-resistant shrubs. The only drawback of the beach here is that it's relatively narrow and separated from the broader, longer sands of Negril's Seven Mile Beach by a rocky barrier. You can opt for all-inclusive rates or, if you want to cook some of your meals yourself (all units contain a kitchenette), you can arrange a stay here without the meal plan. Babysitting services and child care are provided without charge every day from 9am to 5pm, after which "childminders" can be arranged for $5 per child per hour. There's a curve-sided swimming pool on the premises, plus a tennis court, an arts-and-crafts pavilion, a kiddie restaurant, a self-service soda fountain, and a billiards room.

Sandals Negril. Norman Manley Blvd., Negril, Jamaica, W.I. ☎ **800/SANDALS** in the U.S. and Canada, or 876/957-5216. Fax 876/957-5338. www.sandals.com. E-mail: sng@cw. jamaica.com. 215 units. A/C TV TEL. All-inclusive rates for 4 days/3 nights: Winter $1,930–$2,520 double; from $2,690 suite. Off-season $1,900–$2,280 double; from $2,410 suite. Minimum stay of 4 days/3 nights. AE, MC, V. Children not accepted.

Sandals Negril is an all-inclusive, couples-only (male-female) resort, which is for wild and raunchy party types—definitely a young, hip crowd—and far more active and freewheeling than the more formal Sandals properties in either Ocho Rios or Montego

Bay. The resort occupies some 13 acres of prime beachfront land a short drive east of Negril's center, on the main highway leading in from Montego Bay. The crowd is usually convivial, informal, and young. The casual, well-furnished rooms have a tropical motif. Recently renovated, they come in a wide range of styles but are generally spacious. The best units open directly on the beach. Honeymooners usually end up in a Jamaican-built four-poster mahogany bed. For a balcony and sea view, you have to pay the top rates.

Dining/Diversions: Rates include all meals; snacks; unlimited drinks, day and night, at one of four bars (including two swim-up pool bars); and nightly entertainment, including theme parties. Coconut Cove is the main dining room, but guests can also eat at one of the specialty rooms, including the Sundowner, offering white-glove service and Jamaican cuisine, with low-calorie health food served beside the beach. Kimono features Japanese cuisine. In the typical Sandals chain style, the food is rather standardized and nearly everything is imported. But there is quite a variety. At least you get quantity.

Amenities: Three freshwater pools, tennis courts (lit at night), scuba diving, snorkeling, Sunfish sailing, windsurfing, canoeing, aerobics classes, glass-bottom boat, fitness center with saunas and Universal exercise equipment. Laundry, massage, airport transfers.

✪ **Swept Away.** Norman Manley Blvd. (P.O. Box 77), Negril, Jamaica, W.I. ☎ **800/ 545-7937** in the U.S. and Canada, or 876/957-4061. Fax 876/957-4060. www.sweptaway. com. E-mail: sweptaway@infochan.com. 134 units. A/C TEL. All-inclusive rates for 3 nights: Winter $1,684–$2,178 per couple. Off-season $1,650–$2,080 per couple. AE, DC, MC, V. Children not accepted.

Another member of the SuperClubs, this is one of the best-equipped hotels in Negril—it's certainly the one most conscious of both sports and relaxation. All inclusive, it caters to male-female couples eager for an ambience with all possible diversions available but absolutely no organized schedule and no pressure to participate if you just want to relax. As a staff member told us (privately, of course), "We get the health and fitness nuts, and Sandals or Hedonism get the sex-crazed." The resort occupies 20 flat and sandy acres, which straddle both sides of the highway leading in from Montego Bay. The accommodations (the hotel defines them as "veranda suites" because of their large balconies) are in 26 two-story villas clustered together and accented with flowering shrubs and vines, a few steps from Seven Mile Beach. Each lovely, airy, and spacious unit has a ceiling fan, a king-size bed, and (unless the vegetation obscures it) sea views. Twenty of the units contain a combination tub/shower, the rest showers only; all have hair dryers.

Dining/Diversions: The resort's social center is its international restaurant, Feathers, which lies inland, across the road from the sea. There's also an informal beachfront restaurant and bar, and four bars scattered throughout the property, including a "veggie bar."

Amenities: Racquetball, squash, and 10 lit tennis courts; fully equipped gym; aerobics; yoga; massage; steam; sauna; whirlpool; billiards; bicycles; beachside pool; scuba diving; windsurfing; reef snorkeling. Room service (for continental breakfast only), laundry, tour desk for arranging visits to other parts of Jamaica, airport transfers.

2 Where to Dine

Although many visitors in Negril dine at their hotels, there are several other atmospheric and intriguing dining possibilities around.

EXPENSIVE

Le Vendôme. In the Charela Inn, Negril Beach. ☎ **876/957-4648.** Reservations recommended for Sat dinner. Continental breakfast $5; English breakfast $10; main courses $20–$30; fixed-price meal $24–$35. MC, V. Daily 7:30am–10pm. JAMAICAN/FRENCH.

This place, some 3¹/₂ miles from the town center, enjoys a good reputation. You don't have to be a hotel guest to sample the cuisine, which owners Daniel and Sylvia Grizzle describe as a "dash of Jamaican spices" with a "pinch of French flair." Dine out on the terra-cotta terrace, where you can enjoy a view of the palm-studded beach. Start off with a homemade pâté or perhaps a vegetable salad, and then follow with baked snapper, duckling à l'orange, or a seafood platter. You may have had better versions of these dishes at other places, of course, but the food is quite satisfying here, and there's rarely an unhappy customer. The wines and champagnes are imported from France.

Rick's Café. Lighthouse Rd. ☎ **876/957-0380.** Reservations accepted for parties of 6 or more. Main courses $12–$28. MC, V. Daily noon–1pm. SEAFOOD/STEAKS.

At sundown, everybody in Negril heads toward the lighthouse along the West End strip to Rick's Café, whether or not they want a meal. Of course, the name was inspired by the old watering hole of Bogie's *Casablanca*. There was a real Rick (Richard Hershman), who first opened this bar back in 1974, but he's long gone. This laid-back cafe was made famous in the '70s as a hippie hangout, and ever since it's attracted the bronzed and the beautiful (and some who want to be). The sunset here is said to be the most glorious in Negril, and after a few fresh-fruit daiquiris (pineapple, banana, or papaya), you'll give no argument. Casual dress is the order of the day, and reggae and rock compose the background music. There are several stateside specialties, including imported steaks along with a complete menu of blackened dishes, Cajun style. You might begin with the smoked-marlin platter. The fish—red snapper, fresh lobster, or grouper—is always fresh. The food is rather standard fare, and expensive for what you get, but that hardly keeps the crowds away. You can also buy plastic bar tokens at the door, which you can use instead of money, à la Club Med.

✪ Rockhouse Restaurant. West End Rd. ☎ **876/957-4373.** Reservations recommended for dinner in high season. Main courses J$350–J$1,000 ($10–$28.50). MC, V. Daily 7am–11pm. INTERNATIONAL.

This is the most architecturally dramatic restaurant, with some of the best food, in Negril. Set on the premises of the previously recommended Rockhouse, it was developed by a team of Australian and Italian entrepreneurs who designed a bridgelike span, equivalent to a railway trestle, high above the surging tides of a rocky inlet on Negril's West End. Come here for a sense of vertigo (if you happen to lean over the railing), flashes of decor you might have expected on the Great Barrier Reef of Australia, and one of the most worldly and international crowds in town. Enjoy a drink or two at the Blue Maho Bar, which was built with glossy tropical hardwoods and coral stone, before your meal. Delectable menu items, which are always supplemented with daily specials, might include a seasonal platter of smoked marlin or an upscale version of Jamaican peppered pork with yams and root vegetables.

MODERATE

✪ Cosmo's Seafood Restaurant & Bar. Norman Manley Blvd. ☎ **876/957-4784.** Main courses $7–$21. AE, MC, V. Daily 9am–10pm. SEAFOOD.

One of the best places to go for local seafood is centered on a Polynesian thatched *bohio* (beach hut) open to the sea and bordering the main beachfront. This is the dining spot of Cosmo Brown, who entertains locals as well as visitors. You can order his famous conch soup, or conch in a number of other ways, including steamed or cur-ried. He's also known for his savory kettle of curried goat, or you might prefer freshly caught seafood or fish, depending on what the catch turned up. It's a rustic establish-ment, and prices are among the most reasonable at the resort.

Da Gino's. In the Hotel Mariposa Hideaway, Norman Manley Blvd. ☎ **876/957-4918.** Reservations recommended. Main courses $13–$15. MC, V. Daily 8am–11pm. ITALIAN.

Centered beneath a quartet of octagonal, open-sided dining pavilions, and separated from Negril's beachfront by a carefully maintained strip of trees, this restaurant attracts a clientele of sophisticated Italians who remember with fondness the legendary *La Dolce Vita* of Fellini. It evolved as the escapist dream of Gino Travaini, the Brescia (Italy)-born owner, who maintains stringent standards of Italian *haute cuisine*. Part of this derives from pastas and bread that are made fresh on the premises every day and an allegiance to the ingredients and culinary techniques you might have expected in a bountiful restaurant near Milan. House specialties include linguine with lobster, filet of beef with peppercorns, various forms of scaloppini, and heaping platters of grilled seafood. Everything tastes better when preceded with a radicchio salad. On the premises are a dozen very simple huts, each octagonal, rustic, and camplike, that rent for between $60 and $80 each, depending on the season, double occupancy. Each has a TV and a very basic kitchenette, but no air-conditioning.

Hungry Lion. West End Rd. ☎ **876/957-4486.** Main courses $8.50–$24. AE, MC, V. Daily 5:30–10:30pm. JAMAICAN/INTERNATIONAL.

Some of the best seafood and vegetarian dishes are found at this laid-back alfresco hangout on the cliffs. Instead of the usual Red Stripe beer, you can visit the juice bar and sample the tropical punches with or without rum. This is a cozy, two-story, green-painted concrete-and-wood building. The first floor has an open-air section with booths inside, but on the second floor it's all windows. Menus change daily, depend-ing on what's available in the local markets. About seven main courses are offered nightly, not only seafood and vegetarian platters, but many tasty chicken dishes as well, even shepherd's pie, pasta primavera, grilled kingfish steak, and pan-fried snap-per. Lobster is prepared in many different ways, and everything is accompanied by rice and peas along with steamed vegetables. The homemade desserts are luscious, espe-cially the pineapple-carrot cake, our favorite.

Margueritaville. Norman Manley Blvd. ☎ **876/957-4467.** Burgers and sandwiches $5.75–$7.75. Main courses $10.50–$22.50. AE, MC, V. Daily 9am–11pm. AMERICAN/ INTERNATIONAL.

Uninhibited, extroverted, and sometimes raunchy, this place combines a bar and restaurant with an entertainment complex whose slogan might as well be "Funky Jamaica goes Disney." Thanks to the loaded buses that pull in as field trips from some of Negril's all-inclusive hotels, it's a destination in its own right. That's partly because of an ambience that keeps people partying (sometimes frenetically) throughout the day and evening, partly because of the dozens of undraped bodies lying on the nearby beach, and partly because there's more to see and do here than at any other restaurant along Norman Manley Boulevard. There's an on-site art gallery, most of whose works are by the very talented American-born artist Geraldine Robbins, and gift shops where you might actually be tempted to buy something. Every evening beginning around 9pm, there's live music performed, usually loudly, on-site, sometimes accompanied by karaoke facilities. Permanently moored a few feet offshore is a pair of Jamaica's largest trampolines, whale-sized floaters that feature high-jumping contests by any partici-pants whose party-colored cocktails haven't affected them yet. Drinks are deceptively potent, each priced at $5.25, and include everybody's favorite, a rum-based Bonanza. Menu items include shrimp and tuna kebabs, southern-fried chicken, Pacific paella, club steaks, and burgers.

INEXPENSIVE

Big Fish Seafood Restaurant and Bar. Whitehall Rd. ☎ **876/957-4642.** Main courses J$160–J$500 ($4.55–$14.25). No credit cards. Daily 8am–11pm. JAMAICAN.

This restaurant is charming, friendly, and well managed, serving heaping portions of fresh fish and meats. It's set within a party-colored wood-sided building that was created in 1990 by the McIntosh family, most of whose members work inside. Fish and lobster are enduring specialties, as well as fish-and-chips derived mostly from snapper or king-fish. Garlic-flavored lobster is enduringly popular, as are tasty oxtail, curried shrimp or shrimp in brown sauce, and an all-vegetarian casserole. Even if you're not hungry, don't overlook the place as a hangout bar, where interest derives from an intriguing collection of pop-culture Jamaican artifacts that range from raunchy to nostalgic.

✪ **Chicken Lavish.** West End Rd. ☎ **876/957-4410.** Main courses $5–$13. MC, V. Daily 10am–10pm. JAMAICAN.

We've found that Chicken Lavish, whose name we love, is the best of the low-budget eateries. Just show up on the doorstep of this place along the West End beach strip, and see what's cooking. Curried goat is a specialty, as is fried fresh fish. The red snapper is caught in local waters. But the big draw is the restaurant's namesake, the chef's special Jamaican chicken. He'll tell you, and you may agree, that it's the best on the island. What to wear here? Dress as you would to clean up your backyard on a hot August day. Ironically, this utterly unpretentious restaurant has achieved something like cult status among the thousands of counterculture travelers who have eaten here since the 1970s, as it has survived longer, with fewer changes, than any other restaurant on Negril's West End. It's almost amazingly consistent, specializing in chicken, chicken, and more chicken that's fried, served with curry, or served with sweet-and-sour sauce. Dine on the roofed-over veranda if you want, or ask for takeout and dine at home.

Choices. West End Rd. ☎ **876/957-4841.** Lunch main courses J$150–J$230 ($4.30–$6.55). Dinner main courses J$250–J$800 ($7.15–$22.80). No credit cards. Daily 7am–11pm. JAMAICAN.

This no-frills open-air restaurant offers local food in a bustling atmosphere. This is a clapboard-sided roadside hut painted in bright reggae colors of blue, green, and yellow. The inside is totally devoted to the kitchen facilities; customer seating is on plastic tables and chairs beneath an open-air parapet. The food is simple and the portions are hearty. Breakfast includes akee and salt codfish prepared with Jamaican spices, onions, green peppers, and tomatoes. Daily soup specials may include pumpkin or red pea. For a real island experience, try the spicy jerk chicken, fish, or pork. Other dishes might include stewed beef, curried goat, or a dish of oxtail. Most dishes come with salad and your choice of vegetable.

Hunan Garden Chinese Restaurant. In Country, Country, Norman Manley Blvd. ☎ **876/957-4359.** Main courses J$290–J$800 ($8.25–$22.80). MC, V. Daily noon–10pm. HUNAN/CHINESE.

Well known for its authentic Chinese cuisine, this garden restaurant provides a welcome relief from too constant a diet of spicy Jamaican fare. In a previously recommended resort, the restaurant is the best bet for Asian cookery in Negril. It may not match the finest of your Chinese restaurants back home, but it offers decent food at a

Miss Brown's World-Famous Mushroom Tea

No other resort in the Caribbean was as richly associated with ganja and psyche-delic mushrooms as Negril during the 1960s and 1970s. Within a context partly derived from Bob Marley's music, free love, and counterculture partying arose one of the era's most memorable cult figures, Miss Brown (a.k.a. Kathleen Godfrey). Solidly matriarchal and churchgoing and born in St. James Parish "sometime in the 1930s," she began her career running a West Indian restaurant that specialized in steamed fish, curried conch and goat, and jerk chicken. As an added "kicker," her menus included home-brewed pots of a hot drink created from a potent blend of local mushrooms. The very brave (or the very reckless) sometimes combined this with a wholesome-looking chunk of Miss Brown's special brownies. Eventually, her battered premises evolved into the most famous countercultural gathering place in Negril, something akin to a Rastafarian version of a Viennese teahouse where some or all of the guests might have been hallucinating.

Within new quarters set beside Whitehall Road leading south from the center of Negril, Miss Brown continues to dispense her tea and brownies with pride to anyone who stops, as part of an amused defiance of most interpretations of Jamaican law. A brimming cup of tea costs from $10 to $15, based on its strength; brownies that include a whopping dose of baked-in ganja go for $10 each. Between December and May, there's even a half-hearted stab at running the place as a conventional restaurant, wherein full West Indian dinners are priced at J$250 to J$600 ($7.15 to $17.10) each. If you opt to experiment, à la Timothy Leary, with the effects of Miss Brown's recreational desserts, be very alert to their horrendously potent effects, and the heat of the baking process is believed to increase their effects exponentially. For a first-hand reminder of Negril during the heyday of its hippie era, head for the clearly signposted Miss Brown's, Whitehall Road (☎ 876/957-3274), about a half-mile south of the center of town.

Warning: Note that these writers, and this guidebook, in no way advocate the consumption of any illegal or mind-altering substances, and strongly discourage the actual consumption of any of the substances described above. We are merely reporting on a much-patronized local phenomenon that is unique in the Caribbean.

good value in tasty combinations. Begin with the fried spring roll or a combination of barbecued meats, perhaps fish maw and chicken soup, before venturing into the wide selection of chicken, duck, fish, shrimp, lobster, beef, or pork dishes. Our favorite dishes include spicy salt and chili shrimp or honey-roasted chicken. The beef in a satay sauce is equally tasty, as are the pork and yams in a hot pot. A large selection of chow mein dishes is also offered, along with various chop sueys. You'll also be tempted by a dozen fried-rice dishes.

Juicy J's. Negril Square (behind Scotia Bank). ☎ **876/957-4213.** Breakfast platters J$100–J$190 ($2.85–$5.40). Main lunch and dinner courses J$190–J$500 ($5.40–$14.25). No credit cards. Daily 7am–11pm. JAMAICAN.

Despite its funky name and the raffish-looking West Indian house that contains it, this is actually a bastion of solid bourgeois life, as exemplified by Joyce Lindsay, the owner, and her soft-spoken sister Stella, the manager. The more you look at this place, the more you'll probably like it, especially at breakfast, when akee and salt fish or fish stewed in brown sauce and served with plantains are fine, thoughtfully prepared examples of what most Jamaicans consider standard morning fare. To acclimate yourself to the setting, head past the mismatched chairs and tables of the front rooms to the pinewood bar in back, meet the staff, and have a glass of fruit punch, coffee, beer, rum, or whatever. Then, select from a list of good-tasting food that includes grilled, steamed, or (our favorite) escoveitch of fish; four different preparations of chicken, including a version with curry; lasagna; or lobster. The venue is fun and surprisingly conservative, and with a name like Juicy J's, who can possibly not crack a smile?

Kuyaba. In the Sea Gem Resort, Norman Manley Blvd. ☎ **876/957-4318.** Burgers, sandwiches, and salads $5.75–$7.95. Main courses $10.95–$19.95. AE, MC, V. Daily 7am–11pm. INTERNATIONAL.

The engineers who created the dark-stained interconnected decks, gazebos, and pavilions at this restaurant succeeded more extravagantly than those at any other restaurant along Negril Beach. The result is elaborate and stylish—Polynesian in its feeling and a radical departure from the lean-to shanties that are the home of some nearby competitors. Of particular interest is the bar that's nestled beneath a soaring teepee-shaped roof fashioned from rough-textured branches and thatch. The best way to begin a meal here is with such evocatively labeled drinks as a Burning Spear (crème de cacao, Blue Curaçao, and Jamaican rum), priced at $4.95. After that, coconut-curried conch is particularly delicious, as is the blackened snapper and curried chicken.

Pete's. Norman Manley Blvd. ☎ **876/957-3454.** Set-price meals J$200–J$600 ($5.70–$17.10). No credit cards. Daily 9am–11pm. JAMAICAN/SEAFOOD.

Veteran chef Pete Myrie, an intuitive, long-surviving kitchen master whose charm derives from his utter lack of pretension, provides one of the least-formal dining experiences on Negril Beach. Myrie operates from the premises of a cement-floored, lattice-ringed pavilion that has survived recent hurricanes mostly because of its bareboned simplicity. Since it was established in 1991, it has attracted many Europeans, especially Italians, on the lookout for very fresh seafood, especially lobster, prepared with finesse but without artifice. Menu items in this rustic but charming place that have drawn justifiable praise include lobster in garlic and butter sauce, steamed fish (especially snapper), lobster-fried rice, and jerk chicken. The place is hard to find; as you're driving along Norman Manley Boulevard, park near the sign pointing to Merril's, then walk toward the beach. The best way to arrange a meal here involves stopping off during the day, meeting Pete or a member of his staff, and agreeing on a menu and a rendezvous time for the debut of your meal.

Pe-Wees. West End Rd. ☎ **876/957-0111.** Breakfast J$180–J$200 ($5.15–$5.70). Main courses J$300–J$550 ($8.55–$15.70). No credit cards. Daily 8am–2pm and 5–11pm. Closed intermittently Apr–Dec. JAMAICAN.

This is a cheap, cheerful, and very Jamaican enclave of simple but good food and stiff drinks. The setting is an angular concrete structure almost adjacent to the Blue Cave Castle, which, since it doesn't have a restaurant of its own, often directs its clients here. Don't even think of coming here for lunch (it's closed); during the summertime, its hours are laid-back, erratic, and unreliable. In winter, though, it's a good bet for such solid, oft-repeated food as chicken with rice, burgers, grilled chicken, escoveitch of fish, and pork chops. In winter, the bar is open daily from 8am to 11pm.

The Pickled Parrot. West End Rd. ☎ **876/957-4864.** Main courses $5.95–$22.95. AE, MC, V. Daily 9am–midnight. MEXICAN/JAMAICAN/AMERICAN.

With a name like The Pickled Parrot, you know you're heading for a night of fun. It doesn't live up to the riotous times at Rick's, but it's a serious rival for the sundowner market. The restaurant stands at the edge of a cliff and is open to the trade winds. There's a rope swing and a water slide outside to indulge your inner child. The cook claims he serves the best lobster fajitas in town. You can also order the usual array of stateside burgers, sandwiches, and freshly made salads at lunch. Actually, you can order the full dinner menu at lunch if you so desire. They prepare a predictable array of burritos, nachos, and even Mexican pizza (we prefer Italian). You might also be tempted by the fresh fish, lobster (or shrimp) Jamaican style, and the famous jerk chicken.

Restaurant Tan-Ya's/Calico Jack's. In the Sea Splash Resort, Norman Manley Blvd. ☎ **876/957-4041.** Reservations recommended. Main courses $10–$23; breakfast from $6, lunch from $6. AE, MC, V. Daily 11am–3pm and 6:30–10pm. JAMAICAN/INTERNATIONAL.

Set within the thick white walls of a previously recommended resort, these two restaurants provide well-prepared food and the charm of a small, family-run resort. Informal and very affordable lunchtime food is served at Calico Jack's, whose tables are in an enlarged gazebo, near a bar and the resort's swimming pool. The resort's gastronomic showcase, however, is Tan-Ya's. Here, specialties include lemon-flavored shrimp, Tan-Ya's snapper with herb butter, three different preparations of lobster, smoked Jamaican lobster with a fruit salsa, and deviled crab backs sautéed in butter. On many nights, these dishes are filled with flavor and well prepared; on some occasions, they're slightly off the mark.

Sweet Spice. 1 White Hall Rd. ☎ **876/957-4621.** Reservations not accepted. Main courses J$170–J$600 ($4.85–$17.10). MC, V. Daily 8:30am–11pm. JAMAICAN.

This is everybody's favorite mom-and-pop eatery, a real local hangout beloved by locals as well as scantily clad visitors to Negril. It's set beside the road leading south out of Negril, within a clapboard-sided house that seems to grow bigger each year, and which is painted an electric shade of blue. Food is simple, cheap, and bountiful, served amid a decor of plastic tablecloths, tile floors, and windows covered with louvers and screens, but without glass. The Whytes welcome guests warmly and serve them in an alfresco setting. The portions are large and most satisfying, and the cookery is home-style. Bring Grandma, Mom and Dad, and all the kids, as many Jamaican families do. You get what's on the stove or in the kettle that night—perhaps the fresh catch of the day or a conch steak. The grilled chicken is done to perfection, and shrimp is steamed and served with garlic butter or cooked in coconut cream. A number of curry dishes tempt, including concoctions made with goat, lobster, and chicken. Meals come with freshly cooked Jamaica-grown vegetables. The fruit juices served here (in lieu of alcoholic beverages) are truly refreshing, and the menu is the same at lunch and dinner.

3 Hitting the Beach & Other Outdoor Pursuits

HITTING THE BEACH

Beloved by the hippies of the 1960s, ✪ **Seven Mile Beach** is still going strong, but it's no longer the idyllic retreat it once was. Resorts now line this beach, attracting an international crowd. Nudity, however, is just as prevalent, especially along the stretch near Cosmo's (see "Where to Dine," above). The beach promotes a laid-back lifestyle and carefree ambience more than any other on Jamaica, perhaps even in the Caribbean. On the western tip of the island, the white powdery sand stretches from Bloody Bay in Hanover to Negril Lighthouse in Westmoreland; clean, tranquil aquamarine waters, coral reefs, and a backdrop of palm trees add to the appeal. When you tire of the beach, you'll find all sorts of resorts, clubs, beach bars, open-air restaurants, and the like. Vendors will try to sell you everything from Red Stripe beer to ganja.

Many of the big resorts have nude beaches as well. The hottest and most exotic is found at **Hedonism II,** although **Grand Lido** next door draws its fair share. Nude beaches at each of these resorts are in separate and "private" areas of the resort property. Total nudity is required for strolling the beach, and security guards keep Peeping Toms at bay. Photography is not permitted. Most of the resorts also have a nude bar, a nude hot tub, and a nude swimming pool.

SCUBA DIVING & SNORKELING

Negril has the best and most challenging scuba life in Jamaica. Unusual dive sites within an easy boat ride of Negril include **Shallow Plane,** the site of a Cessna aircraft that crashed in 50 feet of water; an underwater cave, called **Throne Room,** which allows divers to enter at one end and ascend into the open air at the other; and two separate sites, each about 66 feet underwater, known as **Shark's Reef** and **Snapper Drop.** Each of these is loaded with flora and fauna whose species change as the elevation changes.

The **Negril Scuba Centre,** in the Negril Beach Club Hotel, Norman Manley Boulevard (☎ 800/818-2963 or 876/957-9641), is the most modern, best-equipped scuba facility in Negril. A professional staff of internationally certified scuba instructors and dive masters teaches and guides divers to Negril's colorful coral reefs. Beginner's dive lessons are offered daily, as well as multiple-dive packages for certified divers. Full scuba certifications and specialty courses are also available.

A resort course, designed for first-time divers with basic swimming abilities, costs $75 and includes all instruction, equipment, a lecture on water and diving safety, and one open-water dive. It begins at 10am daily and ends at 2pm. A one-tank dive costs $30 per dive plus $20 for equipment rental (not necessary if divers bring their own gear). More economical is a two-tank dive, which must be completed in one day. It costs $55, plus the (optional) $20 rental of all equipment. This organization is PADI-registered, although it accepts all recognized certification cards.

Another excellent facility is **Marine Life Divers** at the Drumville Cove Hotel (☎ 876/957-4834). A PADI resort course costs $65, with an open-water certification going for $300. A one-tank dive costs $35.

Water-sports equipment is most easily available at any of at least seven interassociated kiosks that operate at strategic intervals along the sun-flooded beige sands. Each of the informal-looking outlets is operated under the umbrella of **Seatec Water Sports,** Norman Manley Boulevard (☎ 876/957-4401). The staff at each of the kiosks charges roughly the same rates, and in many cases, each has access to the same equipment. Rates for these diversions are as follows: Jet skis cost $35 for a 30-minute ride; snorkeling equipment is $15 per person for a 90-minute excursion by boat to an offshore reef; banana-boat rides are $15 for a 20-minute high-speed, rough-bouncing ride; parasailing is $25 for a 12-minute ride; and water-skiing is $25 for a 15-minute tow-around.

The best area for snorkeling is off the cliffs in the West End. The coral reef here is extremely lively with marine life at a depth of about 10 to 15 feet. The waters are so clear and sparkling that just by wading in and looking down, you'll see lots of marine life. The fish are small but extremely colorful.

GOLF

Negril Hills Golf Course, Sheffield Road (☎ 876/957-4638), is Negril's only golf course. It opened in 1994 on the rolling and arid countryside south of Negril. Although it doesn't begin to have the cachet or allure of such Montego Bay courses as

Tryall, it's the only golf course in western Jamaica, with a par of 72. Greens fees for 18 holes are $57.50, and club rentals go for $18. Carts and caddies, which are not obligatory, cost $34.50 and $14, respectively. Anyone can play, but advance reservations are recommended.

BIKE TOURS

Rusty's X-cellent Adventures, Hilton Avenue, P.O. Box 104 (☎ **876/957-0155**), choreographs some of Jamaica's most hair-raising and best-conceived bike tours. The outfit was founded by Ohio-born Rusty Jones. Tours begin and end at his house, on a side road (Hilton Avenue) just west of Negril's lighthouse. He's the region's expert on the dozens of relatively dry—i.e., nonmuddy—single-track goat and cow paths that provide aerobic exercise and drama for all levels of bike riders. Tours last between 3 and 4 hours, cost from $35 to $40 per person, and never include more than four riders at a time. Riders are exposed to such sites as "the Bat Caves," a huge, relatively dry cave whose 50-foot-high ceilings allow riders and their bikes inside, and visits to a pristine bay not accessible by conventional cars (Little Bay). Tours are primarily geared to "hard-core mountain bikers," even though there are ample opportunities for newcomers to the sport as well. There's a running commentary on cultural and horticultural diversions en route. Bikes, helmets, water canteens, and accessories are included in the price as part of the experience. Advance reservations are essential.

4 Negril After Dark

Evenings in Negril really begin before dark, when everyone heads to Rick's Café for sundowner cocktails or a few Red Stripes (see "Where to Dine," above).

All the resorts have bars. Most offer evening entertainment for their guests, and some welcome nonguests as well.

Alfred's (☎ **876/957-4735**) is a neat Jamaican experience where travelers will still feel welcome. There's no cover, and in addition to grabbing a drink, you can also order a bite to eat until midnight. Particularly interesting is the beach-party area, with a stage for live reggae and jazz acts. You can also boogie on the dance floor inside, shaking to hits you'll hear at clubs stateside.

De Buss, found on Norman Manley Boulevard (☎ **876/957-4405**), is probably the most popular and versatile hangout on Negril Beach and is large enough to accommodate everything from major reggae concerts to simple rums and cola on the beach. It was named after the rusted, crummy looking carcass of a double-decker bus, a long-ago part of Kingston's mass-transit system, that was hauled to this site in the 1960s. Nearby is an imposing-looking courtyard area flanked with a stage that was bashed together from 2 × 4s and plywood, and brightly painted in Rastafarian colors, where live bands perform every Thursday and Saturday in the off-season, and virtually every night in winter. Throughout the year, you can buy heaping platters of jerk chicken with French fries, at between J$220 and J$250 ($6.25 to $7.15). In high season, more substantial platters, priced at J$130 to J$500 ($3.70 to $14.25) are also available. Naturally, the rum and beer flow freely throughout the day and night. It's open daily from 9am to at least 11pm and during show nights till at least 1:30am.

Risky Business, Norman Manley Boulevard (☎ **876/957-3008**), sits a few feet from the waves of Negril Beach on a cement slab that's the base for a high, hip-shaped roof and a battered-looking bar. It can be sleepy or manic depending on whatever music is playing. In midwinter, there's a greater emphasis on food service, when burgers and sandwiches are the norm, than at any other time of the year, when the larder might be bare. Basically, it's a hangout whose traditional party nights are Monday, Thursday, and Saturday beginning at 9pm. Red Stripe costs J$100 ($2.85) a bottle; otherwise, there's no cover, even when the place is rocking and rolling.

Action is also lively at the **Sea Splash Resort,** on Norman Manley Boulevard (☎ **876/957-4041**), whose bar is located amid allamander vines, midway between a swimming pool and the edge of the sea. Sheltered from the sun with a teepee-shaped roof of palm leaves and thatch, it offers a tempting array of tropical drinks. These include such foamy concoctions as Calico Jack's rum punch or a white sands, either of which costs from $3. The bar is open daily from 8am to 11pm.

Mandeville & the South Coast

5

While Negril (see chapter 4) gets the crowds, the **South Coast** of Jamaica has only recently begun to attract large numbers of visitors. The Arawak once lived in sylvan simplicity along these shores before their civilization was destroyed. Early Spanish settlers came here searching for gold; today's traveler comes looking for the untrammeled sands of its secluded beaches. Fishers still sell their catch at colorful local markets, and the prices, as they say here, are "the way they used to be" in Jamaica.

Most visitors to the south head east from Negril through Savanna-la-Mar to the high-country, English-style town of **Mandeville,** then on to a boat tour up the Black River, home of freshwater crocodiles. Those with more time continue southeast along the coast to Treasure Beach before going on to Mandeville. On the South Coast, the best center for overnighting is either the town of Black River or the village of Treasure Beach.

Mandeville, about midway between Negril and Kingston, perches 2,000 feet above sea level in the interior of the island. A large North American contingent employed in the bauxite industry lives here. Although dating from 1814, Mandeville was developed in the late 19th century as a retreat for English visitors attracted to the town's pleasant climate. The temperature in summer averages 70°F, and in winter, a comfortably cool 60°F, which also helped make Mandeville the center of the Jamaican coffee industry during an earlier era. Fortunes were also made in pimento (allspice). The town contains the oldest golf course on Jamaica, and one of its major attractions is Marshall's Pen, an 18th-century great house on a 300-acre cattle farm.

Partly because of its Victorian gingerbread architecture, Mandeville has been called the most English town in Jamaica. Today, it accepts its role as the sleepiest of the larger Jamaican cities—which contributes significantly to its charm.

1 The South Coast

Think of this as undiscovered Jamaica. The arid South Coast is just beginning to attract more visitors every year; they're drawn by Jamaica's sunniest climate. Columbus discovered the Arawak living here when he circumnavigated Jamaica in 1494. When not repelling French pirates, five generations of Spaniards raised cattle on ranches on the broad savannas of St. Elizabeth.

Local adventures are plentiful on the South Coast. Among the most popular is South Coast Safaris' boat tour up the Black River, once a major logging conduit and still home to freshwater crocodiles. Another favorite is the trip to the Y. S. Falls, where seven spectacular cascades tumble over rocks in the foothills of the Santa Cruz Mountains, just north of the town of Middle Quarters, famed for its spicy, freshwater shrimp.

EXPLORING THE AREA

To reach the South Coast, head east from Negril, following the signposts to Savanna-la-Mar. This is known as Sheffield Road, and the highway isn't particularly good until it broadens into the A2 at Savanna. After passing through the village of **Bluefields,** continue southeast to the small town of **Black River,** which opens onto Black River Bay.

After leaving Black River, where you can find hotels and restaurants (see "Where to Stay," below), you can continue north along A2 to Mandeville or else go directly southeast to Treasure Beach. The A2 north takes you to **Middle Quarters,** a village on the plains of the Great Morass, through which the Black River runs. Day visitors often stop here and order a local delicacy, pepper shrimp.

Just north of the town of Middle Quarters is **Y. S. Falls,** where seven waterfalls form crystal pools. Guests take a jitney and go through grazing lands and a horse paddock on the way to the falls, where they cool off in the waters and often enjoy a picnic lunch. After Middle Quarters, the road cuts east toward Mandeville along **Bamboo Avenue,** a scenic drive along 2 miles of highway covered with bamboo. Here, you will see a working plantation, the **Holland Estate,** growing sugarcane, citrus, papaya, and mango.

If you've decided to take the southern coast route to **Treasure Beach,** follow the signs to Treasure Beach directly southeast of Black River. The treasures here are seashells in many shapes and sizes, making for a beachcomber's paradise. Swimming here is tricky because of the undertow, and the sand is gray, but it's secluded and comfortable, and dramatic waves crash onto the shore. This is the site of the Treasure Beach Hotel (see "Where to Stay," below).

To the east of Treasure Beach is **Lovers' Leap,** Smithfield, Yardley Chase (☎ **876/ 965-6634**), the most dramatic and widely publicized attraction along Jamaica's South Coast. It commemorates the story of two runaway slaves, Nizzy (a woman) and Tunkey (a man), who jointly leapt to their deaths rather than be separated and returned to captivity. During the 1990s, beneath a hip-shaped, colonial-inspired roof, the Jamaican government erected an observation deck, a meeting space, and a cafeteria at the site of the famous double suicide, at the top of a 1,600-foot cliff, one of the steepest along the South Coast. If you're adventurous, you can follow a rocky and meandering footpath down to the sea, even though most visitors opt just to enjoy the view that sweeps out over the coastline from the open-air platform. Open Monday to Thursday from 9am to 6pm, and Friday to Sunday from 9am to 7pm, it charges J$105 ($3) for a view of the site, its lighthouse, and its panorama.

The longest stream in Jamaica, the **Black River** has mangrove trees, crocodiles, and the insectivorous bladderwort, plus hundreds of species of birds. You can indeed go on a safari to this wilderness. The best tours are operated by **South Coast Safaris,** Hotel Street in Mandeville (☎ **876/965-2513** for reservations). The cost is $15, and children under 12 go for half price. Tours last 1 hour and 30 minutes and cover 12 miles (6 miles upstream, 5 miles back). Daily tours are at 9am, 11am, 12:30pm, 2pm, and 4pm. Children under 3 go free.

WHERE TO STAY

Invercauld Great House & Hotel. High St. (on the harborfront, a few blocks west of Black River's commercial center), Black River, St. Elizabeth, Jamaica, W.I. ☎ **876/965-2750.** Fax 876/965-2751. 48 units. A/C TV TEL. $78–$84 double, $92–$102 suite. AE, MC, V.

In 1889, when Black River's port was one of the most important in Jamaica, a Scottish merchant imported most of the materials for the construction of this white-sided manor house. Today, the renovated and much-enlarged house functions as a hotel. Only a handful of rooms are within the original high-ceilinged house; most lie within a cement outbuilding that was added in 1991. Rooms are clean, stripped down, and simple, usually with mahogany furniture made by local craftspeople. Gradually, the hotel has added five small houses filled with suites; these come with either a king-size bed or twin beds, and the units also have a fold-out couch and are air-conditioned, with cable TV and phone, plus either a patio or veranda. On the premises are a cement patio and a swimming pool, Jacuzzi, a tennis court, and a conservative restaurant with white tiles and white walls. It's open daily for breakfast, lunch, and dinner.

Irie Sandz Hotel. 67 Crane Rd., Black River, St. Elizabeth, Jamaica, W.I. ☎ **876/966-4844.** Fax 876/965-2466. 10 units. TV. $40–$50 double. MC, V.

Owned by a local doctor, Oliver Myers, and operated by a well-intentioned resident staff, this simple hotel lies on its own beachfront about 1.25 miles south of Black River's commercial core, and about a mile from the banks of the town's namesake, the Black River. Be duly warned: The place is about as Rastafarian as any hotel can possibly be on the South Coast, so if that's not your thing, check in elsewhere. Originally built in the late 1980s, and under present management since 1997, the accommodations are simple and completely unpretentious, with views overlooking the sands. Each has either ceiling or standing fans (or both), and about half have air conditioners. You shouldn't expect luxury—but at these prices, it's still a bargain. There's a bar and a low-key restaurant on the premises. Service is slow, but the staff can arrange 2-hour boat tours (through Jacana Aqua-Tours, the hotel's sibling company) on the nearby river for a fee of $25 per person.

✪ Jake's. Calabash Bay, Treasure Beach, St. Elizabeth, Jamaica, W.I. ☎ **800/OUTPOST** or 877/JAMAIC8 in the U.S. or 876/965-0635. Fax 876/965-0552. 10 units. $75–$95 double; $150–$195 suite, plus 20% service and taxes. AE, MC, V.

This is one of the most eccentric hotels in Jamaica, and if you're the kind of adventurer who appreciates a place that's most definitely *not* the Holiday Inn, you might absolutely adore it. It manages to be memorable, irritating, and delightful at the same time. Perched on a cliffside overlooking the ocean and set within a labyrinth of badly marked roads, adjacent to a rocky beach that benefits from the occasional dumping of truckloads of sand, Jake's is a special haven. It occupies a series of earth-colored Casbah-style buildings, each individually decorated and exploding with colors, everything from funky purple to Pompeiian terra-cotta; each contains mosquito netting, flickering candles, and a CD player with a very hip collection.

The venue was inspired by Sally Henzell, a Jamaican of British ancestry who's married to Perry Henzell, director/producer of *The Harder They Come,* a classic reggae film. Most of the day-to-day operations are skillfully handled by her son, Jason. Sally cites the controversial Catalán architect Antoni Gaudí as her mentor in the creation of Jake's—especially in the generous use of cracked mosaic tile so familiar to Barcelona devotees. Be warned: Except for one unit, where there wasn't any cross-ventilation, there's no air-conditioning and days are hot here in the "desert." Likewise, as a means of avoiding infestations of flying insects, lighting is kept deliberately dim.

There's a raffish-looking bar that attracts guests and well-meaning locals, an amoeba-shaped pool, and a barrage of fishers and drivers who'll familiarize you with local activities and tours. The hotel restaurant is separately recommended in "Where to Dine." This is, incidentally, the only member of the Island Outposts hotel group not owned fully by music-industry mogul Chris Blackwell, and so it carries an extra dose of funkiness that's much, much stronger than that associated with other members of its chain.

Sunset Resort Hotel. Calabash Bay, Treasure Beach, St. Elizabeth, Jamaica, W.I. ☎ **876/ 965-0143.** For reservations, contact South Enterprises, 2875 South Main St., Salt Lake City, Utah 84115. ☎ 800/786-8452 or fax 801/487-2749. www.bizcom.com/sunsetresort. 12 units. A/C TV TEL. $75–$110 double, $140 1-bedroom suite for 2, $225–$230 2-or 3-bedroom suite, with kitchen, for between 2–6 occupants. MC, V.

On a masonry terrace above the seacoast, a short walk from the moored fishing boats of Calabash Bay, this hotel doesn't have the international cachet or the sense of fun of nearby Jake's. Nor does it have the association with the heady worlds of rock music and international media attention. But for an older and more conservative clientele who shuns the idea of a radically offbeat holiday, it's a solid alternative. Built in stages beginning in the late 1970s, Sunset Resort might remind you of an enlarged version of a 19th-century sea captain's house, thanks to a two-story central core and a horseshoe-shaped pair of symmetrical wings that enclose a pool. (Regrettably, for several months prior to our visit, the pool wasn't filled with water.) The bedrooms, however, are larger than those at Jake's, but with none of their decorative, sometimes wild, flair. Each has noncontroversial low-slung furnishings, some made with New England–style knottypine, that evoke a modern version of a mariner's inn in Rhode Island but with none of the decorative flair. Frankly, this place might be more calm and quiet than you might want. But despite that, it has developed a loyal clientele, many from rural areas of the U.S. mainland, who tend to praise the place highly and in some cases, return for repeat visits. There's a restaurant (The Red Lobster) on-site that's sometimes used for meetings of the area's civic and philanthropic groups, plus a bar.

Treasure Beach Hotel. Treasure Beach, Black River, St. Elizabeth, Jamaica, W.I. ☎ **876/ 965-0110.** Fax 876/965-2544. www.treasurebeachjamaica.com. E-mail: treasurebhotel@ cwjamaica.com. 36 units. A/C TV TEL. Winter $110–$143 double. Off-season $99–$113 double. AE, MC, V.

Set on a steep but lushly landscaped hillside above a sandy beach with an active surf, this white-sided hotel was built in the mid-1970s, 1¹/₂ miles west of Pedro Cross. Although its staff is young and inexperienced, this is the largest and most elaborate hotel on Jamaica's South Coast. Its centerpiece is a long and airy rattan-furnished bar whose windows look down the hillside to the beach and the hotel's 11 acres that flank it. Bedrooms lie within a series of outlying cottages, each of which contains between two and six accommodations. Each unit has a ceiling fan and veranda or patio, and in some cases a TV. Amenities include two freshwater pools, a loosely organized array of such activities as volleyball and horseshoes, and a simple restaurant with slow and casual service that's open for lunch and dinner.

WHERE TO DINE

Bridge House Inn. 14 Crane Rd. (on the eastern outskirts of Black River, on the opposite side of the town's only bridge from the commercial center), Black River. ☎ **876/965-2361.** Full meals $15–$30. MC, V. Daily 6am–11:30pm. JAMAICAN.

This is the simple and very Jamaican restaurant that is contained within one of the town's two hotels. The cement-sided structure that houses it was built in the early

1980s; it's done with a beachfront motif and set within a grove of coconut palms and sea grapes. On the premises are 13 bedrooms, each with air-conditioning, a ceiling fan, and simple furniture, but no TV and no telephone. Most clients appreciate this place, however, for its restaurant. Patrons include a cross section of the region, including the occasional conference of librarians or nurses. Menu items—everything is home style—include complete dinners (fish, chicken, curried goat, oxtail, stewed beef, or lobster) with soup and vegetables, served politely and efficiently by a staff of hardworking waiters. A separate bar area off to the side dispenses drinks.

✪ **Culloden Café.** Whitehouse. ☎ **876/963-5344.** Reservations recommended. Main courses J$250–J$350 ($7.15–$10). 3-course set-price meal J$500 ($14.25). AE, MC, V. Wed–Mon noon–9pm. INTERNATIONAL.

Set beside the coastal road stretching between Bluefields and Whitehouse, this restaurant is housed within an aristocratic-looking pink-sided villa that originally functioned as the childhood home of its owners and chef. The cozy and artfully minimalist interior opens to reveal a view of a formal garden, and putting-green lawns that sweep down to the edge of the sea in vistas that evoke a tropical view of the English countryside. The owners include Ann Lyons, a former editor at a New York City publishing house, and her British-born husband, John Belcher. Together, they direct a polite and well-rehearsed staff that prepares flavorful food that's considerably broader in its scope, and more sophisticated, than anything else in the immediate neighborhood. Menu items include locally caught fish that might be blackened in the New Orleans style; escoveitch of fish (a whole fish served in a peppery vinegar sauce); Mexican-style quesadillas stuffed with guacamole; and curried banana soup. Dessert might include key-lime cake or a frothy version of Pavlova—mixed fruit served with whipped cream in a meringue shell.

✪ **Jake's.** Calabash Bay, Treasure Beach, St. Elizabeth. ☎ **876/965-0552.** Reservations recommended for dinner only Dec–Apr. Main courses J$200–J$680 ($5.70–$19.40). AE, MC, V. Daily 12:30–4pm and 6:30–9:30pm. JAMAICAN/INTERNATIONAL.

Even if the sheer eccentricity of Jake's prevents you from an overnight here, you should absolutely and positively descend upon its premises for a meal during your stay on the South Coast. Part of its allure stems from its raffish charm and unpredictability—you never know who might show up to divert and entertain you during a meal. Likely candidates include everyone from Kingston's most prominent and controversial doctors to loquacious local philosophers who will predict your future through a rum-induced haze. Jake's offers two distinctly different dining areas that include a romantic but secluded covered veranda in back, and a much, much more sociable front porch where tables are hand-painted in psychedelic patterns inspired by the 1960s, and where you might see or hear just about anything. Menu items are announced on a chalkboard and might include pumpkin, red bean, or pepper-pot soup; fish tea (a clear broth checkered with herbs); and conch, callaloo or codfish fritters. More substantial fare includes plantain chips or carrot strips served with smoked marlin dip; a marvelous steamed fish in coconut-flavored cream sauce; tender pepper steak; and a revolving array of spicy jerk chicken, beef, pork, and fish.

Tiffany's. Calabash Bay, Treasure Beach. ☎ **876/965-0300.** Reservations recommended. Main courses J$195–J$600 ($5.55–$17.10). AE, DC, MC, V. Daily noon–10pm. Rooftop bar remains open till 2am. JAMAICAN/AMERICAN.

Carmen Sutherland is the hardworking founder of this pleasant and unpretentious restaurant, which sits beside the main street of the scattered community of Treasure Beach, a 2-minute walk from the also-recommended Jake's. Established in 1993, it occupies the premises of a colonial-inspired concrete building whose simple interior is painted in pale tones of blue and pink. Named after one of the owner's favorite books and films (Capote's *Breakfast at Tiffany's*), it features such excellent food items as soups, roast beef, T-bone steaks and peppered steak, three different preparations of chicken (including a version inspired by Waikiki Beach, with pineapple slices), burgers, sandwiches, and salads. There's a bar on the roof sporting a wide-screen TV and a karaoke setup.

2 Mandeville

The "English Town," Mandeville lies on a plateau more than 2,000 feet above the sea, in the tropical highlands. The small commercial part of the town is surrounded by a sprawling residential area popular with the large North American expatriate population (mostly involved with the bauxite-mining industry). Much cooler than the coastal resorts, it's a possible base from which to explore the entire island.

Shopping in the town is a pleasure, whether in the old center or in one of the modern complexes, such as **Grove Court.** The **market** in the center of town teems with life, particularly on weekends when the country folk bus into town for their weekly visit. Among the several interesting old buildings, the square-towered **church** built in 1820 contains fine stained glass, and the little churchyard has an interesting history. The **Court House,** built in 1816, is a fine old Georgian stone-and-wood building with a pillared portico reached by a steep, sweeping double staircase. There's also **Marshall's Pen,** one of the great houses in Mandeville.

WHERE TO STAY

Golf View Hotel. 5¹/₂ Caledonia Rd, Mandeville, Manchester, Jamaica, W.I. ☎ **876/ 962-4477.** Fax 876/962-5640. www.thegolfviewhotel.com. E-mail: gviewrosi@cwjamaica. com. 51 units. TV TEL. $55–$75 double, $60 1-bedroom suite, $80 2-bedroom suite. AE, MC, V.

This hotel doesn't win any prizes for architectural finesse, and some of its detractors even compare its design to something akin to a hospital. But despite its shortcomings, it's the newest (circa 1991) and most efficiently managed hotel, with the best-maintained physical plant, in town. As such, it's the favorite of most of the corporations in town, many of whom advise their workers and suppliers to sleep here, but to avoid the hotel restaurant in favor of the also-recommended Bloomfield Great House (see below). About half of the rooms overlook the verdant fairways of the local golf course (Manchester Golf Club); the others front a swimming pool and a relatively banal-looking courtyard. Rooms are outfitted motel style with relatively comfortable furnishings based on vaguely colonial models. About a third of them have air-conditioning.

Mandeville Hotel. 4 Hotel St. (P.O. Box 78), Mandeville, Jamaica, W.I. ☎ **876/962-2460.** Fax 876/962-0700. E-mail: manhot@cwjamaica.com. 56 units. TV TEL. $65–$125 double, from $95 suite. AE, MC, V.

This ornate hotel was established in the early 1900s and for a while housed part of the British military garrison. In the 1970s, the venerable hotel was replaced with a modern structure, which was completely refurbished in 1982. It lies in the heart of Mandeville, across from the police station. It offers an outdoor and an indoor bar and a spacious lounge, and good food and service. Activity centers mainly on the pool and the coffee shop, where substantial meals are served at moderate prices. Bedrooms, which range in size from small to spacious, are furnished with Jamaican styling, often including a four-poster bed and mahogany furniture. Bathrooms are old-fashioned

Mandeville & Environs

ACCOMMODATIONS
Golf View Hotel **1**
Mandevile Hotel **2**
◆ **DINING**
Bloomfield Great House **3**

JAMAICA
Mandeville ○
⭐ Kingston

Eden St.
JACKASS HILL
New Green Rd.
Clarks Town Rd.
Kendall Rd.
A 2
BATTERSEA
Jones Hwy.
CLARKS TOWN
Battersea Rd.
Knowles Rd.
New Green Rd.
Bonito Crescent
Hanbury Rd.
Winston
Patrick Rd.
BRUMALIA
Gordon Rd.
Brumilla Rd.
GREY ABBEY
Manchester Shopping Centre
CALEDONIA
Rd.
West Rd.
Wint Rd.
TUCKER'S TURN
Caledonia
Main St.
Levy Ln.
Villa Rd.
Ward Ave. ①
Manchester Country Club ⛳
1
GREEN VALE
Brooks Park
Tudor Theatre
Odeon Theatre
Ⓟ
THE VILLA
NEW-LEIGH
De Carteret Rd.
Ward Ave.
2 MANDEVILLE
Greenvale Rd.
PUT TOGETHER
Court House
✝ Parish Church
Park Crescent
BALVENIE HEIGHTS
Manchester School
Market
Wesley Rd.
BLOOMFIELD
Perth St.
3
Manchester Rd.

A 2

LEGEND
✝ Church
⛳ Golf Course
① Information
Ⓟ Police Station
⊠ Post Office

0   1/2 mi
0   .5 km

---

but tidily maintained, although towels are a bit skimpy. There are attractive gardens, and you can play golf or tennis at the nearby Manchester Country Club. Popular with local businesspeople, the hotel restaurant offers a wide selection of sandwiches, plus milk shakes, tea, and coffee. The à la carte menu features Jamaican pepper pot, lobster thermidor, fresh snapper, and kingfish. Potatoes and vegetables are included in the main-dish prices. There is no pretension to the food at all. It's homemade and very basic. From the dining room, you'll have a view of the pool and the green hills of central Jamaica. Main courses range from $12 to $30; reservations are recommended.

WHERE TO DINE

✪ **Bloomfield Great House.** 8 Perth Rd. ☎ **876/962-7130.** Reservations recommended for dinner. Lunch main courses J$250–J$915 ($7.15–$26.10); dinner main courses J$415–J$995 ($11.85–$28.35). AE, DISC, MC, V. Mon–Sat noon–9pm. INTERNATIONAL.

This is the only restaurant in town that's viewed as a destination in its own right. Serving excellent food in an intricately restored setting of historic interest, it's the centerpiece for the leisure hours of many of the town's Australian, British, American, and Scandinavian residents. Surrounded by five acres of landscaping, it's perched on a hilltop about a quarter-mile south of the town's commercial core, in a verdant residential neighborhood of upscale private homes. Although its foundations are about 200 years old, it took its present form in 1838, when it was the centerpiece of a coffee plantation. Today, it evokes a corner of England in the tropics, thanks to the devoted labor of Australia-born Ralph Pearce and his Jamaican-American wife, Pamela Grant, who transformed her family's romantic-looking but sleepy real-estate investment into the well-orchestrated dining enclave you'll see today. Meals taste best when preceded with a drink in the cozy mahogany-trimmed pub that's tucked into a corner adjacent to the dining areas. These include a rambling veranda with views that sweep out over the town and a high-ceilinged dining room whose trim and moldings evoke colonial Jamaica at its most nostalgic. Superb menu items include smoked marlin with black caviar and lime-flavored aioli; curried-chicken ravioli; char-broiled filet mignon with sherry sauce and crispy onions; lobster thermidor; plantain-crusted chicken served with a passion-fruit vinaigrette; and a delicious version of jumbo shrimp stuffed with jalapeño pepper, wrapped in bacon, and served with barbecue sauce. The pastas served here, incidentally, are made fresh on the premises as part of a satellite business that ships fresh pasta to destinations across Jamaica.

EXPLORING THE AREA

Mandeville is the sort of place where you can become well acquainted with the people and feel like part of the community.

One of the largest and driest **caves** on the island is at Oxford, about 9 miles northwest of Mandeville. Signs direct you to it after you leave Mile Gully, a village dominated by St. George's Church, some 175 years old. The **Manchester Country Club,** Brumalia Road (☎ **876/962-2403**), is Jamaica's oldest golf course, but has only nine holes. Beautiful vistas unfold from 2,201 feet above sea level. Greens fees are J$750 ($21.40), with caddy fees running J$500 ($14.25). The course also has a clubhouse. The club is also one of the best venues in central Jamaica for tennis.

Marshall's Pen is one of the great houses, a coffee-plantation home some 200 years old. It has been in the hands of the Sutton family since 1939; they farm the 300 acres and breed Jamaican Red Poll cattle. This is very much a private home and should be treated as such, although guided tours can be arranged. A contribution of $10 is requested for a minimum of four people. For information or an appointment to see the house, contact Ann or Robert Sutton, **Marshall's Pen,** Great House, P.O. Box 58, Mandeville, Jamaica, W.I. (☎ **876/904-5454**).

At Marshall's Pen **cattle estate** and **private nature reserve,** near Mandeville, guided **bird-watching** tours of the scenic property and other outstanding birding spots on Jamaica may be arranged in advance. Six persons are taken on a tour for $200. Self-catering accommodation is sometimes available for bird watchers only, but arrangements must be made in advance. For information, contact Ann or Robert Sutton (co-author of *Birds of Jamaica,* a photographic field guide published by Cambridge University Press), Marshall's Pen, P.O. Box 58, Mandeville, Jamaica, W.I. (☎ **876/904-5454**).

Milk River Mineral Bath, Milk River, Clarendon (☎ **876/995-4099;** fax 876/986-4962), lies 9 miles south of the Kingston–Mandeville highway. It boasts the world's most radioactive mineral waters, recommended for the treatment of arthritis, rheumatism, lumbago, neuralgia, sciatica, and liver disorders. These mineral-laden waters are available to guests of the Milk River Mineral Spa & Hotel, Milk River, Clarendon, Jamaica, W.I., as well as to casual visitors to the enclosed baths or mineral swimming pool. The baths contain water near body temperature (90°F) and are channeled into small tubs 6 feet square by 3 feet deep, each enclosed in a cubicle where participants undress. The cost of a bath is J$50 ($1.45) for adults and J$25 (70¢) for children. Baths usually last about 15 minutes (it isn't good to remain too long in the waters).

The restaurant offers fine Jamaican cuisine and health drinks in a relaxed old-world atmosphere. Some guests check into the adjacent hotel, where there are 25 rooms

You Paid What?

47,000 hotels, 700 airlines, 50 rental car companies. And a few million ways to save money.

Travelocity.com
A Sabre Company

Go Virtually Anywhere.

Will you have enough stories to tell your grandchildren?

Yahoo! Travel

(17 with bath), many with air-conditioning, TV, and phone. Six of the rooms are in the main body of the hotel (a century-old great house that was converted into a hotel in the 1930s). With MAP included, rates for rooms with bath are $105 double. Rates for rooms without bath are $100 double. American Express, MasterCard, and Visa are accepted.

6 Ocho Rios & Runaway Bay

Situated on Jamaica's northeast coast, the resort areas of **Runaway Bay, Ocho Rios,** and **Port Antonio** (see chapter 7) helped to launch large-scale tourism in Jamaica. Known for its abundant rainfall, verdant landscapes, rolling hills, and jagged estuaries, this region was once the preferred hangout for Noël Coward, Errol Flynn, and a host of British and American literati. Ian Fleming, creator of the James Bond spy thrillers, lived at Goldeneye, near Ocho Rios.

Starting from Montego Bay and heading east, you first reach **Discovery Bay,** whose name refers to the belief that Columbus first landed here in 1494. Finding no water, Columbus is said to have named it Puerto Seco (Dry Harbor). Puerto Seco Beach today is a popular stretch of sand, with a few places where you can get lunch or a drink.

Just beyond Discovery Bay is **Runaway Bay,** with some of the best-known resort hotels along the north coast. There is no real town of Runaway Bay; it is mainly a beachfront strip of hotels and sandy shores. Much of the resort area takes up space once occupied by Cardiff Hall, a sprawling plantation owned by one of Jamaica's first English settlers.

From Runaway Bay, continue east along the A3, bypassing the sleepy hamlet of St. Ann's Bay, and you'll reach **Ocho Rios.** Today, this is the north coast's major tourist destination, although it's not up there with Montego Bay.

Although Ocho Rios is the cruise-ship capital of Jamaica, with as many as a half-dozen major vessels anchored offshore at any one time, it is not a port at the mouth of eight rivers, as its Spanish name ("Eight Rivers") might suggest. It was once the lair of pirate John Davis, who remains famous for his plundering of French and Spanish vessels on the nearby seas. One of his best-known exploits was the sacking and burning of St. Augustine, Florida.

The sleepy village of long ago has been enveloped by massive resort hotels (many all inclusive). Ocho Rios is fine for a lazy beach vacation, but it's definitely not for anyone seeking a remote hideaway. You might see calypso and reggae bands greeting cruise-ship passengers, who are then herded onto buses and shuttled off to Dunn's River Falls. Here, they take a sometimes precarious trek across wooded limestone cliffs whose broad waterfalls are among the most frequently photographed sights in Jamaica. To the discomfiture of many visitors, souvenir vendors assail you at almost every point.

1 Ocho Rios

A 2-hour drive east from Montego Bay (see chapter 3) or west from Port Antonio, Ocho Rios was once a small banana and fishing port, but tourism long ago became its leading industry. Now Jamaica's cruise-ship capital, the bay is dominated on one side by a bauxite-loading terminal and on the other by a range of hotels with sandy beaches fringed by palm trees.

Ocho Rios and neighboring Port Antonio have long been associated with celebrities, the two most-famous writers being Sir Noël Coward, who invited the world to his Jamaican doorstep, and Ian Fleming, who created James Bond while writing here.

It is commonly assumed among Spanish-speakers that Ocho Rios was named for eight rivers, its Spanish meaning, but the islanders disagree. In 1657, British troops chased off a Spanish expeditionary force that had launched a raid from Cuba. The battle was near Dunn's River Falls, now the resort's most important attraction. Seeing the rapids, the Spanish called the district *los chorreros*. That battle between the Spanish and the British forces was so named. The British and the Jamaicans weren't too good with Spanish names back then, so *los chorreros* was corrupted into "ocho rios."

Ocho Rios has its own unique flavor, offering the usual range of sports and a major fishing tournament every fall in addition to a wide variety of accommodations, including all-inclusive resorts, couples-only complexes, elegant retreats (some with spas), and inns exhibiting what is left of the area's former colonial culture.

But frankly, unless you're a passenger, you may want to stay away from the major attractions on cruise-ship days. Even the duty-free shopping markets are overrun then, and the street hustlers become more strident in trying to sell their souvenirs. Dunn's River Falls becomes almost impossible to visit at these times.

In our view, you go to overrun Ocho Rios only if you're resort oriented. True, it possesses some of the leading inns of the Caribbean as well as two stellar Sandals properties. When in the area, we prefer to stay away from the center of Ocho Rios itself, perhaps at a resort in Runaway Bay or something really special like Ian Fleming's "Goldeneye."

GETTING THERE

BY PLANE   If you're going to Ocho Rios, you will fly into the **Donald Sangster Airport** in Montego Bay (see chapter 3). Some hotels, particularly the larger resorts, will arrange for airport transfers from that point. Be sure to ask when you book.

BY BUS   If your hotel does not provide transfers, you can go by bus for a $25 one-way fare. We recommend two private companies: **Tour Wise** (☎ 876/979-1027 in Montego Bay, or 876/974-2323 in Ocho Rios) or **Caribic Vacations** (☎ 876/953-9874 in Montego Bay, or 876/974-9016 in Ocho Rios). The bus will drop you off at your hotel. The trip takes 2 hours.

BY RENTAL CAR & TAXI   You can rent a car for the 67-mile drive east along Highway A1 (see "Getting Around" in chapter 2). Or, you can take a taxi; the typical one-way fare from Montego Bay is $70, but always negotiate and agree upon a fare *before* you get into the taxi.

WHERE TO STAY

Some of the accommodations in and around Ocho Rios include the best in all Jamaica.

VERY EXPENSIVE

✪ **Jamaica Inn.** Main St. (P.O. Box 1), Ocho Rios, Jamaica, W.I. ☎ **800/837-4608** in the U.S., or 876/974-2514. Fax 876/974-2449. www.jamaicainn.com. E-mail: jaminn@ intochan.com. 45 units. A/C TEL. Winter including all meals $525–$700 double; from $725 suite for 2. Off-season including MAP (breakfast and dinner) $275–$375 double; from $345 suite for 2. AE, MC, V. Children 13 and under not accepted.

Built in 1950, the Jamaica Inn is a series of long, low, buildings set in a U-shape near the sea, 1.5 miles east of town. Noël Coward, arriving with Katharine Hepburn or Claudette Colbert, was a regular, and Errol Flynn and Ian Fleming used to drop in from time to time. It's an elegant anachronism, a true retro hotel, and has changed little in 4 decades, avoiding the brass and glitter of all-inclusives like Sandals. Lovely patios open onto the lawns, and the bedrooms are reached along garden paths. The rooms of this gracious, family-run inn, long a Jamaican landmark, underwent a $4-million renovation in 1993, but the old charm, including the antique furniture, remains. Guest rooms are very spacious, with colonial two-poster beds, quality carved-wood period pieces, and balustraded balconies opening onto views. Bathrooms are elegant and roomy, gleaming with marble vanities, combination shower/tubs, robes, and deluxe toiletries. The beach is a wide, champagne-colored strip; close to the shore, the sea is almost too clear to make snorkeling an adventure, but farther out it's rewarding.

Dining: The European-trained chef prepares both international and Jamaican dishes. The emphasis is on cuisine that uses fresh local produce. Men must wear a jacket and tie at night in winter.

Amenities: Pool, tennis court, comfortable lounge with books, game room with cards and jigsaw puzzles; Upton Golf Course nearby. Room service, laundry.

EXPENSIVE

High Hope Estate. Box 11, St. Ann's Bay, near Ocho Rios, Jamaica W.I. ☎ **876/972-2277.** Fax 876/972-1607. www.highhopeestate.com. E-mail: info@highhopeestate.com. 6 units. TEL. $125–$270 double. Rates include continental breakfast. MC, V.

Because of the small size of this upscale hotel, your happiness, and the success of your holiday here, will depend a lot on whether you click with the owner and the other guests. It's conceived as a tranquil, private home that accepts paying guests, in the style of the British colonial world at its most rarefied. It was built for a socially prominent heiress, Kitty Spence, granddaughter of prairie-state populist William Jennings Bryan, and later served as the home and laboratory of a horticulturist who successfully bred 560 varieties of flowering hibiscus. Consequently, the estate's 40 acres, set 550 feet above the coast and 7 miles west of Ocho Rios, thrive with flowering plants as well as memories of such luminaries as Noël Coward, who used to play the grand piano that graces one of the public areas. There are absolutely no planned activities here. Basically, it's an upscale private home, the domain of U.S. entrepreneur Dennis Rapaport, whose staff is on hand to help with supervising children, maintaining the property, and preparing meals for anyone who gives advance notice. Bedrooms are a delight—spacious, well thought out, and exceedingly comfortable. The excellent bathrooms have combination shower/tubs. On the premises is a pool, a tennis court, a communal TV room, and a semi-enclosed courtyard modeled on a 15th-century villa. There are sweeping views out over the Jamaican coastline; the nearest beach is a 10-minute ride away. You could rent the entire villa with a group of friends.

Ocho Rios

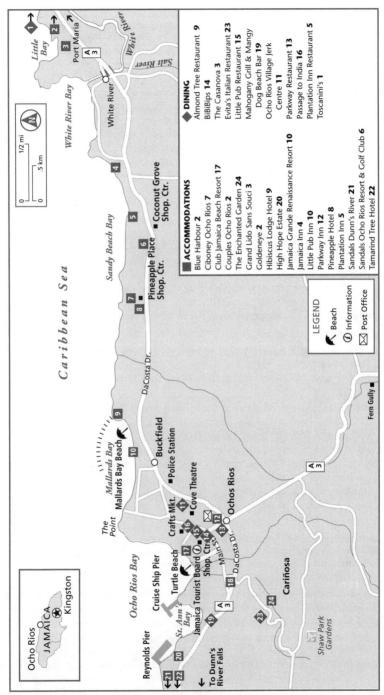

ACCOMMODATIONS
Blue Harbour **2**
Ciboney Ocho Rios **7**
Club Jamaica Beach Resort **17**
Couples Ocho Rios **2**
The Enchanted Garden **24**
Grand Lido Sans Souci **3**
Goldeneye **2**
Hibiscus Lodge Hotel **9**
High Hope Estate **1**
Jamaica Grande Renaissance Resort **10**
Jamaica Inn **4**
Little Pub Inn **10**
Parkway Inn **12**
Pineapple Hotel **8**
Plantation Inn **5**
Sandals Dunn's River **21**
Sandals Ocho Rios Resort & Golf Club **6**
Tamarind Tree Hotel **22**

◆ **DINING**
Almond Tree Restaurant **9**
BiBiBips **14**
The Casanova **3**
Evita's Italian Restaurant **23**
Little Pub Restaurant **15**
Mahogany Grill & Mangy
  Dog Beach Bar **19**
Ocho Rios Village Jerk
  Centre **11**
Parkway Restaurant **13**
Passage to India **16**
Plantation Inn Restaurant **5**
Toscanini's **1**

LEGEND
◤ Beach
ⓘ Information
⊠ Post Office

123

✪ **Plantation Inn.** Main St. (P.O. Box 2), Ocho Rios, Jamaica, W.I. ☎ **800/752-6824** in the U.S., or 876/974-5601. Fax 876/974-5912. www.plantationinn@cwjamaica.com. E-mail: plantationinn@cwjamaica.com. 70 units. A/C TEL. Winter $225–$335 double; $385–$870 suite; $4,375–$5,800 villa for up to 4 (7-night minimum). Off-season $150–$210 double; $230–$550 suite; $2,700–$5,100 villa (7-night minimum). MAP (breakfast and dinner) $70 per person extra. Children under 13 stay free in parents' room. AE, MC, V.

This hotel evokes an antebellum southern mansion. At any moment, you expect Vivien Leigh as Scarlett to come rushing down to greet you. You'll drive up a sweeping driveway and enter through a colonnaded portico, set in gardens, 1.5 miles east of town. Two private beaches are reached via 36 steps down from the garden; seats on the way provide resting spots. All bedrooms open onto balconies and have their own patios overlooking the sea. The rooms are attractively decorated with chintz and comfortable furnishings. Beds are elegantly outfitted with fine linens, and the spacious bathrooms come with hair dryers. Apart from the regular hotel, the Plantana Villa above the eastern beach sleeps two to six people, while the Blue Shadow Villa on the west side accommodates up to eight guests.

Dining: There's an indoor dining room, but most of the action takes place under the tropical sky. A fine Jamaican and continental cuisine is served. You can have breakfast on your balcony and lunch outdoors. English tea is served on the terrace every afternoon.

Amenities: Gym with exercise equipment, sauna, two tennis courts, snorkeling, Sunfish sailing, windsurfing, scuba diving, kayaking, glass-bottom boat; an 18-hole golf course is a 15-minute drive away. Room service, facials, massages, waxing.

INEXPENSIVE

✪ **Hibiscus Lodge Hotel.** 87 Main St. (P.O. Box 52), Ocho Rios, St. Ann, Jamaica, W.I. ☎ **876/974-2676.** Fax 876/974-1874. 27 units. A/C TV. Winter $110.85 double; $157.02 triple. Off-season $99.27 double; $135 triple. Rates include continental breakfast. AE, DC, MC, V.

Hibiscus Lodge Hotel offers more value for your money than any resort at Ocho Rios. The intimate little inn, perched precariously on a cliff along the shore 3 blocks from the Ocho Rios Mall, has both character and charm. All medium-size bedrooms, either doubles or triples, have small, tidy private bathrooms, ceiling fans, and verandas opening to the sea. Singles can be rented for the double rate. After a day spent in a pool suspended over the cliffs, or lounging on the large sundeck, guests can enjoy a drink in the unique swinging bar. Also on the 3-acre site are a Jacuzzi, tennis court, and conference facilities. The owners provide dining at the Almond Tree Restaurant (see below).

Little Pub Inn. 59 Main St. (P.O. Box 256), Ocho Rios, St. Ann, Jamaica, W.I. ☎ **876/974-2324.** Fax 876/974-5825. 22 units. A/C TV TEL. Winter $70 double. Off-season $66 double. Extra person $20 in winter, $15 off-season. Children 11 and under stay free in parents' room. Rates include full American breakfast. AE, MC, V.

If you don't mind a little noise, this place offers simple accommodations at sensible prices. Although this isn't the perfect place for peace and quiet, the hotel is in the heart of Ocho Rios, offering easy access to Turtle Beach, shopping, restaurants, evening entertainment, and a variety of other activities. This hotel is in the Little Pub Complex containing a small nightclub, slot machines, and a restaurant that offers indoor and outdoor dining. The Little Pub Inn pays a small fee to keep a small parcel of the Ocho Rios Beach (which is just below the inn). However, we recommend making the 5-minute walk to Turtle Beach, where the sand is a little nicer. The air-conditioned rooms have a tropical decor; some contain small lofts that can be reached by ladder for extra bed space. The restaurant serves international cuisine and a few local specialties. Hotel guests receive a VIP card good for a 15% discount at the restaurant and night-club.

Parkway Inn. Main St., Ocho Rios, St. Ann, Jamaica, W.I. ☎ **876/974-2667.** 21 units. A/C TV TEL. J$1,500–J$2,500 ($42.75–$71.25) double. AE, MC, V.

Its setting in the commercial heart of Ocho Rios appeals to any budget traveler who wants easy access to the town's inexpensive restaurants, shops, and bars. Built in the early 1990s, the hotel sports a bar on its third floor where patrons can enjoy a grand view over the lights of Ocho Rios. Although there aren't any resort-style facilities on-site, guests are invited to use the pool, tennis courts, and water-sports facilities at the Jamaica Grand Hotel, next door. The closest beach is a 10-minute walk away. There's a Chinese/Jamaican restaurant on the premises serving simple meals. This hotel attracts business travelers hailing from other regions of Jamaica.

Pineapple Hotel. Pineapple Place (P.O. Box 263), Ocho Rios, St. Ann, Jamaica, W.I. ☎ **876/974-2727.** Fax 876/974-1706. 20 units. A/C. $60 double, $85 triple. Children 11 and under stay free in parents' room. AE, MC, V.

Next door to the Pineapple Place Shopping Centre, this hotel offers very basic accommodations at bargain prices. Expect no frills here; stay only if you can't afford the high prices of Ocho Rios, you plan to spend little time in your room, and you are on the north coast only to spend all your time at the beach. The tropically decorated quarters include private baths, tile floors, and air-conditioning, but if you want to make a phone call, you must do it from the front desk. TVs are available in some accommodations. The Pineapple Pizza Pub is on the property, serving a combination of foods that boast Italian, American, and Jamaican influences. Water sports can be arranged at the front desk, and there's a swimming pool on the premises. For a seaside romp, try Turtle Beach, a short walk away.

Tamarind Tree Hotel. P.O. Box 235, Runaway Bay, St. Ann, Jamaica, W.I. ☎ **876/973-4819.** Fax 876/973-5013. 16 units, 3 3-bedroom cottages with kitchenettes. A/C TV TEL. Winter $75–$92 double. Off-season $68–$85 double. Year-round $188 cottage for up to 4. MC, V.

This small family-style hotel was named after a lavishly blossoming tamarind tree (which has since been cut down) that grew near its entrance. Stucco, red-roofed buildings with awnings and pastel-trimmed balconies house cream-colored and carpeted bedrooms. There's a pool terrace and the nearest beach (Cardiff Hall) is within a 5-minute walk. Although the occupants of the cottages usually cook their own meals in their lodgings, there's a simple restaurant (The Bird Wing), which serves three meals a day, and a disco (The Stinger) whose drinks and recorded music create some fun at this otherwise quiet, out-of-the-way hotel. The more appealing bedrooms are on the second floor, partly because they catch more cooling breezes.

NEARBY PLACES TO STAY

Noël Coward's Blue Harbour. On the North Coast Rd. (A4), 80 miles west of Montego Bay and 60 miles north of Kingston (P.O. Box 50), Port Maria, St. Mary's, Jamaica, W.I. ☎ **876/994-0289,** or 505/586-1244 in Questa, New Mexico. Fax 876/586-1087. E-mail: blue-harb@aol.com. 3 villas. $170 double or $4,000 weekly in winter; $3,000 weekly in summer for entire complex (all inclusive). No credit cards.

This 1950s-aura retreat was once owned by Sir Noël Coward, who entertained the rich and famous of his day here. Coward dubbed Blue Harbour, his first Jamaica retreat, "Coward's Folly." Eventually, the place became so popular that Coward built Firefly, a "retreat from his retreat," and stopped staying at Blue Harbour.

Your Own Private Villa

If you're looking for complete immersion in a private Jamaican community of well-maintained homes, and if you prefer a rental wherein you'll prepare your own meals, make your own beds, and do your own laundry (unless you request a housekeeper/cook), consider Ay Caramba. A 15-minute drive east from Ocho Rios, and a short walk from James Bond Beach, Ay Caramba is a well-designed villa offering comfortably furnished, private, one-bedroom units. Each unit has cable TV, ceiling fans, a washing machine, a fully equipped kitchen, and a sofa bed (in addition to the bed in the bedroom). The villa's design is based vaguely on Spanish colonial models and offers views that sweep out over Jamaica's north coast.

Built and maintained by Nicky Richardson, one of the region's most astute tourist advisors, Ay Caramba is one of the best bargains in the area. Rates start at $100 per night, and each unit can accommodate up to four people. For more information, call **876/975-3597** (in Jamaica) or **305/532-1234** (in the States).

Today, the compound is rented in whole or part to paying guests, who appreciate its funky kind of nostalgia. The compound can comfortably accommodate 10 to 12 guests, although the actual bed count is 18. The main house is the Villa Grande, with two bedrooms and two baths, along with a kitchen, dining room, and terrace. Villa Rose, a guest house, contains two large bedrooms, and the smaller Villa Chica is a one-bedroom, one-bath cottage once favored by Marlene Dietrich. Meals, both Jamaican and international, are cooked by a friendly, helpful staff who run the place and see to the needs of guests, some of whom book in here like a house party, renting the entire compound. At other times, individual units are rented separately.

ALL-INCLUSIVE RESORTS

Ciboney Ocho Rios. Main St. (P.O. Box 728), Ocho Rios, St. Ann, Jamaica, W.I. ☎ **800/ 333-3333** in the U.S. and Canada, or 876/974-1027. Fax 876/974-7148. www.ciboney.com. E-mail: ciboney@infochan.com. 254 units. A/C MINIBAR TV TEL. All-inclusive rates for 3 nights per couple: Winter $1,324–$1,474 double; $1,624 junior suite; $1,684 1-bedroom villa suite; $2,434 honeymoon villa; $3,214 2-bedroom villa for 4. Off-season $1,264 double; $1,414 junior suite; $1,474 1-bedroom villa suite; $2,314 honeymoon villa; $2,794 2-bedroom villa for 4. AE, DC, MC, V. Children 15 and under not accepted.

This all-inclusive Radisson franchise is a 1.5-mile drive southeast of town, set on 45 acres of a private estate dotted with red-tile villas. A great house in the hills overlooks the Caribbean Sea. Across from the imposing gate near the resort's entrance are the white sands of a private beach. All but a handful of the accommodations are in one-, two-, or three-bedroom villas, each with a pool, a fully equipped kitchen, and a shaded terrace. Honeymoon villas have their own whirlpools. Thirty-six units are traditional single or double rooms on the third floor of the great house. Accommodations are high-ceilinged, roomy, and decorated in Caribbean colors. They're well furnished, with particularly fine beds, and bathrooms are well maintained.

Dining/Diversions: The Manor Restaurant & Bar offers indoor and outdoor patio dining (classic and good Jamaican food) and entertainment. The Marketplace Restaurant has a contemporary American and Jamaican menu, while Alfresco Casa Nina highlights Italian cuisine. Orchids offers a menu based on *haute cuisine*, as well as healthy food. Late-night entertainment and dancing are featured at Nicole.

Amenities: European-inspired beauty spa with its own health-and-fitness center, six tennis courts (lit for night play), beach club offering an array of water sports, two main pools with swim-up bars (plus 90 other semiprivate pools on the grounds), spa with 20 Jacuzzis.

Club Jamaica Beach Resort. P.O. Box 342, Turtle Beach, Ocho Rios, Jamaica, W.I. ☎ **800/ 818-2964** or 876/974-6632. Fax 876/974-6644. www.jamaicamarketplace.com. E-mail: clubjam@cwjamaica.com. 95 units. A/C TV TEL. Winter $290–$330 double. Off-season $220–$270 double. Rates are all inclusive. AE, DC, MC, V.

The area's newest all-inclusive resort is near the geographic heart of Ocho Rios, adjacent to its crafts market and Turtle Beach. Don't expect a particularly pulled-together staff, as the ambience here is very laid-back and, at least to the observer, not overwhelmingly organized. The completely unpretentious, motel-style bedrooms are outfitted with white tile, bright colors, and contemporary, airy-looking furniture. Bathrooms, a bit small, have shower stalls.

Dining/Diversions: There's lots of emphasis on local color and live music that emanates, beginning at the cocktail hour, from the compound out into the surrounding neighborhood. The resort has three bars and a restaurant, serving local/international cuisine. The food is nothing special, but perfectly fine if you stick to basics. Breakfast and lunch are always served buffet-style. Dinner is also a buffet, except for Tuesday and Sunday nights when there is an à la carte menu. From 2:30 to 5pm, you may also get hamburgers, hot dogs, and other American-style snacks and sandwiches at the snack bar.

Amenities: Pool, glass-bottom boat, snorkeling equipment that's dispensed from a kiosk on the sands of the public beach.

Couples Ocho Rios. Tower Isle, along Rte. A3 (P.O. Box 330), Ocho Rios, Jamaica, W.I. ☎ **800/268-7537** in the U.S., or 876/975-4271. Fax 876/975-4439. www.couples.com. E-mail: couplesresort@couples.com. 212 units. A/C TEL. All-inclusive rates for 3 nights: Winter $1,635–$1,900 double; $2,295 suite. Off-season $1,485–$1,785 double; $2,065 suite. AE, MC, V. The hotel usually accepts bookings for a minimum of any 3 nights of the week, though most guests book by the week; a 4-day stay is sometimes required at certain peak periods, such as over the Christmas holidays. No one 17 or under accepted.

Don't come here alone—you won't get in! The management defines couples as "any *man and woman* in love," and this is a couples-only resort. Most visiting couples are married, and many are on their honeymoon. Everything is in pairs, even the chairs by the moon-drenched beach. Some guests slip away from the resort, which is an 18-minute drive (5 miles) east of town, to Couples' private island to bask in the buff. In general, this is a classier operation than the more mass-market Sandals (the Dunn's River and the Ocho Rios versions). Once you've paid the initial all-inclusive rate, you're free to use all the facilities. There will be no more bills—even the whiskey is free, in addition to the three meals a day and all the wine you want; breakfast is bountiful. Tips aren't permitted. The bedrooms have either a king-size bed or two doubles, pleasantly traditional furnishings, and a patio fronting either the sea or the mountains. Good-size bathrooms have showers and hair dryers.

Dining/Diversions: You get three meals a day, including all the wine you want; breakfast is bountiful. Dinners are five courses, and afterward there's dancing on the terrace every evening, with entertainment. Guests have a choice of six restaurants, including the most recent one to open, Calabash Café, featuring a refined Jamaican cuisine.

Amenities: Five tennis courts (three lit at night), Nautilus gym, scuba diving, snorkeling, windsurfing, sailing, water-skiing, room service (breakfast only), laundry.

✪ **The Enchanted Garden.** Eden Bower Rd. (P.O. Box 284), Ocho Rios, Jamaica, W.I. ☎ **800/847-2535** in the U.S. and Canada, or 876/974-1400. Fax 876/974-5823. www.interknowledge.com. 113 units. A/C TV TEL. All-inclusive rates per couple: Winter $300–$350 double; from $380 suite. Off-season $250–$300 double; from $330 suite. AE, DC, MC, V.

This most verdant of Jamaican resorts sits on a secluded hilltop high above the commercial center of town. Owned and developed by Edward Seaga, former Jamaican prime minister, the land includes 20 acres of rare botanical specimens, nature trails, and 14 cascading waterfalls much loved by such former visitors as Mick Jagger. The lobby is housed in a pink tower accented with white gingerbread; the interior sports marble floors, big windows, and enormous potted palms. Bisected by the Turtle River, the place is of particular interest to botanists and bird watchers. The bedrooms are contained in eight different low-rise buildings amid the resort's carefully landscaped grounds. All of the roomy, elegantly furnished units have sturdy rattan furniture, queen- or king-size beds, and private patios or balconies; some contain kitchens. The spacious bathrooms have combination tub/showers.

Dining: The resort's restaurants serve continental, Thai, Japanese, Indonesian, and regional Chinese meals, and do so rather well. A pasta bar is designed like a tree house in a tropical forest. The Seaquarium offers a cold buffet in a setting surrounded by tropical fish. Annabella's nightclub provides after-dinner entertainment in a setting like something out of the *Arabian Nights.*

Amenities: Spa, beauty salon, pool, two lit tennis courts, walk-in aviary with hundreds of exotic birds (feeding time is every afternoon around 4pm), fitness center. Seaquarium with 15 aquariums for marine-life exotica. Daily transportation to the Beach Club, shuttle for shopping.

✪ **Goldeneye.** Oracabessa, St. Mary's, Jamaica, W.I. ☎ **800/688-7678** or 876/974-3354. Fax 876/975-3679. www.islandoutpost.com. E-mail: goldeneye@cwjamaica.com. 5 villas. TV TEL. $400–$500 1-bedroom villa for 2; $700 2-bedroom villa for up to 4; $1,000 3-bedroom villa for up to 6; $5,000 Ian Fleming's 3-bedroom house for up to 6; $10,000 for entire property of 11 bedrooms (sleeping up to 22). Rates are all inclusive. AE, MC, V.

Few other hotels in the world manage to be as posh, as informal, as appealing, as intimate, and as small-scale as this. The hotel is centered on the villa where the most famous secret agent in the world, James Bond (007) was created in 1952 by then-owner Ian Fleming. Fleming built the imposing but simple main house in 1946, and within its solid masonry walls, wrote each of the 13 original James Bond books. During the resort's heyday, Noël Coward was a frequent guest, along with Graham Greene, Truman Capote, and Evelyn Waugh. In the early 1990s, music publisher Christopher Blackwell bought and restored the by-then dilapidated property to its original modernist dignity, retaining an airy, uncluttered aura within the main house, but unleashing a series of sophisticated British decorators to enrich it with dozens of Balinese antiques and sculptures. Fleming's original desk remains, and the overall decor of oversized Indonesian furniture is enhanced, Hollywood-style, with memorabilia from what later became the most famous spy movies in the world. The main house is usually rented only as a three-bedroom whole for extended house parties, often to rock stars and hideaway celebrities who appreciate the artfully informal venue. More realistic might be your rental of any of four additional villas that were built, in distinct harmony with nature, on the surrounding property. Each evokes a tropical version of a billionaire's summer camp in Maine, thanks to a graceful juxtaposition of indoor and outdoor spaces, ultracomfortable sofas—the kind you want to throw yourself into for a snooze or whatever—and decorative accessories inspired by the literary and/or plantation life of long ago.

Noël's Folly

Arriving in Jamaica in 1944, the gay English playwright, songwriter, raconteur, and actor Noël Coward discovered his dream island.

He returned in 1948 and rented Goldeneye from his friend Ian Fleming, the real-life spy who later created the James Bond character at this estate. During this stopover, Coward found a magical spot 10 miles down the coast at St. Mary's. The land was once owned by Sir Henry Morgan, the notorious buccaneer who had built a small fortress on the property so he could spy on any stray galleon entering local waters. It was here that Coward began construction on what he called his "folly"—Blue Harbour, which can be rented today (see "Nearby Places to Stay," earlier in this chapter).

Once settled in, Coward sent out invitations to his "bloody loved ones." They included Laurence Olivier, Vivien Leigh, Alfred Lunt, Lynn Fontane, Errol Flynn, Katharine Hepburn, Mary Martin, Claudette Colbert, and John Gielgud, among others. Some stayed an entire month.

Blue Harbour became so popular on the north-coast cocktail circuit that in 1956 Coward fled it and built Firefly on a panoramic nearby hilltop. It still stands today much as he left it. Coward lived at Firefly with his longtime companion, Graham Payn.

In 1965, the Queen Mother came to visit Coward, who prepared a lobster mousse for her only to have it melt in the hot sun. He quickly rushed to the kitchen and opened a can of split-pea soup. She found it "divine"—perhaps because Coward had hastily laced it with sherry.

Sir Winston Churchill, who also loved Jamaica, visited Coward several times at Firefly. He told the playwright: "An Englishman has an inalienable right to live wherever he chooses."

Coward died at Firefly and is buried on the grounds. You can still see his plain, flat white-marble gravestone, which is inscribed simply: "Sir Noël Coward, born December 16, 1899, died March 26, 1973."

There's a pool on the premises, but it's reserved only for occupants of the main house. But considering the splendors of the nearby beach, and the intricate labyrinth of masonry paths heading down toward it, no one seems to mind. Each unit has a fully equipped kitchen of its own, and the hotel will provide the groceries and staff you'll need for everything from full banquets to simple platters of fresh fruit. All drinks and food, and most activities, are included in the price. During the lifetime of this edition, look for a dramatic enlargement of this hotel development, as plans are in the works for a series of additional villas near the carefully configured beach and harbor.

✪ **Grand Lido Sans Souci.** Rte. A3 (P.O. Box 103), Ocho Rios, Jamaica, W.I. ☎ **800/ 859-7873** in the U.S., or 876/974-2353. Fax 876/974-2544. www.superclubs.com. 111 units. A/C MINIBAR TV TEL. All-inclusive rates for 3 nights: Winter $2,304 double; from $2,874 suite for 2. Off-season $1,956 double; from $2,064 suite for 2. AE, DC, MC, V.

If a cookie-cutter Sandals resort is the last thing you want, don your best resort finery and head for Sans Souci. Sans Souci is a pink, cliffside fantasy that recently completed a $7-million renovation. It's located 3 miles east of town on a forested plot of land whose rocky border abuts a good beach. There's a freshwater pool, a mineral bath big enough for an elephant, and a labyrinth of catwalks and bridges stretching over rocky chasms filled with surging water. Each unit features a veranda or patio, copies of Chippendale furniture, plush upholstery, and subdued colonial elegance. Some contain Jacuzzis. Accommodations range from rather standard bedrooms to vast suites with large living and dining areas, plus kitchens. Deluxe touches include glazed-tile floors, luxurious beds, and marble bathrooms with whirlpool tubs.

Dining/Diversions: See "Where to Dine," below, for a review of the Casanova restaurant. There's also the Ristorante Palazzina by the beach. The Balloon Bar tries to bring back some 1920s style, and there are several terraces for drinking.

Amenities: Charlie's Spa is the best place on Jamaica for a health-and-fitness vacation. Three Laykold tennis courts (two lit), scuba diving, snorkeling, windsurfing, deep-sea fishing, and Sunfish and catamaran sailing.

Jamaica Grande Renaissance Resort. Main St. (P.O. Box 100), Ocho Rios, St. Ann, Jamaica. ☎ **800/330-8272** in the U.S. and Canada, or 876/974-2201. Fax 876/974-2162. www.changes.com/Grande/Jgrates.html. 720 units. A/C TV TEL. Winter $467–$617 per person. Off-season $430–$490 per person. Rates include meals, drinks, tax, and water sports. AE, DC, MC, V.

This is the largest hotel on Jamaica, a combination of two high-rise beachfront properties constructed in 1975 and 1976. In 1993, an elaborate cluster of waterfalls and swimming pools was inserted into what had been parking lots between the towers, and the entire complex was unified into a coherent whole. The place is pure theatrics and special effects, like a Hollywood production, but is short on true Jamaican style. It seems to be meant to overwhelm guests. Today, the end result boasts more beachfront than any other hotel in Ocho Rios and a comfortable array of public rooms (often filled with members of tour or conference groups). The standard bedrooms are tile-floored and furnished with Caribbean furniture; each opens onto a private balcony.

Dining/Diversions: The restaurants include The Dragon (Chinese) and L'Allegro (Italian), and the less-formal Café Jamique and Mallard's Court (international). The newest restaurant is Cool Runnings, named for the Disney movie about the first Jamaican bobsled team. There's also a beachfront grill and a total of eight bars scattered throughout the premises. The hotel operates the Jamaic'N Me Crazy Disco and a casino (slots only). Every Thursday, the Jamaica Grande is transformed into a village for Jump Up Carnival, with Jamaican food, a live band, and shopping.

Amenities: Tennis courts lit for nighttime play, children's program, a full range of water sports, daily activities program.

Sandals Dunn's River. Rte. A3 (P.O. Box 51), Ocho Rios, Jamaica, W.I. ☎ **800/SANDALS** in the U.S. and Canada, or 876/972-1610. Fax 876/972-1611. www.sandals.com. E-mail: sdrinet@cwjamaica.com. 266 units. TV TEL. All-inclusive rates per couple for 4 days/3 nights: Winter $1,830–$2,410 double; from $2,620 suite. Off-season $1,690–$2,240 double; from $2,500 suite. Minimum stay of 4 days/3 nights. AE, MC, V.

Located on a wide, sugary beach, this is the finest of the Sandals resorts, at least in the opinion of some guests who have sampled them all. Only male-female couples are allowed. Set on the beachfront between Ocho Rios and St. Ann's Bay, the resort is very sports-oriented. It occupies 25 well-landscaped acres, offering attractively furnished and often quite spacious accommodations. All the rooms were reconstructed after the Sandals takeover and given an Italian/Mediterranean motif. The elegant guest rooms are scattered among the six-story main building, two lanai buildings, and a five-story west wing. Extras include coffeemakers, spacious balconies, walk-in closets, and king-size beds.

Dining/Diversions: Before retreating to the disco, guests can choose among several dining options. The International Room is elegant, with fabric-covered walls and rosewood furniture. West Indian Windies serves Caribbean specialties. D'Amore offers Italian cuisine, and Restaurant Teppanyaki serves Chinese, Polynesian, and Japanese dishes.

Amenities: Three Jacuzzis, two whirlpool baths, fitness center, jogging course, beach bar, pitch-and-putt golf course, one of the most spectacular swim-up bars on Jamaica in the lagoon-shaped pool; transport to the Sandals Golf and Country Club. Tours to Dunn's River Falls, shuttles to Sandals Ocho Rios, massages.

Sandals Ocho Rios Resort & Golf Club. Main St. (P.O. Box 771), Ocho Rios, Jamaica, W.I. ☎ **800/SANDALS** in the U.S. and Canada, or 876/974-5691. Fax 876/974-5700. www.sandals.com. 237 units. TV TEL. All-inclusive rates per couple: $400–$520 double; from $570 suite. AE, MC, V.

The resort attracts a mix of coupled singles and married folk, including honeymooners. At times, the place seems like a summer camp for grown-ups (or others who didn't quite grow up). The resort uses the same formula: one price per male-female couple, including everything. This is the most low-key of the Sandals properties. Is it romantic? Most patrons think so, although we've encountered other couples here whose relationship didn't survive the 3-night minimum stay. On 13 well-landscaped acres a mile west of the town center, it offers comfortably furnished but uninspired rooms with either ocean or garden views, plus some cottage units. All units are reasonably large, with king-size beds for loving couples, private safes, coffeemakers, and good-size bathrooms with hair dryers.

Dining/Diversions: You can sip free drinks at an oceanside swim-up bar. Nightly theme parties and live entertainment take place in a modern amphitheater. A unique feature of the resort is an open-air disco. The resort's main dining room is St. Anne's; Michelle's serves standard Italian food, and the Reef Terrace Grill does an above-average Jamaican cuisine and fresh seafood. A new addition is the Arizona Steak House.

Amenities: Three freshwater pools, private artificial beach, sporting equipment and instruction (including water-skiing, windsurfing, sailing, snorkeling, and scuba diving), paddleboats, kayaks, glass-bottom boat, Jacuzzi, saunas, fully equipped fitness center, two tennis courts. Round-trip transfers from the airport, tours to Dunn's River Falls, massages, laundry.

WHERE TO DINE

Since nearly all the major hotels in Ocho Rios have gone all inclusive, smaller independent restaurants are being smothered. There are some, however, struggling to survive.

VERY EXPENSIVE

The Casanova. In the Grand Lido Sans Souci, along Rte. A3, 3 miles east of Ocho Rios. ☎ **876/994-1353.** Reservations required except Tues and Fri. Nonguest evening pass (7pm–2am) of $95 per person includes dinner (beach buffet Tues and Fri), entertainment, and drinks. AE, DC, MC, V. Daily 6:30–9:30pm. FRENCH.

The suave Casanova is one of the most elegant enclaves along the north coast, a super choice when you feel like dressing up. Meals are included for guests of the hotel, but nonguests who purchase a pass can also enjoy dinner and entertainment here. All drinks are included. Jazz wafting in from a lattice-roofed gazebo might accompany your meal. In the late 1960s, Harry Cipriani (of Harry's Bar fame in Venice) taught the staff some of his culinary techniques, and a little more care seems to go into the cuisine here, as opposed to the mass-market chow-downs at some of the other all-inclusives. Salads, vegetarian dishes, and soups are made fresh daily. Typical dishes include an appetizer of smoked chicken breast in a continental berry sauce, or a small vegetable mousse with a fontina cheese sauce. For your main course, you might prefer osso buco (braised veal shanks) or roast Cornish hen with citrus and mild spice. Follow the sumptuous desserts with one of the house's four special coffees.

EXPENSIVE

✪ **Plantation Inn Restaurant.** In the Plantation Inn, Main St. ☎ **876/974-5601.** Reservations required. Main courses $20–$35; fixed-price dinner $38. AE, DC, MC, V. Daily 7:30–10am, 1–2:30pm, 4:30–5:30pm (afternoon tea), and 7–10pm. JAMAICAN/ CONTINENTAL.

You'll think you've arrived at Tara in *Gone with the Wind.* An evening spent here, dining and dancing by candlelight, offers one of the most romantic experiences in Ocho Rios. You're seated at beautifully set tables with crisp linen, either indoors in the dining room or outdoors on the Bougainvillea Terrace. A few steps away is an annex, the Peacock Pavilion, where afternoon tea is served daily. After the dinner plates are cleared, a band plays for dancing. This is definitely the pampered life. The continental cuisine is spiced up a bit by Jamaican specialties. Appetizers are always spicy and tangy; our favorite is "Fire & Spice," a chicken and beef kebab with a ginger-pimiento sauce. For the main course, we always ask the chef to prepare a whole roast fish from the catch of the day. The perfectly cooked fish is served boneless and seasoned with island herbs and spices. It's slowly roasted in the oven and presented with fresh country vegetables. Since the place attracts a lot of meat eaters, the chefs always prepare the classics: lamb chops Provencçale, and the like. The fixed-price menu offered every evening is also a good value. Opt for the banana-cream pie for dessert, if featured— it's creamy and tasty.

MODERATE

Almond Tree Restaurant. In the Hibiscus Lodge Hotel, 87 Main St. ☎ **876/974-2813.** Reservations recommended. Main courses $16–$37. AE, MC, V. Daily 7:30am–10:30; noon–2:30pm, and 6–9:30pm. INTERNATIONAL.

The Almond Tree is a two-tiered patio restaurant with a tree growing through the roof, overlooking the Caribbean at the Hibiscus Lodge Hotel (see "Where to Stay," above). Lobster thermidor is the most delectable item on the menu, but we also like the bouillabaisse (made with conch and lobster). Other excellent choices are the roast suckling pig, medallions of beef Anne Palmer, and a fondue bourguignonne. Jamaican plantation rice is a local specialty. The wine list offers a variety of vintages, including Spanish and Jamaican. Have an aperitif in the unique "swinging bar" (swinging chairs, that is).

Evita's Italian Restaurant. Eden Bower Rd. ☎ **876/974-2333.** Reservations recommended. Main courses $6–$27. AE, MC, V. Daily 11am–11pm. ITALIAN.

Located a 5-minute drive south of the commercial heart of Ocho Rios, in a hillside residential neighborhood that enjoys a panoramic view over the city's harbor and beachfronts, this is one of the most fun restaurants along the north coast of Jamaica. Its soul and artistic flair come from Eva Myers, the convivial former owner of some of the most legendary bars of Montego Bay, who established her culinary headquarters in this white-gingerbread Jamaican house in 1990. An outdoor terrace adds extra seating and enhanced views. More than half the menu is devoted to pastas, including almost every variety known in northern and southern Italy. If you don't want pasta, the fish dishes are excellent, especially the snapper stuffed with crabmeat and the lobster and scampi in a buttery white cream sauce. Italian (or other) wines by the bottle might accompany your main course. The restaurant lies a few steps from the Enchanted Garden, an all-inclusive resort.

Little Pub Restaurant. 59 Main St. ☎ **876/974-2324.** Reservations recommended. Main courses $10–$25. AE, DC, MC, V. Daily 8pm–midnight. JAMAICAN/INTERNATIONAL.

Located in a red-brick courtyard with a fish pond and a waterfall in the center of town, this indoor-outdoor pub's centerpiece is a restaurant in the dinner-theater style. Top local and international artists are featured, as are Jamaican musical plays. No one will mind if you just enjoy a drink while seated on one of the pub's barrel chairs. But if you want dinner, proceed to one of the linen-covered tables topped with cut flowers and candles. Menu items include barbecued chicken, stewed snapper, grilled kingfish, and the inevitable lobster.

✪ **Toscanini's.** Harmony Hall, Tower Isles on Rte. A3, 4 miles east of Ocho Rios. ☎ **876/975-4785.** Main courses $10.85–$26; pastas $9–$16. Tues–Sun noon–2:30pm and 7–10:30pm. AE, DISC, MC, V. ITALIAN.

Parma, Italy, is the birthplace of the trio of partners behind this restaurant, set at an art gallery along the coast. Hailing from the city of a marvelous ham, a peerless cheese, and some of Italy's finest cuisine are Emanuele and Lella Guilivi and her brother, chef Pierluigi Ricci. Coming from a long line of restaurateurs, they bring style and a continental sophistication to their food service and preparation. The menu offers many classic Italian dishes, supplemented by ever-changing specials, depending on what's fresh at the market. Specialties include marinated marlin, various homemade pastas, carpaccio, gnocchi, and a strong emphasis on fresh lobster and seafood. The chef also caters to the vegetarian palate. All this good food is backed up by a fine wine list. For dessert, the chef makes a "wicked" tiramisu.

Inexpensive

BiBiBips. 93 Main St. ☎ **876/974-1287.** Lunch main courses J$160–J$900 ($4.55–$25.65); dinner main courses J$300–J$900 ($8.55–$25.65). AE, MC, V. Daily 11am–5:30pm and 6–11:30pm. INTERNATIONAL.

Set in the tourist core of Ocho Rios, with a name that's inspired by the affectionate nickname of one of the owners (Nancy Chatani), this restaurant occupies a sprawling open-air compound that's sheltered from the sun and rain by an interconnected series of porticos, porches, and verandas. Many clients come here just for the bar, which functions as one of the premier rendezvous points for interested singles in town. Drinks and flirtations sometimes segue into dinner at the adjacent restaurant, where well-prepared menu items include Red Stripe shrimp, which is deep-fried in a beer-based batter; coconut-curried chicken; vegetarian Rasta pasta; and a combination Creole-style seafood platter. Lunches are a bit simpler, focusing mostly on sandwiches, salads, and an especially delicious jerk chicken burger. There's live entertainment (usually some kind of rap or reggae band) every Friday, Saturday, and Sunday beginning at 8pm.

Mahogany Grill and Mangy Dog Beach Bar. Mahogany Beach, Main St. ☎ **876/974-3026.** Reservations not accepted. Lunch platters J$150–J$350 ($4.30–$10); dinner main courses J$250–J$600 ($7.10–$17.10). AE, MC, V. Daily 11am–11pm. JAMAICAN/AMERICAN.

One of the resort's most intriguing small-scale blends of Jamaican and American motifs is set on a 14.5-acre tract of flat, sandy bayfront that's accessible via a steeply sloping winding road from Ocho Rios' main street. Except for the scattering of open-air pavilions, wherein food and drink are dispensed throughout the day, you might assume that this is a popular public park, albeit one that's firmly devoted to paying clients who evoke the young and restless characters on a popular soap opera. Part of its American flavor derives from a pair of California and Washington, D.C.–derived entrepreneurs who deliberately created a Jamaican version of "Baywatch" wherein everyone seems young, sexy, and if not altogether single, at least only loosely attached. The property includes separate dining pavilions for lunch and dinner, an Olympic-size pool, a volleyball court, a reef-sheltered beachfront, a boat-rental facility, and a bar (The Mangy Dog) that gets busy at unpredictable hours of the day and night. There are a lot of things here to remind you of California in the 1980s, and if you're the least bit threatened by intense doses of trendy and exuberant youthfulness, this might not be the place for you. Otherwise, drinks are stiff and party-colored, worthy accompaniments for tempting food items that include grilled tuna panini, marinated salmon with orange-flavored basil sauce, grilled vegetable sandwiches, and jerk versions of both pork and chicken.

✪ **Ocho Rios Village Jerk Centre.** Da Costa Dr. ☎ **876/974-2549.** Jerk pork $3 quarter-pound, $11 pound. Whole jerk chicken $14. MC, V. Daily 10am–11pm. JAMAICAN.

At this open-air restaurant, you can get the best jerk dishes along this part of the coast. When only a frosty Red Stripe beer can quench your thirst, and your stomach is growling for the fiery taste of Jamaican jerk seasonings, head here—and don't dress up. Don't expect anything fancy; it's the food that counts, and you'll find fresh daily specials posted on a chalkboard menu on the wall. The dishes are hot and spicy, but not *too* hot; hot spices are presented on the side for those who want to go truly Jamaican. The barbecue ribs are especially good, and fresh fish is a delight and perfectly grilled—try the red snapper. Vegetarian dishes are also available on request, and if you don't drink beer you can wash it all down with natural fruit juices. If a cruise ship is in port, wait until the evening, as the place is likely to be swamped with passengers during the day.

Parkway Restaurant. 60 DaCosta Dr. ☎ **876/974-2667.** Lunch main courses $5.85–$11.25; dinner main courses $6.40–$22.25. AE, MC, V. Daily 8am–11:30pm. JAMAICAN.

Come here to eat as Jamaicans eat. This popular spot in the commercial center of town couldn't be plainer or more unpretentious, but it's always packed. Locals know they can get some of Ocho Rios' best-tasting and most affordable dishes here. It's the local watering and drinking joint and is a bit disdainful of all those Sandals and Couples resorts with their contrived international food. Hungry diners dig into straightforward fare such as Jamaican-style chicken, curried goat, sirloin steak, and filet of red snapper, topping it all off with banana cream pie. Lobster and fresh fish are usually featured. The restaurant recently renovated its third floor to offer entertainment and dancing. Tuesday's Reggae Night lets local bands do their best "to let the groove ooze," as they say here.

Passage to India. In Soni's Plaza, 50 Main St. ☎ **876/795-3182.** Main courses J$290–J$320 ($8.25–$9.10). MC, V. Tues–Sun 11:30am–10pm. INDIAN.

Within a city that houses a distinctive and influential Indian minority, this is the most visible and desirable Indian restaurant on the north coast. It's set on the second floor of a busy shopping mall in the heart of town and features Indian prints and an earth-toned decor that Indians recognize as inspired by the aesthetic traditions of the North Indian city of Jaipur. Menu items include a wide array of chicken, lamb, vegetable, and fish dishes that appear tableside in whatever degree of spiciness you prefer. Best-selling favorites include a Tandoor sizzler, featuring kebabs of chicken, mutton, and vegetables; minced chicken with garlic, ginger, coriander, and cumin; and a medley of exotic mushrooms served with oregano and spices.

HITTING THE BEACH

The most idyllic sands are at the often-overcrowded **Mallards Beach,** in the center of Ocho Rios, and are shared by hotel guests and cruise-ship passengers. Locals may steer you to the white sands of **Turtle Beach** in the south, between the Renaissance Jamaica Grande and Club Jamaica. It's smaller, more desirable, and not as overcrowded as Mallards.

The most frequented (and to be avoided when cruise ships are in port) is **Dunn's River Beach,** located below the famous falls. Another great spot is **Jamaica Grande's Beach,** which is open to the public. Parasailing is a favorite sport here.

Many exhibitionist couples check into the famous but pricey **Couples Resort,** which is known for its private *au naturel* island. A shuttle boat transports visitors offshore to this beautiful little island with a fine sandy beach. A bar, pool, and hot tub are just a few hundred yards offshore from Couples. Security guards keep the gawkers from bothering guests here.

Our favorite is none of the above. We always follow the trail of 007 and head for ⚫ **James Bond Beach** (☎ 876/975-3663), east of Ocho Rios at Oracabessa Beach. Chris Blackwell, the entrepreneur, reopened writer Ian Fleming's former home, Goldeneye. For $5, nonguests can enjoy its sand strip any day except Monday. Admission includes a free drink (beer or soda) and use of the changing rooms. There's a water-sports rental center here as well.

SPORTS & OUTDOOR PURSUITS

GOLF   **SuperClub's Runaway Golf Club,** at Runaway Bay near Ocho Rios on the north coast (☎ 876/973-4820), charges no fee to guests who stay at any of Jamaica's affiliated SuperClubs. For nonguests, the price is $80 year-round. Any player can rent carts for $35 for 18 holes; clubs are $11 for 18 holes.

Sandals Golf & Country Club (☎ 876/975-0119), a 15-minute ride from the center of the resort, is a 6,500-yard course, known for its panoramic scenery some 700 feet above sea level. From the center of Ocho Rios, travel along the main bypass for 2 miles until you reach Mile End Road (you'll see a Texaco station on the corner). Turn right and drive for another 5 miles until you come to the Sandals course on your right. The 18-hole, par-71 course was designed by P. K. Saunders and opened in 1951 as the Upton Golf Club. Rolling terrain, lush vegetation, and flowers and fruit trees dominate the 120-acre course. A putting green and driving range are available for those who wish to hone their skills first. Sandals guests play free; nonguests pay $50 for 9 holes or $70 for 18 holes.

HORSEBACK RIDING   **Renegade Stables,** Galina, Oracabessa (☎ 876/994-0135), is a riding stable that's home to about 14 horses, half of which are available for riding lessons. A trail ride lasting between 60 and 90 minutes costs $30 per person and incorporates equestrian jaunts along both forest trails and beaches. Everton McKenzie is the owner and stablemaster.

SCUBA DIVING & SNORKELING   The best outfitter is **Resort Divers Shop,** Main Street, Turtle Beach (☎ 876/974-6632), at the Club Jamaica Resort. The skilled staff here can hook you up for dive trips or snorkeling. The best spot for either of these sports is 200 yards offshore (you'll be transported there). A boat leaving daily at 1pm goes to Paradise Reef, where tropical fish are plentiful.

TENNIS   **Ciboney Ocho Rios,** Main Street, Ocho Rios (☎ 876/974-1027), focuses more on tennis than any other resort in the area. It offers three clay-surface and three hard-surface courts, all lit for night play. Guests play free, day or night, but nonguests must call and make arrangements with the manager. An on-site pro offers lessons for $25 per hour. Ciboney also sponsors twice-a-day clinics for both beginners and advanced players. Frequent guest tournaments are also staged, including handicapped doubles and mixed doubles.

EXPLORING THE AREA

A scenic drive south of Ocho Rios along Route A3 will take you inland through **Fern Gully.** This was originally a riverbed, but now the main road winds up some 700 feet among a profusion of wild ferns, a tall rain forest, hardwood trees, and lianas. There are hundreds of varieties of ferns, and roadside stands offer fruits and vegetables, carved-wood souvenirs, and basketwork. The road runs for about 4 miles; at the top of the hill, you come to a right-hand turn onto a narrow road leading to Golden Grove, a small Jamaican community of no tourist interest.

Head west when you see the signs pointing to Lyford, a small community southwest of Ocho Rios. To approach it, take A3 south (the Fern Gully Road) until you come to a small intersection directly north of Walkers Wood. Follow the signpost west to Lyford. You'll pass the remains of the 1763 **Edinburgh Castle,** the lair of one of Jamaica's most infamous murderers, a Scot named Lewis Hutchinson, who used to shoot passersby and toss their bodies into a deep pit. The authorities got wind of his activities, and although he tried to escape by canoe, he was captured by the navy and hanged. Rather proud of his achievements (evidence of at least 43 murders was found), he left £100 and instructions for a memorial to be built. It never was, but the castle ruins remain.

Continue north on Route A1 to **St. Ann's Bay,** the site of the first Spanish settlement on the island. There you can see the **statue of Christopher Columbus,** cast in his hometown of Genoa and erected near St. Ann's Hospital on the west side of town, close to the coast road. There are a number of Georgian buildings in the town—the **Court House** near the parish church, built in 1866, is the most interesting.

THE MAJOR ATTRACTIONS

Brimmer Hall Estate. Port Maria, St. Mary's. ☎ **876/994-2309.** Tours $15. Tours Mon–Fri at 11am, 1:30pm, and 3pm.

Some 21 miles east of Ocho Rios, in the hills 2 miles from Port Maria, this 1817 estate is an ideal place to spend a day. You can relax beside the pool and sample a wide variety of brews and concoctions. The Plantation Tour Eating House offers typical Jamaican dishes for lunch, and there's a souvenir shop with a good selection of ceramics, art, straw goods, wood carvings, rums, liqueurs, and cigars. All this is on a working plantation where you're driven around in a tractor-drawn jitney to see the tropical fruit trees and coffee plants; the knowledgeable guides will explain the various processes necessary to produce the fine fruits of the island. This is a far more interesting and entertaining experience than the trip to Croydon Plantation in Montego Bay. So, if you're visiting both resorts and have time for only one plantation, make it Brimmer Hall.

Coyaba Botanical Gardens and Museum. Shaw Park Rd. ☎ **876/974-6235.** Admission $4.50 adults, free for children under 13. Daily 8am–5pm. Take the Fern Gully-Kingston Rd.; turn left at St. John's Anglican Church, and follow the signs to Coyaba, just half a mile farther.

A mile south of the center of Ocho Rios, at a breezy elevation of 420 feet, this is a well-known botanical garden that's set within what were originally conceived as the gardens of a since-demolished resort built in 1923, the Shaw Park. Its steeply sloping land is artfully bisected with rushing spin-offs from the Milford River, each of which has been channeled into carefully engineered stone-sided canals. Don't expect the sweaty tropics here, as the site's high elevation and frequent breezes keep the place cool, calm, and verdant, factors that keep flowers and shrubs flourishing on virtually every side. On the premises is a museum devoted to the nostalgia of the Shaw Park and its role as the first hotel on Jamaica's north coast. There are also artifacts from the Arawak Indian, Spanish, and English colonial eras in Jamaica.

Cranbrook Flower Forest. Laughland's P.O., Llandovery, near St. Ann's Bay. ☎ **876/770-8071.** Admission J$200 ($5.70), J$100 ($2.85) children under 15. Daily 8:30am–6pm.

Centered on a much-restored water mill that was originally built by a British planter around 200 years ago, this 130-acre commercial nursery welcomes visitors who stroll amid formal lawns, fountains, lakes, and ponds. If you're a devoted botanist, you'll appreciate its diversity of plants. Many Jamaicans value the site as a temporary escape from their apartments, choosing the site for picnics, barbecues, and in some cases, wedding ceremonies. If you opt for a visit, don't miss the view of the open-sided greenhouse whose plants are shaded with cloth mesh from too direct an exposure to the streaming tropical sunlight. Within, you'll find thousands of flourishing orchids and anthuriums. You'll pay a supplement of J$100 ($2.85) for a fishing license, giving you the right to catch one or more of the tilapia stocked in the ponds. For an additional J$100 ($2.85), an on-site chef will gut, clean, and cook whatever fish you catch, serving it within an on-site kitchen. There's a gift shop on the premises, and an on-site facility for shipping thousands of cut flowers to distributors in the U.S.

✪ **Dunn's River Falls.** Rte. A3. ☎ **876/974-2857.** Admission $6 adults, $3 children 2–11, free for children under 2. Daily 8:30am–5pm (8am–5pm on cruise-ship arrival days). From St. Ann's Bay, follow Rte. A3 east back to Ocho Rios, and you'll pass Dunn's River Falls; there's plenty of parking.

For a fee, you can relax on the beach or climb with a guide to the top of the 600-foot falls. You can splash in the waters at the bottom of the falls or drop into the cool pools higher up between the cascades of water. The beach restaurant provides snacks and drinks, and dressing rooms are available. If you're planning to climb the falls, wear old tennis shoes to protect your feet from the sharp rocks and to prevent slipping. Climbing the falls is a chance to experience some 610 feet of cold—but clear—mountain water. In contrast to the heat swirling around you, the splashing water hitting your face and bare legs is quite exhilarating. The problem here is slipping and falling, especially if you're joined to a chain of hands linking body to body. In spite of the slight danger, there seem to be few accidents. The falls aren't exactly a wilderness experience, however; all the tour buses carrying cruise-ship passengers stop here, so at times the place becomes overrun.

Firefly. Grants Pen, in St. Mary, 20 miles east of Ocho Rios above Oracabessa. ☎ **876/997-7201.** Admission $10. Daily 8:30am–5:30pm.

Firefly was the home of Sir Noël Coward and his longtime companion, Graham Payn, who, as executor of Coward's estate, donated it to the Jamaica National Heritage Trust. The recently restored house is more or less as it was on the day Sir Noël died in 1973. His Hawaiian-print shirts still hang in the closet of his austere bedroom, with its mahogany four-poster bed. The library contains a collection of his books, and the living room is warm and comfortable, with big armchairs and two grand pianos (where he composed several famous tunes). When the Queen Mother was entertained here, the lobster mousse Coward planned on serving melted, so, with a style and flair that was the stuff of legend, he opened a can of pea soup instead. Guests were housed at Blue Harbour, a villa closer to Port Maria; they included Evelyn Waugh, Winston Churchill, Errol Flynn, Laurence Olivier, Vivien Leigh, Claudette Colbert, Katharine

Hepburn, and Mary Martin. Paintings by the noted playwright/actor/author/composer adorn the walls. An open patio looks out over the pool and the sea. Across the lawn, his plain, flat white-marble gravestone is inscribed simply: "Sir Noël Coward, born December 16, 1899, died March 26, 1973."

Harmony Hall. Tower Isles on Rte. A3, 4 miles east of Ocho Rios. ☎ **876/975-4222.** Free admission. Gallery Mon–Sat 10am–11pm; restaurant/cafe daily 10am–10pm.

Harmony Hall was built near the end of the 19th century as the centerpiece of a sugar plantation. Today, it has been restored and is now the focal point of an art gallery and restaurant that showcase the painting and sculpture of Jamaican artists as well as a tasteful array of arts and crafts. Among the featured gift items are Sharon McConnell's Starfish Oils, which contain natural additives harvested in Jamaica. The gallery shop also carries the "Reggae to Wear" line of sportswear, designed and made on Jamaica. Harmony Hall is also the setting for one of the best Italian restaurants along the coast, Toscanini's (see "Where to Dine," above).

Prospect Plantation. Rte. A3, 3 miles east of Ocho Rios, in St. Ann. ☎ **876/994-1058.** Tours $12 adults, free for children 12 and under; 1-hour horseback ride $20. Tours Mon–Sat at 10:30am, 2pm, and 3:30pm; Sun at 11am, 1:30pm, and 3pm.

This working plantation adjoins the 18-hole Prospect Mini Golf Course. A visit to this property is an educational, relaxing, and enjoyable experience. On your leisurely ride by covered jitney through the scenic beauty of Prospect, you'll readily see why this section of Jamaica is called "the garden parish of the island." You can view the many trees planted by such visitors as Winston Churchill, Henry Kissinger, Charlie Chaplin, Pierre Trudeau, Noël Coward, and many others. You'll learn about and observe pimento (allspice), bananas, cassava, sugarcane, coffee, cocoa, coconut, pineapple, and the famous leucaena "Tree of Life." You'll see Jamaica's first hydroelectric plant and sample some of the exotic fruit and drinks. Horseback riding is available on three scenic trails at Prospect. The rides vary from 1 hour to 2 hours and 15 minutes. Advance booking of 1 hour is necessary.

SHOPPING

For many, Ocho Rios provides an introduction to Jamaica-style shopping. After surviving the ordeal, some visitors may vow never to go shopping again. Literally hundreds of Jamaicans pour into Ocho Rios hoping to peddle items to cruise-ship passengers and other visitors. Be prepared for aggressive vendors. Pandemonium greets many an unwary shopper, who must also be prepared for some fierce haggling. All vendors ask too much at first, giving them the leeway to "negotiate" until the price reaches a more realistic level. Is shopping fun in Ocho Rios? A resounding no. Do cruise-ship passengers and land visitors indulge in it anyway? A decided yes.

SHOPPING CENTERS & MALLS   There are several main shopping plazas; we've listed them because they're here, not because we heartily recommend them. The originals are Ocean Village, Pineapple Place, and Coconut Grove. Newer ones include the New Ocho Rios Plaza, in the center of town, with some 60 shops. Island Plaza is another major shopping complex, as is the Mutual Security Plaza with some 30 shops. Opposite the New Ocho Rios Plaza is the Taj Mahal, with 26 duty-free stores.

Ocean Village Shopping Centre. ☎ **876/974-2683.** This shopping area contains numerous boutiques, food stores, a bank, sundries purveyors, travel agencies, service facilities, and what-have-you. The **Ocho Rios Pharmacy** (☎ **876/974-2398**) sells most proprietary brands, perfumes, and suntan lotions, among its many wares.

The Potter's Art

The largest and most visible art pottery in Jamaica is found at **Wassi Art, Bougainvillea Drive, Great Pond** (☎ **876/974-5044**). This enterprise is often cited for its entrepreneurial courage by the country's growing core of independent business owners. Established in 1990, it developed from a personal hobby of one of its owners, Theresa Lee, an amateur potter. Today, with her husband Robert, she employs at least 50 artisans and workers in a small-scale beehive of energy about 2.5 miles north of the center of Ocho Rios. You'll reach the place via a winding and impossibly rutted road that's been traveled by thousands of home-owners whose appreciation for the product now approaches something akin to a cult.

Tours of the factory Monday to Saturday 9am to 5pm are free, last about 30 minutes, and include a brief session trying to throw a pot on an electric pot-ter's wheel. Don't expect a high-tech operation here, as virtually every aspect of the manufacturing process, including the digging, hauling, and processing of the Blue Mountain clay, is done the old-fashioned way—by hand. All glazes used in the process are nontoxic and FDA approved.

The finished pottery comes in colors that range from the earth- and forest-toned to the bright iridescent patterns reminiscent of Jamaican music and spice. Prices of objects range from $5 to $2,000, and anything you buy can be shipped by Federal Express. There's a cafe on the premises (try their meat-stuffed patties for an insight into what a Jamaican worker's lunch might include). Part of your experience here includes dialogues with talented artisans hailing from both Jamaica and Cuba.

Although it's a lot more interesting to buy the products directly from the fac-tory, you can also visit the sales outlet, **Wassi Art Gallery and Collectibles** (☎ **876/994-1188**), where prices are the same as at the factory. This outlet is closer to the center of Ocho Rios, across the road from the entrance to the Sans Souci Lido Resort.

Pineapple Place Shopping Centre. Just east of Ocho Rios, this is a collection of shops in cedar-shingle-roofed cottages set amid tropical flowers.

Ocho Rios Craft Park. You can browse some 150 stalls here. A vendor will weave a hat or a basket while you wait, or you can buy a ready-made hat, hamper, handbag, place mats, or lampshade. Other stands stock hand-embroidered goods and will make small items while you wait. Wood carvers work on bowls, ashtrays, statues, and cups.

Coconut Grove Shopping Plaza. This collection of low-lying shops is linked by walkways and shrubs. The merchandise consists mainly of local craft items. Many of your fellow shoppers may be cruise-ship passengers.

Island Plaza. Right in the heart of Ocho Rios is some of the best Jamaican art, all paintings by local artists. You can also purchase local handmade crafts (be prepared to do some haggling), carvings, ceramics, kitchenware, and the inevitable T-shirts.

SPECIALTY SHOPS   In general, the shopping is better in Montego Bay. If you're not going there, wander the Ocho Rios crafts markets, although much of the mer-chandise is monotonous. We list the places that deserve special mention.

Swiss Stores, in the Ocean Village Shopping Centre (☎ 876/974-2519), sells jewelry and all the big names in Swiss watches, including Juvenia, Tissot, Omega, Rolex, Patek Philippe, and Piaget. The Rolex watches here are real, not those fakes touted by hustlers on the streets.

One of the best bets for shopping is **Soni's Plaza,** 50 Main St., the address of all the shops recommended below. **Casa dé Oro** (☎ 876/974-5392) specializes in duty-free watches, fine jewelry, and classic perfumes. **Chulani's** (☎ 876/974-2421) sells a goodly assortment of quality watches and brand-name perfumes, although some of the leather bags might tempt you as well. There's also a wide variety of 14-karat and 18-karat settings with diamonds, emeralds, rubies, and sapphires.

Gem Palace (☎ 876/974-2850) is the place to go for diamond solitaires and tennis bracelets. The shop specializes in 14-karat gold chains and bracelets. **Mohan's** (☎ 876/974-9270) offers one of the best selections of 14-karat and 18-karat gold chains, rings, bracelets, and earrings. Jewelry studded with precious gems such as diamonds and rubies is sold here as well. **Soni's** (☎ 876/974-2303) dazzles with gold, but also cameras, French perfumes, watches, china and crystal, linen tablecloths, and even the standard Jamaican souvenirs. **Taj Gift Centre** (☎ 876/974-9268) has a little bit of everything: Blue Mountain coffee, film, cigars, and hand-embroidered linen tablecloths. For something different, look for Jamaican jewelry made from hematite, a mountain stone. **Taj Mahal** (☎ 876/974-6455) beats most competition with its name-brand watches, jewelry, and fragrances. It also has Paloma Picasso leatherwear and porcelain by Lladró. Other outlets here include **Harjani's Gold Palace** (☎ 876/974-6457), established first in 1940 and still one of the best jewelry stores along the north coast. **Something Jamaican** (☎ 876/974-6428) sells all Jamaican products, including spices and sauces.

We generally ignore hotel gift shops, but the **Jamaica Inn Gift Shop,** in the Jamaica Inn, Main Street (☎ 876/974-2514), is better than most, selling everything from Blue Mountain coffee to Walkers Wood products, even guava jelly and jerk seasoning. If you're lucky, you'll find marmalade from an old family recipe, plus Upton Pimento Dram, a unique liqueur flavored with Jamaican allspice. Local handcrafts include musical instruments for kids, brightly painted country cottages of tin, and intricate jigsaw puzzles of local scenes. The store also sells antiques and fine old maps of the West Indies.

OCHO RIOS AFTER DARK

The **Sports Bar** at the Little Pub Restaurant (see above) is open daily from 10am to 3am, and Sunday is disco night. Most evenings are devoted to some form of entertainment, including karaoke.

Jamaic'N Me Crazy, at the Jamaican Grande Hotel (☎ 876/974-2201), is an all-inclusive spot that's more like a New York nightclub than a Jamaican one. It has the best lighting and sound system in Ocho Rios (and perhaps Jamaica), and the crowd includes everyone from the passing yachter to the curious tourist, who may be under the mistaken impression that he or she is seeing an authentic Jamaican nightclub. It charges nonguests $30 to cover everything you can shake or drink, nightly from 10pm to 3am.

For more of the same without an overbearing Americanized atmosphere, try the **Acropolis,** 70 Main St. (☎ 876/974-2633). The adventurous traveler can rest assured that this is a lot closer to an authentic Jamaican nightclub than Jamaic'N Me Crazy. Cover is required only on nights with a live band, and it's rarely any higher than J$200 ($5.70).

Jamaica Evaluates Its Jerks

Jamaicans, and especially professional drivers, are passionately committed to publicizing the virtues of whatever out-of-the-way stall or kiosk that serves—in their opinion—the country's best jerk pork and chicken. Debates rage in bars and on beaches, but one site that gets consistently good reviews from jerk aficionados is **Blueberry Hill** (☎ **876/996-0263**), located on the coastal road about a half-mile east of the north-shore community of Buff Bay, midway between Port Antonio and Ocho Rios. (It's near the junction of the north-shore coastal highway with one of the roughest roads in the Third World—the one that runs over the Blue Mountains back to Kingston.)

Don't expect a palace. Established in 1980 and flanked by less-famous jerk stalls that have cropped up like clones, it's little more than a roadside lean-to that's caked with the carbonization of years of the slow-cooking jerk process. It serves only jerk pork and jerk chicken, both of which cost J$70 ($2) for a quarter pound; J$120 ($3.40) for a half pound; and J$240 ($6.85) for a full pound. Slices of bread (which you might really want, considering the spiciness of the meat) cost J$5 (15¢) each.

There's no dining room. With an engaging sense of conviviality, clients collect their bounty in aluminum-foil wrappers, and eat with their fingers while standing beside the road, or perhaps sitting on a makeshift stool. Red Stripe and Ting (something akin to Sprite) are the drinks of choice. Overall, it's unpretentious, delicious, friendly, and fun, and is open daily from 10am to 10pm.

2 Runaway Bay

Runaway Bay used to be just a western satellite of Ocho Rios. However, with the opening of some large resorts, plus a colony of smaller hotels, it's now become a destination in its own right. Runaway Bay has developed as a small resort for several reasons, mainly its beaches of white sands, which are superior and less overrun than those of Ocho Rios. The emerging resort is also the place to go if you want to escape the cruise-ship crowds and the aggressive vendors who now overpopulate Ocho Rios.

This part of Jamaica's north coast has several distinctions: It was the first part of the island seen by Columbus, the site of the first Spanish settlement on the island, and the point of departure of the last Spaniards to leave Jamaica following their defeat by the British. Columbus landed at Discovery Bay on his second voyage of exploration in 1494, and in 1509 Spaniards established a settlement called Sevilla Nueva (New Seville) near what is now St. Ann's Bay, about 10 miles east of the present Runaway Bay village. Sevilla Nueva was later abandoned, the inhabitants moving to the southern part of the island.

In 1655, an English fleet sailed into Kingston Harbour and defeated the Spanish garrison there. However, a guerrilla war broke out on the island between the Spanish and English in which the English prevailed. The remnants of the Spanish army embarked for Cuba in 1660 from a small fishing village on the north coast. Some believe that this "running away" from Jamaica gave the name Runaway Bay to the village. However, later historians believe that the name possibly came from the traffic in runaway slaves from the north-coast plantations to Cuba.

WHERE TO STAY & DINE

Runaway Bay offers several unusual accommodations as well as all-inclusive resorts and notable bargains.

EXPENSIVE

Breezes Golf and Beach Resort. P.O. Box 58 (6 miles west of Ocho Rios), Runaway Bay, Jamaica, W.I. ☎ **800/GO-SUPER** or 876/973-2436. Fax 876/973-2352. www.superclubs.com. E-mail: breezesgolf@cwjamaica.com. 238 units. A/C TEL. All-inclusive rates: Winter $500–$830 double. Off-season $440–$790 double. AE, DC, MC, V. Children under 15 not accepted.

This stylish resort operates on a plan that includes three meals a day, all drinks free, and a galaxy of other benefits. Its clubhouse is approached by passing through a park filled with tropical trees and shrubbery. The lobby is the best re-creation of the South Seas on Jamaica, with hanging wicker chairs and totemic columns. Guest rooms are spacious with a light, tropical motif. They're fitted with local woods, cool tile floors, and private balconies or patios. The most elegant are the suites, with Jamaican-made four-poster beds. The good-size bathrooms have combination tub/showers and generous marble counters. There's a miniature jungle with hammocks and a nearby nude beach.

Dining/Diversions: Live music emanates from the stylish Terrace every evening at 7pm, and a nightclub offers live shows 6 nights a week at 10pm. Dine either in the beachside restaurant or in the more-formal Italian restaurant, Martino's.

Amenities: Gym filled with Nautilus equipment, pool, sports-activities center (featuring scuba diving, windsurfing, and a golf school), 18-hole championship golf course. Reggae exercise classes held twice daily.

Chukka Cove Farm and Resort. 4 miles east of Runaway Bay off A1 (P.O. Box 177), Richmond Llandovery, St. Ann's Bay, Jamaica, W.I. ☎ **876/913-4851.** Fax 876/913-4783. E-mail: glascoe@cwjamaica.com. 6 villas. A/C MINIBAR TEL. Winter $2,000 villa per week. Off-season $1,500 villa per week. Rates can be prorated for shorter stays. No credit cards.

Chukka Cove is an ideal center for horse lovers who'd like to live on the grounds. Located 4 miles east of Runaway Bay, it is frequented by Capt. Mark Phillips, former husband of Britain's Princess Anne. On the estate's acreage lie six two-bedroom villas, each suitable for four guests, with a veranda, plank floors, and an architectural plan vaguely reminiscent of 18th-century models. A pampering staff will prepare meals in your villa. Snorkeling is also included.

FDR (Franklyn D. Resort). Main St. (P.O. Box 201), Runaway Bay, St. Ann, Jamaica, W.I. ☎ **800/654-1FDR** in the U.S., or 876/973-4591. Fax 876/973-3071. www.fdrholidays.com. E-mail: fdr@fdrholidays.com. 76 units. A/C TV TEL. Winter $700–$1,000. Off-season $560–$600. Rates are all inclusive. Children 15 and under stay free in parents' suite. AE, MC, V.

Located on Route A1, 17 miles west of Ocho Rios, FDR is geared to families with children and is dedicated to including all meals and activities in a net price. The resort, named after its Jamaican-born owner and developer (Franklyn David Rance), is on 6 acres of flat, sandy land dotted with flowering shrubs and trees, on the main seaside highway. Each of the Mediterranean-inspired buildings has a terra-cotta roof, a loggia or outdoor terrace, Spanish marble in the bathrooms, a kitchenette, and a personal attendant—called a vacation nanny—who cooks, cleans, and cares for children. Although neither the narrow beach nor the modest pools are the most desirable on the island, and most rooms lack a sea view, many visitors appreciate the spacious units and the resort's wholehearted concern for visiting kids.

Dining/Diversions: Two restaurants on the property serve free wine with lunch and dinner (and offer special children's meals), a piano bar provides music every evening, and a handful of bars keeps the drinks flowing. There's live music nightly.

Amenities: An attendant baby-sits for free every day between 9:30am and 4:45pm, after which she can be hired privately for $3 an hour. There's a children's supervisor in attendance at "Kiddies' Centre" (where a computer center, a kiddies' disco, and even kiddies' dinners are regular features). Adults appreciate the scuba lessons, picnics, photography lessons, arts and crafts, and donkey rides that keep the kids entertained. Other amenities include water sports, lit tennis courts, satellite TV room, disco, gym, free use of bicycles for getting around the neighborhood, free tours to Dunn's River Falls, and Ocho Rios shopping.

Hedonism III. Runaway Bay, Jamaica, W.I. ☎ **800/GO-SUPER** in the U.S., or 876/973-5029. Fax 876/973-5402. 225 units. A/C TV TEL. All-inclusive rates for 6 nights: Winter $1,441–$1,603 per person. Off-season $1,089–$1,441 per person. AE, DC, MC, V.

Following a chain format established in Negril, this latest Hedonism is devoted to both singles and couples over 15. Set on 15 acres of landscaped gardens on the eastern end of Runaway Bay, it features ocean views from all rooms and an all-inclusive package deal. The package ranges from fine dining to drinks, plus land and water sports. Ground transfer from and to the Montego Bay airport is included in the rates.

Bedrooms are roomy and freshly decorated, with Jamaica's first-ever block of "swim-up" rooms. All feature large marble bathrooms with Roman Jacuzzi, CD players, and private safes, even irons and ironing boards. Rooms have either twins or one king-size bed. One beach in front of the hotel is au naturel; the other requires clothing.

Dining: The food is quite decent—a choice of four restaurants and a terrace buffet, everything from Italian to Japanese, and, of course, Jamaican.

Amenities: The resort offers three large freshwater pools. Water sports include scuba diving and windsurfing, and there is also a late-night disco along with five bars. Naturally, those notorious toga parties from Negril have been imported here as well.

MODERATE

Club Ambiance Jamaica. Runaway Bay, Jamaica, W.I. ☎ **876/973-4606.** Fax 876/973-2067. 82 units. A/C TV TEL. Winter $115–$135 per person double or triple; $140 per person suite. Off-season $11–$130 per person double or triple; $130 per person suite. Rates are all inclusive. AE, MC, V. Children under 18 not accepted.

Last refurbished in 1995, this is one of the most basic of the all-inclusives, catering mainly to European travelers on a budget. The hotel is laid-back and casual. Lying at the west end of Runaway Bay, it is recommended primarily for its reasonable rates—not for its somewhat bleak two-story appearance (instead of gardens in front, you get a sprawling parking lot). The shoreline near the hotel is rocky, and a small crescent of sand won't win the beach sweepstakes. Units are reasonably comfortable and clean, if not very stylish. Regional art decorates the walls, and the furniture is often upholstered wicker. Accommodations come with either double or king-size beds, with balconies opening onto views of the water.

Dining/Diversions: A standard Jamaican cuisine is served in the Coconut Terrace Dining Room and in Café Calypso. Later, you can work off the calories in the Safari Disco. Sometimes, this sleepy place wakes up with theme nights and cultural shows including beach parties and a live band.

Amenities: Exercise room, swimming pool. For scuba divers, the hotel recently added an accredited PADI center.

✪ **Runaway H.E.A.R.T. Country Club.** Ricketts Ave. (P.O. Box 98), Runaway Bay, St. Ann, Jamaica, W.I. ☎ **876/973-2671.** Fax 876/973-2693. www.discoverjamaica.com. 20 units. A/C TV TEL. Winter $144 double. Off-season $124 double. Rates include MAP (breakfast and dinner). AE, MC, V.

Called "the best-kept secret in Jamaica," this place is located on the main road, and it practically wins hands-down as the bargain of the north coast. One of Jamaica's few training and service institutions, the club and its adjacent academy are operated by the government to provide a high level of training for young Jamaicans interested in the hotel trade. The helpful staff of both professionals and trainees offers the finest service of any hotel in the area. The good-size rooms are bright and airy. Bathrooms have generous shelf space and good towels. The accommodations open onto private balconies with views of well-manicured tropical gardens or vistas of the bay and golf course. Laundry service is available, and facilities include a pool and golf course. Guests enjoy having a drink in the piano bar (ever had a cucumber daiquiri?) before heading for the dining room, the Cardiff Hall Restaurant, which serves Jamaican and continental dishes. Nonguests can also enjoy dinner, served nightly from 7 to 10pm; a well-prepared meal costs around $25. The academy has won awards for some of its dishes, including "go-go banana chicken" and curried codfish.

INEXPENSIVE

Caribbean Isle Hotel. P.O. Box 119, Runaway Bay, St. Ann, Jamaica, W.I. ☎ **876/973-2364.** Fax 876/973-4835. 23 units. A/C. $70 double; $80 triple. AE, MC, V.

This small hotel, located directly on the beach a mile west of Runaway Bay, offers personalized service in an informal atmosphere. Stay here only for the affordable rates; we find the rooms somewhat tattered. But they do all have ocean views, and the superior units have private balconies. The hotel has a TV in the bar-lounge and a dining room leading onto a seaview patio. Meals are served from 7:30am to 11pm daily. Dinner includes lobster, fish, shrimp, pork chops, chicken, and local dishes prepared on request.

NEARBY PLACES TO STAY & DINE

Grand Lido Braco. Rio Bueno P.O. 226, Trelawny, Jamaica. ☎ **888/GOSUPER** in the U.S., or 800/467-8737 or 876/954-0000. Fax 876/954-0020 or 876/954-0021. www.superclubs.com. 226 units. A/C TV TEL. All-inclusive rates for 3 nights: Winter $1,986–$2,220 double; from $2,310 suite for 2. Off-season $1,680–$1,890 double; from $1,980 suite for 2. AE, DC, DISC, MC, V. Children under 16 not accepted.

Established in 1995, this is one of the most historically evocative all-inclusive resorts in Jamaica. Set on 85 acres of land near Buena Vista, a 15-minute drive west of Runaway Bay, it's a re-creation of a 19th-century Jamaican Victorian village, adjacent to an impressive stretch of prime beachfront. A stately copy of a courthouse hosts meetings and entertainment, benches and flowering trees line the symmetrical borders of the town square, and meals are served in four separate venues inspired by an idealized version of Old Jamaica. Employees, most of whom come from the nearby hamlet of Rio Bueno, are encouraged to mingle with guests and share their personal and community stories. You get vivid insights into Jamaican life here that wouldn't be possible at the more cloistered and remote all-inclusive resorts. This is not a place for children; the venue is primarily adult, relaxed, and reasonably permissive. The predominant color scheme throughout the resort is pink and yellow. Accommodations are in 12 blocks of three-story buildings, each trimmed in colonial-style gingerbread and filled with wicker furniture. All units have private patios or verandas and face the ocean, although blocks one through six are closer to the beachfront, while blocks five and six face a strip of sand designated as a "clothing-optional" area. Beds are most comfortable, with extremely good mattresses and fine linen; the bathrooms are well maintained.

Dining/Diversions: Separate dining areas serve Jamaican cuisine, pizza and pasta, and international fare; the Piacere Restaurant serves upscale dinners and has a dress code. The latest restaurant offering, Munahana, serves a Japanese sushi and teppanyaki cuisine. Four bars make getting a drink relatively easy.

Amenities: A soccer field where a local Jamaican team sometimes volunteers to play with (or against) aficionados from the village, a fitness center, a nine-hole golf course, a disco, three fishing ponds, bike and jogging trails, four tennis courts, use of a glass-bottom boat for snorkeling tours, and one of the largest pools in Jamaica. The staff keeps conversations and good times rolling along.

Rio Bueno Hotel. Rio Bueno, Trelawny, Jamaica, W.I. ☎ **876/954-0046.** Fax 876/952-5911. 20 units. $100–$135 double; $200–$250 suite. Rates include continental breakfast. AE, DC, MC, V.

For a 4- or 5-year period in the 1970s, Joe James was a bright flame on the arts scene of Jamaica, with exhibitions of his works in New York, Philadelphia, and Washington, D.C. Although his fame and press coverage have greatly diminished in recent years, the artist continues his endeavors in a concrete-sided compound of buildings set close to the shore of the sheltered harbor of Rio Bueno. Many visitors are fascinated by the showroom, which is loaded with large-scale paintings and wood carvings with Jamaican and African themes. All the objects are for sale, and Mr. James is usually on the premises to explain his artistic theories. Within a few steps of his showroom and the beach, Mr. James has an angular two-story concrete building containing simple and functional accommodations. All have ceiling fans; most have views over the bay and the massive industrial plant whose cranes and smokestacks rise on the opposite side of the harbor. Don't expect luxury here. The primary allure lies in the low cost, the proximity to the studio of one of Jamaica's better-known artists, and the complete lack of pretension.

Dining: The place gets most of its business from the Lobster Bowl Restaurant, serving breakfast, lunch, and dinner daily. The view encompasses the sea, the shore, and one of the neighborhood's largest industrial entities. Lunchtime platters include burgers, salads, sandwiches, and grilled fish. Evening meals are more copious and feature a choice of set menus comprised of grilled fish, broiled lobster, sirloin steak, or chicken, served with soup, salad, dessert, coffee, and Tía María. Meals are served continuously from 8am to 10pm daily. A set-price lunch costs from $12.50 to $18.50, and a set dinner $18.50 to $30. You can dine on a covered wharf, or within the soaring premises that some observers compare to an airplane hangar. Airy, clean, and still evocative of its origins as an industrial building, it's very interesting and with a definite charm.

BEACHES & WATER SPORTS

The two best beaches at Runaway Bay are **Paradise Beach** and **Cardiffall Lot Public Beach.** Both wide, white-sand strips are clean and well maintained—ideal spots for a picnic. There is a great natural beauty in this part of Jamaica, and many foreigners, especially Canadians, seek it out, preferring its more raffish look to the well-publicized tourist Meccas of Ocho Rios. If you're staying in Ocho Rios and want to escape the crowds, come here. You don't get a lot of facilities, however, so you'd better bring along whatever you need.

The waters are calm almost all year. Prevailing trade winds will keep you cool in the mornings and late afternoon. Since there are no lifeguards, be especially careful if you're with children.

Runaway Bay offers some of the best areas for snorkeling in Jamaica. The reefs are close to shore and extremely lively with marine life, including enormous schools of tropical fish such as blue chromis, triggerfish, small skate rays, and snapper. Since boats and fishing canoes can be a problem close to shore, go on a snorkeling excursion with the best diving facility at Runaway Bay: **Resort Divers** (☎ **876/974-5338**), along the beach. This five-star PADI facility takes you out to one of several protected reefs where the water currents aren't dangerous and where fishing boats are required to stay at least 200 yards away from snorkelers. Resort Divers also provides sport-fishing jaunts as well as scuba-diving certification and equipment. A resort dive costs $75, with a one-tank dive going for $35 or a two-tank dive for $65. Parasailing is also available, costing $40 per half hour.

GOLF & HORSEBACK RIDING

SuperClub's Runaway Golf Club (☎ 876/973-7319) charges no admission for guests staying at any of Jamaica's affiliated SuperClubs. For nonguests, the price is $80 year-round.

Jamaica's most complete equestrian center is the **Chukka Cove Polo Club,** at Richmond Llandovery, St. Ann (☎ 876/972-2771), less than 4 miles east of Runaway Bay. A 1-hour trail ride costs $30, while a 2-hour mountain ride goes for $40. The most popular ride is a 3-hour beach jaunt that involves riding over trails to the sea, then swimming in the surf. The $55 cost includes refreshments. A 6-hour beach ride, complete with picnic lunch, goes for $130. Polo lessons are also available, costing $50 for 30 minutes.

EXPLORING THE AREA

Columbus Park Museum, on Queens Highway, in Discovery Bay (☎ 876/973-2135), is a large, open area between the main coast road and the sea at Discovery Bay. Just pull off the road and walk among the fantastic collection of exhibits; admission is free. There's everything from a canoe made from a solid piece of cottonwood (the way Arawaks did it more than 5 centuries ago) to a stone cross that was originally placed on the Barrett estate at Retreat (9 miles east of Montego Bay) by Edward Barrett, brother of poet Elizabeth Barrett Browning. You'll see a tally, used to count bananas carried on men's heads from plantation to ship, as well as a planter's strongbox with a weighted lead base to prevent its theft. Other items are 18th-century cannons, a Spanish water cooler and calcifier, a fish pot made from bamboo, a corn husker, and a water wheel. Pimento trees, from which allspice is produced, dominate the park, which is open daily from 8:30am to 4:30pm.

You can also visit the **Seville Great House,** Heritage Park (☎ 876/972-2191). Built in 1745 by the English, it contains a collection of artifacts once used by everybody from the Amerindians to African slaves. In all, you're treated to an exhibit of 5 centuries' worth of Jamaican history. Modest for a great house, it has a wattle-and-daub construction. A small theater presents a 15-minute historic film about the house. It's open daily from 9am to 5pm; admission is $4.

Port Antonio

From Ocho Rios (see chapter 6), drive east along Highway A4/A3, which will take you through some sleepy fishing villages, including Port Maria, until you reach **Port Antonio.** Since it's situated on the coast just north of the Blue Mountains, Port Antonio is surrounded by some of the most rugged and beautiful scenery in Jamaica. Many visitors prefer to visit the mountains and highlands from a base here, rather than starting out in Kingston, thus avoiding the capital's urban sprawl.

Although Port Antonio was the cradle of Jamaican tourist development, it has been eclipsed by other areas such as Montego Bay, Ocho Rios, and Negril. It remains a preferred hideaway, however, for a chic and elegant crowd that still vacations in its handful of posh hotels. The tourist flow to Port Antonio began in the 1890s, when cruise-ship passengers started to arrive for rest and relaxation. Perched above twin harbors, the estuary was pronounced by the poet Ella Wheeler as "the most exquisite harbor on earth."

Port Antonio is a verdant and sleepy seaport 63 miles northeast of Kingston (you may have seen it as the setting for Tom Cruise's old film *Cocktail*). Here, you can still catch a glimpse of the Jamaica of 100 years ago. The titled and the wealthy have come here before you— European duchesses and barons, along with film stars like Linda Evans, Raquel Welch, and Peter O'Toole. Whoopi Goldberg came here to film *Clara's Heart*.

The small, bustling town itself is like many on Jamaica: clean but ramshackle, with sidewalks around a market filled with vendors. Tin-roofed shacks compete with old Georgian and modern brick and concrete buildings. Lots of people busily shop, talk, and laugh, while others sit and play dominoes (loudly banging the pieces on the table, which is very much part of the game). The colorful market is a place to browse for local craftwork, spices, and fruits.

In the old days, visitors arrived by banana boat and stayed at the Titchfield Hotel (since burned down) in a lush, tropical part of the island unspoiled by modern tourist gimmicks. Captain Bligh landed here in 1793 with his cargo of breadfruit plants from Tahiti, and Port Antonio claims that the breadfruit grown here are the best on the island. Visitors still arrive by water, but now it's on cruise ships, which moor close to Navy Island and send their passengers ashore just for the day.

Navy Island and the long-gone Titchfield Hotel were owned for a short time by film star Errol Flynn. The story is that after suffering damage to his yacht, he put into Kingston for repairs, visited Port Antonio by motorbike, fell in love with the area, and in due course acquired Navy Island (in a gambling game, some say). Later, he either lost or sold it and bought a nearby plantation, Comfort Castle, which is still owned by his widow, Patrice Wymore Flynn, who spends most of her time here. He was much loved and admired by the Jamaicans and was totally integrated into the community. They still talk of him in Port Antonio, especially the men, who refer to his legendary womanizing and drinking in reverent tones.

We find Port Antonio an elite retreat, not as undiscovered as it was when William Randolph Hearst or J. P. Morgan visited, but a virtual Shangri-la when compared to Ocho Rios or Montego Bay. It also has some of the finest beaches in Jamaica and has long been a center for some of the Caribbean's best deep-sea fishing. It's a good place to go to get away from it all.

1 Getting There

BY PLANE
If you're going to Ocho Rios first, you'll fly into the **Donald Sangster Airport** in Montego Bay (see chapter 3) or the **Norman Manley International Airport** in Kingston (see chapter 8). Some hotels, particularly the larger resorts, will arrange for airport transfers from that point. Be sure to ask when you book.

If your hotel doesn't provide transfers, you can fly to Port Antonio's small airport aboard **Air Jamaica Express,** booking your connection through Air Jamaica (☎ **800/ 523-5585** in the U.S.). The one-way fare is $40 from Kingston or $55 from Montego Bay.

BY BUS
The bus costs $25 one-way. We recommend two private companies: **Tour Wise** (☎ 876/979-1027) or **Caribic Vacations** (☎ 876/953-9874). The bus will drop you off at your hotel. The trip takes 2 hours, but for safety's sake, we recommend this option only if you fly into Montego Bay.

BY RENTAL CAR & TAXI
You can rent a car for the 133-mile drive east along Route A1, but we don't advise this 4-hour drive for safety's sake, regardless of which airport you land at. If you take a taxi, the typical one-way fare from Montego Bay is $100, but always negotiate and agree upon a fare *before* you get into the cab.

2 Where to Stay

In spite of the charms of Port Antonio, it is suffering from a lack of business as resort clients are drawn to the more famous Negril, Ocho Rios, and Montego Bay. Many of the hotels below are having to fill up empty rooms with low-cost tour groups hailing from everywhere from Italy to Canada. Because of this, there has been a major deterioration in the physical plants of some of the properties, which are no longer maintained in a state-of-the-art condition.

VERY EXPENSIVE
Trident Villas and Hotel. Rte. A4 (P.O. Box 119), Port Antonio, Jamaica, W.I. ☎ **876/ 993-2602.** Fax 876/993-2960. E-mail: trident@infochan.com. 22 units. A/C TV TEL. Winter $385 double; from $620 suite. Off-season $220 double; from $340 suite. Rates include MAP (breakfast and dinner). AE, MC, V.

Port Antonio

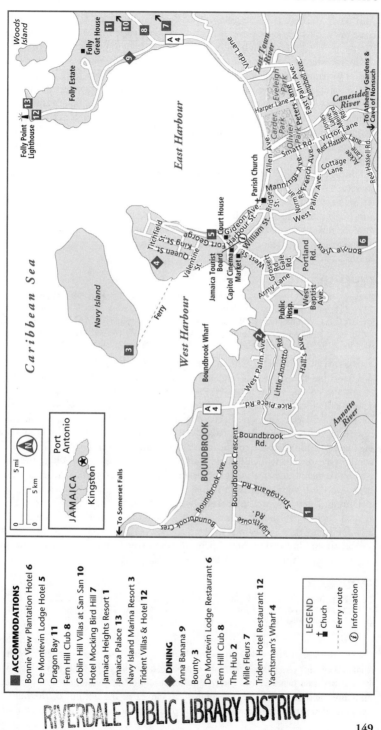

ACCOMMODATIONS
Bonnie View Plantation Hotel **6**
De Montevin Lodge Hotel **5**
Dragon Bay **11**
Fern Hill Club **8**
Goblin Hill Villas at San San **10**
Hotel Mocking Bird Hill **7**
Jamaica Heights Resort **1**
Jamaica Palace **13**
Navy Island Marina Resort **3**
Trident Villas & Hotel **12**

◆ **DINING**
Anna Banana **9**
Bounty **3**
De Montevin Lodge Restaurant **6**
Fern Hill Club **8**
The Hub **2**
Mille Fleurs **7**
Trident Hotel Restaurant **12**
Yachtsman's Wharf **4**

LEGEND
✝ Church
--- Ferry route
ⓘ Information

This rendezvous is about 2½ miles east of Port Antonio along Allan Avenue, on the coast toward Frenchman's Cove. It sits regally above jagged coral cliffs with a seaside panorama. The hotel's main building is furnished with antiques, and flowers decorate the lobby, which is cooled by sea breezes. Your accommodations will be a studio cottage or tower, reached by a path through the gardens. In the cottages, a large bedroom with an ample sitting area opens onto a private patio with a sea view. All units have ceiling fans, plenty of storage space, and tasteful Jamaican antiques and colorful chintzes. Beds are most comfortable with deluxe mattresses, while tiled bathrooms have combination tub/showers. There's a small, private sand beach, and the gardens surround a pool and a gingerbread gazebo. Lounges, tables, chairs, and bar service add to your pleasure.

Dining: The main building has two patios, one covered, where breakfast and lunch are served. You can also have breakfast on your private patio, served by your own butler. Men are required to wear jackets and ties at dinner, when silver service, crystal, and Port Royal pewter sparkle on the tables. Dinner is a multicourse, excellent fixed-price meal, so if you have dietary restrictions, make your requirements known early.

Amenities: Pool, tennis courts, and such water sports as sailing and snorkeling. Room service, laundry, baby-sitting.

EXPENSIVE

Dragon Bay. P.O. Box 176, Port Antonio, Jamaica, W.I. ☎ **876/993-8751.** Fax 876/993-3284. www.dragonbay.com. E-mail: reservations@dragonbay.com. 97 units in 33 bungalows. A/C TEL. Winter $175–$205 double; $240 1-bedroom suite for 2; $360 2-bedroom suite for up to 4; $440 3-bedroom suite for 6–8. Off-season $120 double; $150–$230 1-bedroom suite for 2; $250 2-bedroom suite for up to 4; $320 3-bedroom suite for 6–8. AE, MC, V.

Established in 1969 on 55 acres of forested land that slopes down to a sandy beach, this resort has changed hands frequently during its lifetime and gone through a series of ups and downs. Today, it's a well-managed, carefully designed compound of bungalows and villas that caters to a mostly European clientele, most of whom check in for stays of 2 weeks or more. Accommodations are about 30 pink-and-white, two-story bungalows, some built on flatlands beside the beach, others on the steeply sloping terrain leading uphill to the resort's clubhouse. Furnishings are durable but comfortable; the efficiently organized bathrooms have shower stalls. All but the smallest units contain kitchens, a fact appreciated by guests who prepare at least some of their own meals with supplies purchased at neighborhood grocery stores.

Dining: There are two restaurants, one beside the beach, the other a more substantial eatery. There are three bars—our favorite is the Cruise Bar, which was used as a set for Tom Cruise in *Cocktail.*

Amenities: On-site dive shop, a pool adjacent to the beach, two tennis courts, hiking paths through the forest, and aerobics classes.

MODERATE

Fern Hill Club Hotel. Mile Gully Rd., San San (P.O. Box 100), Port Antonio, Jamaica, W.I. ☎ **876/993-7374.** Fax 876/993-7373. 31 units. A/C TV. $99–$121 double. AE, MC, V. Drive east along Allan Ave. and watch for the signs.

Airy and panoramic but run-down, Fern Hill occupies 20 forested acres high above the coastline, attracting primarily a British and Canadian tour-group clientele. This is a far less elegant choice than its main competitor, Goblin Hill (see below). Technically classified as a private club, the establishment comprises a colonial-style clubhouse and three outlying villas, plus a comfortable annex at the bottom of the hill. The accommodations come in a wide range of configurations, including standard rooms,

TIMBUKTU   KALAMAZOO

AT&T Direct® Service

The easy way to call home from anywhere.

Global connection with the AT&T Network | **AT&T**
direct
service

the easy way to call home, take the attached wallet guide.

Make Learning Fun & Easy

With IDG Books Worldwide

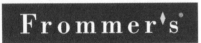

The Hub. 2 West Palm Ave. ☎ **876/993-2149.** Main courses J$180–J$600 ($5.15–$17.10). No credit cards. Daily 8:30am–midnight. JAMAICAN.

Set within a cement-sided, relatively nondescript building just east of the town center, this is the local restaurant that's most often cited by expatriates as their favorite local eatery. Lloyd Bentley, the hardworking owner, maintains a sense of humor about his restaurant's lack of a view. (It overlooks a parking lot and a side yard of the now-defunct local railroad.) But in a town loaded with seafront panoramas, patrons flock here anyway. Menu items are fresh-made and flavorful, featuring a tried-and-true blend of such dishes as pork chops, three different preparations of chicken (including a version in brown-stew sauce), stewed peas with rice, oxtail, and brown-stewed fish.

Yachtsman's Wharf. 16 West St. ☎ **876/993-3053.** Main courses $7–$15. No credit cards. Daily 7:30am–10pm. INTERNATIONAL.

This restaurant beneath a thatch-covered roof is at the end of an industrial pier, near the departure point for ferries to Navy Island. The rustic bar and restaurant is a favorite of the expatriate yachting set. Crews from many of the ultraexpensive boats have dined here and have pinned their ensigns on the roughly textured planks and posts. The kitchen opens for breakfast and stays open all day, serving up menu items such as burgers, ceviche, curried chicken, and akee with salt fish. Main dishes include vegetables. Come here for the setting, the camaraderie, and the usual array of tropical drinks; the food is only secondary.

A NEARBY PLACE TO DINE

✪ **Mille Fleurs.** In the Hotel Mocking Bird Hill, Port Antonio. ☎ **876/993-7267.** Reservations recommended. Fixed-price dinner $21–$25; lunch platters $8.50–$25. AE, MC, V. Daily 8:30am–10am, noon–3pm, and 7–9:30pm. INTERNATIONAL.

This restaurant is terraced into a verdant hillside about 600 feet above sea level with sweeping views over the Jamaican coastline and the faraway harbor of Port Antonio. Sheltered from the frequent rains, but open on the side for maximum access to cooling breezes, it features candlelit dinners, well-prepared food, and lots of New Age charm. Menu items at lunch include sandwiches, salads, grilled fish platters, and soups. At night, you might feast on fresh lobster or else tender lamb and beef dishes, even savory rabbit or smoked marlin. The restaurant has been acclaimed by *Gourmet* magazine for its dishes. You may want to try the coconut-and-garlic soup, and the fish with spicy mango-shrimp sauce is a specialty. Breads and most jams are made on the premises. Some (but not all) of the dishes are designed for vegetarians.

4 Beaches & Outdoor Pursuits

BEACHES   Port Antonio has several white-sand beaches, including the famous **San San Beach,** which has recently gone private, although guests of certain hotels are admitted with a pass.

   Boston Bay Beach is free and often has light surfing; there are picnic tables as well as a restaurant and snack bar. On your way here, stop and get the makings for a picnic lunch at the most famous center for peppery jerk pork and chicken on Jamaica. These rustic shacks also sell the much-rarer jerk sausage. It's 11 miles east of Port Antonio and the Blue Lagoon (see the box below).

   Also free is **Fairy Hill Beach** (Winnifred), with no changing rooms or showers. **Frenchman's Cove Beach** attracts a chic crowd to its white-sand beach combined with a freshwater stream. Nonguests are charged a fee.

Navy Island, once Errol Flynn's personal hideaway, is a fine choice for swimming (one beach is clothing optional) and snorkeling (at **Crusoe's Beach**). Take the boat from the Navy Island dock on West Street across from the Exxon station. It's a 7-minute ride to the island; a one-way fare is 30¢. The ferry runs 24 hours a day. The island is the setting for the Navy Island Marina Resort (see above).

DEEP-SEA FISHING   Northern Jamaican waters are world renowned for their game fish, including dolphinfish (mahimahi), wahoo, blue and white marlin, sailfish, tarpon, barracuda, and bonito. The Jamaica International Fishing Tournament and Jamaica International Blue Marlin Team Tournaments run concurrently at Port Antonio every September or October. Most major hotels from Port Antonio to Montego Bay have deep-sea-fishing facilities, and there are many charter boats.

A 30-foot-long **sportfishing boat** (☎ 876/993-3209) with a tournament rig is available for charter rental. Taking out up to six passengers at a time, it charges $250 per half day or $450 per day, with crew, bait, tackle, and soft drinks included. It docks at Port Antonio's Marina, off West Palm Avenue, in the center of town. Call for bookings.

RAFTING   Although not an adrenaline moment, this is the grand rafting experience on the island and the most fun. It's tame and safe, and you'll have more thrilling moments in the Rocky Mountains. But when in Jamaica, you might give it a try.

Rafting started on the Río Grande as a means of transporting bananas from the plantations to the waiting freighters. In 1871, a Yankee skipper, Lorenzo Dow Baker, decided that a seat on one of the rafts was better than walking, but it was not until Errol Flynn arrived that the rafts became popular as a tourist attraction. Flynn used to hire the craft for his friends, and he encouraged the rafters to race down the Río Grande. Bets were placed on the winner. Now that bananas are transported by road, the raft skipper makes one or maybe two trips a day down the waterway. If you want to take a trip, contact **Río Grande Attractions Limited,** c/o Rafter's Restaurant, St. Margaret's Bay (☎ 876/993-5778).

The rafts, 33 feet long and only 4 feet wide, are propelled by stout bamboo poles; there's a raised double seat about two-thirds of the way back. The skipper, who stands in the front—trousers rolled up to his knees, the water washing his feet—guides the craft down the lively river, about 8 miles between steep hills covered with coconut palms, banana plantations, and flowers, through limestone cliffs pitted with caves, through the "Tunnel of Love" (a narrow cleft in the rocks), then on to wider, gentler water.

The day starts at the Rafter's Restaurant, west of Port Antonio, at Burlington on St. Margaret's Bay. Trips last 2 to 2½ hours and are offered from 8am to 4pm daily at a cost of $45 per raft, which holds two passengers. From the restaurant, a fully insured driver will take you in your rented car to the starting point at Grants Level or Berrydale,

---

A Dip in the Blue Lagoon

Remember Brooke Shields, way back before she tried to become a TV-sitcom star? She made the film *The Blue Lagoon* in this calm, protected cove. The water is so deep, nearly 20 feet or so, that it turns a cobalt blue. There's almost no more scenic spot in all of Jamaica. The Blue Lagoon, with its small, intimate beach, lies 10 miles to the east of Port Antonio. It's a great place for a picnic; you can pick up plenty of the famous peppery delicacy, jerk pork, smoked at various shacks along the Boston Bay Beach area.

Eco-Cultural Tours

Unique Destinations has designed a series of eco-cultural packages for travelers who want to discover the real Jamaica. These "Discover Jamaica Naturally" packages include accommodations in a hotel or villa in Port Antonio, welcome drinks, selected meals and hotel taxes/service charges, and a variety of excursions, such as bamboo rafting and hiking trips to remote waterfalls, scuba diving, snorkeling, and horseback riding. Packages for 3 nights/4 days start at $300 per person (double occupancy). A variety of other packages is also available, including the Birding Adventures package, which journeys into the Río Grande Valley, John Crow Mountains, and Blue Mountains (to observe Jamaica's exotic birds and butterflies); the Maroons of the Río Grande package, which includes a trip to historic Mooretown to meet the Colonel of the Maroons and a hike to the sacred Nanny Falls; and the Hike & Heal Retreat, which includes a visit to a Maroon herbalist for a special garden tour and presentation, followed by a relaxing herbal bath or essential-oil massage. For more information contact **Unique Destinations** via phone at ☎ **401/934-3398** or e-mail at uniquedest@aol.com. You can also visit the Unique Destinations Web site at **www.portantoniojamaica.com**.

where you board your raft. The trip ends back at the Rafter's Restaurant, where you can collect your car, which has been returned by the driver. If you feel like it, take a picnic lunch, but bring enough for the skipper, too, who will regale you with lively stories of life on the river.

SNORKELING & SCUBA DIVING The best outfitter is **Lady Godiva's Dive Shop** in Dragon Bay (☎ **876/993-8988**), 7 miles from Port Antonio. Full dive equipment is available. Technically, you can snorkel off most beaches in Port Antonio, but you're likely to see much more farther offshore. The very best spot is San San Bay by Monkey Island. The reef here is extremely active and full of a lot of exciting marine life. Lady Godiva offers two excursions daily to this spot for $10 per person. Snorkeling equipment costs $9 for a full day's rental.

5 Exploring the Area

Athenry Gardens and Cave of Nonsuch. Portland. ☎ **876/993-3740.** Admission (including guide for gardens and cave) $5 adults, $2.50 children 11 and under. Daily 10am–4pm. From Harbour St. in Port Antonio, turn south in front of the Anglican church onto Red Hassel Rd. and proceed approximately a mile to Breastworks community (fork in road). Take the left fork, cross a narrow bridge, go immediately left after the bridge, and proceed approximately 3.5 miles to the village of Nonsuch.

Twenty minutes from Port Antonio, it's an easy drive and an easy walk to see the stalagmites, stalactites, fossilized marine life, and evidence of Arawak civilization in Nonsuch. The cave is 1.5 million years old, and you can explore its underground beauty by following railed stairways and concrete walkways on a 30-minute walk. The place is dramatically lit. Although the U.S. and Europe have far-greater cave experiences, this is as good as it gets in Jamaica. From the Athenry Gardens, there are panoramic views over the island and the sea. The gardens are filled with coconut palms, flowers, and trees, and complete guided tours are given.

Somerset Falls. 8 miles west of Port Antonio, just past Hope Bay on Rte. A4. ☎ **876/ 913-0108**. Tour $4. Daily 9am–5pm.

Here, the waters of the Daniels River pour down a deep gorge through a rain forest, with waterfalls and foaming cascades. You can take a short ride in an electric gondola to the hidden falls. A stop on the daily Grand Jamaica Tour from Ocho Rios, this is one of Jamaica's most historic sites; the falls were used by the Spanish before the English captured the island. At the falls, you can change into a swimsuit and enjoy the deep rock pools and buy sandwiches, light meals, soft drinks, beer, and liquor at the snack bar. The guided tour includes the gondola ride and a visit to both a cave and a freshwater fish farm. On certain days, the site is likely to be overrun with camera-toting tourists.

Folly Great House. On the outskirts of Port Antonio on the way to Trident Village, going east along Rte. A4. Free admission.

Come here only if you don't have a lot to do that day, and expect to see a roofless structure with weeds growing up through the foundations. Perhaps it'll inspire you to write a Gothic novel. This house was reportedly built in 1905 by Arthur Mitchell, an American millionaire, for his wife, Annie, daughter of Charles Tiffany (founder of the famous New York store). Seawater was used in the concrete mixtures of its foundations and mortar, and the house began to collapse only 11 years after they moved in. Because of the beautiful location, it's easy to see what a fine great house it must have been.

Kingston & the Blue Mountains

8

Kingston, the largest English-speaking city in the Caribbean, is the capital of Jamaica and its cultural, industrial, and financial center. It's home to more than 750,000 people, including those living on the plains between Blue Mountain and the sea. The buildings here are a mixture of the modern, graceful, old, and just plain ramshackle. It's a busy city, as you might expect, with a natural harbor that's the seventh largest in the world. The University of the West Indies has its campus on the edge of the city.

Few other cities in the Caribbean carry as many negative connotations for North American travelers as Kingston, thanks to widely publicized, and sometimes exaggerated, reports of violent crime. Coupled with that is urban congestion, potholed roads, and difficult-to-decipher directional signs that make navigating this city more complicated than navigating any other destination in Jamaica.

But if you're an urban dweller who copes with everyday life in, say, New York, Atlanta, or Los Angeles, Kingston offers resources and charms that aren't duplicated anywhere else. It is here that Jamaica is at its most urbanized and confident, its most witty, its most exciting, and its most challenging. No other place in Jamaica offers as many singles bars, dance clubs, or cultural outlets. And no other place in Jamaica has the creative cauldron wherein ideas and opinions are as sharply focused. Kingston can be very stimulating and very far removed from the tourist-oriented concerns that drive the economic engines of Negril, Ocho Rios, or Montego Bay.

We've carefully screened the recommendations contained within this guidebook, eliminating any that lie within the most dangerous neighborhoods. So, keep an open mind about Kingston—it can be a lot of fun and very exciting.

Nearby Port Royal and Spanish Town are well worth a visit, as Kingston's history is linked to both of these historic towns. Kingston itself was founded by survivors of the great 1692 earthquake that destroyed Port Royal; in 1872, Kingston replaced Spanish Town as Jamaica's capital.

1 Where to Stay

Remember to ask if the 12% room tax is included in the rate quoted when you make your reservation. The rates listed below are year-round unless otherwise noted. All leading hotels in security-conscious Kingston have guards.

Kingston Area

JAMAICA
Kingston

ACCOMMODATIONS

Altamont Court Hotel **9**
The Courtleigh Hotel **13**
Crowne Plaza Kingston **1**
Hotel Four Seasons **8**
Indies Hotel **7**
Kingston Hilton Hotel **12**
Le Meridien Jamaica Pegasus **15**
Strawberry Hill **22**
Terra Nova Hotel **2**

◆ DINING

Akbar **23**
Alexander's **13**
Blue Mountain Inn **20**
Boon Hill Oasis **17**
Chelsea Jerk Centre **11**
Ciaoubella **19**
Devonshire Restaurant/
   The Grogg Shoppe **4**
El Dorado Room **3**
Heather's **16**
The Hot Pot **14**
Indies Pub & Grill **10**
Isabella's **1**
Jade Garden **18**
Norma's on the Terrace **5**
Peppers **3**
The Port Royal Restaurant **15**
Raquel's Restaurant & Seafood **6**
The Restaurant
   at the Four Seasons Hotel **8**
The Upper Crust (Guilt Trip) **21**

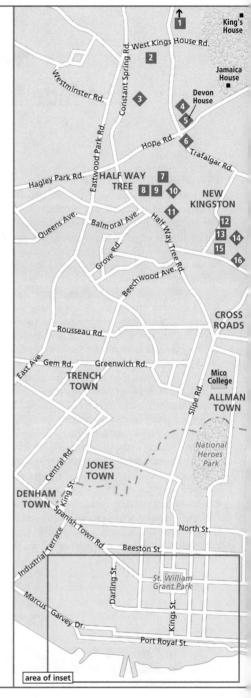

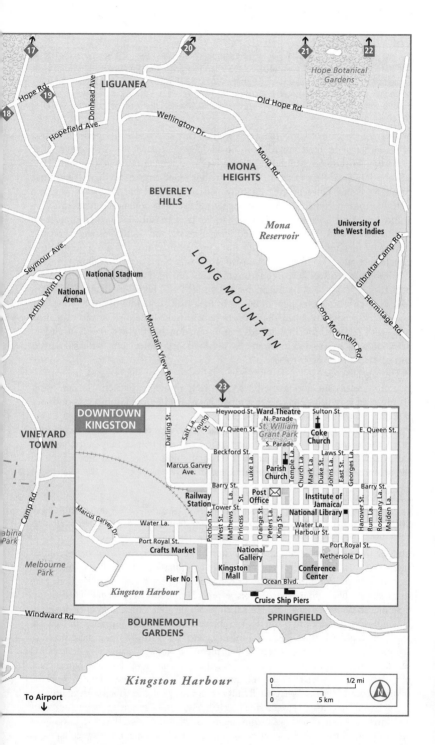

17
20
21
22

Hope Botanical
Gardens

Hope Rd.
19
LIGUANEA
Donhead Ave
18
Hopefield Ave.
Wellington Dr.
Old Hope Rd.

Mona Rd.

MONA
HEIGHTS

BEVERLEY
HILLS

*Mona
Reservoir*

University of
the West Indies

Seymour Ave.

L O N G   M O U N T A I N

Arthur Wint Dr.

National Stadium

**National
Arena**

Gibraltar Camp Rd.

Hermitage Rd.

Long Mountain Rd.

Mountain View Rd.

23

VINEYARD
TOWN

Camp Rd.

abina
Park

*Melbourne
Park*

**DOWNTOWN
KINGSTON**

Darling St.
Salt La.
Young St.

Heywood St.
Ward Theatre
N. Parade
W. Queen St.
St. William
Grant Park
S. Parade

Sulton St.
**Coke
Church**
E. Queen St.

Beckford St.

Marcus Garvey
Ave.

Luke La.

**Parish
Church**

Temple La.
Church La.
Mark La.
Duke St.
Johns La.
East St.
Georges La.
Laws St.

Barry St.

Barry St.

**Railway
Station**

Pechon St.
West St.
Mathews La.
Princess
Tower St.

Orange St.
Peters La.
King St.

**Post
Office**

**Institute of
Jamaica/
National Library**

Hanover St.
Rum La.
Rosemary La.
Maiden La.

Water La.

Marcus Garvey Dr.

Water La.
Port Royal St.

Crafts Market

Water La.
Harbour St.

Port Royal St.
Nethersole Dr.

**National
Gallery**

Pier No. 1

**Kingston
Mall**

Ocean Blvd.

**Conference
Center**

Kingston Harbour

Cruise Ship Piers

Windward Rd.

BOURNEMOUTH
GARDENS

SPRINGFIELD

Kingston Harbour

0 ——— 1/2 mi
0 ——— .5 km

To Airport

VERY EXPENSIVE

✪ **Strawberry Hill.** Irish Town, Blue Mountains, Jamaica, W.I. ☎ **800/OUTPOST** or 876/944-8400. Fax 876/944-8408. www.islandoutpost.com/StrawberryHill/jump.html. E-mail: strawberry@cwjamaica.com. 16 units. TV TEL. $295–$595. AE, DC, MC, V. Guests are personally escorted to the hotel in a customized van or via a 7-minute helicopter ride. It's a 50-min. drive from the Kingston airport or 30 min. via mountain roads from the center of the city.

Music-industry mogul Chris Blackwell worked here to re-create an idealized version of Jamaica that he remembered from his childhood. The setting is a former coffee plantation in the Blue Mountains, on precariously sloping rain-forest terrain 3,100 feet above the sea. Views from its laboriously buttressed terraces overlook the capital's twinkling lights. Eco-sensitive and fully self-contained, it has its own power and water-purification systems, a small-scale spa, and elaborate botanical gardens that horticulturists find thrilling. Accommodations are lavishly nostalgic, draped in bougainvillea and Victorian-inspired gingerbread, and outfitted with gracious mahogany furniture like what you'd expect in a 19th-century Jamaican great house. One former guest described this exclusive resort as a "home away from home for five-star Robinson Crusoes." Maps and/or guides are provided for tours of nearby coffee plantations, hiking and mountain biking through the Blue Mountains, and—if it appeals to you—tours by night or by day of the urban attractions of nearby Kingston. Local craftspeople fashioned the cottages and furnished them in classic plantation style, with canopied four-poster beds and louvered mahogany windows. The elegant bathrooms, each designed in an artfully old-fashioned motif, come with hair dryers and combination shower/tubs.

Dining/Diversions: The food here is good enough that the place is targeted as a glamorous restaurant destination for escapists from throughout eastern Jamaica. Meals are preceded with drinks in a bar that might have been imported from a very posh private home from the Jamaica of long ago.

Amenities: An oval swimming pool was laboriously cantilevered onto a sloping site that architects claimed would never support it. The result is an artfully cascading basin fed by a natural cold-water spring that's very refreshing. There's a full-fledged spa on the premises with hydrotherapy facilities and massage.

EXPENSIVE

Crowne Plaza Kingston. 211A Constant Spring Rd., Jamaica, W.I. ☎ **800/618-6534** or 876/925-7676. Fax 876/925-5757. 130 units. A/C MINIBAR TV TEL. $129 double; $179 suite. Rates include round-trip transfer from airport. AE, DC, MC, V.

One of the most oft-discussed blockbuster hotels in Kingston is an ochre-colored tower that rises dramatically from a hillside in an upmarket suburb, about 15 minutes by taxi from the commercial center of Kingston. Opened in 1997, with a floor plan that's shaped like a four-bladed airplane propeller, it was immediately cited for its desirable accommodations, some of which were quickly claimed as long-term rentals by employees at the nearby American Embassy. (The layout of the place, in fact, has appealed to officials from the U.S. Embassy, who have tried, so far unsuccessfully, to acquire the entire building as part of their premises.) Today, it caters to a discreet and sedate clientele of business travelers, bankers, and high-level political bureaucrats, many of whom appreciate a calm and quiet that's very far from the animated street life of downtown Kingston. What you'll find is a curiously subdued hotel with an unusual lobby layout that clusters several small-scale lounges and a reception facility into cozy and intimate—but sometimes inconveniently small—divisions. These disadvantages are outweighed by such virtues as panoramic terraces that encompass sweeping views of the city and comfortable and fairly spacious bedrooms accented with such high-tech facilities as voice mail and fax modems.

Dining/Diversions: Isabella's is the flagship gourmet restaurant, offering a mix of international cuisine with Jamaica's spicy and stylish flair, accompanied by panoramic views of the harbor and mountains. The Bistro serves meals in an informal poolside setting. The Lobby Bar and Isabella's Lounge (adjoining the main restaurant) are piano bars, often used for informal one-on-one meetings by day. Theme events throughout the week include jazz night, Latin night, Friday-evening happy hour, and Sunday champagne brunch.

Amenities: Swimming pool, tennis, squash, fitness center with sauna and Jacuzzi, business center, jogging and exercise trail, room service, laundry.

Kingston Hilton Hotel. 77 Knutsford Blvd. (in the center of New Kingston, near Oxford Rd.; P.O. Box 112), Kingston 5, Jamaica, W.I. ☎ **876/926-5430.** Fax 876/929-7439. 303 units. A/C TV TEL. $205–$250 double; $320–$525 suite. Children under 12 stay free in parents' room. AE, DC, MC, V.

The Wyndham Kingston is an imposing mass of pink-colored stucco pierced with oversize sheets of tinted glass. The main core of the hotel is a 17-floor tower, containing 220 guest rooms. In addition, poolside units add to the hotel's accommodations. Completely refurbished, bedrooms feature up-to-date amenities, including coffeemakers and remote-control satellite TV.

Dining/Diversions: Fine cuisine is offered at the Terrace Café, providing à la carte Jamaican and international food. The health-conscious appreciate the fare served from the cafe's popular salad and pasta bars. The Rendezvous Bar and Palm Court Restaurant offer more-elegant dining and fine wines.

Amenities: Olympic-size swimming pool, floodlit tennis courts, health club, tour desk, laundry, valet, baby-sitting, massage.

Le Meridien Jamaica Pegasus. 81 Knutsford Blvd. (in the center of New Kingston, off Oxford Rd.; a 12-mile taxi ride from the airport), Kingston 5, Jamaica, W.I. ☎ **876/926-3690.** Fax 876/929-5855. www.meridienjamaica.com. E-mail: jmpegasus@cwjamaica.com. 343 units. A/C TV TEL. $190–$205 double; from $275 suite. AE, DC, MC, V.

A favorite with business travelers, the Jamaica Pegasus outclasses its nearest rival, the Wyndham New Kingston, in a close race. It's located in the banking area of Kingston, which is also a fine residential area. After a major renovation, the hotel is now better than ever and is the site of many conventions and social events. The hotel combines English style with Jamaican warmth. The staff makes an effort to provide activities, such as arranging water sports and sightseeing. Each of the well-furnished bedrooms contains coffee-making equipment, a satellite color TV, and a radio. Several floors of luxuriously appointed suites form the Knutsford Club, which offers special executive services.

Dining: The 4pm tea service is a bit of a social event among some residents. The premier restaurant is The Port Royal (see "Where to Dine," below). The Brasserie is the hotel's informal restaurant that opens onto the swimming pool, where a splashing fountain cools the air. It adjoins a circular bar near the pool at which occasional barbecues are prepared, featuring such dishes as grilled fish and jerk pork. You can also enjoy a drink in the more formal Polo Bar.

Amenities: Jogging track, health club, tennis courts, outdoor pool, laundry and dry-cleaning, 24-hour room service, baby-sitting, therapeutic massage.

MODERATE

The Courtleigh. 85 Knutsford Blvd., Kingston 5, Jamaica, W.I. ☎ **876/929-9000.** Fax 876/926-7744. www.courtleigh.com. E-mail: courtleigh@cwjamaica.com. 126 units. A/C MINIBAR TV TEL. $125–$145 double; $200–$420 suite. AE, MC, V.

In 1997, the Courtleigh abandoned its somewhat run-down premises in another neighborhood of Kingston and moved into a 10-story beige-and-green tower that had originally been built as the site of another hotel, the Skyline. As part of the process, they radically renovated their new home, bringing the bedrooms up to the standards of nearby competitors, the Pegasus and the Wyndham, which lie on either side. Today, you'll find a hardworking, business-oriented hotel with better prices than its neighbors. There's a rectangular swimming pool on the premises, a bar/lounge, and a restaurant (Alexander's), which is separately recommended in "Where to Dine." All rooms contain a safety-deposit box.

Terra Nova Hotel. 17 Waterloo Rd., Kingston 10, Jamaica, W.I. ☎ **876/926-2211.** Fax 876/929-4933. www.cariboutpost.com. 35 units. A/C TV TEL. $132 double. AE, MC, V.

This house is on the western edge of New Kingston, near West Kings House Road. Built in 1924 as a wedding present for a young bride, it was converted into a hotel in 1959. Set in 2.5 acres of gardens with a backdrop of greenery and mountains, it's now one of the best small Jamaican hotels, although the rooms are rather basic and not at all suited for those who want a resort ambience. Most of the bedrooms are in a new wing. The Spanish-style El Dorado Room, with a marble floor, wide windows, and spotless linen, offers local and international food. A buffet breakfast is served on the coffee terrace, and there's a pool at the front of the hotel, with a pool bar and grill.

INEXPENSIVE

Altamont Court Hotel. 1–5 Altamont Terrace, New Kingston, Kingston, Jamaica, WI. ☎ **876/929-4497.** Fax 876/929-2118. www.cariboutpost.com/altamont. E-mail: altamont@n5.com. 55 units. A/C TV TEL. $90 double; $120 suite. AE, DC, MC, V.

Built around 1982 in a three-story white-sided format that's nestled within a walled garden, this hotel offers a less-expensive alternative to such larger competitors as the Hilton or the Meridien. Enlarged around 1993, it might remind you of a motel, thanks to exterior hallways and furniture like you might expect within a well-kept roadside inn in Florida. The staff here is less alert and well informed than you might hope for, but rooms are comfortable and there is a sense of well-ordered decency and thrift. Each of the rooms has either two double beds or one king-size bed. The hotel's most alluring feature is its large swimming pool.

✪ Hotel Four Seasons. 18 Ruthven Rd. (near Halfway Tree Rd.), Kingston 10, Jamaica, W.I. ☎ **800/742-4276** in the U.S., or 876/929-7655. Fax 876/929-5964. 76 units. A/C TV TEL. $76–$90 double. AE, DC, MC, V.

Small-scale, well maintained, and respectable, this is one of the most appealing hotels in Kingston, thanks to a sophisticated design that combines a once-private home with a rambling series of modern wings, courtyards, gardens, and fountains. It was established in 1967 by a pair of German-born sisters (Helga Stoeckert and Christa Lundh) who escaped from then-communist East Germany in 1957, establishing a bootstrap-style operation that's now one of the most noteworthy in the Jamaican capital. Much of what you'll see today, including a series of Chinese-Chippendale balustrades and gazebo bars, was added in the 1980s. Rooms are cozy and comfortable, but the spiritual core of the place is the Elizabethan-inspired bar and restaurant, both of which are recommended separately in "Where to Dine." Because this place is lavishly recommended within most of the travel guides of Germany, it enjoys something approaching cult status within its individual niche, and as such, it welcomes lots of far-ranging German tour groups. Guest rooms evoke the furnishings in a well-maintained, upscale motel, and are usually decorated in wicker or plantation-style furniture. Most rooms have French doors opening onto private balconies or patios, overlooking either the garden or the pool. Don't be confused by the hotel's name: It has absolutely no association with the international hotel chain, the Four Seasons.

Indies Hotel. 5 Holborn Rd. (near the intersection of Trafalgar Rd.), Kingston 10, Jamaica, W.I. ☎ **876/926-2952.** Fax 876/926-2879. E-mail indies@discoverjamaica.com. 15 units. A/C TV TEL. $58–$64 double; $77 triple. AE, MC, V.

On one of the small side streets in the heart of New Kingston, opening onto a flower garden, this half-timbered building with double gables features a small reception area decorated with potted plants, a lounge, and a TV room. The barely adequate bedrooms, restaurant, and bar are grouped around a cool patio. Indies has a reputation among the locals for friendly atmosphere and good-quality budget meals. Their fish-and-chips are good, and they specialize in pizza. They also serve steak with all the trimmings, and when they get fancy, lobster thermidor.

2 Where to Dine

Kingston has a good range of places to eat, whether you're seeking stately meals in plantation houses, hotel buffets, or fast-food shops.

EXPENSIVE

Isabella's. Crowne Plaza Kingston. 211A Constant Spring Rd. ☎ **876/925-7676.** Reservations recommended. Main courses J$525–J$1,400 ($14.95–$39.90). AE, DC, MC, V. Daily 6–10:30pm. JAMAICAN/INTERNATIONAL.

The most formal and elegant hotel restaurant in Kingston, Isabella's is preferred by many business travelers and others who don't like to venture out of their hotel at night into the uncertain streets of Jamaica's capital. The cuisine is good too, combining real Jamaican flavors with an array of international dishes. You might arrive early and enjoy a drink at the marble-topped bar. Seating is available both indoors and on a veranda overlooking the city and harbor. Service is as gracious as the atmosphere. Try the succulent coconut prawns with papaya chutney or the chef's pride, callaloo soup. You can go on to a tender filet mignon, snapper fresh from the sea and sauced with lime curry, Creole shrimp, breast of chicken supreme, or jerked chicken kebabs. For dessert, finish with the crème brûlée and most definitely a coffee from the Blue Mountains.

✪ Norma's on the Terrace. In Devon House, 26 Hope Rd. ☎ **876/968-5488.** Reservations recommended. Main courses J$650–J$1,200 ($18.55–$34.20); Sun brunch J$700–J$800 ($19.95–$22.80). AE, DC, MC, V. Daily 11am–11pm. JAMAICAN.

This is the newest member of a restaurant empire created by one of Jamaica's most famous businesswomen, Norma Shirley, purveyor of food to stylish audiences as far away as Miami and Montego Bay. It's housed beneath the wide porticos of the gallery surrounding Kingston's most famous monument, Devon House. Fans of Ms. Shirley cite her role here as the incentive for improving what had until her arrival been woefully dusty gardens. Today, like the food served inside, they're manicured like something you'd expect on an English estate. Menus change with the season, but usually reflect Ms. Shirley's penchant for creative adaptations of her native Jamaican cuisine. Stellar examples include Jamaican chowder with crabmeat, shrimp, conch, and lobster; grilled whole red snapper encrusted with herbs and served with a thyme and caper sauce; a salad of smoked marlin with citrus segments; grilled smoked pork loin in a teriyaki/ginger sauce, served with caramelized apples.

The Port Royal Restaurant. In Le Meridien Jamaica Pegasus Hotel, 81 Knutsford Blvd. (in New Kingston, off Oxford Rd.). ☎ **876/926-3690.** Main courses $16–$30. AE, DC, MC, V. Mon–Sat 7–11pm. SEAFOOD/CONTINENTAL.

This elegantly furnished restaurant is your best bet if you're looking for upmarket seafood. It's a favorite place for local businesspeople hoping to impress out-of-town clients. We prefer to begin with the Jamaican baby lobster as an appetizer. It's served in a shell with a salad. If you want something hot for a starter, make it the baked stuffed Jamaican crab back presented on vermicelli. Doubloon is one of the chef's better specialties—a medley of chicken supreme and veal presented on a layer of pasta. Many of the main meat and poultry dishes are quite ordinary, although the seafood specialties are more radiant, especially the snapper filet filled with crab mousse and baked in Parmesan cheese and fresh herbs. The Creole shrimp is also good—simmered in beer and flavored with Cajun spices. Service is first-class. You might also visit The Pizza Cellar, the hotel's pizza parlor and wine cellar offering a wide selection of succulent pies and exclusive wines from around the world.

✪ **Strawberry Hill.** Irish Town, Blue Mountains. ☎ **876/944-8400.** Reservations recommended. Lunch main courses $20–$25; set-price Sunday brunch $45; 3-course set-price dinner $49. AE, MC, V. Daily noon–3pm and 6–10pm. Sunday brunch 11:30–3pm. Directions: From Kingston, drive seven miles north, Following Old Hope Road to the northern suburb of Papin. When you get to Papin, turn left onto Gordon Town Road, cross a bridge, and turn left onto Newcastle Road, where you go left. From there, follow the steep uphill road for another 7 miles along dramatic and winding mountain roads, following the signs to Strawberry Hill. MODERN JAMAICAN.

The most charming restaurant venue in the Jamaican capital involves a taxi ride up a meandering Blue Mountain road to the sheltered premises of a hotel that grows more famous every year (see "Where to Stay"). Dining is within an interconnected series of catwalks, verandas, and gazebo-style pavilions that were meticulously re-created along 19th-century patterns. Each manages to seem simultaneously upscale yet unpretentious. The delectable menu items change with the season but are likely to include such Jamaican dishes as grilled shrimp with fresh cilantro; fresh grilled fish with jerk mango and sweet-pepper salsa; or rotis stuffed with curried goat and fresh herbs. It's called "new Jamaican cuisine," and so it is. Meals usually taste better when preceded with a drink in the bar, a setting that might have been removed intact from a cozy enclave within a Jamaican plantation house of long ago. Sunday brunches here are enduringly popular, thanks partly to a lavish array of more than 40 dishes, each arranged in a separate gazebo-like pavilion like a temple to fine gastronomy.

MODERATE

Alexander's. In the Courtleigh Hotel, 85 Knutsford Blvd. ☎ **876/968-6339.** Reservations recommended. Lunch main courses J$265–J$875 ($7.55–$24.95); dinner main courses J$345–J$875 ($9.85–$24.95). AE, MC, V. Daily noon–3pm and 6–10:30pm. INTERNATIONAL.

This is the showplace dining room of one of Kingston's best-respected hotels, and as such, it often attracts business meetings, government delegations, and international travelers who appreciate its good service and culinary savvy. Within a setting inspired by the Jamaican sugar plantations of the 1800s, with muted tropical colors and a view that overlooks the hotel's swimming pool, you can order such starters as smoked marlin or Caribbean crab backs, then move to sirloin steaks; medallions of beef with grilled tomatoes; and filets of pork with brandy, mustard, and cream sauce. After your dinner, consider a drink within the hotel's bar/lounge, Mingles.

✪ **Blue Mountain Inn.** Gordon Town Rd. ☎ **876/927-1700.** Reservations required. Jackets required for men (ties optional). Main courses $9–$16. AE, DC, MC, V. Mon–Sat 7–9:30pm. Head north on Old Hope Rd. into the mountains. CARIBBEAN/INTERNATIONAL.

About a 20-minute drive north from downtown Kingston is an 18th-century coffee-plantation house set high on the slopes of Blue Mountain. Surrounded by trees and flowers, it rests on the bank of the Mammee River. On cold nights, log fires blaze, and the dining room gleams with silver and sparkling glass. The inn is one of Jamaica's most-famous restaurants, not only for its food but also for its atmosphere and service. The effort of dressing up is worth it, and the cool night air justifies it; women are advised to take a wrap.

Ciaoubella. 19 Hillcrest Ave. ☎ **876/978-5002.** Lunch sandwiches and platters J$260–J$700 ($7.40–$19.95); evening tapas J$150–J$900 ($4.30–$25.65). AE, MC, V. Mon–Sat noon–4pm. Tapas and wine Mon–Thurs 6–9pm, Fri–Sat 5:30–11pm. MEDITERRANEAN.

A location in a converted turn-of-the-century house within a short walk of the Bob Marley Museum keeps this place filled with an animated luncheon clientele every day. At night, the scene changes from a restaurant into a busy and convivial bar, where glasses of wine, priced from J$130 to J$400 ($3.70 to $11.40) each, are accompanied by a savory array of tapas. This might include chicken and mushroom quesadillas, Cajun-grilled shrimp, jerk sausage, salt cod cakes, and several kinds of pastas (two or three of these tapas comprise a full meal). Luncheon fare is more conventional, emphasizing dishes such as southwestern grilled chicken salad, sandwiches, and Ciaoubella's baby back ribs. Expect lots of conversations among Kingstonians from the world of business and the arts, especially in the evening, when the building's interconnected verandas reverberate with gossip and dialogue about the day's events and whatever scandal happens to be in vogue at the moment.

Devonshire Restaurant/The Grogg Shoppe. 26 Hope Rd., in Devon House (near Trafalgar Park). ☎ **876/929-7046** or 876/929-7027. Reservations recommended in the Devonshire, not necessary in the Grogg Shoppe. Devonshire main courses $8–$26 at lunch, $8–$28 at dinner. Grogg Shoppe main courses $7–$25 at lunch, $8–$28 at dinner. AE, MC, V. Mon–Sat noon–10pm. JAMAICAN.

These two restaurants are in the brick-sided former servants' quarters of Kingston's most-visited mansion, Devon House. The more formal of the two is the Devonshire, where you can eat on patios under trees, in view of the royal palms and the fountain in front of the historic great house. For true Jamaican flavor, head here, as the kitchen turns out the most authentic dishes in Kingston. Appetizers include a "tidbit" of jerk pork or a bowl of soup (perhaps Jamaican red pea—really bean—or pumpkin). Zesty main dishes feature Jamaican akee and salt fish, barbecued chicken, and curried seafood. Also tasty are unusual homemade ice creams flavored with local fruit, such as soursop. Blue Mountain tea or coffee is also served. The bars for both restaurants serve 11 different rum punches and 10 fruit punches, such as a tamarind fizz or a papaya (pawpaw) punch. Many aficionados opt for these drinks on one of the Grogg Shoppe's two different terraces, labeled "mango" and "mahogany" after nearby trees. Especially popular is the "Devon Duppy," combining into one pastel-colored glass virtually every variety of rum in the bartender's inventory.

Jade Garden. 106 Hope Rd., in Sovereign Centre (north of the town center, west of National Stadium). ☎ **876/978-3476.** Reservations recommended. Main courses J$380–J$1,280 ($10.85–$36.50). AE, MC, V. Daily noon–10pm. CHINESE.

The best Chinese restaurant in Kingston, Jade Garden serves well-prepared food in an elegant, formal setting. The menu is so large we wonder how they manage. The typical chow mein and chop suey dishes are here, but we'd ignore them to concentrate on the more-challenging offers from the chefs. The beef with oyster sauce is delectable, as is the pork with ham choy. For unusual flavors, go shopping in the "China Gems" section of the menu, where you'll find some really savory offerings, including Pi Paw bean curd with chopped Chinese sausage, shrimp, black mushrooms, and water chestnuts.

Also excellent is Subgum War Bar, a combination of meats sautéed with Chinese vegetables and served on a sizzling-hot platter. Count on several good seafood specialties always being featured, especially deep-fried prawns stuffed with prawn mousse and served in a garlic-butter sauce.

Raquel's Restaurant and Seafood. 38A Trafalgar Rd. ☎ **876/920-1588.** Reservations recommended. Lunch platters and main courses J$290–J$800 ($8.25–$22.80); dinner main courses J$400–J$1,400 ($11.40–$39.90). AE, MC, V. Daily 11am–11:30pm. JAMAICAN/INTERNATIONAL.

Set near the big international hotels of New Kingston, this establishment combines aspects of a singles bar, a sports bar, a general rendezvous point for friends, and a restaurant. It's located next door to the country's biggest modeling agency—a prominent player in the annual Miss Jamaica contest—and as such, it's sometimes visited by demimondaines on the body-beautiful circuit, who mingle with famous Jamaican cricket players, or whatever. Piña coladas and fresh pineapple daiquiris cost J$150 ($4.30) each, sometimes accompanying such excellent and savory dishes as lobster thermidor (a signature dish here), curried shrimp, grilled pork chops, chicken à la king in Chardonnay sauce, and New York–style sirloins.

The Restaurant at the Four Seasons Hotel. 18 Ruthven Rd. (near Half Way Tree Rd.). ☎ **876/929-7655.** Reservations recommended. Set-price buffet lunch J$600 ($17.10); lunch and dinner à la carte main courses J$290–J$580 ($8.25–$16.55). AE, MC, V. Daily noon–3pm and 6–10pm. GERMAN/JAMAICAN/INTERNATIONAL.

Set within the previously recommended hotel, this restaurant offers one of the most consistently reliable luncheon buffets in Jamaica, one that's attended on a regular basis by figures from the worlds of Jamaican politics, business, and education. It's supervised by a pair of hardworking East German–born sisters whose unfailing standards have made it a staple on the capital's restaurant scene. No meal would be complete here without a drink in the Elizabethan-style bar, where dark paneling and high ceilings evoke either Old England or Old Thuringia, depending on your point of view. Menu items are freshly made and succulent, with emphasis on everything from Jamaican pepper-pot soup to goulash, from jerk chicken and pork to schnitzels, sauerbraten, and roulades of pork or veal.

INEXPENSIVE

Akbar. 11 Holborn Rd. ☎ **876/926-3480.** Reservations recommended. Main courses J$295–J$850 ($8.40–$24.25). AE, MC, V. Daily noon–4pm and 6–11pm. NORTHERN INDIAN.

This is the best Indian restaurant in Kingston, and as such, it's the focal point for the meetings and rendezvous of many members of Jamaica's Indian community. Set near the big international hotels of New Kingston, within the stucco-sheathed premises of what was originally built as a private home, it contains four dining rooms, each outfitted in earth tones with touches of mint green. Don't overlook the possibility of a meal within the Moghul-style garden, within earshot of a splashing fountain. Menu items are rich with the seasonings of the East, with seafood, vegetarian, lamb, beef, and chicken dishes, as well as a selection of exotic breads. Specific and stellar examples include chicken moghlai cooked in cream sauce with nuts and egg butter; mutton in a spicy sauce; and beef Akbar—one of the most justifiably popular house specialties, skewered and flavored with herbs.

○ **Boon Hall Oasis.** Stony Hill, St. Andrew. ☎ **876/942-3064.** Reservations recommended. Main courses J$250–J$500 ($7.15–$14.25); Sunday brunch J$760 ($21.65). No credit cards. Mon–Sat 11am–8pm (last order); Sun 11am–3pm (last order). Take a taxi from

Kingston, or turn on Seaview Rd. (opposite Petcom Gas Station—Stony Hill Square). Take the third left onto Airy Castle Rd,, then look out for the signs pointing to Boon Hall Oasis. JAMAICAN.

If you opt for a meal at this place, be prepared for more of an exposure to the beauties of the Jamaican forest. It's set about 5 miles north of the commercial core of Kingston on 4 acres of land that, until several years ago, were untamed bush country. Thanks to the dedicated efforts of one of Jamaica's brightest and most talented landscape architects, Stephen Jones, and a staff of eight machete-wielding gardeners, it's now a botanical garden of breathtaking variety and scope. You'll pull into a grassy parking area adjacent to a plant nursery where—if you happen to own a home in Jamaica—you might opt to buy an unusual variety of potted fern, aurelia, orchid, or whatever. Wander down a series of pathways and steps carved into the hillside, some of which run parallel to the rushing waters of a stream that cascades down from the heights of the nearby Blue Mountains. Your meal will be served beneath the galvanized metal roofs of a series of dining pavilions, in the equivalent of a verdant, and intensely manicured, botanical garden. Well-prepared menu items include filet of red snapper with either brown sauce or a vinegar-based escoveitch; three different preparations of shrimp (including a version that's flambéed in a honey-flavored rum sauce); and three different preparations of chicken. Sundays, when residents of some of Kingston's apartment buildings gravitate here for rest and relaxation and, in some cases, art exhibitions and poetry readings, are especially popular.

Chelsea Jerk Centre. 7 Chelsea Ave. (between the New Kingston Shopping Centre and the Wyndham New Kingston Hotel). ☎ **876/926-6322.** Reservations not accepted. Jerk half-chicken J$200 ($5.70); pound of jerk pork J$240 ($6.85). AE, MC, V. Mon–Thurs 10am–10pm, Fri–Sun 10am–1am. JAMAICAN.

Chelsea Jerk Centre is the city's most popular seller of the Jamaican delicacies known as jerk pork and jerk chicken. Set in a low-slung angular concrete building, it offers food to take out or to eat in the comfortably battered dining area. Although no formal appetizers are served, you might order a side portion of what the scrawled-on chalkboard refers to as "festival," which is fried cornmeal dumplings. The best bargain is Chelsea's Special, which is like an old-fashioned blue-plate special at a U.S. roadside diner. It consists of rice, peas, and vegetables, along with jerked pork or chicken. Know in advance that this place does not offer tableside service, but that it functions like a down-home and downscale culinary boutique. You'll order the various components of your meal at different locations of the compound, ordering jerk pork, jerk chicken, and "festival" at one kiosk; rice, peas, oxtail, and stewed fish at another; and beer at yet another. If in doubt, ask someone for guidance through the labyrinth.

El Dorado Room. In the Terra Nova Hotel, 17 Waterloo Rd. (on the western edge of New Kingston, near West Kings House Rd.). ☎ **876/926-9334.** Reservations recommended. Main courses J$650–J$1,200 ($18.55–$34.20) at lunch, J$650–J$2,100 ($18.55–$59.85) at dinner. AE, MC, V. Daily noon–3pm and 7–10:30pm. INTERNATIONAL/JAMAICAN.

Situated in one of the small, respectable hotels of Kingston, this restaurant hosts a crowd of local businesspeople and dignitaries. The grandeur of the portico, the elaborate moldings of the hotel reception area, and the formal dining room are vestiges of the wealthy former owners. The restaurant emphasizes fish and shellfish dishes, and the chef is noted for flambé and fondues. We've found smoked marlin and Jamaican pepper-pot soup to be the most tasty starters, followed by one of the specialties such as a blackened snapper, which is evocative of New Orleans. The best items emerge from the grill, including lobster or a jerk-pork loin. The latter is a real taste of Jamaica, having been marinated with herbs, then "jerked," and served with yams and honey-baked plantain. Among the seafood selections, we gravitate to the steamed ginger snapper with onions and garlic, plus a garnish of okra.

Heather's. 9 Haining Rd., New Kingston. ☎ **876/960-7739.** Reservations recommended. Main courses J$289–J$899 ($8.25–$25.60). AE, DC, MC, V. Mon–Sat noon–3pm and 5pm–midnight. JAMAICAN/SYRIAN.

Loud, convivial, and sometimes boisterous, this establishment combines one of Kingston's most consistently popular singles bars with a somewhat more sedate restaurant. It's housed within a 1950s-era villa, within the shadow of the big hotels of Knutsford Boulevard, and as such, it attracts after-hour office workers from the local embassies, insurance companies, and banks of New Kingston. Dialogues and flirting are de rigeur at this bar, where many of the clients seem to know one another, or show hopes of eventually getting to know one another. Other than its consistently popular bar, its main focal point is a massive mango tree, sheathed in ancient strands of philodendron, that thrusts its way skyward through a hole in the roof. Tasty menu items include grilled fish kebabs, sweet-and-sour fish, Cajun-style blackened fish, Heather's crab cakes, and Heather's special shrimp.

The Hot Pot. 2 Altamont Terrace. ☎ **876/929-3906.** Main courses J$320–J$950 ($9.10–$27.10). MC, V. Daily 7am–10pm. JAMAICAN.

Set within a short walk of both the Pegasus and Hilton hotels, this is a simple local restaurant with an animated crowd of regulars and straightforward, unfussy cuisine. Within a green-and-white interior, near a view of a modest garden, you can drink Red Stripe beer or rum drinks. The chefs are so good you'll want to hire them to cook for you, especially after you've tasted their shrimp with pineapple, their garlic chicken, their akee with salt fish, and their sweet-and-sour fish. The place stays open throughout the day, serving breakfast, lunch, and dinner without interruption. The food is what you'd be served in a typical Jamaican home—nothing fancy, but satisfying and filling—and the prices are astonishingly low.

Indies Pub and Grill. 8 Holborn Rd. (in New Kingston, off Hope Rd.). ☎ **876/920-5913.** Main courses $9–$26.20; pizzas $9–$16.50. No credit cards. Sun–Thurs 10am–midnight, Fri–Sat 10am–2am. JAMAICAN.

Indies, an informal neighborhood restaurant across the street from the Indies Hotel, was designed around a garden terrace, which on hot nights provides the best (and coolest) place to sit. You can also dine in the inner rooms, which are haphazardly but pleasantly decorated with caribou horn, tortoise shells, half-timber walls, an aquarium sometimes stocked with baby sharks, and even a Canadian moose head. There's a full sandwich menu at lunchtime. In the evening, you can enjoy grilled lobster, fish-and-chips, barbecued chicken or pork, chicken Kiev, or roast beef. It's a little better than standard pub grub. Pizza is a specialty. A bottle of Red Stripe, the Jamaican national beer, is the beverage of choice here.

The Upper Crust (Guilt Trip). 20 Barbican Rd., Liguanea. ☎ **876/977-5130.** Lunch main courses J$225–J$495 ($6.40–$14.10); dinner main courses J$395–J$795 ($11.25–$22.65). MC, V. Daily noon–3pm and 6–10:30pm. JAMAICAN/INTERNATIONAL.

Set about a mile north of New Kingston, this open-air restaurant originated as a small-scale pastry shop whose products were so tasty (and so guilt-inducing) that it eventually expanded into a neighborhood institution. Today, amid a funky collection of Jamaican memorabilia and lots of green plants, it's centered on an open-air deck wherein lunches are quicker, and less carefully orchestrated, than dinners. In addition to the pastries, which are made on the premises and displayed behind a glass-fronted display case, menu items include crab-back salads, curried snapper, jerk chicken lasagna, grilled lamb chops with ratatouille, and an especially good grilled filet of snapper with dried-pepper shrimp in a curry sauce.

3 Hitting the Beach

You don't really come to Kingston for beaches, but there are some here. To the southwest of the sprawling city are the black-sanded **Hellshire Beach** and **Fort Clarence.** Both of these beaches are very popular with the locals on weekends. Both have changing rooms, heavy security, and numerous food stands. The reggae concerts at Fort Clarence are legendary on the island.

Just past Fort Clarence, the fisherman's beach at **Naggo Head** is an even hipper destination, or so Kingston beach buffs claim. After a swim in the refreshing waters, opt for one of the food stands selling "fry fish" and *bammy* (cassava bread). The closest beach to the city (although it's not very good) is **Lime Cay,** a little island on the outskirts of Kingston Harbour, reached by a short boat ride from Morgan's Harbour at Port Royal.

4 Seeing the Sights

Even if you're staying at Ocho Rios or Port Antonio, you may want to visit Kingston for brief sightseeing and for trips to nearby Port Royal and Spanish Town.

IN TOWN

One of the major attractions, **Devon House,** 26 Hope Rd. (☎ 876/929-7029), was built in 1991 by George Stiebel, a Jamaican who made his fortune mining in Latin America, becoming one of the first black millionaires in the Caribbean. A striking classical building, the house has been restored to its original beauty by the Jamaican National Trust. The grounds contain crafts shops, boutiques, two restaurants, shops that sell the best ice cream in Jamaica (in exotic fruit flavors), and a bakery and pastry shop with Jamaican puddings and desserts. The main house also displays furniture of various periods and styles. Admission to the main house is $6; hours are Tuesday to Saturday from 9:30am to 5pm. Admission to the grounds (the shops and restaurants) is free.

Almost next door to Devon House are the sentried gates of **Jamaica House** (residence of the prime minister), a fine, white-columned building set well back from the road.

Continuing along Hope Road, at the crossroads of Lady Musgrave and King's House roads, turn left and you'll see a gate on the left with its own personal traffic light. This leads to **King's House,** the official residence of the governor-general of Jamaica, the queen's representative on the island. The outside and front lawn of the gracious residence, set in 200 acres of well-tended parkland, is sometimes open for viewing, Monday to Friday from 10am to 5pm. The secretarial offices are housed next door in an old wooden building set on brick arches. In front of the house is a gigantic banyan tree in whose roots, legend says, *duppies* (ghosts) take refuge when they're not living in the cotton trees.

Between Old Hope and Mona roads, a short distance from the Botanical Gardens, is the **University of the West Indies** (☎ 876/927-1660), built in 1948 on the Mona Sugar Estate. Ruins of old mills, storehouses, and aqueducts are juxtaposed with modern buildings on what must be the most beautifully situated campus in the Caribbean. The chapel, an old sugar-factory building, was transported stone by stone from

Trelawny and rebuilt. The remains of the original sugar factory are well preserved and give a good idea of how sugar was made in slave days.

The **National Library of Jamaica** (formerly the West India Reference Library), Institute of Jamaica, 12 East St. (☎ **876/922-0620**) is a storehouse of the history, culture, and traditions of Jamaica and the Caribbean. It is the finest working library for West Indian studies in the world, offering the most comprehensive, up-to-date, and balanced collection of materials on the region—including books, newspapers, photographs, maps, and prints. Exhibits highlight different aspects of Jamaican and West Indian life. It's open Monday to Thursday from 9am to 5pm, Friday from 9am to 4pm.

The **Bob Marley Museum,** 56 Hope Rd. (☎ **876/927-9152**), is the most-visited sight in Kingston, but if you're not a Marley fan, it may not mean much to you. The clapboard house with its garden and high surrounding wall was the famous reggae singer's home and recording studio until his death on May 11, 1981 in a Miami hospital. You can tour the house and view assorted Marley memorabilia, and you may even catch a glimpse of his children, who often frequent the grounds. Hours are Monday to Saturday from 9:30am to 4pm. Admission is J$350 ($10) for adults, J$230 ($6.55) ages 13 to 18, and J$175 ($5) ages 4 to 12. It's reached by bus 70 or 75 from Halfway Tree, but take a cab to save yourself the hassle of dealing with Kingston public transport.

The entrance to **National Stadium,** Briggs Park, of which Jamaica is justly proud, features an aluminum statue of Arthur Wint, a national athlete. The stadium is used for soccer, field sports, and cycling. Beside the stadium is the **National Arena,** used for indoor sports, exhibitions, and concerts, and there is an Olympic-size pool. Admission prices vary according to activities.

A mile above Kingston, if you go north on Duke Street, lies **National Heroes Park,** formerly known as George VI Memorial Park. This was the old Kingston racecourse. An assortment of large office blocks, including the Ministries of Finance and Education, overlooks the park. There are statues of Simón Bolívar, of Nanny of the Maroons, and of George Gordon and Paul Bogle, martyrs of the Morant Bay revolt. Norman Manley and Alexander Bustamante, national heroes of Jamaica, are buried here, as is Sir Donald Sangster, a former prime minister.

Just north of Heroes Park, at 1A Marescaux Rd., is **Mico College** (☎ **876/929-5260**), a coeducational postsecondary teacher-training institution. Lacy Mico, a rich London widow, left her fortune to a favorite nephew on the condition that he marry one of her six nieces. He did not, and the inheritance was invested, the interest being used to ransom victims of the Barbary pirates. With the end of piracy in the early 19th century, it was decided to devote the capital to founding schools for newly emancipated enslaved persons, and Mico College was established. On the grounds is the Inasca Museum displaying Indian, African, and Caribbean artifacts. It is open Monday to Friday 9am to 4:30pm, charging J$100 ($2.85) for adults and J$30 (85¢) for children.

The central administrative offices of the **Institute of Jamaica,** founded in 1879, are between 12 and 16 East St. (☎ **876/922-0620**), close to the harbor. Open from 8:30am to 5pm Monday through Thursday, and until 4pm on Friday, the institute fosters and encourages the development of culture, science, and history in the national interest. The institute is responsible for several divisions and organizations, of which Junior Centre, the Natural History Division (repository of the national collection of flora and fauna), and the National Library are at the East Street headquarters. Those located elsewhere include the Edna Manley College of Visual and Performing Arts (1 Arthur Wint Dr.), with schools of music, dance, art, and drama; the African-

Caribbean Institute (12 Ocean Blvd.), which conducts research on cultural heritage; the Museums Division, with sites in Port Royal and Spanish Town, which has responsibility for the display of artifacts relevant to the history of Jamaica; the National Gallery (12 Ocean Blvd.); and the Institute of Jamaica Publications Ltd. (4B Camp Rd.), which publishes a quarterly, the *Jamaica Journal,* as well as other works of educational and cultural merit.

5 Shopping

Downtown Kingston, the old part of the town, is centered on Sir William Grant Park, formerly Victoria Park, a showpiece of lawns, lights, and fountains. North of the park is Ward Theatre, the oldest theater in the New World, where traditional Jamaican pantomime is staged from December 26 to early April. To the east is Coke Methodist Church, and to the south is the equally historic Kingston Parish Church.

Cool arcades lead off King Street, but everywhere are many people going about their business. There are some beggars and the inevitable peddlers who sidle up and offer "hot stuff, mon"—which frequently means highly polished brass lightly dipped in gold and fraudulently offered at high prices as real gold. The hucksters accept a polite but firm no, but if you let them keep you talking, you may end up buying. They're very persuasive!

One of the most modern shopping centers in Jamaica, the **New Kingston Shopping Centre,** 30 Dominica Dr., is known for its overall merchandise rather than for a particular merchant. It's sleek and contemporary, and stores are centered on a Maya-style pyramid, down the sides of which cascades of water irrigate trailing bougainvillea. Fast-food outlets, fashion boutiques, and shops selling many other items are here. Free concerts are often presented in the open-air theater. Associated with one of the most beautiful and historic mansions in Jamaica, a building operated by the Jamaican National Trust, **The Shops at Devon House,** 26 Hope Rd. (☎ 876/926-0815), rings the borders of a 200-year-old courtyard once used by slaves and servants. Although about 10 shops operate from these premises, 4 of the largest are operated by Things Jamaican, a nationwide emporium dedicated to the enhancement of the country's handcrafts. Shops include the Cookery, selling island-made sauces and spices; the Pottery, offering crockery; and Elaine Elegance, which sells handcrafts.

The **Wassi Art Gallery and Collectibles,** 26 Hope Rd. (☎ 876/906-5016), is one of the most interesting of the shops that lie on the premises of Kingston's most-visited tourist attraction, Devon House. All the merchandise inside was made within Jamaica's most famous art pottery, Wassi Art, thanks to a labor-intensive, low-tech method that has inspired dozens of newspaper articles across Jamaica. Look for functional, durable kitchenware that's prized by Jamaican homeowners for its eco-sensitive, earthy appeal. Colors range from the jarringly bright to low-key, natural colors inspired by the earth, sea, and forest. Anything you buy can be shipped via FedEx. Prices of objects range from $5 to $2,000, depending on their size and degree of complexity.

For many years, the richly evocative paintings of Haiti were viewed as the most valuable contribution to the arts in the Caribbean basin, but there's a rapidly growing perception that Jamaica is one of the artistic leaders of the developing nations. An articulate group of Caribbean critics is focusing the attention of the art world on the unusual, eclectic, and sometimes politically motivated painting produced in Jamaica. The **Frame Centre Gallery,** 10 Tangerine Place (☎ 876/926-4644), originated as a simple framing shop, and through the personal taste and energy of its founder/owner, Guy McIntosh, it eventually evolved into one of Jamaica's most influential art galleries. The artists whose works are displayed include most of the artistic luminaries of

Jamaica, including the well-respected Colin Garland, David Boxer, Milton George, Laura Facey, and Nelson Cooper. Paintings range in price from $150 for pieces by younger, lesser-known artists to as much as $35,000 for pieces by serious masters such as Colin Garland, whose work is feted as far away as London and Los Angeles. If you're serious about art, don't overlook the upstairs viewing galleries. The **Mutual Life Gallery,** Mutual Life Centre, 2 Oxford Rd. (☎ 876/929-9025), is one of Jamaica's most prominent art galleries, housed in the corporate headquarters of this major insurance company. This center offers an insight into the changing face of Jamaican art. The gallery's exhibitions are organized by Gilou Bauer, who encourages unknowns as well as showcasing established artists with flair. Exhibitions change once a month, but there are usually long-term exhibits as well. The Mutual Life Insurance Company donates the space as part of its effort to improve the status of Caribbean arts. The gallery is a not-for-profit institution.

   Decorators Corner, 19 Hillcrest Ave. (☎ 876/927-0784), is your best shop for gifts, with a wide selection of merchandise, selling not only Jamaican crafts, but British products as well, including crystal and pottery. Now well into its second decade, the **Craft Cottage,** The Village Plaza, 24 Constant Spring Rd. (☎ 876/926-0719), is one of the largest repositories of handcrafts in Kingston, lying in one of the city's major malls. Gift items from all over Jamaica (and other countries) are featured here. A large covered area of individually owned small stalls, the **Kingston Crafts Market,** at the west end of Harbour Street downtown, is reached through thoroughfares like Straw Avenue, Drummer's Lane, and Cheapside. All kinds of Jamaican crafts are on sale—wooden plates and bowls, trays, ashtrays, and pepper pots made of mahoe, the national wood. Straw hats, mats, and baskets are on display, as are batik shirts and cotton shirts with gaudy designs. Banners for wall decoration are inscribed with the Jamaican coat of arms, and wood masks often have elaborately carved faces. Apart from being a good place to buy worthwhile souvenirs, the market is where you can learn the art of bargaining and ask for a *brawta,* a free bonus.

   Loaded with a wider variety of medications than any other pharmacy in Kingston, the **Dick Kinkead Pharmacy, Ltd.** 72–76 Harbour St. (☎ 876/922-6525), has been compared to a civic institution, thanks to the 40-year career of its owner, Dick Kinkead. It functions as a quasi-official dispensary for hundreds of local residents who sometimes head here for advice before they make an appointment with a doctor. Ask for any of the substances that are made on the premises, including a medicinal toothpaste made from tropical roots and herbs that oral hygienists cite for effectiveness against gum diseases such as gingivitis. Its name is Chew Dent, and it's made from chew stick (*gouania lupuliodes*), in a tradition originally brought to Jamaica by West African slaves.

6 Kingston After Dark

Kingston offers a variety of nighttime entertainment. Most events are listed in the daily press, along with a host of other attractions, including colorful carnivals and festivals held islandwide throughout the year. *Caution*: The city is unsafe at night. Be careful!

THE PERFORMING ARTS

Kingston is a leading cultural center of the West Indies. Notable theaters include **Ward Theatre,** on North Parade Road (☎ 876/922-0453), and the **Little Theatre,** on Tom Redcam Drive near the National Stadium (☎ 876/926-6129). Both stage local or imported plays and musicals, light opera, revues, and internationally acclaimed Jamaican dance and choral groups and pop concerts. Ticket prices vary. From downtown Kingston (Parade and Cross roads), buses 90A and 90B run here.

THE CLUB & BAR SCENE

Within the relatively sedate premises of one of Kingston's best-established hotels, **Mingles** (in the Courtleigh Hotel, 85 Knutsford Bd.; ☎ 876/929-9000) is a rich-looking—and richly popular—bar and disco. Sheathed with full-grained mahogany panels, with uniformed bartenders whose look might remind you of Jamaica during the era of Noël Coward, it's a clubby-looking but often rocking site known for a revolving combination of reggae, pop, soca (a danceable form of reggae), and Latino meringue. Folk here tend to flirt, talk, and gossip on Friday nights, and dance, dance, dance on Saturday night. The bar here is open daily from 5pm to 3am. Entrance costs J$200 ($5.70) per person after 10pm.

At **Peppers,** Upper Waterloo Rd. (☎ **876/925-2219**), you can order food from a chalkboard and pay from J$150 to J$300 ($4.30 to $8.55) for a main course. But don't for a moment think that food, or fine dining, is the focal point of this place. Come here for a view of hundreds of hot, hip, young, and young-at-heart Kingstonians who flirt, gossip, debate politics and soccer scores, dance wildly, and generally raise hell most nights of the week. The setting is akin to an oversize parking lot ringed with a chain-link fence, the edges of which are lined with several very animated bars. There is also a series of battered tables for the presentation of such dishes as chicken or shrimp roti, stuffed chicken wings, jerk pork and chicken—sold by the half-pound—and combination platters of fried fish. The place is open only for dinner and late-into-the-night drinks, daily from 6pm till between 2am and 5am, depending on business. Red Stripe flows like a river here.

✪ **The Turntable Club,** 118 Red Hills Rd. (☎ 876/924-0164), established in 1973 and set on the second floor of a battered-looking shopping center, is a vintage nightclub that carries a powerful dose of nostalgia for anyone born between 1940 and 1960. No other club in Jamaica was so richly involved with the emerging sounds of Motown and the early years of reggae. And since most of the political and cultural figures in Jamaica spent quality time here at some stage of their youth, it's sometimes cited as the most appropriate place for a reunion of the country's frequently bickering political factions. Today, it welcomes a high-energy but relatively conservative clientele, many of whom are over 30, into a sprawling purple-and-black room lined with portraits of the great rock-and-roll musicians who preceded Bob Marley. There's a half-moon-shaped dance floor that usually gets very crowded and a long bar whose curved design was inspired by the arm of an old-fashioned record player—the kind that existed before tapes and CDs. It is open Thursday to Saturday 6pm to between 2 and 5am, depending on business. On Thursday night, the cover is J$200 ($5.70); otherwise, the entrance is free.

There's also a simple cafe on the premises, serving cafeteria-style platters priced at J$120 to J$170 ($3.40 to $4.85). Examples include escoveitch of chicken or fish, soups, and fried breadfruit. Thanks partly to this club's aggressive lobbying for a safer neighborhood, and the presence of a police station within a short walk, the once-notorious neighborhood surrounding it is reasonably safe. Any of several taxis waiting outside will take you back to the Hilton or Pegasus hotels for around J$150 ($4.30) each way.

7 Side Trips to Spanish Town & Port Royal

Historic Spanish Town and Port Royal can both be reached easily from Kingston and are well worth a visit.

SPANISH TOWN

Spanish Town, some 10 miles west of Kingston, was the capital of Jamaica from 1662 to 1872 and was founded by the Spanish as Villa de la Vega. But all traces of Roman Catholicism were obliterated by Cromwell's men in 1655.

The English cathedral, surprisingly retaining a Spanish name, **San Jago de la Vega,** was founded in 1666 and rebuilt shortly after being destroyed by a hurricane in 1712. As you drive into the town from Kingston, the ancient cathedral catches your eye, with its brick tower and two-tiered wooden steeple, added in 1831. Because the cathedral was built on the foundation and remains of the old Spanish church, it is half English, half Spanish, showing two definite styles—one Romanesque, the other Gothic.

Of cruciform design and built mostly of brick, San Jago (Spanish for St. James) de la Vega is one of the most interesting historic buildings in Jamaica. The black-and-white marble stones of the aisles are interspersed with ancient tombstones, and the walls are heavy with marble memorials that almost form a chronicle of Jamaica's history, dating back as far as 1662. Episcopalian services, held regularly on Sundays at 7 and 10:30am and at 6:30pm, are sometimes conducted by the bishop of Jamaica, whose see this is.

Beyond the cathedral, turn right and go 2 blocks to Constitution Street and the **Town Square.** Graceful royal palms surround this little square. On the west side is **Old King's House,** residence of Jamaica's British governors until 1872, when the capital was transferred to Kingston. It hosted many celebrated guests—among them Lord Nelson, Admiral Rodney, Captain Bligh of HMS *Bounty* fame, and King William IV. Gutted by fire in 1925, its facade has been restored.

Beyond the house is the **Jamaica People's Museum of Craft & Technology,** Old King's House, Constitution Square (☎ **876/922-0620**), open Monday to Friday from 10am to 1pm. Admission is J$35 ($1) for adults and J$15 (45¢) for children. The garden contains examples of old farm machinery, an old water-mill wheel, a hand-turned sugar mill, a fire engine, and other items. An outbuilding displays a museum of crafts and technology, together with a number of smaller agricultural implements. In the small archaeological museum are old prints, models, and maps of the town's grid layout from the 1700s.

The streets around the old Town Square contain many fine Georgian town houses intermixed with tin-roofed shacks. Nearby is the **market,** so busy in the morning that you'll find it difficult, almost dangerous, to drive through. It provides, however, a bustling scene of Jamaican life.

On the north side of the square is the **Rodney Memorial,** the most dramatic building on the square, commissioned by a grateful assembly to commemorate the 1782 victory of British admiral Baron George Rodney over a French fleet saving the island from invasion.

The remaining side of the square, the east, contains the most attractive building, the **House of Assembly,** with a shady brick colonnade running the length of the ground floor, above which is a wooden-pillared balcony. This was the stormy center of the bitter debates for Jamaica's governing body. Now the ground floor is the parish library. Council officers occupy the upper floor, along with the Mayor's Parlour, all closed to the public.

PORT ROYAL

From West Beach Dock, Kingston, a ferry ride of 20 to 30 minutes will take you to Port Royal, which conjures up visions of swashbuckling pirates led by Henry Morgan, swilling grog in harbor taverns. This was once one of the largest trading centers of the

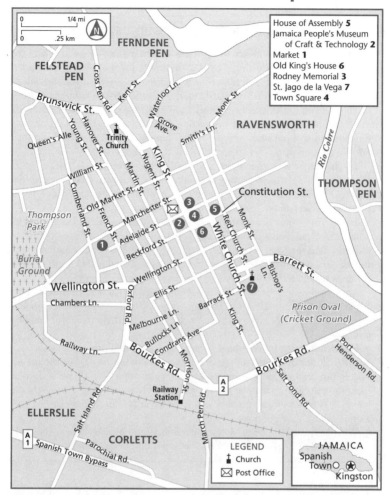

Spanish Town

House of Assembly **5**
Jamaica People's Museum
    of Craft & Technology **2**
Market **1**
Old King's House **6**
Rodney Memorial **3**
St. Jago de la Vega **7**
Town Square **4**

FERNDENE PEN

FELSTEAD PEN

RAVENSWORTH

THOMPSON PEN

Brunswick St.

Cross Pen Rd.

Kent St.

Waterloo Ln.

Grove Ave.

Monk St.

Queen's Alle

Young St.

Hanover St.

Trinity Church

Smith's Ln.

King St.

Rio Cobre

William St.

Cumberland St.

Old Market St.

Old French St.

Martin St.

Nugent St.

Manchester St.

Constitution St.

Thompson Park

Adelaide St.

Beckford St.

Red Church St.

White Church St.

Monk St.

Burial Ground

Wellington St.

Oxford Rd.

Wellington St.

Ellis St.

Barrett St.

Bishop's Ln.

Chambers Ln.

Melbourne Ln.

Barrack St.

King St.

Prison Oval (Cricket Ground)

Railway Ln.

Bullocks Ln.

Condrans Ave.

Bourkes Rd.

Morrison St.

Bourkes Rd.

Salt Pond Rd.

Port Henderson Rd.

Railway Station

A 2

ELLERSLIE

Salt Island Rd.

CORLETTS

March Pen Rd.

A 1 Spanish Town Bypass

Parochial Rd.

LEGEND
✝ Church
✉ Post Office

JAMAICA
Spanish Town ○ ⊛ Kingston

New World, with a reputation for being the wickedest city on earth. Blackbeard stopped here regularly on his Caribbean trips. But it all came to an end on June 7, 1692, when a third of the town disappeared underwater as the result of a devastating earthquake. Nowadays, Port Royal, with its memories of the past, has been designated by the government for redevelopment as a tourist destination.

SEEING THE SIGHTS

Buccaneer Scuba Club, Morgan's Harbour, Port Royal, outside Kingston (☎ 876/967-8061), is one of Jamaica's leading dive and water-sports operators. It offers a wide range of sites to accommodate various divers' tastes, from the incredible *Texas* shipwreck to the unspoiled beauty of the Turtle Reef. PADI courses are also available. One-tank dives begin at $28, while a 1-hour boat snorkeling trip goes for $15, including equipment. A wide array of other water sports is offered, including water-skiing, body boarding, ring skiing, and even a banana-boat ride.

The Wickedest City on Earth

As the notorious pirate Henry Morgan made his way through the streets in the late 17th century, the prostitutes hustled customers, the rum flowed, and buccaneers were growing rich and sassy. The town was Port Royal, at the entrance to the world's seventh-largest natural harbor. It was filled with drinking parlors, gambling dens, billiard rooms, brothels, and joints offering entertainment such as cockfights, target shoots, and bearbaiting. Buccaneers not only got drunk, they fought duels and pursued "foul vices" after long months at sea. All this earned Port Royal the title of "The Wickedest City on Earth."

All this came to a thundering end on the hot morning of June 7, 1692. Without warning, a severe earthquake sank most of the town, killing some 2,000 people. The skies turned copper over this once-vibrant pirate city. To this day, it is known as the famous "Sunken City" of Port Royal.

Today, Port Royal is a small fishing village at the end of the Palisades strip. Some 2,000 residents—and a lot of ghosts—live here. Its seafaring traditions continue, and the town is famous for both its fresh seafood and quaint architecture of old days. Once there were six forts here with a total of 145 guns; some of the guns remain today, but only Fort Charles still stands.

Actually, the 1692 earthquake was only one of nine that descended upon Port Royal. And that's not all: 16 of the worst hurricanes to hit the Caribbean and three devastating fires ravaged the town. It's a wonder anything is still standing today.

Norman Manley International Airport shares the same thin peninsula with Port Royal, but otherwise, all is quiet in the town today. It's easy to conjure up images not only of Morgan but of another buccaneer, Roche Brasiliano, who liked to roast Spaniards alive. To celebrate, he'd break out a keg of wine on the streets of Port Royal; whether they wanted to or not, he forced passersby to have a drink with him at gunpoint.

What happened to Henry Morgan after piracy was outlawed here in 1681? He was knighted in England and sent back to arrest his old hell-raising mateys.

As you drive along the Palisades, you arrive first at **St. Peter's Church.** It's usually closed, but you may persuade the caretaker, who lives opposite, to open it if you want to see the silver plate, said to be spoils captured by Henry Morgan from the cathedral in Panama. In the ill-kept graveyard is the tomb of Lewis Galdy, a Frenchman swallowed up and subsequently regurgitated by the 1692 earthquake.

Fort Charles (☎ 876/967-8438), the only one remaining of Port Royal's six forts, has withstood attack, earthquake, fire, and hurricane. Built in 1656 and later strengthened by Morgan for his own purposes, the fort was expanded and further armed in the 1700s until its firepower boasted more than 100 cannons, covering both the land and the sea approaches. In 1779, Britain's naval hero, Horatio Lord Nelson, was commander of the fort and trod the wooden walkway inside the western parapet as he kept watch for the French invasion fleet. Scale models of the fort and ships of past eras are on display. The fort is open daily from 9am to 5pm; admission is J$140 ($4). Part of the complex, **Giddy House,** once the Royal Artillery storehouse, is another example of what the earth's movements can do. Walking across the tilted floor is an eerie and strangely disorienting experience.

Cays & Mangroves

Although you may be close to the urban sprawl of Kingston, you can return to nature by taking a boat tour leaving from **Morgan's Harbour Hotel Marina** in Port Royal (call ☎ **876/967-8061** to reserve). The nearby mangroves are a natural habitat for Jamaica's bird life, especially pelicans and frigates, which use the area as a breeding ground. Entirely surrounded by water, it is also an important haven for other water-loving birds and wildlife.

Close to Morgan's Harbour and the Kingston airport, the mangroves have survived hurricanes and earthquakes. Jamaican officials created a waterway, allowing small boats to enter. During this trip you can see oyster beds, fish-breeding grounds, and a wide assortment of mangroves, along with wrecks never removed from Hurricane Gilbert's visit in 1988. If you're lucky, you may even spot a pod of dolphins.

After the mangroves, you're taken on a tour of some of Jamaica's most famous cays, including Lime Cay and Maiden Cay. Close to them is Gun Cay, aptly so named for the remains of cannons and large guns. Many a "bloody war" among notorious pirates was fought here.

The cost of this tour is $12, lasting 35 to 40 minutes. Departures can usually be arranged at your convenience.

WHERE TO STAY

Morgan's Harbour Hotel & Beach Club. Port Royal, Kingston 1, Jamaica, W.I. ☎ **800/ 44-UTELL** in the U.S., or 876/967-8030. Fax 876/967-8073. 51 units. A/C MINIBAR TV TEL. $160 double; $210 suite. AE, MC, V. Take the public ferryboat that departs every 2 hours from near Victoria Pier on Ocean Blvd.; many visitors arrive by car or taxi.

The yachtie favorite, Morgan's, which was rebuilt after 1988's Hurricane Gilbert, lies near the end of a long sand spit whose rocky and scrub-covered length shelters Kingston's harbor. On the premises is a 200-year-old red-brick building once used to melt pitch for His Majesty's navy, a swimming area defined by docks and buoys, and a series of wings whose eaves are accented with hints of gingerbread. Set on 22 acres of flat and rock-studded seashore, the resort contains the largest marina facility in Kingston, plus a breezy waterfront restaurant and a popular bar (where ghost stories about the old Port Royal seem especially lurid as the liquor flows on Friday night). Longtime residents quietly claim that the ghosts of soldiers killed by a long-ago earthquake are especially visible on hot and very calm days, when British formations seem to march out of the sea. The well-furnished bedrooms are laid out in an 18th-century Chippendale-Jamaican style. Medium-size bathrooms are tidily maintained. The Buccaneer Scuba Club organizes dives to some of the 170-odd wrecks lying close to shore. Deep-sea-fishing charters and trips to outlying cays can also be arranged.

WHERE TO DINE

Sir Henry Morgan's Restaurant. In Morgan's Harbour Hotel & Beach Club, Port Royal. ☎ **876/967-8075.** Main courses J$385–J$1,200 ($10.95–$34.20). AE, DC, MC, V. Daily 7am–10:30pm. INTERNATIONAL/JAMAICAN.

The bar and restaurant offer guests panoramic views of Kingston Bay and the Blue Mountains. Except for the elegant lobster or seafood salad, lunch is a relatively simple affair. You can order various sandwiches and desserts, along with a daily luncheon special, a traditional Jamaican dish. The catch of the day is steamed or fried. You get more of a choice at dinner; your best bet is either the fresh Jamaican lobster, which can be prepared in a number of ways—everything from thermidor to grilled with garlic butter. The traditional Jamaican pepper steak, with hot and sweet peppers, is excellent, as is the selection of homemade ice creams to finish your meal.

8 Exploring the Blue Mountains

Jamaica has some of the most varied and unusual topography in the Caribbean, including a mountain range laced with rough rivers, streams, and waterfalls. The 192,000-acre **Blue Mountain–John Crow Mountain National Park** is maintained by the Jamaican government. The mountainsides are covered with coffee fields, producing a blended version that's among the leading exports of Jamaica. But for the nature enthusiast, the mountains reveal an astonishingly complex series of ecosystems that change radically as you climb from sea level to the fog-shrouded peaks.

HIKING

The most popular climb begins at **Whitfield Hall** (☎ 876/927-0986), a high-altitude hostel and coffee estate about 6 miles north of the hamlet of **Mavis Bank.** Reaching the summit of Blue Mountain Peak (7,400 feet above sea level) requires between 5 and 6 hours, each way. En route, hikers pass through acres of coffee plantations and forest, where temperatures are cooler than you might expect, and where high humidity encourages thick vegetation. Along the way, watch for an amazing array of bird life, including hummingbirds, many species of warblers, rufous-throated solitaires, yellow-bellied sapsuckers, and Greater Antillean pewees.

Dress in layers and bring bottled water. If you opt for a 2am departure in anticipation of watching the sunrise from atop the peak, carry a flashlight as well. Sneakers are usually adequate, although many climbers bring their hiking boots. Be aware that even during the "dry" season (from December to March), rainfall is common. During the "rainy" season (the rest of the year), these peaks can get up to 150 inches of rainfall a year, and fogs and mists are frequent.

You can opt to head out alone into the Jamaican wilderness, but considering the dangers of such an undertaking, and the crime you might encounter en route, it isn't advisable. A better bet involves engaging one of Kingston's best-known specialists in eco-sensitive tours, **Sunventure Tours,** 30 Balmoral Ave., Kingston 10 (☎ 876/920-8348). The staff here can always arrange an individualized tour for you and your party but offers a mainstream roster of choices as well. The **Blue Mountain Sunrise Tour** involves a camp-style overnight in one of the most remote and inaccessible areas of Jamaica. For a fee of $140 per person, participants are picked up at their Kingston hotels, driven to an isolated ranger station, Wildflower Lodge, that's accessible only via four-wheel-drive vehicle, in anticipation of a two-stage hike that begins at 4:30pm. A simple mountaineer's supper is served at 6pm around a campfire at a ranger station near Portland Gap. At 3am, climbers hike by moonlight and flashlight to a mountaintop aerie that was selected for its view of the sunrise over the Blue Mountains. Climbers stay aloft until around noon that day, then head back down the mountain for an eventual return to their hotels in Kingston by 4pm.

A second popular offering from the same company is an excursion from Kingston to **Y's Waterfall** on the Black River, in southern Jamaica's Elizabeth Parish. Participants congregate in Kingston at 6:30am for a transfer to a raft and boating party near the hamlet of Lacovia, and an all-day waterborne excursion to a region of unusual ecological interest. Depending on the number of participants, fees range from $80 to $100 per person, including lunch.

WHERE TO STAY

Whitfield Hall. c/o John Allgrove, 8 Armon Jones Crescent, Kingston 6, Jamaica, W.I. ☎ **876/927-0986.** 7 units (none with bathroom), 1 2-bedroom cottage. J$500 ($14.25) per person; J$2,000 ($57) cottage for up to 4 occupants. No credit cards.

One of the most isolated places in Jamaica, this hostel is located more than halfway up Blue Mountain at some 4,000 feet above sea level. The main draw here is the opportunity to see the Blue Mountains from a hill climber's point of view. Whitfield Hall is a coffee plantation dating from 1776, and it is the last inhabited house from that period. It provides basic accommodation for 30 guests in rooms containing two or more beds. Blankets and linen are provided, but personal items, such as towels, soap, and food, are not. There is no restaurant, but there's a deep freeze, a refrigerator, and good cooking facilities including crockery and cutlery. All water comes from a spring, and lighting is by kerosene pressure lamps called *tilleys*. A wood fire warms the hostel and its guests, as it gets cold in the mountains at night. You bring your own food and share the kitchen. To get here, you can drive to Mavis Bank, about 20 miles from Kingston. Head northeast along Old Hope Road to the suburb of Papine, then proceed to Gordon Town. At Gordon Town, turn right over the bridge near the police station and drive into the hills for some 10 miles until you reach Mavis Bank. You can also reach Mavis Bank by bus from the Kingston suburb of Papine. The bus departs from the northeast edge of town, at the end of Old Hope Road. Mavis Bank is the terminus of this bus line. Transportation from Mavis Bank to Whitfield costs $20 each way. Most guests simplify matters by requesting pickup in Kingston by the hostel's Land Rover, which costs $40 each way for up to six passengers.

WHERE TO DINE

The Gap Cafe & Gift Shoppe. Main Rd., Hardwar Gap in the Blue Mountains, John Crow Mountain National Park. ☎ **876/997-3032.** Main courses J$550–J$700 ($15.70–$19.95). AE, MC, V. Mon–Thurs 9am–5pm, Fri–Sun 9am–6pm. JAMAICAN.

As you venture outside Kingston, heading for the Blue Mountains, consider a luncheon stopover here on the main road to Newcastle. The location is 4,200 feet above sea level in the mountain overlooking Newcastle with vistas over Kingston and the surrounding hills. The cafe is 20 miles from the center of Kingston, and the place makes an ideal rest stop for your trek into the Blue Mountains. A mule path, which originally led to Newcastle, was widened by British army engineers, allowing horse and buggy traffic. The Gap is some 2 miles past the Jamaica Defense Force Hill station and was built in the late 1930s. Ian Fleming wrote parts of *Dr. No.* in the house. Donald Sangster (1911–1967), then prime minister of Jamaica, used to come here to prepare some of his speeches. The Blue Mountain coffee alone is worth the visit, and it's individually ground and brewed as you sit back taking in the scenery. You can later partake of curry or sautéed shrimp and our favorite dish, pasta with jerk chicken. The chef is also proud—and rightly so—of his crab backs.

Appendix:
Jamaica in Depth

Most visitors already have a mental picture of Jamaica before they arrive: its boisterous culture of reggae and Rastafarianism; its white sandy beaches; and its jungles, rivers, mountains, and clear waterfalls. Jamaica's art and cuisine are also remarkable.

Jamaica can be a tranquil and intriguing island, but there's no denying that it's plagued by crime and drugs. There is also palpable racial tension here. But many visitors are unaffected; they're escorted from the airport to their hotel grounds and venture out only on expensive organized tours. These vacationers are largely sheltered from the more unpredictable and sometimes dangerous side of island life. Those who want to see "the real Jamaica," or at least to see the island in greater depth, should be prepared for some hassle. Vendors on the beaches and in the markets can be particularly aggressive.

Most Jamaicans, in spite of hard times, have unrelenting good humor and genuinely welcome visitors to the island. Others, certainly a minority, harm the tourism business, so that many visitors vow never to return. Jamaica's appealing aspects have to be weighed against its poverty and problems, the legacy of traumatic political upheavals that have characterized the island in past decades, beginning in the 1970s.

So, should you go? By all means, yes. Be prudent and cautious—just as if you were visiting New York, Miami, or Los Angeles. But Jamaica is worth it! The island has fine hotels and terrific food. It's well geared to couples who come to tie the knot or celebrate their honeymoon. As for sports, Jamaica boasts the best golf courses in the West Indies, and its landscape affords visitors a lot of activities that often aren't available on other islands, like rafting and serious mountain hiking. The island also has some of the finest diving waters in the world.

This country lies 90 miles south of Cuba, with which it was chummy in the 1970s (when much of the world feared that Jamaica was going Communist). It's the third largest of the Caribbean islands, with some 4,400 square miles of predominantly green, lush land; a mountain ridge that climbs to 7,400 feet above sea level; and many beautiful white-sand beaches with clear blue sea.

1 History 101

IN THE BEGINNING Jamaica has long been viewed as one of the most desirable islands of the West Indies, richer and more diverse than many of the sandier, smaller, and less dramatic islands that lie nearby.

Attempts by outsiders to control Jamaica have influenced much of its history.

Jamaica was settled around 6000 B.C. by Stone-Age people about whom little is known. They were displaced around A.D. 600 by the Arawak, Indians who originated in northern South America (probably in the area of modern Guyana). Skillful fishers and crafters of pottery and bead items, they had copper-colored skin and lived in thatch-covered huts similar to those used in parts of Jamaica today. The Arawak made flint knives and spears tipped with sharks' teeth, but they never developed the bow and arrow. They lived mainly on a diet of fish and turtle steak. The Arawak were completely unprepared for the horrors brought by the Spanish conquest.

CRUEL COLONY In 1494, during his second voyage to the New World, Christopher Columbus visited Jamaica and claimed the island for the Spanish monarchy. Although he quickly departed to search for gold and treasure elsewhere, he returned accidentally in 1503–1504, when he was stranded with a group of Spanish sailors for many months off Jamaica's northern coastline while they repaired their worm-eaten ships.

Beginning in 1509, Spaniards from the nearby colony of Santo Domingo established two settlements on Jamaica: one in the north (Nueva Sevilla, later abandoned) in modern St. Ann Parish and another in the south, San Jago de la Vega (St. James of the Plain), on the site of present-day Spanish Town. Pirates estimated the Arawak population in Jamaica at the time to be about 60,000.

In 1513, the first African slaves reached Jamaica, and in 1520 sugarcane cultivation was introduced. In the 1540s, the Spanish Crown grudgingly offered the entire island to Columbus's family as a reward for his service to Spain. Columbus's descendants did nothing to develop the island's vast potential, however. Angered by the lack of immediate profit (abundantly available from gold and silver mines in Mexico and Peru), the Spanish colonists accomplished very little other than to wipe out the entire Arawak population. Forced into slavery, every last Arawak was either executed or died of disease, overwork, or malnutrition.

Dateline

- **ca. 6000 B.C.** Indian groups settle Jamaica.
- **ca. A.D. 600** Arawak Indians come to the island.
- **1494** Columbus visits Jamaica.
- **1503–1504** Columbus is stranded on the north coast.
- **1509** Spain establishes colony at St. Ann's Bay.
- **1513** First enslaved Africans arrive.
- **1520** Sugarcane cultivation introduced.
- **1655** British troops overrun Jamaica.
- **1658** English repel Spanish invaders.
- **1661** Major English colonization begins.
- **1670** Hundreds of privateers given royal protection in Jamaica.
- **1692** Earthquake destroys Port Royal.
- **1739** Rebellious Maroons sign treaty with English.
- **1800** Census reveals huge majority of blacks in Jamaica.
- **1808** Slave trade abolished by Great Britain.
- **1838** Slavery ended.
- **1866** Jamaica becomes a British Crown Colony.
- **1930** Jamaicans push for autonomy.
- **1943** Bauxite mining begins.
- **1944** Universal adult suffrage instituted.
- **1960s** Tourist industry grows.
- **1962** Jamaica achieves independence on August 6.
- **1970s** Bob Marley and reggae gain world fame.
- **1972** Michael Manley, a socialist, becomes prime minister.
- **1980** Edward Seaga, a moderate, succeeds Manley.
- **1980s** High unemployment spreads, though tourism thrives.

continues

- **1988** Hurricane Gilbert devastates Jamaica.
- **1989** Manley, now moderate, returns to power.
- **1992** P. J. Patterson becomes prime minister.
- **1997** Patriarch Michael Manley dies; elections retain Patterson and People's National Party.

RAISING THE UNION JACK After 146 years as a badly and cruelly administered backwater of the Spanish Empire, Jamaica met with a change of fortune when a British armada arrived at Kingston Harbour in 1655. The fleet had sailed on orders from Oliver Cromwell, but it had failed in its mission to conquer the well-fortified Spanish colony of Santo Domingo. Almost as an afterthought, it went on to Jamaica. Within a day, the Spaniards surrendered the whole island to the British, who allowed them to escape. Most of the Spaniards emigrated to nearby Cuba, although a handful remained secretly on the island's north coast.

Six months later, British colonists arrived, but many died from poisoning and disease. In 1657, Spaniards based in Cuba initiated a last-ditch effort to recapture Jamaica. Two of the fiercest and biggest battles in Jamaican history pitted the Spanish against the English. The defection from the Spanish by some Maroons (escaped slaves and their descendants living in the Jamaican mountains) led to the permanent exit in 1660 of Spanish troops from Jamaica. Humiliated, these soldiers escaped to Cuba in canoes.

In 1661, the British began to colonize Jamaica in earnest. They appointed a governor directly responsible to the Crown, with orders to create a governing council elected by the colonists. All children born of English subjects in Jamaica became free citizens of England. In 2 years, the population of Jamaica grew to more than 4,000. Hostilities between England and Spain continued, with occasional skirmishes and richly successful raids by the English on Spanish colonies in Cuba and Central America.

The Maroons formed an important subculture in Jamaica. They lived independently in the mountainous interior, often murdering every white person who transgressed their boundaries. In the coastal areas, the population swelled with the importation of many slaves from Africa and the immigration of more than 1,000 settlers from Barbados. Additional settlers came from the ranks of semiautonomous bands of privateers, who with the full approval of the British Crown plundered any ship or settlement belonging to nations hostile to England. Under Governor Thomas Modyford, Britain initiated a policy of full protection of privateers at Port Royal, near Kingston. Modyford simultaneously encouraged cacao, coffee, and sugarcane cultivation, tended by an increasing number of slaves.

A few years later, Britain committed one of the most cynical, yet practical, acts in the history of Jamaica when it appointed the notorious privateer, Welsh-born Henry Morgan, as the island's lieutenant governor. Morgan's previous bloody but profitable exploits had included plundering Panama City and Porto Bello on the Isthmus of Panama, both laden with treasure from the mines of Peru awaiting shipment to Spain. Despite the well-known torments and atrocities he had inflicted on non-English colonists throughout the Caribbean, Morgan was buried with honors in 1688 at Port Royal. By then, more than 17,000 persons lived in Jamaica. Port Royal reveled in its reputation as "the wickedest city on earth." It likely contained more houses of dubious repute than any other contemporary city in the Western Hemisphere.

EARTHQUAKES, FIRES & PROSPERITY British interest in Jamaica grew as opportunities for adding profits and territory increased. In 1687, Sir Hans Sloane, physician to powerful aristocrats of Britain and namesake of

London's Sloane Square, wrote two influential scholarly books on the geography, flora, fauna, and people of Jamaica. The volumes helped convince Britain to continue its investments in the island.

In 1690, a slave rebellion was crushed by the British, who executed its leaders. Some participants escaped to the mountains, where they joined the independent Maroons.

On June 7, 1692, just before noon, one of the most violent earthquakes in history struck the city of Port Royal. In less than 20 minutes the three shocks, ascending in intensity, caused the sea to recede and then rush back with terrible force, drowning the virtuous and wicked alike. Much of the city actually dropped into the sea. A handful of survivors attempted to rebuild parts of the city, but in 1704 a great fire destroyed every building except a stone-sided fort.

Although the centerpiece of Jamaica had disappeared, the countryside was becoming one of the world's great producers of sugar. This corresponded neatly with the increasing demand in England for sugar to sweeten the flood of tea imported from Asia. Within 4 years of the destruction of Port Royal, Jamaica contained more than 47,000 inhabitants. They were divided into three main classes: white property owners (planters, traders, and professionals, many of whom prospered), slaves from Africa and their descendants (by far the largest in number but with little power), and white indentured servants.

In 1694, a French fleet led by Admiral Du Casse invaded the north shore of Jamaica at Carlisle Bay. At the time, France and Britain were at war in Europe as well, and the French plan was meant to divert English warships from Europe. Although the French were eventually driven back to their ships, they destroyed at least 50 sugar plantations and captured some 1,300 slaves. Six years later, the French fleet was counterattacked by the English off the coast of Colombia, but after 5 days of concentrated fighting, the battle ended in a draw. Back in Kingston, the captains responsible for the early withdrawal of the British fleet from the fighting were convicted of misconduct and shot.

POWER STRUGGLES   The struggle for control of Jamaica intensified over the next 50 years as the island became one of the most profitable outposts of the British Empire, despite hurricanes, pirate raids, and slave rebellions. For ease of government, it was divided into 13 parishes, whose boundaries remain today.

Most troublesome for the English were the Maroons, who escaped control by fleeing into the mountains and forests. In 1734, in one of many dramatic battles, the English captured the Maroon stronghold of Nanny Town, destroying its buildings and killing many of its inhabitants. The survivors committed suicide by jumping off a cliff, preferring death to enslavement. By 1739, however, both the English and the Maroons recognized the virtues of increased cooperation, and they signed a series of peace agreements. The Maroons were given tax-free land in different parts of the island. They were allowed to govern themselves and to be tried and punished by their own leaders, who could not, however, sentence a subject to death. Also very important, the Maroons agreed to capture all runaway slaves and return them to their masters and to assist in suppressing any slave rebellion.

In 1741, the British navy used Jamaica as a base of operations for mostly unsuccessful military strikes against Spanish strongholds in Cartagena, Colombia, and on the Isthmus of Panama. Caused by harsh conditions, slave rebellions in 1746 and 1760 led to many deaths. The British ended both revolts, killing many, and sending most survivors to Honduras to work in swamps and sweltering timberlands.

Jamaica Natural

Jamaica and the rest of the Caribbean archipelago are summits of a submarine string of mountains, which in prehistoric times probably formed a land bridge between modern Mexico and Venezuela. Covering about 4,240 square miles, it's approximately the size of Connecticut, yet offers a diverse landscape. The island is some 146 miles long, with widths ranging from 22 to 58 miles.

Millions of years ago, volcanoes thrust up from the ocean floor, forming Jamaica's mountains, which range to 7,402 feet high (loftier than any along the eastern seaboard of North America). These mountains, located in an east-to-west line in central Jamaica, contain more than 120 rivers and many waterfalls as well as thermal springs. In the high mountains of the east, the landscape features semitropical rain forest and copses of mist-covered pines. The mountains are bordered on the north and east by a narrow coastal plain fringed with beaches. The flat, arid southern coastline reminds visitors of African savanna or Indian plains, whereas the moist, fertile north coast slopes steeply from hills down to excellent beaches. Much of Jamaica is underlaid by limestone, dotted with dozens of caves that store large reservoirs of naturally filtered drinking water.

Almost everything grows in Jamaica, as proved by colonial British botanists who imported flowers and fruits from Asia, the Pacific, Africa, and Canada. The island contains unique orchids, ferns, bromeliads, and varieties of fruit, like the Bombay mango, that don't flourish elsewhere in the Western Hemisphere. Birds, insects, and other animals are also abundant.

Framing the capital of Kingston, the Blue Mountains dominate the eastern third of the island. This is the country's most panoramic area, and it's split by a network of paths, trails, and bad roads—a paradise for hikers. From this region comes Blue Mountain coffee, the most expensive in the world. Younger than the Blue Mountains, the John Crow Mountains rise at the northeastern end of the island. Only the most skilled mountain climbers or advanced hikers should attempt this rugged karstic terrain. It rains here almost daily, creating a rain-forest effect.

Jamaica's longest river is called Black River, and it's bordered by marshes, swamps, and mangroves where bird and animal life, including reptiles, flourishes. Black River, which is also the name of a small port, is in the southwestern section, lying east of Savanna-la-Mar and reached by Route A2.

By the time of the American Revolution, the population of Jamaica had reached almost 210,000, some 193,000 of whom were slaves. After 1776, some Loyalist residents of the United States moved to Jamaica. France, which sided with the Americans against the British, sent an opportunistic militia to the West Indies. It captured many British islands in the eastern Caribbean, and Jamaicans trembled with anticipation of a French invasion. Admiral Horatio Nelson, later famous for defeating Napoleon's French fleet at the Battle of Trafalgar, drilled the Jamaican garrisons to repel the expected attack. It never came, however.

Naval skirmishes among the British, Spanish, and French continued offshore, with Jamaica usually serving as the stronghold for British forces. In

1782, Admiral George Brydges Rodney defeated a huge French force off Dominica, killing more than half of the 6,000 men intended for an invasion of Jamaica. Rodney brought the captured French ships to the rebuilt Port Royal. Appreciative colonists voted to spend £3,000 to erect a statue in his honor, and the British government made him a peer.

In 1793, Britain tried to influence a rapidly disintegrating situation in nearby Haiti, a dependency of France. Although several Haitian cities were captured by English troops, an outbreak of disease and the fierce opposition of the noted leader Toussaint L'Ouverture (who later ruled all Haiti) soon ended the venture.

Also in 1793, some 5,000 British troops equipped with specially trained bloodhounds imported from Cuba fought another bloody war against the Maroons in the Jamaican highlands. The British sent the captured Maroons first to Canada, then to Sierra Leone, in West Africa. Those not involved were allowed to remain in Jamaica.

An official census in 1800 revealed a Jamaican population of 300,000 blacks and 20,000 whites. This disparity was not lost upon either the powers in London or the leaders of the increasingly politicized blacks.

Despite revolts by blacks and military expeditions to neighboring islands, Jamaica in 1803 exported the largest sugar crop in the country's history. In part, the island's wealth resulted from acts of Parliament that imposed high tariffs on sugar imported into Britain from Cuba, Haiti, Martinique, Guadeloupe, and other areas. The Jamaican planters maintained one of the best-organized political machines in London, lobbying hard and spending great amounts of money to retain the trade barriers that kept sugar prices artificially high in England. Adding to the wealth was coffee; in 1814, the island exported a record crop.

After Nelson defeated Napoleon at Trafalgar in 1805, the huge sums expended by Jamaica to defend against French raiders decreased dramatically. At the same time, Jamaica's role as a depot for smuggling contraband British goods to Cuba and Spanish colonies of South America also diminished. Within 20 years, the island's economy worsened considerably, signaling an end to a great era of Jamaican prosperity.

SLAVERY & PROSPERITY END   After the United States became independent in 1776, Britain imposed an embargo on U.S. products and cut off trade between North America's eastern seaboard and Jamaica, a condition that caused great hardship throughout the island.

Adding to Jamaica's woes was increasing popular sentiment in Britain against the slave trade. The importation of forced laborers from Africa was outlawed in 1807, and in 1838 slavery itself was made illegal in all British dependencies, including Jamaica. Parliament voted £20 million to compensate the slave owners. Partly because of Jamaica's influence in Parliament, almost £6 million of that money was designated for the island's slave owners. Freed blacks celebrated throughout Jamaica, with credit for the legislation going (rightly or wrongly) to Queen Victoria.

The problem then arose of finding workers for the labor-intensive sugar plantations. Planters offered blacks only low wages (about 9 pence a day) for the difficult labor, and in addition many former enslaved persons refused to work under any circumstances for their former owners. As a result, the large sugar industry declined.

The Jamaica Railway opened in 1845, having been built by inexpensive laborers from India. Any benefits the line might have offered the sugar planters, however, were quickly undercut by passage in 1847 of the Free Trade Act. Designed to encourage untaxed trade in the British Empire, the act removed the protection enjoyed by Jamaican sugar in Britain, placing it on an even par with the plentiful, cheap sugar produced in other parts of the Caribbean.

Between 1850 and 1852, epidemics of Asian cholera and smallpox ripped through the island's overcrowded shantytowns, whose sanitation facilities were minimal. More than 32,000 people died from the maladies brought from other parts of the British Empire. At the same time, Jamaica suffered from an exodus of creative entrepreneurs, a lack of funds to run the government, and a continuing decline of the agricultural base. The island's workforce vehemently protested low wages and competition from cheap labor brought in from British dependencies in India and China.

REVOLTS & REFORMS   As a result of the American Civil War fought between 1861 and 1865, many vital shipments formerly brought to Jamaica from North America were blocked or rendered very expensive. During this period, the lieutenant governor of the colony, at odds as usual with both planters and laborers, publicly described the colony as being "in a state of degeneration." Labor unrest, attempts by blacks to overturn the government, and interference in Jamaican affairs by committees of English Baptists and London-based liberals plagued the planters. In 1866, Jamaican laborers mounted an extremely bloody revolt, which was put down by English troops. Many changes were initiated thereafter, however, including the recall of the very unpopular lieutenant governor of the island. Eventually, a more liberal form of government emerged, and island residents had a larger voice in Jamaican affairs. The police and judicial systems were reorganized into a fairer system directly responsible to the British Crown, rather than to local potentates who had often abused their power. Also, administrative divisions of the island's parishes were changed and their numbers reduced.

Meanwhile, telegraph communication with Europe was established in 1869, the Jamaica Railway was extended, and nickel coins, guaranteed by the Bank of England, were issued for the first time. The education system was improved, great irrigation works were initiated, and the dependency became known for the enlightened application of British ways. Hurricanes seemed to demolish parts of the island at regular intervals, however, and the power struggle between British authorities in London and local administrators in Kingston went on.

British tourism to Jamaica began in the 1890s, and a quintet of hotels was built to house the administrators and investors who showed keen interest in developing the island's fertile land. A Lands Department was organized to sell government-held land to local farmers cheaply and on easy terms. The island's teachers were organized into unions, and the railroad was extended to Jamaica's northeast tip at Port Antonio. New bridges and improved roads also helped open the island. Frustrated by low sugar prices, Jamaican planters invested heavily in the production of bananas.

On January 14, 1907, another great earthquake shattered much of the city of Kingston, destroying or damaging just about every building. More than 800 lives were lost, and total damage was estimated at £2 million. It seemed to be a repeat of the earthquake that had shattered Port Royal 215 years earlier. Parliament and the Church of England sent massive funds to rebuild Kingston. The new street plan remains the basis for the city's layout today.

JAMAICA IN THE WORLD WARS   During World War I, Jamaica sent about 10,000 men to fight with British forces. They were eventually deployed in Palestine, where they battled heroically against the Ottoman Empire. Many ships used in peacetime to export Jamaican agricultural products were commandeered for use in European waters. Martial law was imposed on Jamaica, and local volunteers were organized to defend the island from attack. In 1915, 1916, and 1917, the war effort was complicated by hurricanes that devastated the island's banana crop. But some progress was made: In May 1917, Jamaican women were given the right to vote.

In 1938 Alexander Bustamante organized Jamaica's first officially recognized labor union. At first imprisoned but later freed and knighted by the British, he is today regarded as a founder of modern Jamaica.

At the outbreak of World War II in 1939, Jamaica was placed under rigid control, and the governor set prices and censored the press, the telephones, the telegraph, and international mail. In 1940, the United States was granted the right to establish army and navy bases in British territories, including Jamaica, where two bases were quickly built. By 1943, many Jamaicans had moved to the United States to work in munitions factories. In the same year, bauxite, the raw material for making much-needed aluminum, was mined for the first time in St. Ann Parish. The next year, a new constitution provided for universal adult suffrage.

In 1947, after the war, Jamaica served as the meeting place for discussions concerning the amalgamation of English-speaking lands of the Caribbean area into a single political unit. The countries sending representatives to the meetings included Barbados, Trinidad and Tobago, the Leeward Islands, the Windward Islands, British Guiana (now Guyana), and British Honduras (now Belize). The union never developed fully, however, mainly because of political infighting and local attachments.

FREEDOM ARRIVES In 1950, newly formed Radio Jamaica Ltd. (RJR) provided an outlet for the ideologies rapidly being shaped in Jamaica.

In 1951, the worst hurricane in almost 100 years completely demolished Port Royal for the third time. No serious attempt was made thereafter to rebuild the city, which had played a vital part in developing Jamaica.

In 1957, Jamaica attained full internal self-government under a system based on well-established English models. Lengthy celebrations marked the event. The same year, nearly 17,000 Jamaicans emigrated to England to find work because the Jamaica's economy was not growing as quickly as the population. Concurrently, bauxite and alumina (processed bauxite) exports surged, and the government demanded and received a higher percentage of profits from the mining companies. With the advent of the intercontinental jet airliner, Jamaica's tourist industry also expanded, and hotels were built to accommodate visitors from North America and Europe.

After the rise to power in 1959 of Fidel Castro, Jamaica cut many ties with Cuba and established trade and cultural links with other islands, especially Puerto Rico. In 1959 Montego Bay airport was opened, and Kingston airport was expanded to handle the flood of visitors. Despite economic growth, however, large-scale emigration to Great Britain continued.

In 1961, Jamaica withdrew from the Federation of the West Indies, which had been formed in 1958, after Jamaicans voted to seek independence as a separate nation. The next year, on August 6, Jamaica achieved its independence, although still recognizing the British monarch as the formal head of state and maintaining other ties as a member of the Commonwealth of Nations. Sir Alexander Bustamante, head of the Jamaica Labour Party (JLP), became the country's first prime minister. Also in 1962, the Royal Hampshire

Regiment—the last British troops in Jamaica—departed the island, thus ending the colonial era begun in 1655.

RECENT TIMES In 1966 Haile Selassie I, emperor of Ethiopia, came to Jamaica on a 3-day state visit. The stay sparked national interest in the emperor's life, and as a result there was a notable increase in Jamaican converts to Rastafarianism, a religion that venerates the late emperor, known earlier as Ras Tafari (see "Rastafarianism" later in this appendix). During the 1970s, the popularity of Rastafarian musician Bob Marley and other Jamaican reggae performers spread around the world, giving the country an important role on the international music stage.

In 1972, Michael Manley, a trade unionist who headed the left-wing People's National Party (PNP), was sworn in for the first of what would eventually be several terms as Jamaica's prime minister. For many historians, this marked the beginning of full-scale ideological battles for the heart and soul of the Jamaican people. Jamaicans argued vehemently over whether the young nation should embrace socialism, and over its relationship with the United States. A noteworthy event of Manley's Democratic Socialism occurred in 1977, when Cuban President Fidel Castro paid a 6-day official visit to Jamaica, which led to a perception in Washington that Jamaican politics were increasingly shifting leftward. Despite Manley's political prowess, the months leading up to the 1980 elections were particularly violent, with episodes of civil disobedience and numerous deaths on both sides. The elections were won by the moderate, free-enterprise JLP, led by relatively conservative Edward Seaga, who became prime minister. Shortly afterward, Jamaica broke diplomatic ties with Cuba. Seaga's mandate was solidified in the 1983 elections, which the PNP claimed were unfairly run. Seaga attempted to promote economic growth and cut inflation but with little success. Unemployment rose, as did violent crime.

In September 1988, the island was devastated by Hurricane Gilbert, which destroyed some 100,000 homes.

A much-more-moderate Manley returned to power in 1989. This time, he sought friendly ties with the United States. In the early 1990s, Jamaica continued to face daunting economic difficulties, as unemployment hovered near 18% of the workforce. In Kingston, there was gang violence, some reputedly tied to the country's main political parties. Tourism boomed, however. Manley retired in 1992 because of ill health and was succeeded by an associate, Percival J. Patterson, also a moderate. Patterson was confirmed in office when his PNP won 53 of 60 seats in the House of Representatives in elections in March 1993.

In the elections of 1997, Patterson continued his reign over Jamaica, consolidating his power. The Peoples National Party continued to hold the loyalty of the majority of voters.

The island also laid to rest one of its all-time major power brokers, the controversial former premier Michael Manley, who became prime minister in 1972, succeeding his father, Norman Manley. His left-wing politics, and especially his ties with Fidel Castro, brought on increasing strain with the United States. Manley later accused the U.S. of "overreacting" to his friendship with Castro. Manley also became one of the most forceful boosters of the Black Power movement that swept the Caribbean in the 70s and 80s.

In 1998, the prime minister, Patterson, launched a crackdown on those who badger tourists to buy or barter for drugs, sex, and merchandise. Jamaica also established night courts, making it possible for law-enforcement officers to appear in court without having to abandon their beats.

Did You Know?

- Jamaica is the third largest of the 51 inhabited islands in the Caribbean—only Cuba and Hispaniola are bigger.
- Akee, though cooked and used as a vegetable, is actually a fruit that is a poison until it bursts open and its gases escape. It is part of Jamaica's national dish, akee and salt fish.
- Blue Mountain coffee, grown on the slopes of Jamaica's loftiest mountain, is among the tastiest and most sought-after coffees in the world.
- In 1503–1504, Christopher Columbus spent about a year off the north coast of Jamaica because his worm-eaten vessels weren't seaworthy.
- In the 17th century, the notorious privateer, Henry Morgan, presided over Jamaica's Port Royal, known as the "wickedest city on earth."
- Annie Palmer, the "white witch" of Rose Hall (near Montego Bay), famed for murdering husbands and lovers, was herself strangled to death by an unknown assailant.
- On August 6, 1962, England's Princess Margaret and U.S. Vice President Lyndon B. Johnson watched as the British Union Jack was lowered and a new flag raised as Jamaica attained independence. The new flag featured a gold cross on a black-and-green background.
- Rastafarians, a Jamaican religious group, venerate the late Ethiopian emperor, Haile Selassie.
- Some Jamaicans regard ganja (marijuana) as a sacred plant and testify to its healing power.

Patterson told the press, "People are going to refuse to come to Jamaica, resulting in a virtual collapse of the tourism industry because of harassment. No matter how enjoyable the beaches, the views, or the music, if visitors are the subject of constant harassment, they simply will not return. While most Jamaicans are hospitable, the miscreants have to be dealt with decisively—and that means stiff fines."

2 Jamaican Style

ART

Since the Arawak first inscribed interiors of Jamaican caves with petroglyphs, the island has produced many artists. Although its artistic production is less renowned than neighboring Haiti's, Jamaica nonetheless is considered a Caribbean art capital, with a vibrant tradition ranging from street art to formal canvases that receive acclaim in chic galleries of London and New York. Jamaican art tends to be less stylized than Haiti's, less uniform in its assumptions, and more broadly based on a wide array of differing philosophical traditions. The bulk of Jamaican artwork has been executed since 1940, when the yearning for independence and a sense of national destiny colored many aspects of the country's life. Whereas reggae, the national musical form, is strongly influenced by a subculture (the Rastafarians), Jamaican painting is much wider-ranging and diverse.

The most easily accessible Jamaican artwork is "yard art," which rises from the concrete, litter, and poverty of the island's cities. Punctuated with solid blocks of vivid color, and sometimes interspersed with graffiti, these murals are often viewed as an authentic reflection of the Jamaican soul. Subjects include political satire, naive (or intuitive) depictions of an artist's friends and family, idealized Jamaican landscapes, and kaleidoscopic visions of heaven and hell. Examples of yard art seem to increase, along with graffiti and political slogans, before each election. Predictably, however, a flood of uninspired wood carvings, handcrafts, and banal painting has appeared in recent years because of worldwide commercial and sociological interest in yard art. *Caveat emptor.*

Much yard art is a legacy of a group of self-taught intuitive artists (sometimes known as "primitives") who rose to fame in the 19th century. Most famous was John Dunkley (b. 1891), a Kingston barber, whose spare time was devoted almost entirely to covering the walls, ceilings, and furniture of his shop with flowers, vines, trees, and abstract symbols that a psychologist might describe as Jungian. Although his painting was scorned by mainstream art critics during his lifetime, it survives as the most sought after, and among the most expensive, artwork in the Caribbean today. Jamaican artists who followed Dunkley's lead include Mallica Reynolds, Gaston Tabois, Allan Zion, and Sydney McLaren.

Despite the artistic merits of these painters, it required the organizational efforts of Edna Manley, wife and mother of two of Jamaica's prime ministers and an acclaimed sculptor in her own right, to foster the development of Jamaican art. Beginning around 1940, she encouraged self-taught artists and organized art classes at the Institute of Jamaica, thereby inspiring islanders to view local artwork in a more respectful way.

Jamaican nationalists view as pivotal the day in 1939 when a group of about 40 highly politicized artists stormed the annual meeting of the Institute of Jamaica, then the island's most visible art museum. Demanding freedom from the domination of Jamaican art by European aesthetics, the nationalists insisted that the English-inspired portraits of the colonial age be replaced in galleries by works of Jamaica's artists. In response, Edna Manley and some volunteers started a series of informal art lessons, which in 1950 blossomed into the Jamaican School of Art and, several years later, the Cultural Training Centre. Based in Kingston, these two schools have trained many of Jamaica's established artists, dancers, and actors.

Today, Jamaica's leading painters include Carl Abrahams, whose recurrent theme is the Last Supper; Barrington Watson, known for a romanticized, charming view of the Jamaican people; Eugene Hyde, one of the country's first modern abstract artists; and English-born Jonathon Routh, whose illustrations of Queen Victoria during elaborate state visits to Jamaica—none of which really occurred—provoke laughter as far away as London. Also noteworthy are Christopher Gonzalez, who won a commission by the Jamaican government for a statue of reggae superstar Bob Marley; David Boxer, one of the first Jamaican surrealists; and Osmond Watson, known for his sharp-angled and absorbing depictions of the human face.

A discussion of Jamaican art would not be complete without mentioning the rich tradition of art left by the colonial English and wealthy planters. The earliest published illustrations of Jamaica include the Spillsbury prints, which show in subtle detail the harbors and fine Georgian buildings of 18th-century Jamaica. English-born Philip Wickstead painted portraits of the island's wealthiest families. George Robertson, following in the great tradition of English landscape painting exemplified by John Constable, depicted the lush forests and sugarcane fields of Jamaica during the peak of their commercial prosperity.

Other artists, some white and itinerant, captured the charm and sorrow of 19th-century Jamaica. Isaac Mendes Belisario, an English-born Jew whose family stemmed from Italy, set up a studio in Kingston and produced portraits of enslaved persons and sketches of carnivals and musical parades. Scottish-born Joseph Bartholomew Kidd executed finely detailed sketches of Kingston buildings and the homes of wealthy planters. Also noteworthy are statues erected by the British in honor of military heroes, among the finest in the Caribbean. A good example is the Rodney Memorial Statue, by John Bacon, Sr., in the heart of Spanish Town.

More scandalous, and perhaps more famous, are the Jamaica-inspired works produced during the 18th century by William Hogarth, whose reputation as a satirist had already been assured by the publication and wide distribution of a series of engravings titled *A Harlot's Progress*. Equally ribald was Hogarth's series titled *The Sugar Planter, at Home and Abroad*. Savagely satirical, the engravings showed a grossly bloated planter alternately whipping forced laborers and hoarding gold, while surrounded by his mulatto children. In the same series, a better-behaved London incarnation of the planter is shown dressed in urban finery entertaining the peerage, manipulating votes in Parliament, and smiling benignly as lines of impoverished English housewives pay artificially inflated prices for his sugar. The release of this effective series was carefully timed to coincide with popular movements in Parliament to curtail price-fixing by Jamaica sugar barons.

ARCHITECTURE

The colonization of Jamaica occurred during a great period of British expansion. Much effort was expended in displaying the cultural allegiance of Jamaican planters to their native England, and one of the most obvious methods of doing so was to adapt the contemporary architectural motifs of Britain to the tropics. Partly because of a desire to protect their political prerogatives in Parliament, Jamaican planters returned to England frequently, maintaining their political links with Parliament, their investments, their social status, and an elevated price for sugar, which had made them rich. The obsession of Jamaican planters with contemporary English taste helped create an architectural elegance rivaled by only a handful of other English colonies, notably Pennsylvania, Massachusetts, and Barbados. Although the island style began with an allegiance to Georgian models, concessions were made to the heat, humidity, bugs, hurricanes, and earthquakes of the tropics. Later, after Jamaica became recognized as the leading outpost of English military power and agrarian skill in the West Indies, Jamaican architectural principles spread to other parts of the Caribbean.

Georgian-type design, manifest in Jamaica's port facilities, Customs houses, and civic buildings, was most graceful in the island's many great houses. Intended as centerpieces for enormous sugar plantations, these buildings include some of the finest examples of domestic architecture in the West Indies. Among common design elements are wide verandas on at least two sides, balustrades, intricate fretwork, sophisticated applications of contrasting types of lattice, deep and sometimes ornate fascia boards, and a prevalence of pineapple-shaped finials above cornices and rooflines. Individual houses varied with the personality of the architects and the wealth and taste of the owners. Unlike great houses in other English-speaking Caribbean islands, the first floors of Jamaican buildings were usually elevated by low stilts or pilings to allow air to circulate. This prevented rot, cooled the ground floor, and helped keep rats, snakes, insects, and scorpions out of living quarters. Jamaican masonry and wood pilings are radically different from showplace buildings on St. Kitts, for example, where lower foundations were usually crafted from massive bulwarks of stone.

Not all of Jamaica's 18th-century buildings were designed along Georgian lines. Smaller, less pretentious houses were built in styles appropriate to the income of the owners and demands of the sites. Jamaican vernacular architectural style was developed by tenant farms and indentured servants, many from Scotland, and by the children of freed enslaved persons. These houses usually received the prevailing trade winds, and typically were angled to prevent smoke from the kitchen from blowing into living quarters. Known for the pleasing proportions of their inner spaces, the buildings continue to surprise contemporary architectural critics by their appropriate placement and convenient interior traffic patterns.

Since the end of World War II, architecture in Jamaica has followed two distinct variations on colonial themes. Banks, civic buildings, and commercial structures have generally been inspired by the thick walls, small windows, and massive dignity of the island's 18th- and 19th-century English forts. Hotels and private dwellings, on the other hand, typically trace their inspiration to the island's great houses or to the unpretentious wooden cottages that still dot the landscape. Other commercial buildings draw inspiration from the International Style that swept over most of the industrialized world between 1945 and 1980.

Noteworthy on virtually all Jamaican houses is the technique of attaching porch roofs and verandas to the main body of the house. In the hurricane-prone area, an experienced carpenter would deliberately not interconnect the beams of a porch with the beams supporting the main roof of the house. Because of their tendency to be destroyed during hurricane-strength wind gusts, porch roofs were usually built as separate, loosely attached architectural adornments not considered vital to the building's main core. Roofs were covered with split mahogany shingles until the 1930s, when Canadian cedar shingles became readily available. In the English tradition, gardens were usually considered important adjuncts to the great house. Altogether, Jamaican houses were graceful reflections of the good life, with only one major drawback: easy destruction by fire.

Jamaica today boasts an important contingent of locally born architects trained in the United States and Canada. The dean of Jamaican architects, Vayden McMorris, whose practice began in the mid-1950s, is credited with nurturing Jamaica's young architects. McMorris designed such New Kingston towers as the Panjam Building, the Citibank Building, the Doyall Building, and the Victoria Mutual Building Society's head office.

Wilson Chong, a Jamaican of Chinese descent, is responsible for the design of one of Jamaica's most-visited buildings, the football (soccer) stadium. Viewed as a master of the shell-shaped concrete curve, Chong flourished in the 1960s. A dramatic, but rarely visited, Chong design is the grandstand of Marley Racetrack, whose triple cantilever is considered an engineering marvel. The racetrack, located some 23 miles west of Kingston, has not been operated for several years.

Another bright star among Jamaican architects is H. Denny Repol, whose firm designed about a dozen major hotels on the north shore. In the 1980s, Repol also designed the administrative headquarters of the Jamaica Tourist Board (21 Dominica Dr., in Kingston), considered a model version of the "work-related open space." Another Repol commission is the Life of Jamaica

Head Office Building, whose four floors of reinforced concrete shelter a sun-flooded atrium spanned with a bridge and thousands of verdant plants.

3 The Jamaican People & Their Culture

Jamaica's 2.5 million people form a spectrum of types that bespeak the island's heritage. Most Jamaicans are black, but there are also people of Chinese, Asian Indian, Middle Eastern, and European background. About 75% of the people are classified as black African and about 15% as Afro-European.

Jamaicans are above all friendly, funny, opinionated, talented, and almost impossible to forget. The sense of humor is dry and understated but robust and physical; one makes fun of oneself and others. It is also both subtle and direct. National pride is specific—beating the English at cricket, winning gold medals in the Olympics, or attaining world boxing titles. Individuals take pride in outstandingly bright and successful family members, a new house, a successful business, and the ability to survive, not easy in some urban slums.

To grow sugarcane, the English long ago brought in Africans to do forced work. Most came from the west coast of Africa, notably the area of modern Ghana, and belonged to the Fanti and Ashanti ethnic groups. Others are descended from the Ibo and Yoruba people of present-day Nigeria. When the forced laborers were freed in 1838, most deserted the plantations and settled in the hills to cultivate small plots of land. They founded a peasantry that is still regarded as the backbone of Jamaica.

After slavery was abolished, the English brought in Chinese and later East Indians as indentured laborers for the plantation.

Jews are among the oldest residents of Jamaica. Some Jewish families have been here from the time of the earliest Spanish settlements. Although small in number (about 400), the Jewish community has been influential in government and commerce.

When the English came, the Spaniards fled to neighboring islands and their black forced workers escaped into the mountains and formed independent groups called Maroons.

In 1991, the birthrate in Jamaica was about 24 per 1,000 persons, and the death rate 6 per 1,000. Life expectancy at birth was 76 years for females, 72 years for males. There was a net out-migration of 9 persons per 1,000 inhabitants. The annual population growth rate was 0.9%.

RASTAFARIANISM

Although relatively small in number (they had about 14,000 firm adherents in the early 1980s), Rastafarians have had wide-ranging influence on Jamaican culture. Their identifying dreadlocks (long, sometimes braided, hair) can now be seen at virtually every level of Jamaican society.

To understand the origins of Rastafarianism, it's necessary to introduce Marcus Garvey. Born in 1887 in Jamaica's St. Ann Parish, Garvey did much to build black pride in the United States as well as in the West Indies. To combat the vast cultural upheavals wrought by slavery, Garvey founded the Universal Negro Improvement Association (UNIA) to raise the consciousness of blacks about a diaspora unmatched since the first-century scattering of the Jews. Advocating a "back to Africa" kind of self-reliance, he aroused the loyalty of blacks and the hostility of whites. Garvey died in London in 1940, almost forgotten, but his body was later returned to Jamaica, where he received a hero's burial.

None of the power of Garvey, however, could match the later revival of African consciousness by the Rastafarians. Stressing the continuity of black African culture throughout history, Rastas believe in their direct spiritual descent from King Solomon's liaison with the queen of Sheba. Rastafarianism, according to some, is based on an intuitive interpretation of history and scripture—sometimes with broad brush strokes—with special emphasis on the reading of Old Testament prophecies. Rastafarians stress contemplation, meditation, a willingness to work inwardly to the "I" (inner divinity), and an abstractly political bent. Their assumptions are enhanced through sacramental rites of ganja (marijuana) smoking, Bible reading (with particular stress on references to Ethiopia), music, physical exercise, art, poetry, and cottage industries like handcrafts and broom making. Reggae music developed from Rasta circles and produced such international stars as the fervently religious Bob Marley. Jamaica's politicians, aware of the allure of Rastafarianism, often pay homage to its beliefs.

A male Rastafarian's beard is a sign of his pact with God (Jah or Jehovah), and his Bible is his source of knowledge. His dreadlocks are a symbol of his link with the Lion of Judah and Elect of God, the late Emperor of Ethiopia Haile Selassie, who, while a prince, was known as Ras Tafari (hence the religion's name). During the emperor's 1966 visit to Jamaica, more than 100,000 visitors greeted his airplane in something approaching religious ecstasy. The visit almost completely eclipsed Queen Elizabeth's a few months earlier. Rastas believe Haile Selassie to be their personal savior.

LANGUAGE

The official language of Jamaica is English, but the unofficial language is a patois. Linguists and a handful of Jamaican novelists have recently transformed this oral language into written form, although for most Jamaicans it remains solely spoken—and richly nuanced. Experts say that more than 90% of its vocabulary is derived from English, with the remaining words largely borrowed from African languages. There are also words taken from Spanish, Arawak, French, Chinese, Portuguese, and East Indian languages.

Although pronounced similarly to standard English, the patois preserves many 17th- and 18th-century expressions in common use during the time of early British colonial settlement of Jamaica. This archaic and simplified structure, coupled with African accents and special intonation, can make the language difficult to understand. Some linguists consider it a separate language, whereas others view it as just an alternate form of English. Some of the most interesting anecdotes and fables in the Caribbean are usually told in the patois, so understanding its structure can add to your insight into Jamaican culture.

Proverbs and place-names express some of the vitality of Jamaican language. For "Mind your own business," there is "Cockroach no business in fowl-yard." For being corrupted by bad companions, "You lay wid dawg, you get wid fleas." And for the pretentious, "The higher monkey climb, the more him expose." Both British and biblical place-names abound in Jamaica. Examples include Somerset and Siloah, Highgate and Horeb. One also sees Arawak names like Linguanea, Spanish ones like Oracabessa, Scottish names like Rest-and-Be-Thankful, and entirely Jamaican names like Red Gal Ring.

A final note: The patois has been embellished and altered with the growth of Rastafarianism. Rastas have injected several grammatical concepts, one of the most apparent being the repeated use of "I"—a reminder of their reverence of Ras Tafari. "I" is almost always substituted for the pronoun "me." It is also substituted for many prefixes or initial syllables. Thus, "all right," becomes

"I're," "brethren" becomes "Idren," and "praises" becomes "Ises." The Rasta-farian changes of Jamaica's patois are a recent phenomenon and have not always been adopted by non-Rastas.

FOLKLORE

Nothing shaped the modern culture of the Caribbean more than the arrival of slaves from various parts of Africa. They brought gods, beliefs, superstitions, and fears with them. Although later converted to Christianity, they kept their traditions vibrant in fairs and festivals. Jamaican cultural and social life revolved mostly around the church, which was instrumental in molding a sense of community. Storytellers helped maintain ties to the past for each new generation, since little was written down until the 20th century. Since the advent of television, however, Jamaicans rarely gather to hear stories of the old days.

The folklore and ancient oral traditions of Jamaicans have fascinated English colonizers as well as modern-day visitors searching for a pattern to the mysticism that sometimes seems to pervade the countryside. Oral tradition forms a powerful undercurrent in this devoutly religious island; many folk beliefs were brought from Africa by slaves during the 17th and 18th centuries. Despite the later impact of Christian missionaries, a strong belief in magic remains, as does a wide array of superstitions.

Some folk beliefs are expressed in music, notably in the lyrics of reggae. Others are expressed in rhythmic chanting, whose stresses and moods once accompanied both hard labor and dancing. Other beliefs can be found in fairy tales and in legends about the island's slaves and their owners. The telling of oral narrations is a highly nuanced art form. Repetition and an inspired use of patois are important features.

Healing arts make use of Jamaican tradition, especially in the "balm yard," an herb garden-cum-healing place where a mixture of religion and magic is applied by a doctor or "balmist" of either sex. Some medicines brewed, dis-tilled, or fermented in the yard are derived from recipes handed down for many generations and can be effective against ailments ranging from infertil-ity to skin disease. A balm yard is usually encircled by a half-dozen thatch-covered huts, which house supplicants (patients). Bright-red flags fly above each hut to chase away evil spirits. Ceremonies resembling revival meetings are held nightly, with a "mother" and a "father" urging the crowd to groan ecsta-tically and in unison. The threat of damnation in hellfire may be mentioned as punishment for anyone who doesn't groan loudly enough or believe fer-vently enough. It is believed that prayer and supplications to Jesus and various good and evil spirits will help relieve the sick of their ailments.

The two most famous spirits of Jamaica are Obeah and the jumbie. Originating in the southern Caribbean, Obeah is a superstitious force that believers hold responsible for both good and evil. It is prudent not to tangle with this force, which might make trouble for you. Because of a long-established awareness of Obeah, and an unwillingness to tempt it with too positive an answer, a Jamaican is likely to answer, "Not too bad," if asked about his or her health.

There's no agreement on the nature of a jumbie. It's been suggested that it is the spirit of a dead person that didn't go where it belonged. Some islanders, however, say that "they're the souls of live people, who live in the bodies of the dead." Jumbies are said to inhabit households and to possess equal capacities for good and evil. Most prominent are Mocko Jumbies, carnival stilt-walkers seen in parades.

Ganja

Marijuana use is the island's biggest open secret, and you'll no doubt encounter it during your vacation. (To be honest, it's the big draw for some visitors.) Vendors seem to hawk it at random, often through the chain-link fences surrounding popular resorts.

Ganja is viewed with differing degrees of severity in Jamaican society, but it's still officially illegal. We should warn you that being caught by the authorities with marijuana in your possession can lead to immediate imprisonment or deportation.

Marijuana and Jamaica have long endured a love-hate relationship. The plant was brought here by indentured servants from India in the mid-19th century. Revered by them as a medicinal and sacred plant, and referred to by the British as "Indian hemp," it quickly attracted the attention of the island's plantation owners because its use significantly reduced the productivity of those who ingested it. Legislation against its use quickly followed—not for moral or ethical reasons, but because it was bad for business.

During the 1930s, the slow rise of Rastafarianism (whose adherents believe marijuana use is an essential part of their religion) and the occasional use of marijuana by U.S. bohemians, artists, and jazz musicians led to a growing export of the plant to the United States. A massive increase in U.S. consumption occurred during the 1960s. Since the mid-1970s, after more stringent patrols were instituted along the U.S.–Mexico border, it is estimated that between 75% and 95% of all marijuana grown in Jamaica is consumed in the United States.

Cultivation of the crop, when conducted on the typical large scale, is as meticulous and thorough as that of any horticulturist raising a prize species of tomato or rose. Sold illegally by the quart, seeds must first be coaxed into seedlings in a greenhouse, then transplanted into fields at 2-foot intervals. Popular lore claims that the most prolific seedlings are raised in Jamaica's red, bauxite-rich soil and nurtured with all-organic fertilizers such as bat dung or goat droppings. As the plants mature, tattered scarecrows, loud reggae music, fluttering strips of reel-to-reel recording

One folk tradition that can while away hours of a Jamaican's time is reciting Anansi stories. Such narration is an authentic performing art, which celebrates the nuances of Jamaican patois as well as the cunning, or lack thereof, of the stories' protagonists. Partly reflecting the tellers, the richly funny stories can include repeated key phrases whose rhythms add dramatic effect. Some stories concern Anansi, the spider-man. Like ancient Greeks, Africans invested the spider with human characteristics and intelligence. Whereas the Greeks linked the spider with Arachne, who taught humans to weave and spin, Africans emphasized the wiles and craft of a poisonous and vaguely repulsive eight-legged animal. By the time the tradition reached Jamaica, the spider had become a spider-man and had been given both a name (Anansi) and a distinctive personality.

A notorious trickster, with a distinctly Jamaican humor, Anansi manipulates those around him and eventually acquires whatever spoils happen to be available. In one well-known story, Anansi steals sheep from a nearby plantation; in another, he pilfers half of every other person's plantain. Among the tape, and slingshots manned by local laborers are used to fend off the birds that feed off the seeds.

Even more feared than natural predators, however, are the Jamaican police. The constables periodically raid fields and destroy the crop by burning it or spraying it with herbicide.

Marijuana plants reach maturity 5 to 6 months after transplanting, often with a height of about 9½ feet. Stalks and stems are then pressed for hash oil; leaves are dried for smoking, baking into pastries, or use in herbal teas. Most seeds are saved for the next planting.

Various types of ganja can be grown in a single field, each identified by names like McConey, Cotton, Burr, Bush, Goat's Horn, Lamb's Breath, and Mad. Bush and Mad are the least potent of the crop, whereas the strongest are acknowledged to be Lamb's Breath, Cotton, and Burr. The last three are marketed in the United States under the name of sinsemilla (Spanish for "without seeds"). Rastafarians typically prefer specific types of marijuana, much the way a gastronome might prefer specific types of caviar or red wine. To each his own.

Smuggling of the dried and packaged final product is disconcertingly efficient. A small plane lands at any of the country's hundreds of outlaw airstrips, which are sometimes disguised immediately before and after use by huts and shacks moved into place by crews of strong-armed men. The planes then whisk away the crop, much of it to Florida. Undoubtedly, in a country with chronically low wages and constant fear of unemployment, the temptation to accept bribes runs high among government officials in both high and low positions.

Now that we have told you all we know about ganja, we remind you again that marijuana is illegal in Jamaica despite its widespread presence. Whatever you choose to do while you're on the island, we implore you above all not to try to buy a bag and bring it home to the United States—drug-sniffing dogs are employed at the airports, and we don't want you to end your vacation in jail.

funniest are episodes in which Anansi exposes the indiscretions of an Anglican priest. Anansi's traits include a lisp, a potent sense of greed, and a tendency to be wicked. The stories are sometimes funny, sometimes poignant, sometimes sexually suggestive. They often are parables, teaching a basic lesson about life. Each narrative has a well-defined and often charming ending, which tends to be followed by an explosion of laughter from the storyteller. Several collections of Anansi stories have been published.

DANCE & DRAMA

A sense of drama and theatrics is innate to virtually every Jamaican, as shown in the easy laughter, irreverent humor, and loose-limbed style that are the island's pride and joy. In Kingston in particular, everyone is a star, if only for a moment, during one or another of any day's interpersonal exchanges.

The natural flair of Jamaicans has been channeled into many different drama and dance groups. One of the most visible is the **National Dance**

Theatre Company (NDTC), whose goal is to assemble a body of dancers, actors, and singers to express and explore the Jamaican sense of stylized movement. Applauded by audiences around the world, the company offers abstract interpretations of the Jamaican experience, going far beyond the priorities of a purely folkloric dance troupe. Members are mostly volunteers (lawyers, secretaries, laborers, and nurses by day, highly motivated performers by night), and the troupe has usually refused to accept funds from the government. Among the troupe's most famous performers are Rex Nettleford, a dancer and cofounder, and Louise Bennett, pantomime artist and storyteller, and an early proponent of Jamaican patois as a literary language. Established in 1962, NDTC holds a season running from July to December, with most performances in August. It performs at several locations, so you'll need to inquire about where to attend on a particular day.

4 Calypso, Reggae & Rap: The Rhythms of Jamaica

Many people visit Jamaica just to hear its authentic reggae. Reggae is now known around the world and recognized in the annual Grammy awards run by the U.S. music industry.

The roots of Jamaica's unique reggae music can be found in an early form of Jamaican music called **mento.** This music was brought to the island by African slaves, who played it to help forget their anguish. Mento is reminiscent of the rhythm and blues that in the mid-20th century swept across North America. It was usually accompanied by hip-rolling dances known as dubbing, with highly suggestive lyrics to match. Famous Jamaican mento groups reaching their prime in the 1950s included the Ticklers and the Pork Chops Rhumba Box Band of Montego Bay.

In the late 1950s, Jamaican musicians combined boogie-woogie with rhythm and blues to form a short-lived but vibrant music named **ska.** Jamaican artists in this form included Don Drummond, Roland Alphanso, Lloyd Knibbs, Theophilus Beckford, and Cluet Johnson. The five often played together during a vital chapter in Jamaica's musical history. It was the politicization of ska by Rastafarians that led to the creation of reggae.

CALYPSO

No analysis of Jamaican music would be complete without the inclusion of Jamaican-born musician, actor, and political activist Harry Belafonte. Recognizable to more North American and British listeners than any other Jamaican singer in the 1950s and early 60s, he became famous for his version of the island's unofficial anthem, "Jamaica Farewell," in which the singer leaves a little girl in Kingston Town. Although he worked in other musical forms, Belafonte is particularly known for his smooth and infectious calypsos. *Note:* Some purists in the crowd will point out that calypso is really a product of Trinidad, but it remains very popular in Jamaica (and Barbados).

REGGAE

The heartbeat of Jamaica, reggae is the island's most distinctive musical form, as closely linked to Jamaica as soul is to Detroit, jazz to New Orleans, and blues to Chicago. The term *reggae* is best defined as "coming from the people." It is taken from a song written and performed in the late 1960s by Jamaica-born "Toots" Hibbert and the Maytals ("Do the Reggay"). With a beat some fans claim is narcotic, it has crossed political and racial lines and temporarily drained the hostilities of thousands of listeners, injecting a new kind of life into their pelvises, knees, fingertips, and buttocks. It has influenced the music of international stars like the Rolling Stones, Eric Clapton, Paul Simon, the B-52s, Stevie Wonder, Elton John, and Third World as well as lesser-known acts like Black Uhuru, Chicago's Blue Riddim Band, and rap groups. Most notably, it propelled onto the world scene a street-smart kid from Kingston named Bob Marley. Today, the recording studios of Kingston, sometimes called "the Nashville of the Third World," churn out hundreds of reggae albums every year, many snapped up by danceaholics in Los Angeles, Italy, and Japan.

Reggae's earliest roots lie in the African musical tradition of mento. Later, the rhythms and body movements of mento were combined with an improvised interpretation of the then-fashionable French quadrille to create the distinctive hip-rolling and lower-body contact known as dubbing. Lyrics became increasingly suggestive (some say salacious) and playful as the musical form gained confidence and a body of devoted adherents.

In the 1950s, calypso entered Jamaica from the southern Caribbean, especially Trinidad, whereas rhythm and blues and rock and roll were imported from the United States. Both melded with mento into a danceable mixture that drew islanders into beer and dance halls throughout Jamaica. This music led to the powerful but short-lived form called ska, made famous by the Skatalites, who peaked in the mid-1960s. When their leader and trombonist, Drummond, became a highly politicized convert to Rastafarianism, other musicians followed and altered their rhythms to reflect the African drumbeats known as kumina and burru. This fertile musical tradition, when fused with ripening political movements around 1968, became reggae.

One of the most recent adaptations of reggae is **soca,** which is more upbeat and less politicized. Aficionados say that reggae makes you think, but soca makes you dance. The music is fun, infectious, and spontaneous—perfect for partying—and often imbued with the humor and wry attitudes of Jamaican urban dwellers. Soca's most visible artists include Byron Lee and the Dragonaires. A skillful entrepreneur and organizer, Lee is the force behind the growing annual Jamaica Carnival, which draws more than 15,000 foreign visitors.

Leading early reggae musicians included Anton Ellis and Delroy Wilson. Later, Bob Marley and (to a lesser degree) Jimmy Cliff propelled reggae to world prominence. Marley's band, the Wailers, included his Kingston friends Peter MacIntosh (later known as Peter Tosh), Junior Brathwaite, and Bunny Livingston (now known as Bunny Wailer). Since the death of Marley in 1981, other famous reggae musicians have included his son Ziggy Marley, Roy Parkes, Winston "Yellowman" Foster, and Roy Shirley. Among noteworthy bands are Third World and The Mighty Diamonds.

RAP

After 1965, the influx of Jamaican immigrants to North America's ghettos had a profound (and profitable) influence on popular music. Such Jamaican-born stars as Clive Campbell, combining the Jamaican gift for the spoken word with reggae rhythms and high electronic amplification, developed the roots of what eventually became known as rap. Taking on a street-smart adaptation of rhyming couplets, some of which were influenced by Jamaica's rich appreciation of word games and speech patterns, he organized street parties where the music of his groups—Cool DJ Herc, Nigger Twins, and the Herculords—was broadcast to thousands of listeners from van-mounted amplifiers.

Designed to electrify rather than soothe, and reflecting the restlessness of a new generation of Jamaicans bored with the sometimes mind-numbing rhythms of reggae, popular Jamaican music became less awestruck by Rastafarian dogmas, less Afrocentric, and more focused on the urban experiences of ghetto life in New York. Music became harder, simpler, more urban, and more conscious of profit-searching market trends. Dubbed dance-hall music, the sounds seemed inspired by the hard edge of survival-related facts of life ("girls, guns, drugs, and crime") on urban streets.

One of the major exponents of the new form is Super Cat (William Maragh), who wears his hair cut short ("bald-head") in deliberate contrast to the dreadlocks sported by the disciples of Marley. The sounds are hard and spare, the lyrics as brutal and cruel as the ghetto that inspires them. Super Cat's competitors include Kris Kross, an Atlanta-based rap duet who affect Jamaican accents and speech patterns, and Shabba Ranks, known for often blatant sexual references and unconcealed black machismo. Whereas Marley during the peak of his reggae appeal sold mainly to young whites, the new sounds appeal mostly to young black audiences who relate to the sense of raw danger evoked by dance-hall music's rhythms and lyrics. During some of Shabba Ranks's concerts, audiences in Jamaica have shown their approval by firing gunshots into the air in a gesture known locally as a "salute of honor."

RECOMMENDED RECORDINGS

Jamaica's culture is indicative of and certainly can be defined by its main musical export—reggae. The undisputed king of reggae, the late Bob Marley, popularized the genre, which is musically stylized by percussive guitar riffs and lyrically peppered with political and social activism.

Legend (Best of Bob Marley and the Wailers) chronicles the late artist's body of work. Termed a poet and a prophet, Marley brought reggae into the American conscience and mainstream. The album features a collection of hits such as "Get Up, Stand Up," "Jamming," "One Love," and perhaps his biggest hit, "Stir It Up." *Legend* was released in 1984 and has already outsold such megahits as Michael Jackson's *Thriller,* The Beatles' *Sgt. Pepper's Lonely Hearts Club Band,* and Pink Floyd's *Dark Side of the Moon.* (Tuff Gong/Island Records, 422846210-2.)

Honorary Citizen, a three-CD box set, covers the career of Marley's contemporary, Peter Tosh, a reggae legend in his own right and termed also a poet, prophet, preacher, and philosopher. *Honorary Citizen* brings out the best of Tosh's work, including some unreleased and live tracks with artists such as Marley, Bunny Wailer (of the Wailers), and Mick Jagger and Keith Richards. Tracks include "Fire Fire," "Arise Blackman," and "Legalize It." (Columbia/Legacy, C3H 65064.)

Liberation by Bunny Wailer is another important album of the reggae movement. When *Newsweek* selected the three most important musicians in the Third World, Bunny Wailer was among them. He has controlled his artistic development, despite tragedies in his career, while avoiding any compromising of his vision. (Shanachie Records, 43059.)

One Love by Bunny Wailer, Bob Marley, and Peter Tosh (Three Greats) offers the three biggest legends of reggae together on one album, a "Three Tenors" of reggae. This compilation is the first chronological and definitive study of Bob Marley and the Wailers and Peter Tosh in their formative years. The music, the cornerstone of the ska era, includes previously unreleased alternate takes and rarely recorded Jamaican singers. (Heartbeat Records, CDH111/112.)

Ziggy Marley and the Melody Makers, Best of 1988–1993 spans the successful and ongoing career of one of Bob's many children. Ziggy is largely responsible for reggae's 1990s mainstream acceptance, penning such crossover hits as "One

Bright Day," "Joy and Blues," and "Brothers and Sisters," which are contained in this collection. His debut album, *Conscious Party*, is still his best work. (Virgin, 724384490821.)

Liberation—The Island Anthology by Black Uhuru is a box set of collective works from the band's 1980s Island Records catalog. The 1980s were still dominated by the Marley effect, and Black Uhuru was the band that passed the reggae torch along to Ziggy Marley. (Island Records, 314518282-2.)

The Lee "Scratch" Perry Arkology is another recent box-set release of another "old skool" reggae artist from "back in the day." Covering his entire career, it contains recordings from the many different bands he formed, as well as solo works, including two never-before-released tracks. (Island/Jamaica, 61524 3792.)

In Concert—Best of Jimmy Cliff is a recording of a legendary pedigree. Produced by legends Andrew Loog Oldham and Cliff, this album features Ernest Ranglin on lead guitar and Earl "Baga" Walker on bass. Includes the classic, "Many Rivers to Cross" and "The Harder They Come." (Reprise, 2256-2.)

Jah Kingdon by Burning Spear is known for its strongly political lyrics. This record could serve as a definition for hard-core reggae. Includes "World Power" and "Land of My Birth." (Mango/Island Records, 162539915-2.)

Too Long in Slavery is an album by one of Ziggy Marley's contemporaries, Culture. All songs were written and performed by J. Hill, K. Daley, and A. Walker. (Virgin, CDFL9011.)

The recordings by the Marleys, Tosh, and the Wailers are considered to be the purist reggae, defined as such today because of reggae's splintering into many different forms such as dance/house music and rap.

Best Sellers by Mikey Dread is a compilation album spanning the career of Dread, Jamaica's best-known DJ. With material ranging from 1979 to 1990, it was Dread (along with the band Maxi Priest) who ushered reggae into the new dance movement. (Rykodisc Records, 20178.)

Many Moods of Moses by Beenie Man is the latest release by an artist whose political lyrics maintain all the criteria for purist reggae, but adds a dance beat heard only from the likes of Dread before the 1990s. Tracks from this album include "Who I Am (Zim Zamma)" and "Oysters and Conch." (VP Records, VPCD1513-2.)

Sawuri, the self-titled release by Sawuri, offers a Creole taste to the Jamaican sound. It features the Caribbean artists Marcel Komba and Georges Marie. If you have trouble finding this record in your favorite store, try www.worldmusic. com, a site devoted to promoting world music that has yet to become mainstream. (Dom Records, CD 1067.)

Militant, by newcomer Andrew Bees, is a signal that the purist reggae will always remain *en vogue* in Jamaica. Tracks such as "Struggle and Strive," "Militant," and "Life in the Ghetto" evoke modern realizations of the same themes Marley, Tosh, and Wailer sang about in the past—except now with mounting frustrations of citizens from a Third-World society. (Ras Records, ML 81811-2.)

5 Jamaican Food & Drink

A visit to Jamaica doesn't mean a diet of just local cuisine. The island's eating establishments employ some of the best chefs in the Caribbean, hailing from the United States and Europe, and they can prepare a sumptuous cuisine of elegant French, continental, and American dishes.

When dining in Jamaica, try some fish, which is often delectable, especially dolphin (the game fish, not the mammal), wahoo, yellowtail, grouper, and red snapper. These fish, when broiled with hot lime sauce as an accompaniment, may represent your most memorable island meals. Sweet-tasting Caribbean lobster is different from the Maine variety.

Elaborate buffets are often a feature at the major resorts. These buffets display a variety of dishes along with other more-standard fare, and they are almost always reasonably priced. Entertainment is often a reggae band. Even if you are not staying at a particular hotel, you can call on any given night and make a reservation to partake of a buffet.

Before booking a hotel, it's wise to have a clear understanding of what is included in the various meal plans offered.

To save money, many visitors prefer the Modified American Plan (MAP), which includes room, breakfast, and one main meal per day, nearly always dinner. The visitor is then free to take lunch somewhere else. If the hotel has a beach, guests often will order a light à la carte lunch at their hotel, which is added to the bill. The American Plan (AP), on the other hand, includes all three meals per day. Drinks, including wine, are usually extra.

If you want to eat your main meals outside the hotel, book a Continental Plan (CP), which includes only breakfast. To go one step further, choose the European Plan (EP), which includes no meals.

Frankly, it's difficult for first-time visitors driving rented cars to navigate the Jamaican roads at night, looking for that special little restaurant, as roads are narrow and poorly lit. To complicate matters, Jamaica requires motorists to drive on the left, as in Great Britain. If you go out for dinner, consider taking a taxi. All taxi drivers know the badly marked roads well. Once at the restaurant, you can arrange for the taxi to pick you up at an agreed-upon time or else have the restaurant call a taxi when you are ready to leave. Some restaurants, such as the first-class establishments in Montego Bay, will arrange to have a minivan pick you up and return you to your hotel if you call in advance.

APPETIZERS

Except for soup, appetizers don't loom large in the Jamaican kitchen. The most popular appetizer is *stamp and go*, or salt-fish cakes. *Solomon Gundy* is made with pickled shad, herring, and mackerel, and seasoned with onions, hot peppers, and pimiento berries. Many Jamaicans begin their meal by enjoying plantain and banana chips with their drinks.

The most famous soup, pepper pot, is an old Arawak recipe. It is often made with callaloo, okra, kale, pig's tail (or salt beef), coconut meat, yams, scallions, and hot peppers. Another favorite, akee soup, is made from akees (usually from a dozen ripe open pods), flavored with a shin of beef or a salted pig's tail. Pumpkin soup is seasoned with salted beef or a salted pig's tail. Red-pea soup is also delicious (note that it's actually made with red beans).

Tea in Jamaica can mean any nonalcoholic drink, and fish tea, a legacy of plantation days, is made with fish heads or bony fish, along with green bananas, tomatoes, scallions, and hot pepper and other spices.

MAIN COURSES & SIDE DISHES

Because Jamaica is an island, there is great emphasis on seafood, but many other tasty dishes are also offered. Rock lobster is a regular dish on every menu, presented grilled, thermidor, cold, or hot. Salt fish and akee is the national dish, a mixture of salt cod and a brightly colored vegetablelike fruit that tastes something like scrambled eggs. *Escoveitch* (marinated fish) is usually fried and then simmered in vinegar with onions and peppers.

Among meat dishes, *curried mutton* and *goat* are popular, each highly seasoned and likely to affect your body temperature. *Jerk pork* is characteristic of rural areas, where it is barbecued slowly over wood fires until crisp and brown.

Apart from rice and peas (usually red beans), usually served as a sort of risotto with added onions, spices, and salt pork, some vegetables may be new to you. They include *breadfruit*, imported by Captain Bligh in 1723 when he arrived aboard HMS *Bounty*; *callaloo*, rather like spinach, used in pepper-pot soup (not to be confused with the stew of the same name); *cho-cho*, served boiled and buttered or stuffed; and *green bananas* and *plantains*, fried or boiled and served with almost everything. Then there is *pumpkin*, which goes into a soup, as mentioned, or is served on the side, boiled and mashed with butter. *Sweet potatoes* are part of main courses, and there is also a sweet-potato pudding made with sugar and coconut milk, flavored with cinnamon, nutmeg, and vanilla.

You'll also come across intriguing *dip and fall back*, a salty stew with bananas and dumplings, and *rundown*, mackerel cooked in coconut milk and often eaten for breakfast. The really adventurous can try *manish water*, a soup made from goat offal and tripe said to increase virility. Patties (meat pies) are a staple snack; the best are sold in Montego Bay. Boiled corn, roast yams, roast salt fish, fried fish, soups, and fruits are available at roadside stands.

DRINKS

Tea, as mentioned above, is a word used in Jamaica to describe any nonalcoholic drink, a tradition dating back to plantation days. Fish tea (see "Appetizers," above) is often consumed as a refreshing pick-me-up and is sometimes sold along the side of the road. *Skyjuice* is a favorite Jamaican treat for a hot afternoon. It's sold by street vendors from not-always-sanitary carts. It consists of shaved ice with sugar-laden fruit syrup and is offered in small plastic bags with a straw. *Coconut water* is refreshing, especially when a roadside vendor chops the top off a nut straight from a tree.

Rum punches are available everywhere, and the local beer is Red Stripe. The island produces many liqueurs, the most famous being *Tía María*, made from coffee beans. *Rumona* is another good one to bring back home with you. *Bellywash*, the local name for limeade, will supply the extra liquid you may need to counteract the tropical heat. Blue Mountain coffee is considered among the world's best coffees—it's also very expensive. Tea, cocoa, and milk are also usually available to round out a meal.

6 Recommended Books & Films

BOOKS
GENERAL

Catch a Fire: The Life of Bob Marley, by Timothy White (Guernsey Press, 1983), chronicles the reggae musician's life and career, from poverty in Kingston's Trench Town to international fame. It's an insightful exploration of the historic, cultural, religious, and folkloric milieu that shaped Marley's spiritual and political beliefs, from which reggae emerged.

The Real Bob Marley Story, by Don Taylor (Barricade, 1995), is a memoir by the reggae star's manager. Taylor strays from the subject, often turning the Bob Marley story into the Don Taylor story, but there is much Marley lore here in spite of that. The most fascinating part concerns the attempt on

Marley's life in the 1970s. Taylor was there and was seriously injured himself. Because the book is so poorly written, it is recommended only for the most diehard fans.

Tales of Old Jamaica, by Clinton V. Black (Longman Caribbean, reprinted 1991), brings together 10 of the most intriguing tales of the island's famous personalities, including Three-Fingered Jack (the terror of Jamaica) and the notorious Annie Palmer of Rose Hall.

Jamaican Folk Tales and Oral Histories, by Laura Tanna (Institute of Jamaica Publications, 1984), is a collection culled from the best Jamaican storytelling, such as spicy Anansi or Nancy stories and lore told with humor and style.

West Indian Folk-tales, retold by Philip Sherlock, illustrated by Joan Kiddell-Monroe (Oxford University Press, 1990), offers a colorful selection of West Indian myths and legends recounted with warmth and humor.

The Rebel Woman in the British West Indies during Slavery, by Lucille Mathurin, illustrated by Dennis Ranston (African Caribbean Publications, 1975), explores the variety of methods used to express resentment toward the institution of slavery. The quiet, subtle methods of protest, which today might be termed civil disobedience, are examined as is violent armed rebellion.

The Cimaroons, by Robert Leeson (William Collins, 1978), is the story of enslaved persons who refused to accept their status. Wherever the Cimaroons took off their chains, they fought stubbornly for their freedom. Their story does not appear in many history books, yet is true and exciting.

X/Self, by Edward Kamau Brathwaite (Oxford University Press, 1987), one of the finest of the Caribbean poets, traces his African/Caribbean ancestry. In *X/Self*, the four landscapes—European, African, Amerindian, and Maroon—meet and mingle in an extraordinarily rich, imaginative sequence of poems.

The How to Be Jamaican Handbook, by Kim Robinson, Harclyde Walcott, and Trevor Fearon (Jamrite Publications, 1987), is a candid look at Jamaican characters and humorous aspects of island life. It is mandatory reading for anyone who wants to blend into Jamaican society.

Jamaica Talk: Three Hundred Years of the English Language in Jamaica, by Frederic G. Cassily (Macmillan Caribbean, 1982), is a thorough study of English as spoken in Jamaica. It covers the language, both past and present, of Jamaicans of all ranks. Chapters deal with composition, pronunciation, grammar, and vocabulary.

Garvey's Children: The Legacy of Marcus Garvey, by Tony Sewall (Macmillan Caribbean, 1990), is a look at a great Jamaican's philosophy and opinions. It is said that Garvey linked the Caribbean, the United States, and Africa in a vision that saw all black people working together to determine their own destiny.

HISTORY

The Gleaner Geography & History of Jamaica (Gleaner Company, 22nd edition, 1991) is a textbook through which Jamaican schoolchildren learn about their country. Visitors can also learn about the history and geography of the island from the book. The latest edition is available in major bookstores around Jamaica.

TRAVEL

Tour Jamaica, by Margaret Morris (Gleaner Company, 1988), describes an island of infinite variety with interesting and warmhearted people. Covering six regions, the book provides data on places of interest, local personalities, and historic and topical anecdotes. Featured are 19 recommended tours.

The Adventure Guide to Jamaica, by Steve Cohen (Hunter Publishing, 1988), leads you on a tour of unforgettable parts of the island few visitors know how to reach. The book emphasizes walking, cycling, river travel, and horseback touring. Includes a guide to hundreds of roadside vendors.

Jamaica Guide, by Clinton V. Black (William Collins & Sangster, Jamaica, 1973), provides much information a visitor will find interesting, including a detailed introduction to the history of the people and country.

CUISINE

The Jamaican Chef, by Byron Murray and Patrick Lewin (Life Long Publishers, 1990), provides recipes for an array of sumptuous and mouthwatering dishes that get high marks from even the most critical gourmets.

Traditional Jamaican Cookery, by Norma Benghiat (Penguin, 1985), includes recipes never before written down, having been passed from generation to generation by word of mouth.

FILMS

More than any other island in the Caribbean, Jamaica has offered itself to the movie industry as a site for fabricating celluloid dreams. Partly the result of savvy marketing, partly the result of a landscape varied enough to offer diverse filmmaking settings, the island might at any time during your visit host crews for filming movies, documentaries, or TV shows and commercials.

This is to some extent the heritage of 1940s and 50s film star Errol Flynn, whose parties and personal shenanigans added a Hollywood gloss to Port Antonio and other areas of Jamaica. The actor owned both a hotel and a house in Port Antonio for years, and the town is still the home of his widow, ex-film actor Patrice Wymore. Hollywood filmmakers first visited the island in 1941 to shoot exteriors for the George Brent and Ann Sheridan comedy, *Honeymoon for Three*, and again in 1954 to shoot the climax of *20,000 Leagues Under the Sea*. Altogether, more than 50 motion pictures, and dozens of documentaries, music videos, and TV commercials have been filmed amid the shantytowns, great houses, Spanish and English colonial forts, deserts, beaches, and seascapes of Jamaica.

The best-selling novels of the 20th century include the James Bond spy series written by Ian Fleming at his house on Jamaica's northeast shore. The movie versions of some, such as *Dr. No.* and *Live and Let Die*, were partly filmed in Jamaica. The filming of other, even larger, adventure films followed shortly after the first Bond films. Although its story is set mostly on Devil's Island off French Guyana, *Papillon*, starring Steve McQueen, was largely filmed in Jamaica, near the crowded north-shore town of Falmouth. A make-believe French colonial prison was constructed, using British overseers and an army of Jamaican carpenters and masons.

During the 1970s, when Jamaican politics took an abrupt turn to the left, foreign filmmakers (as well as investors in other industries) stayed away from the island. In 1984, however, the newly elected centrist prime minister, Edward Seaga, relaxed import-export laws and enacted tax incentives for the film industry, making Jamaica again an important site for international films. The government also cut red tape. Filmmakers were lured by Jamaica's trained technicians and actors (all nonunion, offering services priced much lower than their U.S. or British counterparts), and occasional access to army and navy facilities. Because of the various advantages, Jamaica snared the location rights for Tom Cruise's *Cocktail*, Whoopi Goldberg's *Clara's Heart*, Bill Murray and

Peter O'Toole's *Club Paradise*, and a 1988 remake of *Lord of the Flies*. Each was filmed near Errol Flynn's old stomping ground, Port Antonio.

For the 26-episode remake of the "Flipper" TV series, which presented the adventures of two young brothers with a herd of tame dolphins, the locale was shifted from the Florida Keys to Jamaica, and the script was updated to include a Jamaican actor as one of the young protagonists.

Documentaries have been filmed in Jamaica as well. Heritage Films chose the Blue Mountains as a cost-effective substitute for Kenya and Tanzania when producing a biography of zoologist Dian Fossey. Titled *The Strange Life and Death of Dian Fossey*, this film should not be confused with Sigourney Weaver's *Gorillas in the Mist*, shot in Africa. Several films dealing with reggae have also been produced in Jamaica.

Even in films not requiring a Caribbean setting, Jamaica retains a strong pull on the imaginations and budgets of Hollywood filmmakers. One such example is the humorous horror movie *Popcorn*, which a viewer might easily believe had been filmed in Los Angeles. Actually, the film was shot with English and American actors in Kingston and has nothing to do with swaying palms and coral reefs. Most challenging to the film's art directors was the creation of a giant mosquito poised menacingly atop the protagonists' car.

The Lunatic, released in 1992, is a ribald comedy. Set in a tiny Jamaican hamlet, it tells the madcap story of a vagabond with a good heart, a "randy" German visitor, and a butcher of many talents. The film has been called "a Caribbean fantasy."

Wide Sargasso Sea (1993), an adaptation of the Jean Rhys novel of 1966, received good critical notices. Rich in imagery of 19th-century Jamaica, it tells the story of a young English aristocrat named Rochester (played by Nathaniel Parker), who arrives in Jamaica and marries a Creole sugar-plantation heiress (played by Karina Lombard). Rochester turns out to be *the* Rochester—that is, the brooding man of *Jane Eyre* by Charlotte Brontë. In her novel, Rhys attempted to "fill in" the doomed saga of Rochester's first marriage as a prelude to *Jane Eyre*.

Stepping Razor-Red X (1993) has been called a "reggae *Malcolm X*." This politically galvanizing portrait tells the tragic story of reggae legend Peter Tosh, who was murdered in 1988. The voice in the film is that of Tosh himself, culled from the "Red X" tapes he was working on for a planned autobiography. Much vintage footage of life in Jamaica in the 1960s is shown in the film, along with re-creations of Tosh's childhood.

Cool Runnings (1993) is loosely based on the story of a Jamaican bobsled team that achieved massive publicity at the 1988 Winter Olympics. The team had practiced without ever having seen snow. The film was shot not only in Calgary (site of the Olympics) but in Ocho Rios and Montego Bay. One critic suggested it was a snowbound *Chariots of Fire* with reggae music.

Index

See also Accommodations and Restaurant indexes, below.

General Index

ACCOMMODATIONS

RESTAURANTS

FROMMER'S® COMPLETE TRAVEL GUIDES

Alaska
Amsterdam
Arizona
Atlanta
Australia
Austria
Bahamas
Barcelona, Madrid &
  Seville
Beijing
Belgium, Holland &
  Luxembourg
Bermuda
Boston
British Columbia & the
  Canadian Rockies
Budapest & the Best of
  Hungary
California
Canada
Cancún, Cozumel &
  the Yucatán
Cape Cod, Nantucket &
  Martha's Vineyard
Caribbean
Caribbean Cruises & Ports
  of Call
Caribbean Ports of Call
Carolinas & Georgia
Chicago
China
Colorado
Costa Rica
Denmark
Denver, Boulder & Colorado
  Springs
England
Europe

European Cruises & Ports
  of Call
Florida
France
Germany
Greece
Greek Islands
Hawaii
Hong Kong
Honolulu, Waikiki &
  Oahu
Ireland
Israel
Italy
Jamaica
Japan
Las Vegas
London
Los Angeles
Maryland & Delaware
Maui
Mexico
Miami & the Keys
Montana & Wyoming
Montréal & Québec City
Munich & the Bavarian
  Alps
Nashville & Memphis
Nepal
New England
New Mexico
New Orleans
New York City
New Zealand
Nova Scotia, New Brunswick
  & Prince Edward Island
Oregon
Paris

Philadelphia & the
  Amish Country
Portugal
Prague & the Best of the
  Czech Republic
Provence & the Riviera
Puerto Rico
Rome
San Antonio & Austin
San Diego
San Francisco
Santa Fe, Taos & Albuquerque
Scandinavia
Scotland
Seattle & Portland
Singapore & Malaysia
South Africa
Southeast Asia
South Pacific
Spain
Sweden
Switzerland
Thailand
Tokyo
Toronto
Tuscany & Umbria
USA
Utah
Vancouver & Victoria
Vermont, New Hampshire
  & Maine
Vienna & the Danube Valley
Virgin Islands
Virginia
Walt Disney World &
  Orlando
Washington, D.C.
Washington State

FROMMER'S® DOLLAR-A-DAY GUIDES

Australia from $50 a Day
California from $60 a Day
Caribbean from $70 a Day
England from $70 a Day
Europe from $60 a Day

Florida from $60 a Day
Hawaii from $70 a Day
Ireland from $60 a Day
Italy from $70 a Day
London from $85 a Day

New York from $80 a Day
Paris from $85 a Day
San Francisco from $60 a Day
Washington, D.C.,
  from $60 a Day

FROMMER'S® PORTABLE GUIDES

Acapulco, Ixtapa &
  Zihuatanejo
Alaska Cruises & Ports of Call
Bahamas
Baja & Los Cabos
Berlin
California Wine Country
Charleston & Savannah
Chicago

Dublin
Hawaii: The Big Island
Las Vegas
London
Maine Coast
Maui
New Orleans
New York City
Paris

Puerto Vallarta, Manzanillo
  & Guadalajara
San Diego
San Francisco
Sydney
Tampa & St. Petersburg
Venice
Washington, D.C.

FROMMER'S® NATIONAL PARK GUIDES

Family Vacations in the
National Parks
Grand Canyon

National Parks of the
American West
Rocky Mountain

Yellowstone & Grand Teton
Yosemite & Sequoia/
Kings Canyon
Zion & Bryce Canyon

FROMMER'S® MEMORABLE WALKS

Chicago
London

New York
Paris

San Francisco
Washington D.C.

FROMMER'S® GREAT OUTDOOR GUIDES

New England
Northern California

Southern California & Baja
Southern New England

Washington & Oregon

FROMMER'S® BORN TO SHOP GUIDES

Born to Shop: China
Born to Shop: France

Born to Shop: Italy
Born to Shop: London

Born to Shop: New York
Born to Shop: Paris

FROMMER'S® IRREVERENT GUIDES

Amsterdam
Boston
Chicago
Las Vegas

London
Los Angeles
Manhattan
New Orleans

Paris
San Francisco
Seattle & Portland
Vancouver

Walt Disney World
Washington, D.C.

FROMMER'S® BEST-LOVED DRIVING TOURS

America
Britain
California

Florida
France
Germany

Ireland
Italy
New England

Scotland
Spain
Western Europe

THE UNOFFICIAL GUIDES®

Bed & Breakfasts in
California
Bed & Breakfasts in
New England
Bed & Breakfasts in
the Northwest
Beyond Disney
Branson, Missouri
California with Kids
Chicago

Cruises
Disneyland
Florida with Kids
Golf Vacations in the
Eastern U.S.
The Great Smoky &
Blue Ridge
Mountains
Inside Disney

Hawaii
Las Vegas
London
Miami & the Keys
Mini Las Vegas
Mini-Mickey
New Orleans
New York City
Paris

Safaris
San Francisco
Skiing in the West
Walt Disney World
Walt Disney World
for Grown-ups
Walt Disney World
for Kids
Washington, D.C.

SPECIAL-INTEREST TITLES

Frommer's Britain's Best Bed & Breakfasts and
Country Inns
Frommer's Britain's Best Bike Rides
The Civil War Trust's Official Guide
to the Civil War Discovery Trail
Frommer's Caribbean Hideaways
Frommer's Food Lover's Companion to France
Frommer's Food Lover's Companion to Italy
Frommer's Gay & Lesbian Europe
Frommer's Exploring America by RV
Hanging Out in Europe
Israel Past & Present

Mad Monks' Guide to California
Mad Monks' Guide to New York City
Frommer's The Moon
Frommer's New York City with Kids
The New York Times' Unforgettable
Weekends
Places Rated Almanac
Retirement Places Rated
Frommer's Road Atlas Britain
Frommer's Road Atlas Europe
Frommer's Washington, D.C., with Kids
Frommer's What the Airlines Never Tell You